ADVANCED ACCOUNTING
FOR A2

IAN HARRISON

Hodder & Stoughton

A MEMBER OF THE HODDER HEADLINE GROUP

ACKNOWLEDGEMENTS

Gratitude is due to many people when writing any book; this book is no exception. I thank the team at Hodder Arnold – in particular Alexia Chan for her support, understanding and patience, also Tessa Heath who has offered similar support. I must thank my wife Sandie for her proofreading and word-processing and for her comments and guidance which are very much appreciated and most of all for her tolerance and good humour during the preparation of this book. I am also indebted to David Austen for his comments on the raw text before final submission.

There may be occasions when a critical reader might feel that I have over-simplified some concepts. However, I make no apologies for this as the main readership will be the average 18-year-old studying at Advanced Level or first-year degree level and my explanations are written with a view to aiding their understanding of what is often seen as a more difficult subject.

Orders: please contact Bookpoint Ltd, 130 Milton Park, Abingdon, Oxon OX14 4SB. Telephone: (44) 01235 827720. Fax: (44) 01235 400454. Lines are open from 9.00–6.00, Monday to Saturday, with a 24-hour message answering service. You can also order through our website: www.hodderheadline.co.uk.

British Library Cataloguing in Publication Data
A catalogue record for this title is available from the British Library

ISBN 0 340 87312 4

First Published 2004
Impression number   10 9 8 7 6 5 4 3 2 1
Year   2008 2007 2006 2005 2004

Copyright © 2004 Ian Harrison

Papers used in this book are natural, renewable and recyclable products. They are made from wood grown in sustainable forests. The logging and manufacturing processes conform to the environmental regulations of the country of origin.

Artwork by David Graham
Typeset by Fakenham Photosetting Ltd, Fakenham, Norfolk
Printed in Spain for Hodder & Stoughton Educational, a division of Hodder Headline, 338 Euston Road, London NW1 3BH.

CONTENTS

INTRODUCTION

You have just completed an AS course in Accounting. This has been an ideal foundation course for your A2 year. You should have laid a solid foundation necessary to help you build up to the more difficult and complex topics that you will now encounter.

At AS Level much emphasis was placed on knowledge and understanding of the various topics. You learned how to apply that knowledge and understanding to various situations.

The Advanced Level course that you are embarking on requires higher-order skills, especially those involving the ability to analyse and evaluate a topic.

As an A Level student you will be assessed on your ability to:

- demonstrate your knowledge and understanding of accounting information systems
- assemble and classify accounting data, presented to you, in an understandable way
- know and apply accounting concepts in a variety of scenarios
- interpret and analyse accounting information in a way that will enable you to evaluate alternative courses of action and make reasoned judgements
- communicate your results and findings in a variety of ways that will suit the many users of accounting information
- understand and appreciate the value of accounting information as well as its inherent limitations.

Studying and revising for any examinations should not be a last-minute affair. In order to gain the grade that you deserve, you should make detailed notes throughout the duration of the course.

Jot down notes of interesting items from the radio and television, from newspapers and from what friends and relatives tell you about the business world.

Accounting needs much practice. If you have run out of questions on a particular topic, revisit questions or borrow past question papers from your school or college library. Visit the appropriate web sites to 'get the feel' of recent examination papers and check your answers against any mark schemes that are available.

Practise the topics with your friends – this will help you, as well as them.

Certain items have to be learned by heart in any subject – there is no substitute for this. Layouts must be learned, as well as certain definitions and formulae. This is vitally important. There can be no excuses. Practise for 5 or 10 minutes per day – you will soon master any topic you wish to remember. This is how you learn the words of pop songs – regular practice.

Why is it that your teachers know so much about their subject areas? Yes, they did study it at a high level at university, but the other reason is that they have probably repeated certain topics to many classes over many years and this practice has meant perfection!

REVISION

Start to revise in plenty of time – please do not leave it to the last minute. The A2 year is not as long as it seems: it is not 12 months – it can be as short as seven or eight months. Deduct holidays from this and an odd few days off with a sports injury or a cold and you could be looking at five and a half months – work it out!

Remember to spread your revision across all your subjects – no employer or university wants a grade A in one subject and two or three fail grades. Be like the juggler and keep all your subjects going at the same time.

Try to find spare times at school or college to revise – this will free up some time at home.

Prepare a revision timetable for each week – and stick to it – it is easier to stick to a regular routine of study than it is to do it in a haphazard way. Regular study works best.

The more you put in, the more you will get out of it!

If you revise while listening to music, remember that this is not possible in a crowded examination hall so you need to have practice sessions in complete silence – sounds awful, doesn't it? But this is necessary because you will have to spend up to two and a half hours in the examination room at one time, sitting and working in silence.

Varying your methods of revision will help you to avoid getting bored – have regular breaks or a change of subjects or topics.

Try:

- reading aloud
- talking yourself through a difficult topic
- giving yourself tests
- working with a friend and testing each other (make sure that when you set a question, you know the answer!). Try to avoid gossip sessions when working with a friend!
- summarising answers to written questions
- using mnemonics
- practising sections of questions before building up to the whole question.

As a guide to how well you know a topic, ask yourself: 'Could I explain this topic to someone who does not know much (if anything) about accounting so that they would understand it?' If you can answer 'Yes', then you probably understand the topic. If you have to answer 'No' – then more revision is necessary.

When you are waiting outside the examination hall, ready to start your examination, I bet that some of your friends will wish you good luck. Luck has nothing to do with the result you obtain – the result will be a reflection of the time spent revising and practising.

Examination results are awards for honest endeavour. Remember this as you go through this book!

CHAPTER
ONE

Loose Ends

The aim of this book is to take you one stage further in the study of accounting. *Introducing Accounting* covered the topics that you needed to cover for tackling your AS examinations; this book covers the topics that you will encounter on your A2 course. It has been written with, I hope, the minimum of jargon, to make it as understandable as possible. Clearly, there are some topics that cannot be completely de-mystified, but an attempt has been made.

As in *Introducing Accounting*, chapter objectives identify the key points to be covered in the chapter you are about to read and there are references to the sections of the specifications covered.

Each time a new term is introduced it will appear in a definition box.

Examination tips are also identified as the chapters progress. Each chapter will explain the topic, then there will follow examples of questions that an examiner may ask. Each worked example is followed by the answer. It is a good idea to cover over the answer with a spare sheet of paper while you attempt it. If you get stuck you can then uncover the answer and hopefully carry on and perhaps finish the example.

Throughout the text there are numerous questions for practice purposes. Questions are graded, starting with simpler ones and building up to more complex questions as you proceed through the chapter.

Odd-numbered questions have the answers at the end of the book. Even-numbered questions do not have the answers.

In the main, even-numbered questions are very similar to the odd-numbered questions so if you get stuck you can use the odd-numbered question to help you out.

Past examination questions have deliberately been omitted as these can be readily obtained from the examination boards. These will then provide a further useful resource for you to use in addition to the questions provided for you in this book.

Details of past papers available can be obtained from the appropriate website.

Do have a look at these sites because they will give you an idea of how questions look in the context of each paper. The mark schemes will give an indication of what the examiner is looking for in your answer. But do remember that the mark schemes have been prepared for use by examiners who have had a full day's training on the papers, followed by several hours of instruction from senior examiners.

Try www.aqa.org.uk and www.ocr.org.uk.

It is so very important that you practise questions from each topic. The old adage 'practice makes perfect' still applies today and the more practice you get, the better your grade will surely be.

The more time you spend on your studies, the greater will be your reward when the results are announced.

Specification coverage:
OCR 5.2.2

By the end of this chapter you should be able to:
- prepare departmental accounts
- prepare a reconciliation statement of control account balances with schedules of debtors and creditors
- prepare and use a suspense account.

DEPARTMENTAL ACCOUNTS

Accounting is an information system. It is used to communicate information to the users of final accounts. It communicates information to managers, to owners, to lenders of finance and to many others. Sometimes the information that is obvious hides other information that is less obvious.

Tony owns and runs a newsagent's shop. As well as newspapers, Tony sells magazines, sweets and chocolates, cigarettes and bottles of fizzy drinks. His profits have been fairly static over the past five years or so at around £26,000. 'Quite a nice living', you might say.

However, if we look more closely at Tony's profits and analyse them very carefully, we may discover that all is not quite what it seems:

- profit from the sale of newspapers is £12,000 per annum
- profit from the sale of magazines is £8,500 per annum
- profit from sales of sweets and chocolates is £4,400 per annum
- profit from the sale of cigarettes is £1,870 per annum
- loss on sales of fizzy drinks is £770 per annum.

If Tony ceased to sell fizzy drinks, his profit would rise to £26,770. So perhaps Tony should close down the section of the shop that is devoted to stocking and selling the drinks.

But Tony may be prepared to sell the drinks as a 'loss leader' because he knows that very few of his customers buy only a drink. They usually buy a drink and a magazine or a drink and a chocolate bar etc. So if he stopped selling the drinks, other products might suffer too.

Accounting information might not tell us the whole story. We need as much accounting information as possible to enable us to make informed business decisions.

Departmental accounts provide us with information that will enable us to assess the profitability of separate sections of a business.

WORKED EXAMPLE

Sanjay owns and runs a shop that sells baby linen, prams and cots. He provides the following information relating to the year ended 31 March 20*5:

Departments	Baby linen £	Prams £	Cots £
Stock as at 1 April 20*4	1,380	2,350	560
Stock as at 31 March 20*5	1,540	1,970	430
Purchases	23,760	35,780	2,350
Sales	45,980	60,460	5,890
Wages	12,560	16,670	2,340

The following expenses cannot be attributed to any particular department:

	£
Rent and rates	4,200
Lighting and heating expenses	6,600
Administration costs	1,200
Other expenses	900

Sanjay has decided to apportion rent and rates and lighting and heating expenses in proportion to the floor space occupied by each department. Administration and other expenses are to be shared equally.

Required Prepare a departmental trading and profit and loss account for the year ended 31 March 20*5.

	Baby linen £	£	Prams £	£	Cots £	£
Sales		45,980		60,460		5,890
Less Cost of sales						
Stock as at						
1 April 20*4	1,380		2,350		560	
Purchases	23,760		35,780		2,350	
	25,140		38,130		2,910	
Stock as at						
31 March 20*5	1,540		1,970		430	
		23,600		36,160		2,480
Gross profit		22,380		24,300		3,410
Less Expenses						
Wages	12,560		16,670		2,340	
Rent and rates	2,100		1,400		700	
Heat and light	3,300		2,200		1,100	
Administration	400		400		400	
Other expenses	300		300		300	
		18,660		20,970		4,840
Net profit/(loss)		3,720		3,330		(1,430)

Answer

It can clearly be seen from the results that the cots department is unprofitable. If Sanjay closed down the cots department his profit would rise to £7,050.

Or would it?

We have already mentioned the interdependency of one department to another in Tony's business; this may also be true in the case of Sanjay's business.

Let us consider the way in which expenses have been shared between the departments. Apart from the wages, the other expenses have been apportioned on a purely arbitrary basis. Their apportionment may not reflect accurately the amount of the resources actually used by each department. The accurate way to apportion the expenses is to ask how much rent and rates would be saved if the cots department was closed. If we said that £380 would be saved then that must be the amount of rent and rates that should be charged to the cots department. How much would be saved on heating and lighting if the department was closed? If the answer was £620 then that is the correct charge to the cots department. This method, although time consuming, would reveal the true extent of the profitability of each department.

As well a considering the profitability of the department and its impact on other departments, other factors should be considered: the impact on customer confidence and workers' morale, among others.

A better approach is to take the **marginal cost approach**. This is considered in depth in Chapter Fourteen.

QUESTION 1

The following information is given for Jan's electrical store:

Stock	at 1 January 20*4 £	at 31 December 20*4 £
Kitchen goods	6,980	7,450
DIY goods	4,870	5,090
Leisure goods	8,820	7,690

	Kitchen goods £	DIY goods £	Leisure goods £
Sales for the year	97,876	73,752	102,653
Purchases for the year	42,631	30,884	38,005

Required Prepare departmental trading accounts for the year ended 31 December 20*4.

QUESTION 2

Cedric provides the following information relating to his business:

	Nail bar £	Hairdressing £	Cosmetics £
Stock as at 1 March 20*4	230	860	340
Stock as at 28 February 20*5	185	1,010	350
Sales	18,357	46,679	28,763
Purchases	4,784	25,879	8,472

Required Prepare departmental trading accounts for the year ended 28 February 20*5.

QUESTION 3

Maurice Duvall owns and runs a shop specialising in continental cheeses and meats. He provides the following information for the year ended 31 October 20*4.

	£
Stocks of cheeses – 1 November 20*3	2,860
31 October 20*4	1,790
Stocks of meats – 1 November 20*3	1,540
31 October 20*4	1,680
Purchases – cheeses	29,960
meats	43,750
Sales – cheeses	88,630
meats	125,330

	£
Wages of sales assistants – cheeses	12,660
meats	21,110
Administrative salaries	8,560
Insurances	4,800
Repairs to meat fridge	840
Electricity	2,400
Rent and rates	7,200
Lighting and heating expenses	1,680
General expenses	8,550
Motor expenses (including depreciation)	11,500

The cheese department occupies two-thirds of the total floor area; the meat department occupies the remainder.

Overheads are to be apportioned as follows:

■ according to **floor area** – electricity, rent and rates and lighting and heating
■ **equally** between the two departments – administrative salaries, insurances and general expenses
■ **motor expenses** are to be apportioned one-fifth to cheeses and four-fifths to meats.

Required Prepare a departmental trading and profit and loss account for the year ended 31 October 20*4.

QUESTION 4

The following information is given for Sandra's boutique:

	£
Wages	108,000
Rent and rates	9,400
Insurances	9,500
Depreciation	24,000
General expenses	17,400
Purchases – Department A	72,000
Department B	64,000
Department C	18,000
Sales – Department A	180,000
Department B	120,000
Department C	60,000
Stock as at 1 February 20*4 – Department A	5,800
Department B	4,600

	£
Department C	1,800
Stock as at 31 January 20*5 – Department A	5,500
Department B	4,900
Department C	1,600

■ Departments A and B each occupy 4,400 m²; Department C occupies 2,200 m².
■ Wages and depreciation are to be apportioned in proportion to sales revenue.
■ Rent and rates are to be apportioned according to floor area occupied.
■ Insurances and general expenses are to be apportioned equally.

Required Prepare a departmental trading and profit and loss account for the year ended 31 January 20*5.

CONTROL ACCOUNTS – FURTHER CONSIDERATIONS

In *Introducing Accounting* we prepared control accounts and used them to verify the entries in the sales ledgers and purchases ledgers. It is unusual at A2 Level to require candidates to prepare a straightforward control account. (The exception to this is, of course, when it is part of a larger synoptic question.)

Questions at A2 Level generally deal with errors and events that are discovered after the schedule of debtors and the control accounts have been drawn up.

These questions are designed to test candidates' knowledge of:

■ how control accounts are prepared
■ the sources of information used to write up the personal ledger accounts
■ the sources of information used to prepare the control accounts
■ the relationship between the control account and the personal ledger accounts.

It is worth spending a little time revisiting *Introducing Accounting* to remind yourself how the day books are used to write up both the personal ledger accounts and the control accounts.

Remember that some control accounts are kept as part of the double-entry system; they are **integrated** into the double-entry system. Some control accounts are kept purely as memorandum accounts and the personal accounts are kept as part of the double-entry system.

Whether control accounts are part of the double-entry system or whether they are memorandum accounts, they are always prepared in the same way.

A **schedule of debtors** is a list of all debit balances extracted from the sales ledger(s).

A **schedule of creditors** is a list of all credit balances extracted from the purchases ledger(s).

● EXAMINATION TIP

Remember that any credit balances extracted from the sales ledger must be shown in the trial balance (and later the balance sheet) as creditors.

Any debit balances extracted from the purchases ledger must be shown as debtors.

The most popular type of question to be set at A2 Level requires candidates to reconcile the balance shown in the control account with the total of the balances extracted from the appropriate personal ledger.

This type of question will give a list of errors. Some of the errors will require:

- an adjustment to a personal account in the sales ledger (or purchases ledger) only – hence this will have an effect on the schedule of debtors (or creditors) extracted from the ledger
- an adjustment to the appropriate control account only – hence this will have an effect on the balance brought down in the control account
- an adjustment to both a personal account in the sales ledger (or the purchases ledger) and an adjustment to the control account too.

WORKED EXAMPLE

Amandeep Bola maintains control accounts as part of her general ledger. She has prepared a sales ledger control account for February 20*5 with information derived from her subsidiary books. The debit balances shown in the control account at 28 February 20*5 amounted to £9,040. This failed to agree with the schedule of debtor balances extracted from the sales ledger on that date. This showed total debtors of £9,372.

After preparing the control account and the schedule of debtors, the following errors were discovered:

1. The debit side of John Taylor's account in the sales ledger had been overcast by £100.
2. A credit sale of £340 to Akit Patel had been debited in error to the account of Anjni Patel. Akit's account had been debited to correct the error but no entry had been made in Anjni's account.
3. A credit sale to Janice Mulch of £108 had been correctly entered in the sales day book but had not been entered in her sales ledger account.

Required   Prepare a statement reconciling the total debtors shown by the schedule of debtors with that shown in the control account at 28 February 20*5.

Answer

	£	
Total debtor balances as per schedule	9,372	All these errors have an effect on one
Less Overcast	(100)	of the accounts in the sales ledger.
Entry in Anjni' account	(340)	None of them has any effect on the
Add Entry to Janice's account	108	sales ledger control account.
Control account balance	9,040	

WORKED EXAMPLE

Leslie Buttersby has prepared a purchases ledger control account as a memorandum account for December 20*4. The creditors shown in the control account at 31 December 20*4 amounted to £6,488; this amount failed to agree with the total of creditors' balances extracted from the purchases ledger at that date. The schedule of creditors totalled £4,316.

The following errors were discovered during January 20*5:

1. A page of the purchases day book was overcast by £1,000.
2. The balance of £7,937 on the purchases ledger control account at the end of November 20*4 had been carried forward into the December control account as £9,737.
3. Credit balances amounting to £1,372 had been transferred to the sales ledger. These 'set-offs' had not been entered in the purchases ledger control account.

WORKED EXAMPLE *continued*

Required Prepare a statement showing the adjustments to the balance shown by the purchases ledger control account.

Answer

	£
Balance as per control account 31 December 20*4	6,488
Add Amount of overcast	1,000
Less Transposition error	(1,800)
Set-offs	(1,372)
Corrected control account credit balance	4,316

WORKED EXAMPLE

Charlie Parlez maintains control accounts as part of his general ledger. He has prepared a sales ledger control account for the month of August 20*4. The debit balance shown in the sales ledger control account at 31 August 20*4 failed to agree with the schedule of debtors extracted from the sales ledger at that date. The total of the balances extracted from the sales ledger at that date was £16,561. The following errors were subsequently discovered:

1. The debit side of Melvyn Chan's account in the sales ledger had been undercast by £10.
2. A credit sale of £427 to David Austen had been debited to the account of Darren Morris in error.
3. A credit sale of £633 to I. Gourd had not been entered in the sales day book.
4. A page in the returns day book had been undercast by £100.
5. The account of Juan Badun shows a debit balance of £137. Although an entry to write this debt off as being bad had been entered in the journal, no entries had been made in any ledgers.
6. The provision for doubtful debts was increased in August from £1,740 to £1,930; no entry has been made in any ledger.

Required Calculate:

a the corrected total of sales ledger balances after the errors have been corrected
b the total of debtor balances at 31 August 20*4 as shown in Melvyn's sales ledger control account **before** the errors had been corrected.

Answer

a)

	£
Debtor balances as per uncorrected schedule	16,561
Add Adjustment to Melvyn's account (1)	10
Add Missing entry from account of I. Gourd (3)	633
Less Bad debt (5)	(137)
Corrected debtors' balances	17,067

WORKED EXAMPLE *continued*

b)

	£
Correct debtors balance as per control account	17,067
Add Sale to I. Gourd (3)	633
Less Sales returns day book undercast (4)	(100)
Less Bad debt written off (5)	(137)
Original debit balance on incorrect control account	17,463

- Correction (2) does not affect the schedule of debtor balances nor does it affect the sales ledger control account – it is a transfer from one debtor to another.
- Correction (6) does not affect the sales ledger – it is a book entry only: debit profit and loss account; credit the provision account.

● EXAMINATION TIP

Remember that the solution to this type of problem is not dependent on whether the control accounts are integrated or kept as memorandum accounts. The time when there will be a difference in your answers is when you are required to show the double entries.

WORKED EXAMPLE

A credit sale to R. Dickens for £97 had been omitted from the sales day book.

Required Journal entries to correct the error.

Answer

For an integrated system:
    Dr Sales ledger control account   97
        Cr Sales   97

For control accounts kept as memorandum accounts:
    Dr R. Dickens   97
        Cr Sales   97

QUESTION 5

Alex Brown has prepared a schedule of debtors which has totalled £4,775. He has discovered the following errors which he believes may affect the list of debtors balances that he has extracted from his sales ledger at 31 May 20*4:

1. A balance on the account of T. Stamp, a credit customer, of £146 has been brought down on 1 June as £416.
2. The sales day book has been undercast by £1,000.
3. An entry for C. Oyne of £718 in the sales day book has not been posted to his account in the sales ledger.
4. P. Ence, who owes Alex £316, could not settle his debt and the amount was to have been written off in May – no entries had been made in the books of account to record this.

Required Calculate the corrected total of debtors at 31 May 20*4.

QUESTION 6

Melody Gnobu has prepared a purchases ledger control account for May 20*4. The balance carried down was £11,319. In June 20*4 she discovered the following errors:

1. The purchases returns day book had been undercast by £100 in May 20*4.
2. A payment to I. Gloope for £612 on 12 May 20*4 had been entered in the cash book but had not been entered in Gloope's account.
3. Transfers of balances (set-offs) amounting to £4,372, in May 20*4, had not been entered in any control account.
4. The total discount allowed account had not been entered in any control account.

Required Calculate the correct balance to be carried forward into the purchases ledger control account for June 20*4.

QUESTION 7

Julie Blackwell maintains control accounts as an integral part of her double-entry system. She has prepared a sales ledger control account for January 20*5.
She has also extracted a schedule of debtors from her sales ledger. The total of debtors failed to agree with the balance carried forward to the February control account of £4,361.
The following errors have been discovered:

1. A copy of the sales invoice sent to Clax & Co for £301 had been destroyed and no record of the transaction had been made in the books of account.
2. Discounts received of £126 had not been entered in the control account.
3. The balance brought down on 1 January amounting to £2,717 had not been entered in the control account.
4. A credit sale to J. Fitzwilliam of £991 had been entered in the sales day book but had not been posted to the ledger.
5. Cash sales for 4 January 20*5 amounting to £1,488 had not been entered in the books of account.
6. A credit sale of £637 to Betty Cluck had been entered in the sales day book as £376.

Required

a The correct total of debtors shown in the sales ledger control account for January 20*5.
b The total of debtors balances at 31 January 20*5 before the errors were corrected.

QUESTION 8

Rita Blundiski maintains control accounts as memorandum accounts. Her purchases ledger control account prepared for September does not agree with the £27,520 total of creditors extracted from her purchase ledger. On examination, Rita discovers the following errors:

1. A purchases invoice for £543 for goods purchased on credit from J. Bull has not been received. No entry has been made in the book of prime entry.
2. The total of the discount received column in the cash book had been overcast by £101.
3. One whole page in the payments cash book totalling £4,728 had been posted to the wrong side of the individual creditors' accounts.
4. Bad debts for September amounting to £1,342 have not been written off in the books of account.
5. A purchases invoice received from Pough & Blow Ltd, for £1,467, had been entered in the purchases day book as £7,164.
6. Transfers (set-offs) from the sales ledger, to the purchases ledger, amounting to £1,467, had not been entered in either control account.
7. A balance of £211 in the account of Patsy D. Khan at 31 July 20*4 had been carried down on 1 August as £1,121.

Required

a Calculate the corrected total creditors at 30 September **after** errors 1–7 have been taken into account.
b Calculate the original balance on the purchases ledger control account at 30 September 20*4 **before** errors 1–7 were taken into account.

SUSPENSE ACCOUNTS

Suspense accounts are sometimes examined at A2 Level, especially as part of the synoptic assessment. Remember that if a trial balance does not balance, you cannot reasonably expect your final accounts to balance if you use the figures from the trial balance to prepare your final accounts.

To allow a set of draft final accounts to be prepared, a suspense item is included in the trial balance in order to make it balance. If the 'balancing' amount is a debit, the suspense item is included in the balance sheet as a current asset. If the suspense item is a credit, then this will appear in the balance sheet as a current liability.

Here are three examples to remind you of how a suspense account is used.

WORKED EXAMPLE

The sales day book has been overcast by £100.

Required Prepare journal entries to correct the error.

Answer

The sales day book provides the entry to the double-entry system (remember the ticket booths into the football ground in *Introducing Accounting*).

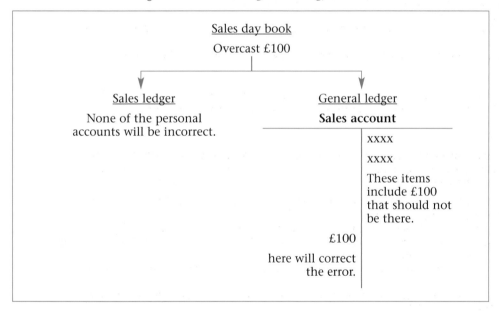

So we have put in £100 on the debit side of the double-entry system. Where can we put a credit entry to maintain our system? In the rent account? In the wages account? Of course not! If you cannot find a corresponding entry easily and comfortably, you will need to use a suspense account.

So:

	Dr	Cr
Sales account Dr	£100	
Suspense account		£100
Correction of error – sales overcast by £100.		

Rent paid of £4,000 has been entered in the rates account in error.

Required Prepare journal entries to correct the error.

Answer

Rates account		
xxxx	4,000	
xxxx		

We need to credit the rates account to get it right and debit the rent account

Rent account		
xxxx		
xxxx		
4,000		

Do we have a debit entry and a credit entry? Of course – easy – so no need for entries in any other account.

So:

	Dr	Cr
Rent account Dr	£4,000	
Rates account		£4,000

Correction of error of commission £4,000 paid for rent incorrectly entered in rates account.

WORKED EXAMPLE

The discounts received column in the cash book totalling £953 has been posted to the debit of the discounts allowed account as £539.

Required Prepare journal entries to correct the error.

Answer

Discounts allowed		
xxxx	539	

Entry to remove incorrect posting of discount received.

Discounts received		
	xxxx	
	xxxx	
	953	

Entry to post correctly discount received.

Do we have a debit entry and a credit entry (of the same amount)? No – we have credit entries totalling £1,492 – we need a debit entry of £1,492. Where can we put the debit

QUESTION 9

Patricia Gooi extracted a trial balance from her ledgers at close of business on 31 May 20*4. The trial balance totals failed to agree. (Patricia maintains an integrated set of control accounts in her general ledger.) In June 20*4 Patricia found the following errors:

1. The advertising account had been overcast by £100.
2. A cheque paid to Ralph Simpson for £720 had been posted to the credit of his account.
3. Goods to the value of £120 withdrawn for Patricia's own use had been included in the books as sales.
4. Repairs of £1,600 to a machine had been debited to the Machinery account.

When these errors had been corrected, the trial balance totals agreed.

Required Prepare:

a journal entries to correct the errors that Patricia discovered
b a suspense account showing clearly the original trial balance error

(narratives are not required).

QUESTION 10

Vincent Schelling extracted a trial balance from his ledgers at close of business on 30 April 20*4. The trial balance totals failed to agree. (Vincent does not maintain integrated control accounts in his general ledger.) In early May Vincent discovered the following errors:

1. Purchases returns of £702 had been incorrectly debited to the purchases account as £207.
2. £450 drawings for April had been posted to the wages account.
3. The sales day book had been overcast by £1,001.
4. A cheque paid to Sammy Lim for £71 had been posted to the credit of his account.

When the trial balance errors had been corrected, the trial balance totals agreed.

Required Prepare:

a journal entries to correct the errors (narratives are not required)
b a suspense account showing clearly the original trial balance difference.

QUESTION 11

Bert Aked extracted a trial balance from his ledgers at close of business on 31 January 20*5. The trial balance totals failed to agree. (Bert maintains integrated control accounts in his general ledger.) The following errors were discovered in early February 20*5:

1. Bert had injected £5,000 additional capital into his business. This sum had been included in the sales account.
2. Commission payable of £2,100 had been entered in the general ledger as commission receivable £1,200.

3. A credit sale of £650 to Pippa Bramley had been debited to the account of Pippin Cox.
4. £73 discount allowed entered in the cash book to Shirley Knott had been debited to the account of Andy Knott as £37.
5. Purchase returns of £140 sent to D. County had been entered in the account of S. County.

Required Prepare:

a journal entries to correct the errors (narratives are not required)
b a suspense account showing clearly the original trial balance difference.

QUESTION 12

Joyce McIntyre extracted a trial balance from her ledgers at close of business on 31 December 20*4. The trial balance totals failed to agree. (Joyce does not maintain integrated control accounts in her general ledger.) Joyce found the following errors in early January:

1. Goods returned by Sanaa Malik of £302 had been completely omitted from the books of account.
2. Rent receivable amounting to £650 had been posted to the rent payable account as £560.
3. A debit balance of £240 in the sales ledger account of S. Neal had been transferred to her purchase ledger account as £420.
4. The bank overdraft figure of £1,750 on 1 December had been included in the debit bank column in the cash book.
5. Goods purchased on credit from D. Hickson £903 had been entered in the account of H. Dickson.

When these errors had been corrected, the trial balance totals agreed.

Required Prepare:

a journal entries to correct the errors (narratives are not required)
b a suspense account showing clearly the original trial balance differences.

CHAPTER TWO

Incomplete Records

There are two main types of organisation that may not keep a full set of double-entry records. They are

- small cash-based businesses
- clubs and societies.

Both types of organisation are the frequent subject of examination questions.

Both types rely on similar skills and techniques in order to prepare a full set of final accounts.

In this chapter we shall consider the former; the final accounts of clubs and societies will be dealt with in the next chapter.

SMALL CASH-BASED BUSINESSES

Much of the work of any professional accountant is taken up with the preparation of the final accounts of small businesses; because many of these businesses carry on their business on a cash basis they will not keep a full set of ledgers in which to record their business transactions.

QUESTION

Name three businesses that conduct most of their business on a cash basis.

Answer
Your answer could have included businesses like Roland's Hair salon; Wong's Chinese take-away; Wendy's Mini-market.

Since there will be few (if any) credit customers in my answer it is extremely unlikely that Roland, Wong or Wendy will keep a sales ledger.

Remember that a sales ledger will contain the accounts of all credit customers. Since the vast majority of the customers of those businesses pay cash, there is no need to open an account for them.

Also, many (if not all) of the purchases of goods for resale and the services consumed will be paid for by using cash or by writing cheques. Roland will buy his perms from his local hairdressing cash and carry; Wong will pay by cheque for the gas used to cook the food that he sells; Wendy will pay for her telephone calls by cheque or by using cash. None of these traders will find it necessary to keep a purchases ledger.

The main book for the recording of transactions for these businesses will be a cash book in which all transactions using cash or cheques will be recorded. The information contained in the cash book will be supplemented by bank statements, till rolls, invoices and receipts.

The task that is faced in this situation is to build up a more complete picture of the financial transactions that have taken place during the financial year than the one that is shown by the cash book on its own.

There are two main types of questions set in examinations:

- where candidates are required to calculate the organisation's profit or loss
- where candidates are required to prepare a trading and profit and loss account for the organisation.

It is important that you are able to recognise each type of question.

Specification coverage:
AQA 14.1; OCR 5.2.4.

By the end of this chapter you should be able to:
- calculate net profit or loss using the net asset method
- prepare final accounts for businesses who do not keep a full set of financial records
- calculate cash and stock losses.

CALCULATION OF THE PROFIT OR LOSS OF A CASH-BASED BUSINESS

The key to recognising this type of question is found in the word used in the question. That word is 'required'. It is quite simple really – if you read the question very carefully.

This type of question will always ask you to calculate the profit or loss.

There are five stages to this procedure. You will recognise them. They have already been used in Chapter 2 of *Introducing Accounting*.

Since in this type of business there is no ledger, therefore no accounts. There can be no balances, so there can be no sheet for balances (ie a balance sheet).

Can you remember how you calculated the profit or loss for a business using the net asset method?

> A **statement of affairs** is exactly the same as a balance sheet.

- **Stage 1: Calculate the opening capital** (net assets) of the business either by listing the assets and then deducting the liabilities or by preparing a statement of affairs.
- **Stage 2: Calculate the closing capital** (net assets).
- **Stage 3: Deduct the opening capital from the closing capital**. This will indicate the profit or loss retained in the business.
- **Stage 4**: Some profits may have been taken out of the business during the year in the form of cash and/or goods (or services) as drawings. These **drawings** (profits) **have to be added to the retained profits**.
- **Stage 5**: Sometimes the proprietor of a business may inject new capital into the business. This extra capital will increase the assets owned by the business at the end of the year; in turn this will increase the figure we have calculated as retained profit (it could reduce the figure calculated as a retained loss).

  Obviously, the amount of capital introduced is not an increase in net assets earned by the business so it must be disregarded in our calculation. So **deduct capital introduced**.

We can summarise these stages:

	Closing capital
Deduct	Opening capital
Retained profit	xxxxxxxxxxxx
Add	*Drawings*
	xxxxxxxxxxxx
Deduct	Capital introduced
Profit for the year	xxxxxxxxxxxxxx

WORKED EXAMPLE

As at 1 January 20*4 Gemma had the following assets and liabilities: vehicle at valuation £2,400; equipment at valuation £5,400; stock £670; debtors £45; bank balance £1,730; creditors £260.

One year later, at 31 December 20*4, she had the following assets and liabilities: vehicles at valuation £12,400; equipment at valuation £4,860; stock £590; debtors £55; bank balance £2,540; creditors £180.

During the year Gemma withdrew £16,750 cash from the business for her household expenses. She also withdrew goods for her personal use, to the value of £1,230.

Required   Calculate the business profit or loss for the year ended 31 December 20*4.

WORKED EXAMPLE *continued*

Answer

	£
Closing capital	20,265 (12,400+4,860+590+55+2,540−180)
Less Opening capital	9,985 (2,400+5,400+670+45+1,730−260)
Retained profits	10,280
Add Drawings	17,980 (16,750+1,230)
Profit for the year ended	
31 December 20*3	28,260

Note the wording of the question: it said 'calculate'.

WORKED EXAMPLE

Dreyfus supplies the following information relating to his business:

	at 1 April 20*3 £	at 31 March 20*4 £
Premises at cost	60,000	60,000
Machinery at valuation	36,000	32,400
Vehicles at valuation	12,600	11,340
Stock	1,650	2,120
Debtors	135	120
Creditors	470	430
Bank balance	1,450	3,560

During the year ended 31 March 20*4 Dreyfus made drawings of £23,700.

In February Dreyfus inherited £7,800 from a distant relative; he paid this sum into the business bank account.

Required Calculate the business profit or loss for the year ended 31 March 20*4.

Answer

	£	
Closing capital	109,110	(60,000+32,400+11,340+2,120+120+3,560−430)
Less Opening capital	111,365	(60,000+36,000+12,600+1,650+135+1,450−470)
Retained profits	(2,255)	
Add Drawings	23,700	
	21,445	
Less Capital introduced	7,800	
Net profit for the year ended		
31 March 20*4	13,645	

○ **EXAMINATION TIP**

Always show your workings – they may gain you marks if part of your answer is incorrect.

QUESTION 1

Chesney supplies the following information:

Assets and liabilities	at 30 November 20*3 £	at 30 November 20*4 £
Machinery	40,000	48,000
Equipment	10,000	14,000
Vehicles	17,000	15,000
Stock	1,250	1,300
Debtors	500	700
Creditors	910	1,000
Long-term loan	20,000	30,000
Bank balance	1,750	2,000

During the year Chesney withdrew £13,500 cash from the business for private use.

Required Calculate the profit or loss for the year ended 30 November 20*4.

QUESTION 2

Marion supplies the following information:

Assets and liabilities	at 31 May 20*3 £	at 31 May 20*4 £
Vehicles	12,000	19,000
Stock	140	610
Debtors	–	400
Creditors	–	160
Bank balance	730	1,270
Bank loan	–	7,500
Cash in hand	20	30

During the year Marion withdrew £8,400 cash from the business for private use.

Required Calculate the profit or loss for the year ended 31 May 20*4.

QUESTION 3

Pat provides the following information:

Assets and liabilities	at 31 December 20*3 £	at 31 December 20*4 £
Premises	40,000	40,000
Machinery	10,000	14,000
Vehicles	16,000	12,000
Stock	2,400	2,500
Debtors	180	200
Creditors	930	1,000
Bank balance	1,650	2,840

During the year Pat withdrew £24,500 from the business for private use. She also paid a National Lottery win of £12,500 into the business bank account.

Required Calculate the profit or loss for the year ended 31 May 20*4.

QUESTION 4

Nicky had net assets valued at £67,800 on 1 October 20*3; one year later, on 30 September 20*4, her net assets were valued at £72,450. During the year ended 30 September 20*4 she withdrew £18,950 cash from the business for private use. She also took £875 of goods from the business for her own use.

During the year an uncle gave her a gift of £25,000 which she paid into the business bank account.

Required Calculate the profit or loss for the year ended 30 September 20*4.

PREPARATION OF FINAL ACCOUNTS OF A CASH-BASED BUSINESS

We have seen how we can calculate the profit or loss by comparing closing and opening capital values. In real life this is usually not sufficient to satisfy the Inland Revenue (for taxation purposes) or to satisfy the Customs and Excise authorities (for VAT purposes).

Both of these government departments would require more detailed records to be kept.

These records do not have to be a full set of double-entry records – there is no statutory requirement that sole traders or partnerships should maintain a full set of accounting records.

To satisfy the authorities, most traders would keep a record of all cash and bank transactions. They would also keep all source documents received and copies of those sent.

QUESTION

Identify **four** source documents kept by a sole trader who does not keep a full set of accounting records.

Answer

Your answer should have identified: purchases invoices; copies of sales invoices; bank statements; cheque book counterfoils; paying-in counterfoils; till rolls; invoices from the utilities (gas, electricity, water) – the list could go on. The source documents are a record of all monies received and paid out.

These source documents will:

■ help us build up a picture of the financial transaction that have taken place throughout the financial year
■ verify the receipts and payments made
■ be necessary if the business is VAT registered. A record of VAT paid to suppliers and charged to customers is essential to determine whether VAT has to be paid to Customs and Excise or claimed back from it.

In an examination any question that asks for the preparation of a trading account, a profit and loss account and a balance sheet will require the following procedures. So we must read the question very carefully.

● EXAMINATION TIP

Questions that start with the word 'calculate' require the techniques used above. Those starting with the words 'prepare a trading and profit and loss account' require the following techniques. Learn the difference – it will save you time and possible anguish.

In order to be able to use this second method it is essential that we have the following information to hand:

■ valuations of assets and liabilities at the start of the financial year
■ debtors and creditors totals at the start of the financial year
■ accrued expenses at the start of the year
■ pre-payments made at the start of the financial year
■ payments made by debtors during the financial year
■ payments made to creditors during the financial year
■ cash payments made during the financial year
■ cash receipts during the financial year
■ valuations of assets and liabilities at the end of the financial year
■ debtors and creditors totals at the end of the financial year
■ accrued expenses at the end of the financial year
■ pre-payments made at the end of the financial year.

There are four stages to preparing the final accounts from a set of records that are incomplete:

■ Stage 1: Prepare an opening statement of affairs. You may have to calculate the capital figure if it is not given in the question.
■ Stage 2: Compile a summary of cash and bank transactions.
■ Stage 3: Construct adjustment accounts (some teachers call these 'control accounts').
■ Stage 4: Prepare the final accounts by using all the information gained from Stages 1, 2 and 3.

REVISION TIP

Learn these four stages – they are so important.

It is essential to follow these stages methodically each time you are asked to produce a set of final accounts from incomplete records.

The stage that gives most people a problem is Stage 3. Stage 3 is necessary because most of the records kept by traders who keep less than a full set of books of account are records of cash spent to acquire the necessary resources to carry on business or records of cash when it is received.

As accountants we must be aware of and apply the **accruals concept** – the payment to acquire a resource is not the same as the use of that resource.

Consider two examples:

Jack receives £120 on 15 February 20*4 for a sale of goods that took place on 21 December 20*3.

Cash was recorded in February – the profit was earned in December (realisation concept which is part of the accruals concept).

Electricity meter was read on 28 July for electricity used in May, June and July.

The electricity bill was received on 13 August and the amount was paid (very late!) on 12 October.

Electricity (a resource) used in May, June and July – even though the payment was not paid until October.

Stage 3 sounds very complicated, but if we rely on first principles that we learned in our AS year it should be simplified.

Rely on your knowledge of double entry.

Rely on using 'T' accounts.

We will concentrate on Stage 3 since this is the stage that seems to cause the main problem.

WORKED EXAMPLE

Saleem Zain does not keep full accounting records. He is able to provide the following information for the year ended 29 February 20*4:

Summarised bank account			
	£		£
Balance as at 1 March 20*3	1,456	Payments to creditors	43,675
Receipts from debtors	86,494	General expenses	24,911
		Purchase of fixed asset	17,500
		Balance as at 29 February 20*4	1,864
	87,950		87,950

Additional information

	at 1 March 20*3	at 29 February 20*4
	£	£
Debtors	752	918
Creditors	857	633
Stock	2,152	2,779

Required Prepare a trading account for the year ended 29 February 20*4.

Answer

We must prepare an adjustment account to determine the amount of sales for the year (remember that this may be different to the cash received from debtors during the year).

We also need to construct a similar account to determine the amount of the purchases for the year.

'Missing figures' for sales and purchases are italicised

	Debtors				Creditors		
Balance b/d	752	Cash received	86,494	Cash paid	43,675	Balance b/d	857
Sales	*86,660*	Balance c/d	918	Balance c/d	633	*Purchases*	*43,451*
	87,412		87,412		44,308		44,308
Balance b/d	918					Balance b/d	633

To avoid making an error with your debtors and creditors, always put the closing balances under the account totals and 'bring them up'.

Debtors on the debit *under the account.* Creditors on the credit *under the account.*

WORKED EXAMPLE *continued*

Saleem Zain
Trading account for the year ended 29 February 20*4

	£	£
Sales		86,660
Less Cost of sales		
Stock as at 1 March 20*3	2,152	
Purchases	43,451	
	45,603	
Stock as at 29 February 20*4	2,779	42,824
Gross profit		43,836

QUESTION 5

Tamsin Rook does not keep a full set of accounting records. She is able to provide the following information for the year ended 31 August 20*4:

Summarised bank account

	£		£
Balance as at 1 September 20*3	2,963	Payments to creditors	59,846
Receipts from debtors	121,367	General expenses	60,957
		Balance as at 31 August 20*4	3,527
	124,330		124,330

Additional information

	at 1 September 20*3 £	at 31 August 20*4 £
Stock	8,467	9,566
Debtors	1,792	2,468
Creditors	815	1,067

Required Prepare a trading account for the year ended 31 August 20*4.

QUESTION 6

Barbara Vun does not keep a full set of accounting records. She provides the following information for the year ended 31 March 20*4:

Summarised bank account

	£		£
Receipts from debtors	68,499	Balance as at 1 April 20*3	852
Balance as at 31 March 20*4	2,467	Payments to creditors	32,814
		General expenses	37,300
	70,966		70,966

Additional information

	at 1 April 20*3 £	at 31 March 20*4 £
Stock	488	637
Debtors	214	376
Creditors	1,496	2,841

Required Prepare a trading account for the year ended 31 March 20*4.

We can use the same approach to determine the amount of any expenses to be debited to the profit and loss account if we know the cash paid and the amount of any accruals and pre-payments outstanding at the end of each financial year.

WORKED EXAMPLE

Harry Cary does not keep a full set of accounting records but he is able to provide the following information for the year ended 31 July 20*4:

Amounts paid for staff wages	£21,387
Amounts paid to landlord for rent	£3,400
Amounts paid for electricity	£2,162
Amounts paid for insurances	£3,467

Additional information

Amounts owed	at 1 August 20*3 £	at 31 July 20*4 £
for staff wages	212	297
for rent	118	136
for electricity	167	48
Amount paid in advance for insurances	196	346

Required Calculate the amounts for wages and rent to be included in the profit and loss account for the year ended 31 July 20*4.

Answer

Wages	£21,472
Rent	£3,418
Electricity	£2,043
Insurances	£3,317

Workings

Use the same procedure that was used to determine sales and purchases earlier.

Wages			
Cash	21,387	Balance as at 1 August 20*3	212
Balance as at 31 July 20*4	297	P & L a/c	21,472
	21,684		21,684
		Balance as at 1 August 20*4	297

WORKED EXAMPLE *continued*

Rent

Cash	3,400	Balance as at 1 August 20*3	118
Balance as at 31 July 20*4	136	P & L a/c	3,418
	3,536		3,536
		Balance as at 1 August 20*4	136

Electricity

Cash	2,162	Balance as at 1 August 20*3	167
Balance as at 31 July 20*4	48	P & L a/c	2,043
	2,210		2,210
		Balance as at 1 August 20*4	48

Insurances

Balance as at 1 August 20*3	196	P & L a/c	3,317
Cash	3,467	Balance as at 31 July 20*4	346
	3,663		3,663
Balance as at 1 August 20*4	346		

Notice that the balances have been brought down. This is important since often there are marks in an examination for these balances.

QUESTION 7

Eric provides the following information for the year ended 31 January 20*4:

	at 1 February 20*4 £	at 31 January 20*5 £
Amount owed for motor expenses	78	461
Amount paid in advance for rates	120	145
Cash paid during the year ended 31 January 20*5 for motor expenses		£8,166
Cash paid during the year ended 31 January 20*5 for rates		£1,534

Required Calculate the amounts to be entered in the profit and loss account for the year ended 31 January 20*4.

QUESTION 8

Tanya provides the following information for the year ended 30 September 20*4:

	at 1 October 20*3 £	at 30 September 20*4 £
Amount owed for advertising	467	88
Amount paid in advance for rent	200	360
Cash paid during the year ended 30 September 20*4 for advertising		£2,784
Cash paid during the year ended 30 September 20*4 for rent		£6,160

Calculate the amounts to be entered in the profit and loss account for the year ended 30 September 20*4.

We shall now work through an example that incorporates the techniques outlined above.

Work carefully through this example. We will be using the four stages outlined at the start of this section.

Can you remember the four stages?

WORKED EXAMPLE

Roger Guillaume owns a florist's shop. He does not maintain proper books of account.

He provides the following information for the year ended 30 April 20*4:

Summarised bank account

	£		£
Balance as at 1 May 20*3	1,793	Payments to creditors	22,497
Takings banked	74,887	Rates	2,430
		Rent	2,800
		Other expenses	20,075
		Drawings	8,409
		Purchase of vehicle	17,000
		Balance as at 30 April 20*4	3,469
	76,680		76,680

All takings were paid into the bank account with the exception of the following:

Wages £14,280
Drawings £12,000

Additional information

Assets and liabilities	at 1 May 20*3 £	at 30 April 20*4 £
Stock	212	164
Debtors	48	130
Creditors	467	328
Cash in hand	142	237
Rates paid in advance	1,080	1,340
Rent owed	102	120
Fixtures at valuation	720	648
Vehicles at valuation	4,200	16,500

Required

Prepare a trading and profit and loss account for the year ended 30 April 20*4 and a balance sheet as at that date.

Note that because the question asks for the preparation of a set of final accounts, we must go carefully and methodically through each of the four stages outlined earlier.

If the question had asked for a calculation of the profit or loss, we could have used the much quicker net asset method.

Both methods will give us the same profit figure but the net asset method would not give us the same amount of detail that a full set of accounts will.

WORKED EXAMPLE *continued*

Answer

Stage 1: Prepare an opening statement of affairs

As an Advanced Level student you should be able to do this almost as quickly as you can write the items down.

Do not be concerned with categories of assets and liabilities.

Stage 1 is part of your workings **BUT** do write the figures down neatly as well as quickly.

	Statement of affairs as at 1 May 20*3		
		£	
Assets	Stock	212	
	Trade debtors	48	
	Rates in advance	1,080	
	Cash	142	
	Fixtures	720	
	Vehicles	4,200	
Don't forget . . .	Bank balance	1,793	
		8,195	
Liabilities	Trade creditors	467	
	Rent owed	102	
		569	
	Net assets	7,626	This is also Roger's capital

Note that the assets have been written down in the order that they have appeared in the question; no attempt has been made to categorise them.

Do take care to include the bank balance if it is not included in the list of assets and liabilities given in the question.

● EXAMINATION TIP

Do not just key the assets and liabilities into your calculator. If you do make an error then you cannot be rewarded for the parts that you got correct. Write the items down before you key them in.

Stage 2: Compile summarised cash and/or bank accounts

A bank summary has been given in the question (one less task to be done!). But we do need to prepare a cash summary.

Cash account				
Balance as at 1 May 20*3 (from list of assets)	142	Takings banked (from bank summary)	74,887
Total takings for year (missing figure)	*101,262*	Wages paid	14,280
		Drawings	12,000
		Balance as at 30 April 20*4 (from list of closing balances)	237
	101,404		101,404

Stage 3: Construct adjustment accounts

You may be uncertain how many adjustment accounts to use. Initially you may not be confident enough to decide which accounts to open and which items do not need to be adjusted.

WORKED EXAMPLE *continued*

If you are not confident, then open an account for every item listed in your statement of affairs.

Stock – we will adjust the stock in a special account in Stage 4. The special account is the trading account! You are well used to adjusting stock – you have done this in every trading account that you have ever done!

Open an adjustment account for each of:

trade debtors; rates; (not cash – we adjusted our cash figures in Stage 2); fixtures; (not bank – this has been adjusted for us in the question); trade creditors, and finally rent.

Do each adjustment in turn.

Open a 'T' account for each:

1. Enter the opening balance (debit for an asset; credit for a liability).
2. Enter the closing balance under your 'T' account.
3. Take the closing balance up diagonally into the body of the account.
4. Debit cash paid from the bank or cash account.
5. Credit cash received into the bank or cash account.
6. Total the account.
7. Calculate the *missing figure* to be posted to the trading account or profit and loss account.

Let us prepare the adjustment accounts. Numbers are given as a guide to the order in which the entries are made.

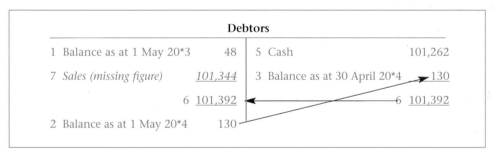

Debtors

1 Balance as at 1 May 20*3	48		5 Cash		101,262
7 *Sales (missing figure)*	*101,344*		3 Balance as at 30 April 20*4		130
	6 101,392			6	101,392
2 Balance as at 1 May 20*4	130				

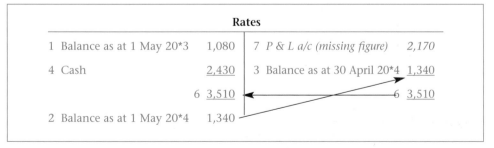

Rates

1 Balance as at 1 May 20*3	1,080		7 *P & L a/c (missing figure)*		*2,170*
4 Cash	2,430		3 Balance as at 30 April 20*4		1,340
	6 3,510			6	3,510
2 Balance as at 1 May 20*4	1,340				

WORKED EXAMPLE *continued*

Fixtures

Balance as at 1 May 20*3	720	*P & L a/c missing figure (depreciation)*	*72*
		Balance as at 30 April 20*4	648
	720		720
Balance as at 1 May 20*4	648		

Vehicles

Balance as at 1 May 20*3	4,200	*P & L a/c missing figure (depreciation)*	*4,700*
Cash	17,000	Balance as at 30 April 20*4	16,500
	21,200		21,200
Balance as at 1 May 20*4	16,500		

Creditors

Cash	22,497	Balance as at 1 May 20*3	467
Balance as at 30 April 20*4	328	*Purchases missing figure*	*22,358*
	22,825		22,825
		Balance as at 1 May 20*4	328

Rent

Cash	2,800	Balance as at 1 May 20*3	102
Balance as at 30 April 20*4	120	*P & L a/c missing figure*	*2,818*
	2,920		2,920
		Balance as at 1 May 20*4	120

Generally at this point in an examination you will have scored no marks unless you have specifically been asked to prepare the opening statement of affairs or one or two of the adjustment accounts in detail. The question asked us to prepare a trading and profit and loss account and balance sheet and as yet we have not done that. All that we have done is the preparatory work – we have got all our information ready.

An accountant in practice would call all the workings that we have done 'working papers'.

It is now time for Stage 4 where we bring all our workings together to prepare the final accounts.

● EXAMINATION TIP

Show all your workings, no matter how trivial they seem to be. If you have made an error in compiling your final accounts or even in your workings, you will be rewarded for the parts that you have got correct. Every mark counts towards that final grade.

WORKED EXAMPLE *continued*

Stage 4: Preparation of final accounts

Roger Guillaume
Trading and profit and loss account for the year ended 30 April 20*4

	£	£
Sales		101,344
Less Cost of sales		
Stock	212	
Purchases	22,358	
	22,570	
Stock	164	22,406
Gross profit		78,938
Less Expenses		
Rates	2,170	
Rent	2,818	
Wages	14,280	
Other expenses	20,075	
Depreciation Fixtures	72	
Vehicles	4,700	44,115
Net profit		34,823

Balance sheet as at 30 April 20*4

	£	£	£
Fixed assets			
Fixtures at valuation			648
Vehicles at valuation			16,500
			17,148
Current assets			
Stock		164	
Trade debtors		130	
Bank balance		3,469	
Cash		237	
Rates paid in advance		1,340	
		5,340	
Less Current liabilities			
Trade creditors	328		
Rent accrued	120	448	4,892
			22,040
Capital			7,626
Add Net profit			34,823
			42,449
Less Drawings			20,409
			22,040

CALCULATION OF MISSING CASH

Examination questions sometimes indicate that cash has been stolen during the course of the year. Part of the question might require the candidate to calculate the amount of cash that is missing.

The procedure involves working out what the cash position would have been had the mishap not occurred, and comparing that position with the actual position.

Imagine that you receive £80 wages from a part-time job. On the way home you buy a DVD costing £14.99 and a magazine costing £2.30.

Later, you are in the shower when your brother asks you to lend him some money.

You call to him 'Help yourself from my wallet'.

How would you calculate the amount of cash he had taken?

Use the same technique in an accounting problem where cash has gone missing.

WORKED EXAMPLE

Adele owns a general store. At 1 January her cash in hand was £167. At the end of the year, on 31 December, cash in hand was £143. Her till rolls show her takings to be £53,788. During the year she banked £21,894 after taking £13,600 cash for private use and paying wages of £17,840.

Adele believes that some cash has been stolen in a burglary over the Christmas period.

Required

Calculate the amount of cash stolen.

Answer

Cash summary			
Cash in hand as at 1 January	167	Cash banked	21,894
Takings	53,788	Drawings	13,600
		Wages	17,840
		Cash stolen (missing figure)	*478*
		Cash in hand as at 31 December	143
	53,955		53,955

Note that the question asked for a calculation; it did not ask for an account. The answer has been given in account form but full marks could have been gained by other means.

There are a variety of ways of arriving at the correct answer; each would be acceptable. However, do show full workings if you choose another method of arriving at your answer.

The answer shows an account as this fits in with the workings used throughout the chapter.

CALCULATION OF MISSING STOCK

To calculate the value of stock that has gone missing during a financial year, a trading account that uses *actual figures* is compared with the figures that ought to have applied.

WORKED EXAMPLE

Gary owns a hairdressing salon. Several boxes of expensive perms have been stolen. Gary is unsure of the value of the stolen perms. He provides the following information for the year ended 30 April 20*4:

stocks of perms as at 1 May 20*3 £210; stocks of perms as at 30 April 20*4 £70; purchases of perms during the year ended 30 April 20*4 £4,690; sales of perms during the year £7,080. (All perms carry a uniform mark-up of 50%.)

WORKED EXAMPLE *continued*

Answer

	Actual figures are		They should be	
	£	£	£	£
Sales		7,080		7,080
Less Cost of sales				
Stock as at 1 May 20*3	210		210	
Purchases	4,690		4,690	
	4,900		4,900	
Stock as at 30 April 20*4	70		180	4,720
Stolen stock *missing figure*	110	4,720		
Gross profit		2,360		2,360

Note: The closing stock of £70 appears as a current asset on the balance sheet; the mark-up percentage was used to calculate the gross profit; the stolen stock of £110 must also appear as an expense on the profit and loss account to complete the double entry.

Chapter summary

- Net profit can be calculated by comparing net assets at the start of a period (usually a year) with net assets at the end of the period.
- This is a very accurate way of determining profit but it has the major drawback that it does not show all the financial details of exactly how this profit was earned. These details are essential for stewardship and management purposes.
- If a set of final accounts is to be prepared then the four-step approach must be adopted:
  - prepare an opening statement of affairs
  - compile a bank and/or cash summary
  - construct adjustment accounts
  - prepare final accounts.

Self-test questions

- A statement of affairs is the same as a ——————.
- Total assets less total liabilities =——————.
- Opening capital + net profit − drawings =——————.
- Closing capital less opening capital =——————.
- Profits retained in the business + drawings =——————.
- Profits retained in the business —— drawings —— capital introduced = net profit.
- Opening balance in a vehicles account is £23,000; no purchases or sales of vehicles takes place over the year. The closing balance is £18,000. What does the difference in balances represent?
- Cash paid to creditors during the year is credited to the creditors' adjustment account. True or false?
- Cash received from debtors during the year is credited to the debtors' adjustment account. True or false?
- Sole traders are required by law to keep a full set of double-entry books. True or false?

TEST QUESTIONS

QUESTION 9

Fatima Aakloo provides the following information for the year ended 30 April 20*4: Her net assets at 30 April 20*3 were £47,682; her net assets at 30 April 20*4 were £37,901. During the year ended 30 April 20*4 she withdrew goods to the value of £831 and cash amounting to £17,467 from the business for private use.

Required Calculate the profit or loss for the year ended 30 April 20*4.

QUESTION 10

Fred Gray provides the following information for the year ended 31 March 20*4: his capital at 31 March 20*3 was £67,583; his capital at 31 March 20*4 was £37,901. During the year he withdrew £14,500 cash and £276 goods from the business for his own use.

Required Calculate the profit or loss for the year ended 31 March 20*4.

QUESTION 11

Angus McToff provides the following information:

Assets and liabilities	at 1 September 20*3 £	at 31 August 20*4 £
Machinery at valuation	84,000	100,000
Vehicles at valuation	26,000	20,000
Stock	1,278	1,472
Debtors	3,461	3,824
Creditors	2,138	3,167
Bank balance	1,796	812
Cash in hand	232	472
Long-term loan	10,000	20,000

During the year ended 31 August 20*4 Angus withdrew £18,750 cash and goods to the value of £1,798 from the business for his own use.

In February 20*4 Angus paid a legacy of £21,000 into the business bank account.

Required Calculate the profit or loss for the year ended 31 August 20*4.

QUESTION 12

Hoi Yin provides the following information:

Assets and liabilities	at 1 December 20*3 £	at 30 November 20*4 £
Premises at valuation	140,000	138,000
Machinery at valuation	48,000	36,000
Vehicles at valuation	28,000	42,000
Stock	4,862	4,807

Assets and liabilities	at 1 December 20*3 £	at 30 November 20*4 £
Debtors	1,296	2,468
Creditors	632	1,277
Bank balance	840	–
Bank overdraft	–	3,592
Cash in hand	148	210
Long-term loan	2,000	22,000

During the year ended 30 November 20*4 Hoi made drawings of £19,750. In August she paid £26,000 into the business from a premium bond win.

Required Calculate the profit or loss for the year ended 30 November 20*4.

QUESTION 13

Jack Hay provides the following information for the year ended 30 June 20*4:

	at 1 July 20*3 £	at 30 June 20*4 £
Stock	1,791	2,348
Debtors	840	512
Creditors	3,461	3,790

During the year cash received from customers was £73,498; cash paid to suppliers was £38,910.

Required Prepare a trading account for the year ended 30 June 20*4.

QUESTION 14

Selina Szeto provides the following information for the year ended 31 May 20*4:

	at 1 June 20*3 £	at 31 May 20*4 £
Stock	14,887	12,347
Debtors	1,277	2,003
Creditors	8,766	7,942

During the year cash received from customers was £146,781; cash paid to suppliers was £81,313.

Required Prepare a trading account for the year ended 31 May 20*4.

QUESTION 15

Alice Band provides the following information for the year ended 31 December 20*4:

	at 1 January 20*4 £	at 31 December 20*4 £
Stock	982	1,271
Debtors	146	287
Creditors	1,999	1,871

During the year cash received from customers was £61,803; cash paid to suppliers was £28,718. Discounts allowed during the year were £310.

Required Prepare a trading account for the year ended 31 December 20*4.

QUESTION 16

Jane Lopez provides the following information for the year ended 29 February 20*4:

	at 1 March 20*3 £	at 29 February 20*4 £
Stock	477	528
Debtors	316	349
Creditors	1,792	1,981

During the year cash received from customers was £48,777; cash paid to suppliers was £11,466. Discounts allowed during the year were £523; discounts received were £291.

Required Prepare a trading account for the year ended 29 February 20*4.

QUESTION 17

Dai Johns did not keep a full set of accounting records for the year ended
31 December 20*4, however he is able to provide the following information:

Cash book summary

	£		£
Balance as at 1 January 20*4	2,347	Payments to creditors	23,457
Cash sales	64,534	General expenses	34,561
Receipts from debtors	16,409	Drawings	17,900
		Purchase of equipment	4,500
		Balance as at 31 December 20*4	2,872
	83,290		83,290

Additional information

	at 1 January 20*4 £	at 31 December 20*4 £
Premises at cost	65,000	65,000
Equipment at valuation	14,000	15,000
Stock	2,519	2,331

	at 1 January 20*4 £	at 31 December 20*4 £
Debtors	1,339	1,570
Creditors	2,910	2,341
General expenses accrued	145	276

Required

Prepare:

a a trading and profit and loss account for the year ended 31 December 20*4
b a balance sheet as at 31 December 20*4.

QUESTION 18

Noel Neal did not keep a full set of accounting records for the year ended 30 September 20*4, however he is able to provide the following information:

Cash book summary

	£		£
Balance as at 1 October 20*3	3,762	Payments to creditors	27,884
Cash sales	63,711	Purchase of vehicle	23,560
Cash received from debtors	12,674	Drawings	7,821
Rent received	3,000	Wages	13,759
Balance as at 30 September 20*4	11,440	General expenses	21,563
	94,587		94,587

Additional information

	at 1 October 20*3 £	at 30 September 20*4 £
Land and buildings at valuation	64,000	60,000
Machinery at valuation	34,000	30,600
Vehicles at valuation	16,600	30,000
Stock	2,892	3,007
Debtors	238	541
Creditors	5,935	5,442
Wages accrued and unpaid	239	1,671
General expenses paid in advance	679	395

Required

Prepare:

a a trading and profit and loss account for the year ended 30 September 20*4
b a balance sheet as at 30 September 20*4.

QUESTION 19

Andre Lefevre did not keep a full set of accounting records for the year ended 31 March 20*4 but he was able to provide the following information:

Cash book summary

	£		£
Cash sales	43,734	Balance as at 1 April 20*3	452
Cash received from debtors	46,880	Cash paid to creditors	34,872
Commission receivable	2,000	Cash purchases	5,761
		Drawings	23,560
		Purchase of fixtures	4,800
		Rent	6,600
		Wages	24,797
Balance as at 31 March 20*4	21,971	General expenses	13,743
	114,585		114,585

Additional information

	at 1 April 20*3 £	at 31 March 20*4 £
Premises at valuation	56,000	54,000
Fixtures at valuation	18,000	20,000
Vehicle at valuation	8,000	4,000
Stock	1,638	1,744
Debtors	1,649	459
Creditors	2,225	2,619
Rent paid in advance	600	2,200
General expenses owed	127	981
Commission receivable owing	–	1,000

Required

Prepare:

a a trading and profit and loss account for the year ended 31 March 20*4
b a balance sheet as at 31 March 20*4.

QUESTION 20

Ravi Ollie did not keep proper accounting records for the year ended 29 February 20*4, but he is able to supply the following information:

Cash book summary

	£		£
Balance as at 1 March 20*3	4,619	Drawings	34,600
Cash sales	25,890	Cash paid to creditors	32,842
Cash paid to debtors	76,882	Cash purchases	16,931
Rents received	2,400	Wages	17,805
Capital introduced	5,000	General expenses	13,775
Balance as at 29 February 20*4	1,162		
	115,953		115,953

Additional information

	at 1 March 20*3 £	at 29 February 20*4 £
Equipment at valuation	36,000	31,000
Vehicle at valuation	12,000	6,000
Stock	8,467	9,106
Debtors	499	882
Creditors	3,821	4,166
Rent received in advance	120	240
Wages owed	–	236
Wages paid in advance	341	–
General expenses owed	1,639	838

Required

Prepare:

a a trading and profit and loss account for the year ended 29 February 20*4
b a balance sheet as at 29 February 20*4.

QUESTION 21

Joe Duff provides the following information:

	at 1 January 20*3 £	at 31 December 20*4 £
Stock	17,993	18,501
Creditors	16,381	15,491

During the year sales amounted to £240,000. All goods sold are subject to a mark-up of 33⅓%.

All goods are purchased on credit. Cash paid to creditors during the year amounted to £189,373.

Just before the end of the financial year Joe's business was burgled and a significant amount of stock was stolen. Joe is unsure of the exact amount of stolen stock.

Required Calculate the value of stolen stock.

QUESTION 22

Alice Band provides the following information.

	at 1 May 20*3 £	at 30 April 20*4 £
Stock	10,411	1,249
Creditors	18,791	16,427

During the year sales amounted to £361,920. All goods are sold at a margin of 20%.

All goods are purchased on credit. Cash paid to creditors during the year amounted to £290,929.

During the final week of the financial year an amount of stock was stolen. Alice is unsure of the exact amount.

Required Calculate the value of the stolen stock.

QUESTION 23

Akit Patel did not keep a full set of accounting records. However, he is able to provide the following information for the year ended 30 September 20*4:

Summary of bank account

	£		£
Balance as at 1 October 20*3	1,764	Wages	23,761
Cash banked	102,250	Drawings	10,470
Receipts from debtors	6,479	Purchases	1,328
		General expenses	37,328
		Purchases of equipment	2,600
		Payments to creditors	34,107
		Balance as at 30 September 20*4	899
	110,493		110,493

Akit's till rolls show his takings to be £120,698. Before banking any of the business takings, Akit paid the following:

	£
Wages	4,380
Rent	2,400

He also withdrew £8,460 for his own personal use.

Akit provides the following additional information:

	at 1 October 20*3 £	at 30 September 20*4 £
Equipment at valuation	9,700	11,000
Vehicle at valuation	3,000	1,000
Stock	984	1,358
Debtors	126	211
Creditors	1,477	1,086
Cash in hand	238	326

Akit knows that a dishonest casual worker stole some cash before leaving the business; he is uncertain of the precise amount. His insurance company has agreed to pay £3,000 compensation for the loss on 20 October 20*4.

Required

a   Calculate the amount of cash stolen.
b   Prepare a trading and profit and loss account for the year ended 30 September 20*4.
c   Prepare a balance sheet as at 30 September 20*4.

QUESTION 24

Jane Seager did not keep proper books of account for the year ended 31 July 20*4. However, she provides the following information:

Summary of bank account

	£		£
Cash banked	118,739	Balance as at 1 August 20*3	3,168
Received from debtors	4,783	General expenses	12,792
Capital introduced	8,000	Motor expenses	8,461
		Insurance	2,170
		Purchase of vehicle	23,000
		Payments to creditors	48,672
		Drawings	31,798
		Balance as at 31 July 20*4	1,461
	131,522		131,522

Before banking her business takings which amounted to £133,432, Jane paid the following:

	£
Wages	9,461
Electricity	1,240

She also withdrew £3,560 for personal use.

Jane provides the following additional information:

	at 1 August 20*3 £	at 31 July 20*4 £
Premises at valuation	126,000	124,000
Equipment at valuation	17,000	15,300
Vehicles at valuation	2,400	19,000
Stock	4,618	4,883
Debtors	422	637
Creditors	3,419	3,066
Cash in hand	816	528
Electricity bill unpaid	171	–
Garage bill unpaid	–	355
General expenses paid in advance	217	–
General expenses owed	–	333
Insurance paid in advance	210	326

During the week-end before her financial year-end, Jane's business was burgled and cash was stolen. Jane is unsure of the exact amount.

Required

a Calculate the amount of cash stolen.
b Prepare a trading and profit and loss account for the year ended 31 July 20*4.
c Prepare a balance sheet as at 31 July 20*4.

CHAPTER THREE

Clubs and Societies

The principles involved in calculating the surplus or deficit or of preparing a set of final accounts for a club or society are the same as those learned in Chapter Two.

[For ease, both clubs and societies will be referred to in this chapter as 'clubs'.]

There are a number of superficial changes to be made to some of the headings used when preparing the final accounts.

Clubs and societies require a different form of final accounts to those of a trading organisation.

Specification coverage:
AQA 14.2; OCR: 5.3.1.

By the end of this chapter you should be able to:
- calculate the surplus or deficit by using the net asset method
- prepare a set of final accounts
- prepare subscriptions accounts; life membership funds
- make entries to record donations.

> The revenue statement of a club is not called a profit and loss account. It is headed 'Income and expenditure account'.

> Any profit (or loss) made by a club is called an **excess of income over expenditure**. It is often shortened to **surplus** (or **excess of expenditure over income** sometimes shortened to **deficit**).

> The capital account of a club is known as the **accumulated fund**.

> The summarised cash book may be called a **receipts and payments account**.

The main function of a club or society is not to trade. Its existence is to provide facilities for members or to provide an opportunity for people to meet and further their common interest.

Often the members of a club have little or no knowledge of accounting or book-keeping and because of this many club treasurers present a receipts and payments account to the club's annual general meeting as a set of final accounts.

A receipts and payments account does not show the members:

- the true financial position of the club
- any accrued expenses or any pre-payments made
- the asset base of the club or by how much the assets have depreciated during the year
- any liabilities that are outstanding at the year-end.

To present a more complete picture of the club's financial activities and position, an income and expenditure account and a balance sheet should be prepared.

An income and expenditure account is prepared using the accruals concept and so:

- all incomes and expenditures for the period under review are recorded
- it includes all expenditures accrued and as yet unpaid for the period
- it includes all incomes due that have not yet been received
- it includes non-cash expenses such as depreciation
- the completed income and expenditure account will reveal a surplus or deficit for the period
- it shows whether the club is generating sufficient income to pay for members' activities.

ANCILLARY ACTIVITIES

Many clubs organise activities that are not the core activity of the club. These activities are useful in:

- raising additional funds which means that subscriptions may be lower than if profitable activities were not undertaken
- keeping members interested at times when major club activities are quiet – a cricket club may organise activities (eg discos) during the winter months.

For each ancillary activity, the club treasurer should calculate whether the activity is profitable or not and include the profit or loss in the income and expenditure account.

BAR/SNACK BAR TRADING ACCOUNT

If a club has a bar and/or snack bar, in order to raise additional funds for the club, a bar trading account should be prepared. The profit or loss generated should be transferred to the income and expenditure account.

The trading account prepared is no different to any of the other trading accounts that you have produced on a regular basis during your studies.

You may have to do an adjustment account in order to determine the amount of the purchases to use in the trading account.

WORKED EXAMPLE

The treasurer of the Apes Rugby Club provides the following information for the year ended 31 May 20*4:

- 1 June 20*3 – amount owed to supplier of drinks and snacks: £213
- 31 May 20*4 – amount owed to supplier of drinks and snacks: £186
- bar takings for the year: £27,759
- amounts paid to the supplier of drinks and snacks: £14,621
- stocks of drinks and snacks as at 1 June 20*3: £165
- stocks of drinks and snacks as at 31 May 20*4: £191.

Required Prepare a bar trading account for the year ended 31 May 20*4.

Answer

Apes Rugby Club
Bar trading account for the year ended 31 May 20*4

	£	£
Takings		27,759
Less Cost of sales		
Stock	165	
Purchases	14,594	
	14,759	
Stock	191	14,568
Bar profit *(to income and expenditure account)*		13,191

Workings

Creditors adjustment

	£		£
Cash	14,621	Balance b/d	213
Balance c/d	186	*Bar trading a/c missing figure*	14,594
	14,807		14,807
		Balance b/d	186

DINNER DANCES, DISCOS, LOTTERIES AND BINGO NIGHTS

These activities are often used as fund-raisers. A profit and loss account should be prepared for each of them and the profit or loss generated should be transferred to the income and expenditure account.

It is important to prepare these 'extra' revenue accounts so that members are able to identify one figure (profit or loss) relating to the activity. This means that members can then decide whether or not the activities should continue in the future. Clearly, if an activity is profitable the membership is likely to agree to the continuation of that activity. If the activity is unprofitable it is likely that the members will wish to discontinue the activity.

CALCULATION OF RESULTS FOR CLUBS AND SOCIETIES

To calculate the surplus or deficit for a club requires a comparison of net assets at the start of the period with the net assets at the end of the period.

Exactly the same technique is used as in Chapter Two.

WORKED EXAMPLE

Higworth Tennis club had the following assets and liabilities at 1 January 20*4:

nets £112; stock of tennis balls £26; creditor for tennis balls £72; stock of fertiliser £54; line paint £8; balance at bank £136.

At 31 December 20*4 the club assets and liabilities were: nets £80; stock of tennis balls £20; stock of fertiliser £48; balance at bank £207.

Required Calculate the surplus or deficit for the year ended 31 December 20*4.

Answer

	£
Closing net assets (accumulated fund)	355 (80 + 20 + 48 + 207)
Opening net assets (accumulated fund)	264 (112 + 26 +54 + 8 +136 − 72)
Surplus for the year	91

PREPARATION OF THE FINAL ACCOUNTS FOR CLUBS AND SOCIETIES

As in Chapter Two, a question may require the preparation of a set of final accounts. In such a question we need to go carefully through the four stages used in Chapter Two.

Can you remember the four stages?

■ Stage 1: Prepare an opening statement of affairs.
■ Stage 2: Compile a summarised cash and/or bank account.
■ Stage 3: Construct adjustment accounts.
■ Stage 4: Prepare the final accounts.

An **honorarium** is a payment made to a club official to cover expenses and time spent on club activities.

Once again Stage 3 is the stage that will take up much of our time since this is the area that seems to cause most problems.

WORKED EXAMPLE

The following receipts and payments account for the year ended 31 October 20*4 has been prepared by the treasurer of the Danbury Gardening Club:

	£		£
Bank balance as at 1 November 20*3	146	Payments to seed supplier	407
Seed sales	612	Rotavator purchase	2,842
Subscriptions received	5,040	Meeting room rent	750
Show entry fees	326	Secretary's honorarium	100
Annual dinner dance ticket sales	2,250	Speakers' expenses	240
Equipment hire	420	Bank charges	28
		Advertising	126
		Insurances	348
		Postages and telephone	142
		Dinner dance expenses	1,874
		Printing for dinner dance	128
		Show prizes	247
		Show expenses	148
		Balance at bank as at 31 October 20*4	1,414
	8,794		8,794

The following additional information is available:

	£	£
Equipment at valuation	840	3,000
Creditor for seed purchases	128	84
Creditor for printing for dinner dance	62	75
Pre-payment for insurance	112	206
Subscriptions paid in advance	360	135
Subscriptions owing at year-end	180	225

Required Prepare an income and expenditure account for the year ended 31 October 20*4 and a balance sheet as at that date.

Answer

Stage 1: Prepare an opening statement of affairs

	£	£	
Assets			
Equipment	840		Subscriptions owing –
Pre-payment – insurance	112		members who owe the club
Subscriptions owing	180	1,278	money are debtors
Bank balance	146		
Liabilities			
Creditors – seed merchants	128		Subscriptions in advance –
Printing	62		members who could
Subscriptions paid in advance	360	550	demand their money back
Accumulated fund		728	are creditors

Stage 2: Compile a summarised cash and/or bank account
No need – it has been given in the question.

WORKED EXAMPLE *continued*

Stage 3: Construct adjustment accounts
This is the important stage.

Use one account for each item used in Stage 1 statement of affairs:

Equipment

Balance as at 1 November 20*3	840	I & E a/c (missing figure)		682
Bank	2,842	Balance as at 31 October 20*4		3,000
	3,682			3,682
Balance as at 1 November 20*4	3,000			

Insurance

Balance as at 1 November 20*3	112	I & E a/c missing figure		254
Bank	348	Balance at as 31 October 200*4		206
	460			460
Balance as at 1 November 20*4	206			

Seeds

Bank	407	Balance as at 1 November 20*3	128
Balance as at 31 October 20*4	84	I & E a/c missing figure	363
	491		491
		Balance as at 1 November 20*4	84

Printing

Bank	128	Balance as at 1 November 20*3	62
Balance as at 31 October 20*4	75	I & E a/c missing figure	141
	203		203
		Balance as at 1 November 20*4	75

The next adjustment account is the one that seems to cause the most problems. It is the subscriptions account.

It is worth spending some time getting this sorted out in your own mind.

Put yourself in the position of a club treasurer.

■ People or organisations who owe your club money are **debtors (debit balances)**.
■ Members who owe your club money are **debtors (debit balances)**.
■ So subscriptions owing at the end of the year are debtors (**debit balances**).
■ Subscriptions in arrears are **debtors (debit balances)**.

At the end of any year there may be some members of a club who have paid their subscriptions for the following year. If they have taken up a place at university or moved out of the area to take a job, they may wish to cease their membership of the club, in which case the club owes them money. Until the club pays the ex-member they will be a creditor of the club.

■ People or organisations who are owed money by your club are **creditors (credit balances)**.
■ Members who are owed money are **creditors (credit balances)**.

WORKED EXAMPLE *continued*

■ Subscriptions paid in advance at the end of the year are **creditors (credit balances)**.
■ Subscriptions in advance are **creditors (credit balances)**.

Monies received during the year from members are debited in the cash book. We need to complete the double entry in the subscriptions (adjustment) account.

It will be shown as a debit in the receipts and payments account (the cash book summary); we complete the double entry by *crediting* the subscriptions account.

You must spend time on these entries in the subscriptions account. It is well worth the effort; there can be up to 6 or 7 marks for the correct entry for subscriptions in an income and expenditure account.

● EXAMINATION TIP

Subscriptions accounts are also often asked for as a short question in some examinations.

REVISION TIP

You will make fewer errors if you use the technique outlined earlier. Put your closing balances below the account and then bring them back up into the account.

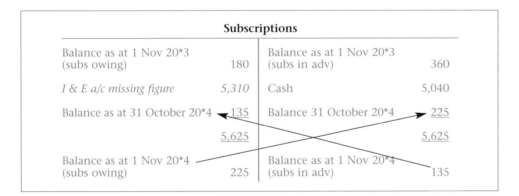

Subscriptions

Balance as at 1 Nov 20*3 (subs owing)	180	Balance as at 1 Nov 20*3 (subs in adv)	360
I & E a/c missing figure	5,310	Cash	5,040
Balance as at 31 October 20*4	135	Balance 31 October 20*4	225
	5,625		5,625
Balance as at 1 Nov 20*4 (subs owing)	225	Balance as at 1 Nov 20*4 (subs in adv)	135

I am sure you can see why there are often a lot of marks for the figure of £5,310 for subscriptions.

Once again; you have up to this stage scored no marks (unless a question has asked you to calculate or prepare one of the adjustment accounts). However, the end is in sight and you have already done all of the really hard work.

● EXAMINATION TIP

Show your adjustment accounts neatly – an examiner may have to refer to them in order to reward you with part marks.

WORKED EXAMPLE *continued*

Stage 4 (At last!): Prepare an income and expenditure account

Danbury Gardening Club
Income and expenditure account for the year ended 31 October 20*4

	£	£	
Income – Subscriptions	5,310		
Profit on seed sales	249		(612 − 363)
Profit on dinner dance	235		(2,250 − 1,874 − 141)
Equipment hire	420	6,214	
Less Expenditure			
Loss on show	69		(326 − 395)
Rent	750		
Secretary's honorarium	100		
Speakers' expenses	240		
Bank charges	28		
Advertising	126		
Insurance	254		
Postages and telephone	142		
Depreciation of equipment	682	2,391	
Excess of income over expenditure		3,823	

Balance sheet as at 31 October 20*4

	£	£	£
Fixed assets			
Equipment at valuation			3,000
Current assets			
Bank balance	1,414		
Pre-payments – insurance	206		
subscriptions	225	1,845	
Less Current liabilities			
creditors – seeds	84		
printing	75		
Subscriptions in advance	135	294	1,551
			4,551
Accumulated fund			728
Add Surplus			3,823
			4,551

Note that each of the ancillary activities (ie sales of seeds, dinner dance and the show) have all been netted to reveal whether the activity has been beneficial to the club or whether it has drained resources from the club.

The workings have been shown to help you. Do show your workings but show them separately, outside the main body of your answer.

Label your working so that the examiner can see which figure you have been calculating.

Notice also the change in the terms used (ie 'income and expenditure account', 'excess of income over expenditure' and 'accumulated fund').

QUESTION 1

A tennis club has paid its landlord £600 rent for the year. At the beginning of the year rent paid in advance amounted to £200. At the end of the year rent paid in advance amounted to £100.

Calculate the amount to be included in the club's income and expenditure account for rent.

QUESTION 2

During the year a cricket club has paid £712 to the local authority for rates. At the beginning of the year £126 had been pre-paid. At the end of the year the rates paid in advance amounted to £112.

Required Calculate the amount to be included in the club's income and expenditure account for rates.

QUESTION 3

A choral society has paid £2,467 for the hire of concert halls. At the beginning of the year the society owed £183 for use of a hall. At the end of the year the society owed £206 for use of the hall.

Required Calculate the amount to be included in the society's income and expenditure account for hire of halls.

QUESTION 4

At the beginning of a year a cricket club owed £420 to a garage for repairs and maintenance of equipment. During the year £1,840 was paid to the garage. At the end of the year an invoice for repairs totalling £312 remained unpaid.

Required Calculate the amount for repairs and maintenance to be included in the club's income and expenditure account.

QUESTION 5

A club treasurer provides the following information for the year ended 31 March 20*4:

	£
Cash received for subscriptions	875
Subscriptions in arrears as at 31 March 20*3	50
Subscriptions in arrears as at 31 March 20*4	75

Required Calculate the amount for subscriptions to be included in the income and expenditure account for the year ended 31 March 20*4.

QUESTION 6

The treasurer of an operatic society provides the following information for the year ended 31 August 20*4:

	£
Cash received for subscriptions	1,460
Subscriptions paid in advance as at 31 August 20*3	210
Subscriptions paid in advance as at 31 August 20*4	140

Required Calculate the amount for subscriptions to be included in the income and expenditure account for the year ended 31 August 20*4.

QUESTION 7

The treasurer of a badminton club provides the following information for the year ended 31 May 20*4. Cash received during the year for subscriptions was £1,240.

	at 31 May 20*3 £	at 31 May 20*4 £
Subscriptions paid in advance	40	60
Subscriptions in arrears	30	20

Required Calculate the amount for subscriptions to be included in the income and expenditure for the year ended 31 May 20*4.

QUESTION 8

The treasurer of a squash club provides the following information for the year ended 29 February 20*4. Cash received during the year for subscriptions was £3,460.

Additional information

	at 28 February 20*3 £	at 29 February 20*4 £
Subscriptions paid in advance	200	80
Subscriptions in arrears	110	130

Required Calculate the amount for subscriptions to be included in the income and expenditure account for the year ended 29 February 20*4.

In practice, many clubs write off any subscriptions not paid by the end of the club's financial year, since if a member has not paid their subscription by the end of the year there is a strong likelihood that the membership has lapsed.

If an examiner expects you to take this line of action, the question will indicate this.

WORKED EXAMPLE

During the year ended 30 June 20*4 cash received for subscriptions to the Dropkick Rugby Club amounted to £1,860.

At 1 July 20*3 subscriptions paid in advance amounted to £140; at 30 June 20*4 subscriptions paid in advance were £80.

At 30 June 20*4 subscriptions totalling £60 remained unpaid.

It is club policy to write off any subscriptions that remain unpaid at the financial year-end.

Required Prepare a subscriptions account for the year ended 30 June 20*4.

Answer

Subscriptions

I & E a/c	1,980	Balance b/d	140	£1,980 is shown as income on
Balance c/d	80	Cash	1,860	I & E a/c
		I & E a/c (subs w/o)	60	£60 is shown as an expense
	2,060		2,060	on I & E a/c
		Balance b/d	80	

Some clubs gain income from other sources.

LIFE MEMBERSHIP

This is a lump sum paid by a member. It entitles the member to use the club's facilities for the rest of their life, without any further payment. Money received from the member is debited to the bank account and credited to a life membership fund.

The balance on the life membership fund is credited to the income and expenditure account in equal annual instalments over a period that has been agreed by the club committee.

The balance on the life membership fund is shown on the balance sheet as a long-term liability.

WORKED EXAMPLE

The Old Jacks Bowling Club operates a life membership scheme. The life membership subscription is £350. The balance standing on the life membership fund at 30 September 20*3 was £2,940.

During the year ended 30 September 20*4 five members took out life membership, paying a total of £1,750. The club transfers 10% of the balance standing in the life membership fund at the end of the year to the income and expenditure account.

Required Prepare a life membership fund for the year ended 30 September 20*4.

Answer

Life membership fund			
Income and expenditure account	469	Balance b/d	2,940
Balance c/d	4,221	Bank	1,750
	4,690		4,690
		Balance b/d	4,221

£469 is shown as income on the income and expenditure account.

£4,221 is shown as a long-term liability in the balance sheet.

ENTRANCE FEES PAID BY NEW MEMBERS

In their first year of membership a member may be charged an entrance fee in addition to the normal annual subscription. Generally, these entrance fees are regarded as revenue income and are credited to the income and expenditure account. However, some clubs treat this form of income as a capital income and in these cases they would be added to the accumulated fund.

DONATIONS

Small donations should be treated as revenue income. However, if a large donation is received it should be treated as a capital receipt.

I hear you say 'What is a large donation and what would be a small donation?'

An examination question ought to indicate the club's policy towards any donations received – the question should indicate whether donations are capital or revenue income.

If a club receives a large donation (or legacy) that has been given for a particular purpose, it should be credited to a special trust fund and a special bank account should be opened. This avoids the money being used for general club expenditure.

The trust fund should be debited each year with the amount of the annual expenditure on the special purpose; the debit entry is in the income and expenditure account.

(The entries are similar to those used in a life membership fund account.)

WORKED EXAMPLE

On 1 January 20*4 the Stumps Cricket Club received a donation of £50,000 to build a new pavilion. In August 20*4, A. Wellie, a builder, was paid £3,874 after laying the foundations.

In September 20*4 another building firm, C. Means, was paid £4,751 for work done.

Required Prepare the necessary accounts to record the transactions.

Answer

Bank – building account

1 Building fund	50,000	4 Wellie		3,874
		5 Means		4,751
		Balance c/d		41,375
	50,000			50,000
Balance b/d	41,375			

Trust fund – pavilion

6 I & Ex a/c	8,625	1 Bank		50,000
Balance c/d	41,375			
	50,000			50,000
		Balance b/d		41,375

Pavilion account

2 Wellie	3,874	
3 Means	4,751	

Wellie

4 Bank	3,874	2 Pavilion	3,874

Means

5 Bank	4,751	3 Pavilion	4,751

The numbers refer to the sequence of events. There will be a credit (an income) in the income and expenditure account for the year.

Chapter summary

- The skills involved in preparing club accounts are similar to those employed in the preparation of small cash-based businesses.
- There is a change in some of the headings. 'Profit and loss account' becomes 'Income and expenditure account'.
- 'Profit' becomes 'Excess of income over expenditure' or 'Surplus'.
- 'Loss' becomes 'Excess of expenditure over income' or 'Deficit'.
- 'Capital' becomes 'Accumulated fund'.
- Any ancillary activities should be netted to appear as one figure on the income and expenditure account.

Self-test questions

- What is the name given to the summarised cash book of a club?
- Name two ancillary activities that might be organised by a club.
- Why would a club organise ancillary activities?
- Give one advantage that a club will obtain by running a life membership scheme.
- Give one disadvantage of running a life membership scheme.
- How would entrance fees be treated in the final accounts of a club?
- What is the name of the capital account of a club?
- Subscriptions in arrears is a current asset. True or false?
- Subscriptions paid in advance is a current asset. True or false?
- Equipment at valuation at the beginning of a year = £3,400; equipment at valuation at the end of a year = £2,700. There have been no additions or disposals during the year. What has caused the £700 difference?

TEST QUESTIONS

QUESTION 9

A club operates a life membership scheme. Life membership costs £800. The subscriptions are to be credited to the club's income and expenditure account in equal instalments over eight years. The balance in the fund at 1 September 20*3 was £7,600. During the year ended 31 August 20*4 life membership subscriptions amounted to £2,400.

Required Prepare a life membership fund for the year ended 31 August 20*4.

QUESTION 10

A club operates a life membership scheme. Members pay £1,200 for life membership. The subscriptions are to be credited to the income and expenditure account in equal instalments over 10 years. The balance in the fund at 1 June 20*3 was £62,000. During the year ended 31 May 20*4 life membership subscriptions amounted to £8,400.

Required Prepare a life membership fund for the year ended 31 May 20*4.

QUESTION 11

The treasurer of Netters Angling Club provides the following receipts and payments account for the year ended 30 September 20*4:

	£		£
Balance as at 1 October 20*3	453	Photocopying – club newsletter	372
Subscriptions	7,650	Coach hire	2,770
Donations	235	Competition prizes	1,340
Competition entry fees	625	Purchase of boat	2,120
		Fuel and servicing costs	342
		Secretary's honorarium	120
		Balance as at 30 September 20*4	1,899
	8,963		8,963

The committee believes that the boat will have a useful life of four years, it will have no residual value. It agrees that the donations should be treated as revenue income.

Required Prepare an income and expenditure account for the year ended 30 September 20*4 and a balance sheet as at that date.

QUESTION 12

The treasurer of the Fifteen-All Tennis Club provides the following receipts and payments account for the year ended 31 December 20*4:

	£		£
Balance as at 1 January 20*4	2,864	Purchase of equipment	5,740
Subscriptions	10,980	General expenses	6,750
Competition fees	1,176	Competition prizes	977
Dinner dance receipts	2,590	Dinner dance expenses	2,392
Donation	2,000	Coaches fees	560
		Balance as at 31 December 20*4	3,191
	19,610		19,610

Depreciation of equipment is to be provided for at 10% per annum, using the straight line method.
The donation is to be treated as capital income.

Required Prepare an income and expenditure account for the year ended 31 December 20*4 and a balance sheet as at that date.

QUESTION 13

The treasurer of the Buliov Hockey Club provides the following receipts and payments account for the year ended 31 March 20*4:

	£		£
Balance as at 1 April 20*3	1,672	Purchases of equipment	730
Subscriptions	2,775	General expenses	3,657
Interest	124	Team travel costs	348
Balance as at 31 March 20*4	164		
	4,735		4,735

Additional information
At 1 April 20*3 subscriptions remaining unpaid were £125; subscriptions paid in advance amounted to £25. One year later, on 31 March 20*4, unpaid subscriptions were £50 while subscriptions paid in advance were £75.
Equipment is expected to have a useful life of five years and is to be depreciated using the straight-line method.

Required Prepare an income and expenditure account for the year ended 31 March 20*4.

QUESTION 14

The treasurer of Crawlers Swimming Club provides the following receipts and payments account for the year ended 30 June 20*4:

	£		£
Balance as at 1 July 20*3	769	Pool hire	4,672
Subscriptions	7,995	General expenses	763
Functions – income	1,560	Functions – expenses	673
Swimming lessons	542	Grants to young swimmers	3,400
		Balance as at 30 June 20*4	1,358
	10,866		10,866

Additional information
At 30 June 20*3 subscriptions in arrears amounted to £130; subscriptions paid in advance were £520.
At 30 June 20*4 subscriptions in arrears amounted to £195; subscriptions paid in advance were £455.

Required Prepare an income and expenditure account for the year ended 30 June 20*4

QUESTION 15

The treasurer of the Scrimmage Rugby Club provides the following information for the year ended 31 July 20*4:
Bar takings £103,671; payments to brewery £52,768.

Additional information

	at 31 July 20*3 £	at 31 July 20*4 £
Creditor – brewery	453	621
Bar stocks	2,518	2,661

Required Prepare a bar trading account for the year ended 31 July 20*4.

QUESTION 16

The treasurer of Kinton Stanley Football Club provides the following information for the year ended 31 August 20*4:
Bar takings £130,005; payments to brewery £67,449.

Additional information

	at 31 August 20*3 £	at 31 August 20*4 £
Creditor – brewery	2,341	1,833
Bar stocks	4,449	4,802

Required Prepare a bar trading account for the year ended 31 August 20*4.

QUESTION 17

The treasurer of Fretters Sports Club provides the following information for the year ended 30 November 20*4:

	Cash received £	Cash payments £
Subscriptions	2,970	
Bar takings	61,385	
Other income	270	
Payments to bar creditors		27,483
Rent		3,900
General expenses		26,742

Additional information

	at 30 November 20*3 £	at 30 November 20*4 £
Bar creditors	436	629
Rent paid in advance	600	900
Subscriptions paid in advance	90	270
Subscriptions in arrears	180	120
Bar stocks	1,789	1,904

Required Prepare a bar trading account and an income and expenditure account for the year ended 30 November 20*4.

QUESTION 18

The treasurer of the Gholic Cricket Club provides the following information for the year ended 31 December 20*4:

	Cash receipts £	Cash payments £
Bar takings	75,906	
Subscriptions	18,760	
Profits on functions	1,642	
Payments to bar creditors		46,283
Wages		26,645
General expenses		25,971

Additional information

	at 31 December 20*3 £	at 31 December 20*4 £
Bar creditors	812	1,278
Wages owing	112	148
Subscriptions in arrears	140	350
Subscriptions in advance	70	210
Bar stocks	2,197	2,844

Required Prepare a bar trading account and an income and expenditure account for the year ended 31 December 20*4.

QUESTION 19

The treasurer of the Green Lane Bowling Club provides the following information for the year ended 31 October 20*4:

Assets and liabilities	at 1 November 20*3 £	at 31 October 20*4 £
Land and buildings at valuation	120,000	120,000
Equipment at valuation	21,000	23,000
Bar stock	2,750	2,451
Bar creditors	219	473
Subscriptions in advance	160	80
Rates pre-paid	342	452

A summary of the club's receipts and payments for the year shows:

	£		£
Balance as at 1 November 20*3	1,456	Bar creditors	21,761
Subscriptions	8,480	Purchase of equipment	4,560
Bar takings	34,879	General expenses	16,843
Competition fees	562	Rates	1,764
		Competition prizes	340
		Balance as at 31 October 20*4	109
	45,377		45,377

Required

Prepare:

a a bar trading account for the year ended 31 October 20*4
b an income and expenditure account for the year ended 31 October 20*4
c a balance sheet as at 31 October 20*4.

QUESTION 20

The treasurer of Cholerton Athletics Club provides the following information for the year ended 31 March 20*4:

Assets and liabilities	at 31 March 20*3 £	at 31 March 20*4 £
Land and buildings at valuation	64,000	64,000
Equipment at valuation	2,640	3,000
Snack bar stock	439	357
Creditors for snack bar stock	43	227
Insurances paid in advance	324	461
Advertising owing	230	–
Subscriptions in advance	192	128
Subscriptions in arrears	64	160

The following is the club's receipts and payments account for the year:

	£		£
Balance as at 1 April 20*3	342	Insurances	2,876
Income from sports days	3,568	Advertising	867
Subscriptions	4,464	Payments to snack bar creditors	7,684
Snack bar takings	9,644	General expenses	3,220
		Sports days expenses	2,990
		Purchases of equipment	810
Balance as at 31 March 20*4	429		
	18,447		18,447

Required
Prepare:

a a snack bar trading account for the year ended 31 March 20*4
b an income and expenditure account for the year ended 31 March 20*4
c a balance sheet at 31 March 20*4.

QUESTION 21

The treasurer of Cloggers Rugby Club provides the following information for the year ended 31 December 20*4:

Assets and liabilities	at 1 January 20*4 £	at 31 December 20*4 £
Land and buildings at cost	245,000	245,000
Equipment at valuation	3,470	6,000
Life membership fund	13,600	?
Bar stocks	3,249	4,032
Bar creditors	2,165	1,908
Subscriptions in arrears	1,260	540
Subscriptions paid in advance	180	300
Creditor for general expenses	387	672

The following receipts and payments account is available:

	£		£
Balance as at 1 January 20*4	2,447	Bar steward's wages	7,452
Bar takings	34,759	Groundsman's wages	8,661
Subscriptions – annual	48,720	Payments to bar creditors	23,002
life membership	3,500	Dinner dance expenses	4,673
Sale of dinner dance tickets	5,720	Disco expenses	1,342
Income from discos	1,560	General expenses	38,011
		Purchase of equipment	4,220
		Balance as at 31 December 20*4	9,345
	96,706		96,706

Prepare:

a a bar trading account for the year ended 31 December 20*4
b an income and expenditure account for the year ended 31 December 20*4
c a balance sheet as at 31 December 20*4.

QUESTION 22

The treasurer of the Boundary Cricket Club provides the following information for the year ended 30 September 20*4:

Assets and liabilities	at 30 September 20*3 £	at 30 September 20*4 £
Land and buildings at valuation	120,000	120,000
Equipment at valuation	26,000	27,000
Life membership fund	12,800	?
Bar stocks	1,790	2,146
Bar creditors	248	302
Subscriptions in arrears	350	140
Subscriptions paid in advance	630	490
General expenses paid in advance	387	842

The following receipts and payments account is available:

	£		£
Balance as at 1 October 20*3	10,830	Purchase of land	25,000
Subscriptions – annual	22,470	Purchases of equipment	6,540
life membership	5,850	Payments to creditors	39,672
Dinner dance receipts	2,480	Dinner dance expenses	2,360
Disco receipts	3,726	Disco expenses	1,988
Bar takings	83,444	Bar staff wages	12,791
Balance as at 30 September 20*4	5,491	Ground staff wages	18,477
		General expenses	27,463
	134,291		134,291

Prepare:

a a bar trading account for the year ended 30 September 20*4
b an income and expenditure account for the year ended 30 September 20*4
c a balance sheet as at 30 September 20*4.

CHAPTER FOUR

Partnership Accounts

Up to now we have concentrated much of our studies on the simplest form of business organisation, that is, the accounts of sole traders.

Although being a sole trader does have many advantages, many people in business form partnerships.

> **Limited liability** means that the liability of shareholders, for the debts of a limited company of which they are members, is limited to the amount they agreed to subscribe. Sole traders and partners have **unlimited liability**: this means that they are fully responsible for any debts incurred by the business, even if this means using private assets to discharge business debts.

Specification coverage:
AQA 14.3; OCR: 5.3.1.

By the end of this chapter you should be able to:
- prepare profit and loss appropriation accounts
- prepare partners' capital and current accounts and explain their uses.

ADVANTAGES OF BEING A SOLE TRADER

- The sole trader has complete control over how the business is run, so success or failure is dependent on the trader.
- The business can be established with the minimum of legal formalities.
- The financial results of the business do not need to be divulged to other members of the general public.

DISADVANTAGES OF BEING A SOLE TRADER

- The sole trader has unlimited liability.
- May involve long hours of work.
- Illness or other reasons that cause absence may affect the running of the business.
- No one with whom to share problems or ideas.
- May be difficult to raise extra finance when it is needed.

Expansion of a business usually involves raising extra finance. Raising the necessary finance is very difficult without involving other people. This generally means that a sole trader is faced with the choice of converting the business into either

- a partnership or
- a limited liability company.

We shall deal with limited companies later, in Chapter Six.

PARTNERSHIP ACCOUNTING

The Partnership Act of 1890 defines a partnership as 'the relationship which subsists between persons carrying on business with a view of profit'.

Forming a partnership overcomes some of the disadvantages associated with being in business as a sole trader.

ADVANTAGES OF BEING IN PARTNERSHIP

- Access to more capital.
- Partners can share the workload.
- Partners can pool ideas and share problems.

DISADVANTAGES OF BEING IN PARTNERSHIP

- Partners have less independence than sole traders. Decisions have to be agreed by all partners. So, a partner's ideas for development of the business may be frustrated by other partners.

- The number of partners is limited to 20 (as far as 'A' level examinations are concerned); there are exceptions to this limit (eg firms of solicitors, accountants etc).
- Partners have unlimited liability.

It is usual for a partnership to have a written partnership agreement (although it is possible that the agreement could be a verbal one); this will reduce the possibility of any disputes arising.

The agreement usually covers:

- the duties of the individual partners
- the amount of capital to be subscribed by each of the partners
- the ways in which profits are to be shared (see later)
- the financial arrangements if there are any changes to the structure of the partnership.

If there is no agreement, the Partnership Act of 1890 lays down the following rules which must apply:

- partners should contribute equal amounts of capital
- no partner should be entitled to interest on capital
- no partner is entitled to a salary
- no partner is to be charged interest on drawings
- residual profits or losses are to be shared equally
- any loan made to the partnership by a partner will carry interest at the rate of 5% per annum.

● EXAMINATION TIP

If no details of the way in which profits are to be shared are given in a question, you must assume that no partnership agreement exists and so the Partnership Act of 1890 applies to the question.

PARTNERSHIP PROFIT AND LOSS APPROPRIATION ACCOUNTS

(Often shortened to 'partnership appropriation accounts'.)

The internal final accounts for all businesses are shown in the same way in most respects:

It is only after the calculation of net profit that a change in layout may take place. When you prepared the final accounts of a sole trader the profit (or loss) was entered in the trader's capital account.

The profit (or loss) earned by a partnership has to be shared between the partners in accordance with any agreement (or according to the Partnership Act of 1890 if there is no agreement).

The profit sharing is shown in detail in the profit and loss appropriation account.

Partners usually agree to share profits in ways that will reflect the:

■ workload of each partner
■ amount of capital invested in the business by each partner
■ risk-taking element of being in business.

Residual profits (or losses) are the profits (or losses) that remain once all appropriations of net profit have been allocated to the appropriate partners.

Although partners, like all entrepreneurs, receive a share of profits, for convenience's sake the profit division is shown in the appropriation account under the headings of:

■ salaries
■ interest on capital
■ share of residual profits.

PARTNERSHIP SALARIES

WORKED EXAMPLE

Ash and Ben are in partnership, sharing residual profits in the ratio of 2:1 respectively.

Their net profit for the year ended 31 July 20*4 was £36,450.

Required A profit and loss appropriation account for the year ended 31 July 20*4.

Answer

Ash and Ben Profit and loss appropriation account for the year ended 31 July 20*4		
	£	£
Net profit		36,450
Share of profit		
Ash	24,300	
Ben	12,150	36,450

Note the heading – 'for the year ended'. Fairly straightforward!

If a partner is entitled to a partnership salary, this is taken from the net profit before the residual profit shares are calculated.

WORKED EXAMPLE

Charlie and Divya are in partnership, sharing residual profits in the ratio 3:2 respectively after crediting Divya with a partnership salary of £4,200.

The net profit for the year ended 31 December 20*4 was £29,460.

Required Prepare a profit and loss appropriation account for the year ended 31 December 20*4.

WORKED EXAMPLE *continued*

Answer

Charlie and Divya
Profit and loss appropriation account for the year ended 31 December 20*4

	£	£
Net profit		29,460
Less salary – Divya		4,200
		25,260
Share of profit		
Charlie	15,156	
Divya	10,104	25,260

Note:

- Divya's salary is deducted before the sharing of residual profits.
- Divya's share of profits is £14,304 (she does not earn a salary in the same way that employees earn a salary; she is a part owner of the business and as such she earns profits no matter how they are described).

INTEREST ON CAPITAL

WORKED EXAMPLE

Ed and Fred are in partnership. They maintain fixed capital accounts the balances of which are £30,000 and £20,000 respectively. Their partnership agreement provides that profits and losses are shared 2:1 after interest on capital is provided at 8% per annum.

The net profit for the year ended 31 March 20*4 was £32,269.

Required Prepare a profit and loss appropriation account for the year ended 31 March 20*4.

Answer

Ed and Fred
Profit and loss appropriation account for the year ended 31 March 20*4

	£	£
Net profit		32,269
Less Interest on capital		
Ed	2,400	
Fred	1,600	4,000
		28,269
Share of profit		
Ed	18,846	
Fred	9,423	28,269

Note the use of the 'inset' to show clearly the individual appropriations and the total appropriation.

- Ed's share of the profit is £21,246 (interest £2,400 and £18,846 share of residual profit).
- Fred's share of the profit is £11,023.

WORKED EXAMPLE

Gervais and Hannah are in partnership. They maintain fixed capital accounts at £50,000 and £32,000 respectively. The net profit for the year ended 31 August 20*4 was £47,632.

The partnership agreement provides that:

■ Hannah be credited with a partnership salary of £3,750 per annum
■ interest at the rate of 7% per annum be credited for partners' capital account balances
■ residual profits be shared in the ratio 4:1 respectively.

Required Prepare a profit and loss appropriation account for the year ended 31 August 20*4.

Answer

Gervais and Hannah
Profit and loss appropriation account for the year ended 31 August 20*4

	£	£
Net profit		47,632
Less Salary – Hannah		3,750
		43,882
Less Interest on capital –		
Gervais	3,500	
Hannah	2,240	5,740
		38,142
Share of profit –		
Gervais	30,514	
Hannah	7,628	38,142

Note that the residual profit shares have been rounded.

○ EXAMINATION TIP

If figures do not divide exactly, quickly check that you have not overlooked an entry somewhere (do not spend too much time doing this. Remember: time = marks).

If nothing has been missed then 'round' your figures, unless the question asks you to work in pence.

QUESTION 1

Ian and Jenny are in partnership. The net profit for the year ended 31 January 20*5 was £26,900. Their partnership agreement provides that Ian be credited with a partnership salary of £5,000 and that residual profits or losses be shared in the ratio of 2:1 respectively.

Required Prepare an appropriation account for the year ended 31 January 20*5.

QUESTION 2

Kelly and Larry are in partnership. The net profit for the year ended 30 November 20*4 was £48,270.
Their partnership agreement provides that Larry be credited with a partnership salary of £2,500 and that residual profits or losses be shared in the ratio of 3:2 respectively.

Required Prepare an appropriation account for the year ended 30 November 20*4.

QUESTION 3

Maria and Nelly are in partnership. They have fixed capital accounts of £40,000 and £60,000 respectively. Their partnership agreement provides that Maria be credited with a partnership salary of £4,800 and that partners be credited with 8% interest on capital. Any residual profits or losses are to be shared in the ratio 3:1 respectively.
The net profit for the year ended 31 March 20*5 amounted to £74,868.

Required Prepare a profit and loss appropriation account for the year ended 31 March 20*5.

QUESTION 4

Ollie and Paul are in partnership. They have fixed capital accounts of £100,000 and £120,000 respectively. Their partnership agreement provides that Ollie be credited with a partnership salary of £8,000 and that partners be credited with interest on capital at 7% per annum. Any residual profits or losses are to be shared equally.
The net profit for the year ended 31 December 20*4 was £123,671.

Required Prepare a profit and loss appropriation account for the year ended 31 December 20*4.

QUESTION 5

Queenie and Rusty are in partnership, sharing profits and losses equally after providing for interest on capital of 6% per annum. The partners maintain fixed capital accounts of £30,000 and £20,000 respectively. The partners have agreed that from 1 August 20*3 Rusty be credited with a salary of £10,000 per annum.
The net profit for the year ended 29 February 20*4 was £63,842.

Required Prepare a profit and loss appropriation account for the year ended 29 February 20*4.

QUESTION 6

Steve and Tajinder are in partnership, sharing profits and losses in the ratio 3:2 respectively after providing for interest on capital of 9% per annum. The partners maintain fixed capital accounts of £40,000 and £60,000 respectively. The partners agreed that from 1 March 20*4 Steve be credited with a salary of £6,000 per annum.
The net profit for the year ended 31 August 20*4 was £31,450.

Required A profit and loss appropriation account for the year ended 31 August 20*4.

QUESTION 7

Ursula and Vincent are in partnership. They maintain fixed capital accounts of £10,000 and £60,000 respectively. Their partnership agreement provides that Ursula be credited with a partnership salary of £6,000 and that partners be credited with interest on capital of 5% per annum. Any residual profits or losses are to be shared in the ratio 3:2 respectively.
The net profit for the year ended 31 December 20*4 was £8,400.

Required Prepare a profit and loss appropriation account for the year ended 31 December 20*4.

QUESTION 8

Wanda and Yvonne are in partnership, sharing residual profits and losses in the ratio 3:1 respectively. They maintain fixed capital accounts of £60,000 and £70,000. Their partnership agreement provides that Yvonne be credited with a salary of £14,000 and that partners be credited with interest on capital of 7% per annum.
The net profit for the year ended 30 April 20*4 was £22,780.

Required Prepare a profit and loss appropriation account for the year ended 30 April 20*4.

INTEREST ON DRAWINGS

Some partnership agreements provide that partners will be charged interest on any drawings made during the financial year. This is supposed to deter partners from drawing cash from the business in the early part of the financial year.

We say 'supposed' since, if a partner needs to draw cash from the business, an interest charge is hardly likely to deter him or her.

WORKED EXAMPLE

The partnership agreement of Arbuthnot and Brennan provides that interest be charged on drawings, at 5% per annum. The business year-end is 31 December.

During the year, the partners made drawings as follows:

	Arbuthnot £	Brennan £
31 March	3,000	2,000
30 June	5,000	6,500
30 September	4,300	5,600
31 December	7,900	4,000

Required Calculate the amount of interest to be charged to each partner for the year.

Answer

Arbuthnot will be charged **£294.25** interest on drawings.

Workings   £3,000 × 5% × ¾ year = £115.50
£5,000 × 5% × ½ year = £125.00
£4,300 × 5% × ¼ year = £53.75

Brennan will be charged **£307.50** interest on drawings.

Workings   £2,000 × 5% × ¾ year = £75.00
£6,500 × 5% × ½ year = £162.50
£5,600 × 5% × ¼ year = £70.00

Note that no interest has been charged for drawings made on the last day of the year.

The entries in the partnership accounts are:

   Debit the profit and loss appropriation account and

   Credit the partners' current accounts.

The credit entry in the partners' current accounts has the effect of increasing the amount withdrawn during the year. It is, in effect, an additional amount of drawings.

○ EXAMINATION TIP

The amount of interest on drawings will generally be given in the question, so you will not be required to calculate the amounts to be charged to each partner.

WORKED EXAMPLE

Greta and Hanif are in partnership. They supply the following information for the year ended 31 August 20*4.

The partnership agreement provides that:

- Greta be credited with a partnership salary of £5,600
- partners be credited with interest on capital of 8% per annum
- partners be charged interest on their drawings at 5% per annum
- residual profits be shared equally

- Greta's fixed capital account stands at £42,000 while Hanif's fixed capital account stands at £50,000.
- The profit for the year before appropriations was £56,934.
- During the year Greta made drawings of £32,900 and Hanif's drawings were £21,750.
- Interest on drawings was calculated at £348 for Greta and £180 for Hanif.

Required Prepare a profit and loss appropriation account for the year ended 31 August 20*4.

Answer

Greta and Hanif
Profit and loss appropriation account for the year ended 31 August 20*4

	£	£
Net profit		56,934
Add Interest on drawings – Greta	348	
Hanif	180	528
		56,406
Less Salary – Greta		5,600
		50,806
Less Interest on capital – Greta	3,360	
Hanif	4,000	7,360
		43,446
Share of profit – Greta	21,723	
Hanif	21,723	43,446

QUESTION 9

Gareth and Darius are in partnership. The partnership agreement provides that partners are to be charged interest on drawings and that residual profits or losses are to be shared equally.
The following information is available for the year ended 31 January 20*5:

	£
Net profit for the year	27,362
Interest on drawings for the year – Gareth	146
Darius	238

Required Prepare a profit and loss appropriation account for the year ended 31 January 20*5.

QUESTION 10

Ali and Brenda are in partnership. They share profits and losses equally. They have also agreed that interest be charged on any drawings made during the financial year.
They provide the following information for the year ended 31 December 20*4:

	£
Net profit for the year	17,614
Interest on drawings for the year – Ali	542
Brenda	104

Required Prepare a profit and loss appropriation account for the year ended 31 December 20*4.

QUESTION 11

Tramp and Hobo are in partnership, sharing profits and losses in the ratio 3:2 respectively. They have also agreed that Hobo be credited with a partnership salary of £2,000 and that interest be charged on drawings made during the financial year.
They provide the following information for the year ended 30 June 20*4:

	£
Net profit for the year	25,570
Interest on drawings for the year – Tramp	267
Hobo	303

Required Prepare a profit and loss appropriation account for the year ended 30 June 20*4.

QUESTION 12

Jacques and Gillian are in partnership. Their partnership agreement provides that profits and losses be shared in the ratio 4:1 respectively. It also provides that Jacques be credited with a partnership salary of £3,500 and that partners be charged interest on drawings made during the financial year.
The following information is available for the year ended 31 October 20*4:

	£
Net profit for the year	11,810
Interest on drawings for the year – Jacques	234
Gillian	901

Required Prepare a profit and loss appropriation account for the year ended 31 October 20*4.

QUESTION 13

Mark, Noreen and Oswald are in partnership, sharing profits and losses 3:2:1, respectively. They have agreed that interest be charged on drawings made during the financial year.
The following information is available for the year ended 31 March 20*5:

	£
Net loss for the year	818
Interest on drawings for the year – Mark	261
Noreen	38
Oswald	279

Required Prepare a profit and loss appropriation account for the year ended 31 March 20*5.

QUESTION 14

Wilkinson, Sword and Cutlass are in partnership, sharing profits and losses 2:2:1 respectively. Their partnership agreement provides that they be charged interest on drawings.
The following information is available for the year ended 29 February 20*4:

	£
Net loss for the year	834
Interest on drawings for the year – Wilkinson	240
Sword	732
Cutlass	182

Required Prepare a profit and loss appropriation account for the year ended 29 February 20*4.

PARTNERSHIP CAPITAL AND CURRENT ACCOUNTS

Partners' **capital accounts** show deliberate injections of capital into the business; plus any adjustments of a capital nature, eg goodwill adjustments; plus any profits or losses arising on a revaluation of assets (generally on the admission or the retirement of a partner).

Partners' **current accounts** record entries relating to each partner's share of the profits of the business in the current year. The current account would also be used to adjust for any errors made in the profit share in previous years.

The balance sheet of a partnership differs from that of a sole trader in that, since there is more than one owner, there must be more than one capital account, showing the financial commitment of each partner to the business.

Indeed, the capital employed in the business is usually divided into partners' capital accounts and partners' current accounts.

Capital accounts may change each year if current accounts are not maintained and they would resemble the capital accounts that you have already prepared in your studies. It is more usual for partnerships to maintain fixed capital accounts. However, some examination questions state that only capital accounts are maintained.

WORKED EXAMPLE

The profit and loss appropriation account for the year ended 30 June 20*4 of Tessa and Alexia is shown. They share profits and losses in the ratio 2:3 respectively.

	£	£
Net profit		34,745
Less salary – Tessa		6,000
		28,745
Interest on capital –		
Tessa	2,400	
Alexia	3,000	5,400
		23,345
Share of profit –		
Tessa	9,338	
Alexia	14,007	23,345

The capital account balances as at 1 July 20*3 were £40,000 and £50,000 respectively.

Drawings for the year were £22,350 (Tessa) and £26,850 (Alexia).

Required Prepare the capital accounts of Tessa and Alexia as at 30 June 20*4.

Answer

	Tessa £	Alexia £		Tessa £	Alexia £
Drawings	22,350	26,850	Balance b/d	40,000	50,000
Balance c/d	35,388	40,157	Salary	6,000	
			Interest on capital	2,400	3,000
			Share of profit	9,338	14,007
	57,738	67,007		57,738	67,007
			Balances b/d	35,388	40,157

Notice that a columnar layout has been used. This saves time and space. Do try it. It may be difficult the first time or two that you use it but it does mean that you don't have to repeat the descriptions used in each account.

The capital accounts would generally be shown on the balance sheet of the partnership as follows:

Capital accounts at 30 June 20*4	Tessa £	Alexia £	£
Balance	40,000	50,000	
Add Salary	6,000		
Interest on capital	2,400	3,000	
Share of profit	9,338	14,007	
	57,738	67,007	
Less Drawings	22,350	26,850	
	35,388	40,157	75,545

Both the capital accounts and the layout used above give the same result.

If a question asks you to prepare capital accounts, you must produce the information in account form as shown. If you do not, then you will most probably forfeit some marks. If a question asks for a 'calculation' or does not ask for 'accounts' then the second approach is acceptable.

The use of the accounts will save space in an answer so in many ways it is preferable to draw up the ledger accounts and merely insert the totals of the ledger accounts in the balance sheet.

So, in the above example the balance sheet might be drawn up showing only:

Capital accounts	£	£
Tessa	35,388	
Alexia	40,157	75,545

It is more usual for a partnership to maintain fixed capital accounts and showing all appropriations in the partnership current accounts.

All entries relating to profits earned and profits withdrawn are entered in the current accounts.

WORKED EXAMPLE

Terry and June are in partnership. They provide the following information for the year ended 31 August 20*4.

	Terry £	June £
Capital account balances as at 1 September 20*3	30,000	45,000
Current account balances as at 1 September 20*3	1,542 Cr	238 Cr
Drawings for the year were	20,653	16,234
Interest to be charged on drawings	541	452

The profit and loss appropriation account shows:

	£
Salary – Terry	4,800
Interest on capital – Terry	2,100
June	3,150
Share of residual profits – Terry	18,000
June	9,000

Required Prepare detailed capital accounts and current accounts for the partnership at 31 August 20*4.

Answer

Capital accounts

	Terry £	June £		Terry £	June £
			Balances b/d	30,000	45,000

Current accounts

	Terry £	June £		Terry £	June £
Drawings	20,653	16,234	Balances b/d	1,542	238
Interest on drawings	541	452	Salary	4,800	
			Interest on capital	2,100	3,150
			Share of profits	18,000	9,000
Balance c/d	5,248		Balance c/d		4,298
	26,442	16,686		26,442	16,686
Balance b/d		4,298	Balance b/d	5,248	

The capital accounts have remained 'fixed' and the profits earned and profits withdrawn from the business (drawings) and interest on drawings are recorded in the current account.

It is, of course, possible that a partner may withdraw more profits from the business than he or she has earned. In such a case the partner's current account will show a debit balance.

WORKED EXAMPLE

Vikram and Walter provide the following information for their partnership for the year ended 30 April 2004:

	Vikram £	Walter £
Current account balances	164 Cr	298 Cr
Interest on capital for the year	500	700
Share of residual profits	25,300	12,650
Drawings for the year	20,000	15,000
Interest on drawings	270	460

Required

Prepare:
a a profit and loss appropriation account for the year ended 30 April 20*4
b current accounts as at 30 April 20*4.

Answer
a)

Vikram and Walter
Profit and loss appropriation account for the year ended 30 April 20*4

	£	£
Net profit		38,420 *missing figure*
Add Interest on drawings – Vikram	270	
Walter	460	730
		39,150
Less Interest on capital – Vikram	500	
Walter	700	1,200
		37,950
Share of profits – Vikram	25,300	
Walter	12,650	37,950

WORKED EXAMPLE *continued*

b)

	Vikram	Walter	Current accounts	Vikram	Walter
Drawings	20,000	15,000	Balances b/d	164	298
Interest on drawings	270	460	Interest on capital	500	700
			Share of profits	25,300	12,650
Balance c/d	5,694		Balance c/d		1,812
	25,964	15,460		25,964	15,460
Balance b/d		1,812	Balance b/d	5,694	

Chapter summary

- A partnership exists when two or more people are engaged in business with the aim of making profits.
- A partnership should have a partnership agreement. If there is no agreement then the Partnership Act 1890 lays down the rules by which the partnership is governed.
- Final accounts contain a profit and loss appropriation account that shows how profits (and losses) are shared between the partners.
- Partnerships can maintain fixed or fluctuating capital accounts.
- Most partnerships maintain fixed capital accounts. In such cases all transactions involving appropriations of profits and drawings of profits are entered in current accounts.
- Entries in capital accounts involve capital transactions only.

Self-test questions

- What is limited liability?
- A sole trader has limited liability. True or false?
- Partners have unlimited liability. True or false?
- Explain two advantages of being in partnership.
- Give the date of the Partnership Act that governs the basic rules that apply if a partnership does not have a partnership agreement.
- List four rules that apply if a partnership does not have an partnership agreement.
- What is the difference between an appropriation account and a profit and loss appropriation account?
- A partnership cannot have both interest on drawings and interest on capital shown in the profit and loss appropriation account. True/false?
- Give an example of an entry in a partner's capital account.
- Give two examples of debit entries in a partner's current account.
- Give two examples of credit entries in a partner's current account.

TEST QUESTIONS

QUESTION 15

Rooney and Timms are in partnership. Their net profit for the year ended 31 May 20*4 was £27,967. The partnership agreement provides that Rooney be credited with a partnership salary of £3,000 per annum; that interest on capital be credited to the partners at the rate of 10% per annum on

fixed capital accounts; and that residual profits and losses be shared equally. The agreement also provides that interest be charged on drawings.
The following information is available:

	Rooney £	Timms £
Capital account balance as at 1 June 20*3	12,000	10,000
Interest on drawings	82	179

Required Prepare a profit and loss appropriation account for the year ended 31 May 20*4.

QUESTION 16

Ramtochan and Welsh are in partnership. Their net profit for the year ended 30 November 20*4 was £46,784.
The partnership agreement provides that:

■ Welsh be credited with a partnership salary of £8,000 per annum
■ interest on capital be provided at 10% per annum
■ residual profits be shared 3:2 respectively
■ interest be charged on drawings.

Additional information

	Ramtochan £	Welsh £
Capital account balances as at 1 December 20*3	23,000	27,000
Interest on drawings	480	106

Required Prepare a profit and loss appropriation account for the year ended 30 November 20*4.

QUESTION 17

Gray and Pink are in partnership. Their partnership agreement provides that:

■ Gray be credited with a partnership salary of £4,000 per annum
■ interest on capital be credited to partners at 8% per annum
■ residual profits and losses be shared in the ratio 4:1 respectively
■ interest be charged on drawings.

Additional information
The net profit for the year ended 30 November 20*4 was £37,951.

	Gray £	Pink £
Capital account balances as at 1 December 20*3	30,000	70,000
Interest on drawings	171	298

Required Prepare a profit and loss appropriation account for the year ended 30 November 20*4.

QUESTION 18

Hunter and Carrier are in partnership. Their net profit for the year ended 31 December 20*4 was £5,195.
Their partnership agreement provides that Hunter be credited with a partnership salary of £1,500; that partners be credited with interest on capital of 7% per annum on fixed capital account balances; that interest be charged on drawings; and that residual profits or losses be shared in the ratio 3:2 respectively.
The following information was also available:

	Hunter £	Carrier £
Capital account balances as at 1 January 20*4	20,000	30,000
Drawings for the year	17,500	16,750
Interest on drawings	212	193

Required Prepare a profit and loss appropriation account for the year ended 31 December 20*4.

QUESTION 19

Naylor, Niall and Norbert are in partnership. Their profit for the year ended 31 May 20*4 was £71,560.
The partnership agreement provides that:

- Niall be credited with a partnership salary of £7,500
- partners be credited with interest on capital at the rate of 6% per annum
- residual profits and losses be shared 3:2:2 respectively
- interest be charged on drawings.

Additional information

	Naylor £	Niall £	Norbert £
Drawings for the year	27,200	17,450	19,350
Interest on drawings	460	320	411
Fixed capital account balances as at 1 June 20*3	50,000	30,000	40,000
(On 1 December Niall introduced £10,000 additional capital into the business)			
Current account balances as at 1 June 20*3	85 Cr	162 Dr	131 Cr

Required

Prepare:

a a profit and loss appropriation account for the year ended 31 May 20*4
b current accounts as at 31 May 20*4.

QUESTION 20

Budgert, Grouper and Singh are in partnership. Their net profit for the year ended 30 November 20*4 was £94,082.
The partnership agreement provides that:

- Budgert and Singh be credited with partnership salaries of £1,000 and £2,500 respectively
- interest on fixed capital accounts be credited at 5% per annum
- residual profits be shared 3:2:1 respectively
- interest be charged on drawings.

	Budgert £	Grouper £	Singh £
Drawings for the year	38,000	23,000	21,000
Interest on drawings	210	440	316
Fixed capital account balances as at 1 December 20*3	30,000	20,000	70,000
Current account balances	2,716 Dr	81 Cr	236 Cr

Required

Prepare:

a   a profit and loss appropriation account for the year ended 30 November 20*4
b   current accounts as at 30 November 20*4.

CHAPTER FIVE

Partnership Accounts – Structural Changes

Obviously, during the lifetime of any business there could be changes in the ownership.

Colin, a sole trader, may decide that he no longer wishes to trade as a farmer and that he will sell his business to Jayne on 31 July.

The ownership of a partnership could change because:

■ partners may decide to terminate the partnership
■ partners may decide to admit another partner
■ they may decide to alter their profit-sharing ratios.

When there is any kind of change to the structure of a partnership, the treatment is the same: one business ceases to exist at the date of the change and immediately after the date of the change a new business comes into being.

Specification coverage:
AQA: 14.3; OCR: 5.3.1.

By the end of this chapter you should be able to:
■ account for changes in profit- sharing ratios
■ account for the retirement and admission of partners
■ account for the dissolution of a partnership
■ account for the revaluation of assets and goodwill.

EXAMPLE

1. When Art and Bart admitted Carl as a partner on 1 April 20*4 there were two businesses involved:

| **Up to 31 March 20*4** | **From 1 April 20*4** |
| Owners are Art and Bart | Owners are Art, Bart and Carl |

2. When Iain retired from the partnership of Iain, Janet and Keith on 30 September 20*4 there were two businesses involved:

| **Up to 30 September 20*4** | **From 1 October 20*4** |
| Owners are Iain, Janet and Keith | Owners are Janet and Keith |

3. Dierdre and Ethel were in partnership sharing profits and losses equally. When they changed their profit sharing ratio to 3:2 on 30 June 20*4 there were two businesses involved:

Up to 30 June 20*4	**From 1 July 20*4**
Owners are Dierdre and Ethel	Owners are Dierdre and Ethel
(profit share equal)	(profit share 3:2)
different profit share =	= different business

● EXAMINATION TIP

When there is a structural change to a partnership, treat the information relating to the business before the change separately from the information relating to the business after the change.

THE ADMISSION OF A NEW PARTNER

WORKED EXAMPLE

Adele and Gloria are in partnership, sharing profits and losses equally. Their financial year-end is 31 December. They admit Carolyn as a partner on 1 June 20*4. They all agree that Adele, Gloria and Carolyn will share profits 3:2:1 respectively.

The net profit for the year ended 31 December 20*4 was £40,000. The profit accrued evenly throughout the year.

Required Prepare profit and loss appropriation accounts for the year ended 31 December 20*4.

Answer

Remember that we are dealing with two businesses:

Up to 31 May 20*4	From 1 June 20*4
Owners were Adele and Gloria	Owners are Adele, Gloria and Carolyn

So:

Adele and Gloria
Profit and loss appropriation account for the six months ended 31 May 20*4

	£	£
Net profit		20,000
Profit share – Adele	10,000	
Gloria	10,000	20,000

Adele, Gloria and Carolyn
Profit and loss appropriation account for the six months ended 31 December 20*4

	£	£
Net profit		20,000
Profit share – Adele	10,000	
Gloria	6,667	
Carolyn	3,333	20,000

Note that the profit share has been rounded. Do not work using pence unless you are instructed to do so in the question.

The worked example shown was fairly straightforward (I hope you agree!).

However, common sense would tell us that Adele and Gloria would not simply have allowed Carolyn to become a partner without her contributing some capital to the business.

Common sense would also suggest that Adele and Gloria would have considered the value of their business assets before allowing Carolyn to become a part-owner of those business assets.

Imagine that your grandparents have been in business for 40 years. Their business assets are recorded on the business balance sheet as follows:

	£	
Premises (book value)	18,500	Remember that we value assets at cost,
Equipment (book value)	5,500	not at what they could be sold for –
Other net assets	2,000	the 'going concern' concept.
	26,000	
Capital – Grandpa	11,000	
Grandma	15,000	
	26,000	

Now imagine that your grandparents admit Willy Fox as a partner into their business.

WORKED EXAMPLE *continued*

They ask him to provide £20,000 capital. He agrees and enters the business.

What would the balance sheet look like now?

	£	
Premises (book value)	18,500	Simple!
Equipment (book value)	5,500	Your grandparents are simple if
Other net assets	22,000	they agree to what has taken place!
	46,000	Remember that they have been in
Capital – Grandpa	11,000	business for 40 years.
Grandma	15,000	How much must the premises be
Willy Fox	20,000	worth now? Surely they are worth
	46,000	more than the book value shown?

Can you see your likely future inheritance disappearing into Willy Fox's pocket?

I can!

In fact, what needs to happen when any kind of structural change takes place is that the business assets have to be revalued. The increase in value (or decrease in value) belongs to the **original** partners.

WORKED EXAMPLE

Mike and Jeanette have been in partnership for many years, sharing profits and losses equally. The financial year-end for the business is 31 December. They decide to admit Kiri into the partnership, with effect from 1 May 20*4. Kiri will pay £25,000 capital into the business bank account. The partnership balance sheet at 30 April 20*4 was:

Mike and Jeanette
Balance sheet as at 30 April 20*4

	£	£
Fixed assets		
Premises at cost		28,000
Vehicles at cost		16,000
		44,000
Current assets		
Stock	3,500	
Trade debtors	4,300	
Bank	1,560	
	9,360	
Less **Current liabilities**		
Trade creditors	3,360	6,000
		50,000
Capital accounts – Mike		25,000
Jeanette		25,000
		50,000

Over the years, property prices have risen. The premises were valued at £70,000 at the end of April 20*4.

Required Prepare a balance sheet as at 1 May 20*4, after the admission of Kiri.

Answer

Mike, Jeanette and Kiri
Balance sheet as at 1 May 20*4

	£	£
Fixed assets		
Premises at valuation		70,000
Equipment at cost		16,000
		86,000
Current assets		
Stock	3,500	
Trade debtors	4,300	
Bank	26,560	
	34,360	
Less **Current liabilities**		
Trade creditors	3,360	31,000
		117,000
Capital accounts – Mike		46,000
Jeanette		46,000
Kiri		25,000
		117,000

The rise in the value of the premises (by £42,000) has taken place while Mike and Jeanette have been the only proprietors, so any profits (because of inflation) belong to them. The increase in the value of the premises did not occur when Kiri was a partner, so she should not benefit. As they are equal partners, the increase has been divided equally between Mike and Jeanette.

QUESTION 1

Pat and Danny have been in partnership for a number of years, sharing profits and losses in the ratio of 2:1 respectively. Their balance sheet as at 31 December 20*4 showed:

	£	£
Fixed assets (book value)		110,000
Current assets	15,000	
Current liabilities	10,000	5,000
		115,000
Capital accounts – Pat	60,000	
Danny	55,000	115,000

On 1 January 20*5 Pat and Danny admitted Janice as a partner. She introduced £25,000 as her capital. They agree that the fixed assets are to be valued at £155,000.

Required Prepare a balance sheet as at 1 January 20*5, immediately after Janice was admitted as a partner.

QUESTION 2

Bert and Vanessa have been in partnership for several years. They share profits and losses equally. The business balance sheet as at 31 January 20*4 showed:

	£	£
Fixed assets (book value)		21,000
Current assets	4,500	
Current liabilities	2,350	2,150
		23,150
Capital accounts – Bert		10,950
Vanessa		12,200
		23,150

On 1 February 20*4 it was agreed to admitted Ellie as a partner. She introduced £12,500 as her capital. It was further agreed that the fixed assets be valued at £50,000.

Required Prepare a partnership balance sheet as at 1 February 20*4, after Ellie was admitted as a partner.

It is more usual to find a balance sheet showing details of all assets and liabilities. When a structural change takes place in such instances we use an account to record any changes to the values of assets and liabilities shown on the balance sheet and hence to calculate the (inflationary) profit or loss resulting from the changes.

A temporary account is opened and it is only used to record adjustments to the account balances from the ledgers shown on the balance sheet.

This is how the temporary account works:

WORKED EXAMPLE

Sandie and Ian are in partnership, sharing profits and losses in the ratio 4:3 respectively. They admit Laura as a partner on 1 August 20*4; she pays £35,000 to the partnership as her capital.

The partnership balance sheet at 31 July 20*4 was:

	£	£
Fixed assets		
Premises at cost		48,000
Equipment (book value)		12,000
Vehicle (book value)		15,000
		75,000
Current assets		
Stock	2,400	
Trade debtors	1,750	
Bank balance	2,200	
	6,350	
Current liabilities		
Trade creditors	2,790	3,560
		78,560
Capital accounts – Sandie	40,000	
Ian	30,000	70,000
Current accounts – Sandie	3,410	
Ian	5,150	8,560
		78,560

It was agreed that the assets on 31 July 20*4 be revalued as follows:

	£
Premises	100,000
Equipment	4,500
Vehicle	6,000
Stock	2,000
Trade debtors	1,650

WORKED EXAMPLE *continued*

Required Prepare a balance sheet as at 1 August 20*4, after the admission of Laura as a partner.

Answer

Workings

We open an account for each asset that is to be revalued:

Premises

Bal b/d	48,000		
Revaluation	52,000	Bal c/d	100,000
	100,000		100,000
Bal b/d	100,000		

Equipment

Bal b/d	12,000	Revaluation	7,500
		Bal c/d	4,500
	12,000		12,000
Bal b/d	4,500		

Vehicle

Bal b/d	15,000	Revaluation	9,000
		Bal c/d	6,000
	15,000		15,000
Bal b/d	6,000		

Stock

Bal b/d	2,400	Revaluation	400
		Bal c/d	2,000
	2,400		2,400
Bal b/d	2,000		

Trade debtors

Bal b/d	1,750	Revaluation	100
		Bal c/d	1,650
	1,750		1,750
Bal b/d	1,650		

The revaluation account is used to adjust the asset accounts and to calculate any profit or loss on revaluation. The profit or loss is transferred to the existing partners' capital accounts **before** the new partner is admitted.

WORKED EXAMPLE *continued*

Revaluation account

Equipment	7,500	Premises	52,000
Vehicle	9,000		
Stock	400		
Debtors	100		
Capital – Sandie	20,000		
Ian	15,000		
	52,000		52,000

Capital – Sandie

		Bal b/d	40,000
Bal c/d	60,000	Revaluation a/c	20,000
	60,000		60,000
		Bal b/d	60,000

Capital – Ian

		Bal b/d	30,000
Bal c/d	45,000	Revaluation a/c	15,000
	45,000		45,000
		Bal b/d	45,000

Sandie, Ian and Laura
Balance sheet as at 1 August 20*4

	£	£
Fixed assets		
Premises at valuation		100,000
Equipment at valuation		4,500
Vehicle at valuation		6,000
		110,500
Current assets		
Stock	2,000	
Trade debtors	1,650	
Bank balance	37,200	
	40,850	
Current liabilities		
Trade creditors	2,790	38,060
		148,560
Capital accounts – Sandie	60,000	
Ian	45,000	
Laura	35,000	140,000
Current accounts – Sandie	3,410	
Ian	5,150	8,560
		148,560

Note that the changes to the capital structure of the business are entered in the partners' capital accounts. The current accounts have not been used. The current accounts will change only when trading profits or losses are shared between partners or as partners make drawings.

Notice that the fixed assets are now labelled 'at valuation' since they do not now appear 'at cost'.

When you get used to making adjustments to the partnership balance sheet because of a structural change you may find that you do not have to open an account for each asset and liability. However, it will be safer for you always to open a revaluation account to 'collect' the changes that have been implemented.

QUESTION 3

Umair and Tim are in partnership, sharing profits and losses in the ratio 3:2 respectively. Their balance sheet as at 30 September 20*4 was as follows:

	£	£	£
Fixed assets			
Premises at cost			30,000
Equipment at cost			8,900
Vehicles at cost			14,100
			53,000
Current assets			
Stock		4,500	
Trade debtors		6,500	
		11,000	
Current liabilities			
Trade creditors	2,700		
Bank overdraft	1,300	4,000	7,000
			60,000
Capital accounts – Umair			30,000
Tim			30,000
			60,000

Eddie was admitted as a partner on 1 October 20*4; he paid £10,000 as his capital.
It was agreed that the following assets be revalued at 30 September 20*4:

	£
Premises	100,000
Equipment	1,400
Vehicles	12,000
Stock	4,200
Trade debtors	6,400

Required Prepare a balance sheet as at 1 October 20*4, after the admission of Eddie as a partner.

QUESTION 4

George and Bernard are in partnership, sharing profits and losses 2:1 respectively. Their balance sheet as at 31 March 20*4 was as follows:

	£	£
Fixed assets		
Premises at cost		36,000
Equipment at cost		23,900
Vehicles at cost		34,700
		94,600
Current assets		
Stock	9,870	
Trade debtors	4,670	
Bank balance	850	
	15,390	
Current liabilities		
Trade creditors	9,990	5,400
		100,000

Capital accounts – George	£	£
Bernard		50,000
		50,000
		100,000

Shore was admitted to the partnership on 1 April 20*4; he paid £40,000 as his capital. It was agreed that the following assets be revalued:

	£
Premises	110,000
Equipment	16,000
Vehicles	20,000
Stock	9,800
Trade debtors	4,340

Required Prepare a balance sheet as at 1 April 20*4, after the admission of Shore.

Goodwill is the cost of acquiring a business less the total value of the assets and liabilities that have been purchased.

Goodwill is an **intangible asset**. It cannot be seen; it has no physical presence, unlike tangible assets such as premises or machinery or vehicles.

When a successful business is sold, the vendor will generally price the business at a level greater than the total of the net assets being sold.

The balance sheet of a local fish and chip shop may be as follows:

	£	£
Fixed assets		
Equipment		34,000
Fixtures and fittings		8,400
		42,400
Current assets		
Stock	840	
Bank balance	2,345	
Cash in hand	455	
	3,640	
Current liabilities		
Creditors	1,420	2,220
		44,620
Capital – Terri		44,620

Terri decided to sell her business. She advertised it at £90,000.

Henry bought the business for £90,000.

Two points emerge:

- Terri sold her business at a profit of £48,180. (She would not sell the bank balance or cash in hand.) She sold fixed assets of £42,400 and stock of £840 less current liabilities of £1,420 for £90,000.
- Henry purchased the business net assets for £90,000. He has purchased net tangible assets for £41,820 and an intangible asset (goodwill) for £48,180.

○ EXAMINATION TIP

Goodwill is not sold; it is only purchased. The seller makes a profit; the purchaser buys net assets including goodwill.

We have already said that when there is a structural change to a partnership the change involves **two** businesses:

■ the business that existed before the change and
■ the business that comes into existence **because** of the change.

When a new partner is admitted to a partnership we have already seen that the assets need to be revalued. We also need to place a value on the intangible asset goodwill.

THE VALUATION OF GOODWILL

We cannot give a definitive method that can be used in every type of business when goodwill has to be valued. If a business were being purchased then goodwill would represent how much would be paid in excess of the value of the net assets being purchased. We have already seen this when Terri sold her fish and chip shop to Henry in the example used above.

How can we value goodwill when there is a structural change to a partnership; when no one is actually purchasing the business?

The value placed on goodwill has to be acceptable to the partners in the 'old' partnership as well as being acceptable to the new partner(s).

The following are the most commonly used methods of determining the value of goodwill.

Goodwill is valued at a multiple of the:

■ average profits generated over the past few years
■ average weekly sales generated over the past financial year
■ average of 'gross fees' earned over a number of years
■ 'super profits' earned by the business.

1. **A multiple of average profits generated over the past few years.**

WORKED EXAMPLE

It has been agreed that goodwill be valued at two years' purchase of the average profits taken over the past five years.

Profits for the past five years were:

Year	£
1	12,450
2	12,560
3	14,890
4	8,450
5	11,650

Required Calculate the value to be placed on goodwill.

Answer

Goodwill is valued at £24,000.

Workings Total profits for 5 years £60,000/5 = £12,000 × 2 = £24,000

2. **A multiple of average weekly sales generated over the past financial year.**

WORKED EXAMPLE

It has been agreed that goodwill be valued at four weeks' purchase of average weekly sales over the past financial year.

Last year's annual sales were:

£
322,400

Required Calculate the value to be placed on goodwill.

Answer

Goodwill is valued at £24,800.

Workings £322,400/52 = £6,200 × 4 = £24,800

3. **A multiple of an average of the gross fees earned over a number of years.**

This method is used by many professional businesses, such as accountants, doctors, solicitors and vets etc, when a partner retires or a new partner enters the business.

WORKED EXAMPLE

It has been agreed that goodwill be valued at two years' purchase of the average gross fees over the past four years.

Gross fees are the equivalent of sales income for a professional business.

Year	£
1	98,000
2	77,000
3	72,000
4	69,000

Fees for the past 4 years were:

Required Calculate the value to be placed on goodwill.

Answer

Goodwill is valued at £158,000.

Workings £98,000 + £77,000 + £72,000 + £69,000 = £316,000
£316,000/4 = £79,000 × 2 = £158,000

4. **A multiple of 'super profits' earned by the business.**

Opportunity cost is the cost of making a decision in terms of the benefit lost by not using a resource in the next best alternative.

Super profits are calculated using the principle of opportunity cost.

WORKED EXAMPLE

Dirgen, an estate agent, has £50,000 capital invested in his business. If he were working for another estate agent he could earn £23,000 salary per annum. His business is presently earning profits of £38,000.

Required Calculate the amount of super profits earned by Dirgen's business.

Answer

Super profits earned were £12,500.

Workings	£
If Dirgen worked for another estate agent he could earn:	23,000
If Dirgen invested his capital outside his business he could earn (say) 5%:	2,500
	25,500

By carrying on as a self-employed estate agent he earns £12,500 more than he would earn by using his capital and talents in the next best alternative.

WORKED EXAMPLE

Homer owns and runs a small plumbing business. Profits for the past few years have averaged £18,000. Homer has £14,000 capital invested in his business. He could earn £12,000 as a plumber working locally. He currently earns 5% per annum on a building society account. Goodwill is to be valued at three years' super profits.

Required Calculate the value to be placed on goodwill.

Answer

Goodwill is valued at £15,900.

Workings

£18,000 − £12,700 = £5,300 × 3= £15,900
(£12,000 earnings + £700 interest on the £14,000 invested)

FACTORS THAT CONTRIBUTE TO THE ESTABLISHMENT OF GOODWILL

The factors that determine the value of goodwill placed on business are varied. They include:

- a good reputation because of the quality of a product
- a good reputation because of good service
- a good reputation for the helpfulness of staff
- a good after-sales service
- a prominent physical position of premises
- popularity among customers.

No doubt you can think of one or two other factors that might contribute to the establishment of goodwill.

So, why might you pay £30,000 more than the net asset value placed on a business in order to purchase it?

- You cannot purchase a good reputation – you could destroy that overnight.
- You cannot buy popularity.
- You certainly cannot purchase customers.

The reason you might pay the 'extra' £30,000 is because you can see the prospect of earning high profits in the future – you can envisage yourself earning lots of profits.

Goodwill is paid by the purchaser of a business in order to gain access to future profits that may be generated by that business.

Let us see how goodwill is dealt with when a partner is **admitted** into a business.

WORKED EXAMPLE

Issmail and Gary are in partnership as door-to-door salesmen selling cleaning materials. They share profits and losses in the ratio 3:1 respectively. Their balance sheet at 31 August 20*4 showed:

		£
Bank balance		370
Capital accounts – Issmail		200
Gary		170
		370

Issmail and Gary admit June to the partnership, with effect from 1 September 20*4. June contributes £2,000 as her capital. They agree that goodwill be valued at £8,000.

Required   A balance sheet as at 1 September 20*4, immediately after June was admitted to the partnership.

Answer

Issmail, Gary and June
Balance sheet as at 1 September 20*4 (after admission of June)

		£
Bank balance		2,370
Goodwill		8,000
		10,370
Capital accounts – Issmail		6,200
Gary		2,170
June		2,000
		10,370

Notice that a new asset has appeared on the balance sheet: an asset (intangible) that has built up over the years while Issmail and Gary have been in business as partners. The two original partners have been responsible for creating the goodwill through their personality, products, after-sales service etc, so it is only *their* capital accounts that have been credited in the profit-sharing ratios.

The book-keeping entries to record the introduction of goodwill into the partnership books would look like this:

Capital (Issmail)

Balance c/d	6,200		Balance b/d	200
	6,200		Goodwill	6,000
				6,200
			Balance b/d	6,200

WORKED EXAMPLE *continued*

Capital (Gary)

		Balance b/d		170
Balance c/d	2,170	Goodwill		2,000
	2,170			2,170
		Balance b/d		2,170

Goodwill

Capital – I	6,000
Capital – G	2,000

QUESTION 5

Mo and Doug are in partnership, sharing profits and losses in the ratio 2:1 respectively. They provide the following information:

Balance sheet as at 31 March 20*4

	£
Bank balance	1,760
Capital accounts – Mo	1,010
Doug	750
	1,760

They admit Tracey to the partnership, with effect from 1 April 20*4. Tracey pays £3,000 into the business bank account as capital. It was agreed that goodwill be valued at £12,000.

Required Prepare a balance sheet as at 1 April 20*4 after the admission of Tracey as a partner.

QUESTION 6

Meena and Talha are in partnership, sharing profits and losses in the ratio of 3:2 respectively. They provide the following information:

Balance sheet as at 31 October 20*4

	£
Bank balance	7,500
Capital accounts – Meena	5,000
Talha	2,500
	7,500

Divya is admitted to the partnership, with effect from 1 November 20*4. She pays £1,000 into the business bank account as her capital. It was agreed that goodwill be valued at £10,000.

Required Prepare a balance sheet as at 1 November, after the admission of Divya as a partner.

Goodwill only appears in a balance sheet when it is purchased. If you see the asset on any balance sheet you can say with some certainty that:

■ either the ownership has changed recently
■ or the business has recently purchased another business.

This applies no matter what type of business balance sheet you are examining.

Inherent goodwill is the goodwill that has been generated internally, it has not been purchased, it is the goodwill that is enjoyed by a business while it is still ongoing.

Inherent goodwill is not entered in the books of account so it is never shown on a balance sheet.

Well-established businesses such as Marks and Spencer plc or McDonald's enjoy much inherent goodwill but this will not be shown on their balance sheets. Both these businesses are going concerns.

The going concern concept tells us that assets should be shown at cost price, not at what they would fetch if sold. Neither of the businesses is due to be sold in the next few days so as a going concern they would not show inherent goodwill.

Goodwill can appear in the books of any business when it is purchased.

Goodwill is generally written off immediately after purchase in examination questions involving partnerships.

[But see Chapter Eight on FRS 10 goodwill and intangible assets.]

WORKED EXAMPLE

Arthur and Bruce are in partnership, sharing profits and losses equally. They provide the following information:

Balance sheet as at 31 July 20*4

	£
Bank balance	6,500
Capital accounts – Arthur	3,500
Bruce	3,000
	6,500

They admit Ches as a partner, with effect from 1 August 20*4. Ches pays £5,000 into the partnership bank account as his capital. They agree that goodwill be valued at £18,000 and that the account will not appear in the balance sheet. They further agree to share profits 3:2:1 respectively.

Required Prepare a balance sheet as at 1 August 20*4, after the admission of Ches as a partner.

Answer

Arthur, Bruce and Ches
Balance sheet as at 1 August 20*4 (after the admission of Ches)

	£
Bank balance	11,500
Capital accounts – Arthur	3,500
Bruce	6,000
Ches	2,000
	11,500

The book-keeping entries showing the above transactions are:

Bank

Balance b/d	6,500		
Capital – Ches (3)	5,000		

Capital (Arthur)

Goodwill (4)	9,000	Balance b/d	3,500
Balance c/d	3,500	Goodwill (1)	9,000
	12,500		12,500
		Balance b/d	3,500

Capital (Bruce)

	£		£
Goodwill (5)	6,000	Balance b/d	3,000
Balance c/d	6,000	Goodwill (2)	9,000
	12,000		12,000
		Balance b/d	6,000

Capital (Ches)

	£		£
Goodwill (6)	3,000	Bank (3)	5,000
Balance c/d	2,000		
	5,000		5,000
		Balance b/d	2,000

Goodwill account

	£		£
Capital – Arthur (1)	9,000	Capital – Arthur (4)	9,000
Bruce (2)	9,000	Bruce (5)	6,000
		Ches (6)	3,000
	18,000		18,000

Numbers in brackets have been placed next to each entry so that you can trace each entry individually to each account.

Notice that the goodwill account has disappeared and is not shown in the final balance sheet.

QUESTION 7

Victor and Ffiona are in partnership-sharing profits and losses in the ratio 3:1 respectively. They provide the following information:

Balance sheet as at 30 September 20*4

	£
Bank balance	1,500
Capital accounts – Victor	800
Ffiona	700
	1,500

They agree to admit Eric as a partner, with effect from 1 October 20*4. The new profit-sharing ratio would be 2:2:1 respectively. Eric will provide £7,500 as his capital. The partners agreed that profits in future would be shared equally. It was further agreed that goodwill be valued at £10,000 and that it would not appear on the balance sheet.

Required Prepare a balance sheet as at 1 October 20*4, after the admission of Eric to the partnership.

QUESTION 8

Clarissa and Gareth are in partnership-sharing profits and losses equally. They provide the following information:

Balance sheet as at 29 February 20*4

	£
Bank balance	6,000
Capital accounts – Clarissa	4,000
Gareth	2,000
	6,000

They admit Hugo to the partnership, with effect from 1 March 20*4. The partnership agreement provides that profits and losses will be shared equally. Goodwill is valued at £7,500 and will not appear in the balance sheet.

Required Prepare a balance sheet as at 1 March 20*4, after Hugo was admitted to the partnership.

Clearly, it is very unusual for a business to have a bank balance as its only asset. The above examples were used to highlight the way goodwill is treated when it does not remain in the books of account.

Let us put together a more realistic scenario – a situation where the assets are revalued and a value is placed on goodwill.

WORKED EXAMPLE

Len, Don and Ben are in partnership, sharing profits and losses in the ratio 3:2:1 respectively. They provide the following information:

Balance sheet as at 31 May 20*4

	£	£
Fixed assets at cost		26,000
Current assets	9,000	
Current liabilities	2,000	7,000
		33,000
Capital accounts – Len		10,000
Don		15,000
Ben		8,000
		33,000

They agree that Cat be admitted as a partner, with effect from 1 June 20*4. Profits in future will be shared equally. They further agree that fixed assets be revalued at £28,000 and that goodwill be valued at £10,000. Goodwill should not remain in the business books of account.

Cat is to pay £5,000 into the business bank account as capital.

Required

Prepare:
a a revaluation account
b a goodwill account
c capital accounts for each partner
d a balance sheet as at 1 June 20*4, after the admission of Cat as a partner.

Answer

Revaluation account

	£		£
Capital – Len	6,000	Fixed assets	2,000
Don	4,000	Goodwill	10,000
Ben	2,000		
	12,000		12,000

Goodwill account

	£		£
Revaluation a/c	10,000	Capital – Len	2,500
		Don	2,500
		Ben	2,500
		Cat	2,500
	10,000		10,000

WORKED EXAMPLE *continued*

Capital accounts

Note: All figures are in £000

	Len	Don	Ben	Cat		Len	Don	Ben	Cat
Goodwill	2.5	2.5	2.5	2.5	Balances b/d	10	15	8	
Balances c/d	13.5	16.5	7.5	2.5	Revaluation a/c	6	4	2	
					Bank				5
	16	19	10	5		16	19	10	5
					Balances b/d	13.5	16.5	7.5	2.5

Len, Don, Ben and Cat
Balance sheet as at 1 June 20*4 (after the admission of Cat)

	£	£
Fixed assets at valuation		28,000
Current assets	14,000	
Current liabilities	2,000	12,000
		40,000
Capital accounts – Len		13,500
Don		16,500
Ben		7,500
Cat		2,500
		40,000

Note the use of columnar capital accounts; this technique saves a little time. Four partners have been involved in the partnership, to show that the techniques do not change when a question has more than three partners. Examination questions usually have two or three partners.

Note the heading too. All accounting statements need a heading which includes the name of the business.

● EXAMINATION TIP

Write figures out in full. Many examination candidates make errors when they forget that they are using thousands and put a figure in their answers as, say, £13.5 when it should say £13,500. Careless mistakes cost valuable marks – do not throw marks away.

QUESTION 9

Shubratha and Ciaran are in partnership, sharing profits and losses in the ratio 4:1. Their balance sheet is shown.

Balance sheet at 31 December 20*4

	£	£
Fixed assets at cost		34,000
Current assets	11,000	
Current liabilities	10,000	1,000
		35,000
Capital accounts – Shubratha		20,000
Ciaran		15,000
		35,000

Jim was admitted to the partnership on 1 January 20*5. The following terms have been agreed:

	£
Fixed assets to be revalued at	50,000
Goodwill to be valued at	24,000
Jim introduces capital of	15,000

It was further agreed that goodwill should not remain in the books of account, and that in future profits and losses would be shared equally.

Required
Prepare:

a a revaluation account
b a goodwill account
c partners' capital accounts (in columnar form)
d a balance sheet as at 1 January 20*5.

QUESTION 10

Therese and Jean-Luc are in partnership; they share profits and losses equally.
Their balance sheet shows:

Balance sheet at 31 January 20*5

	£	£
Fixed assets at cost		46,000
Current assets	9,450	
Current liabilities	5,450	4,000
		50,000
Capital accounts – Therese	35,000	
Jean-Luc	15,000	
		50,000

They admitted Frebus to the partnership, with effect from 1 February 20*5, under the following terms:

	£
Frebus introduced capital of	25,000
Fixed assets were revalued at	60,000
Goodwill was valued at	26,000

Goodwill was not to remain in the business books of account.
Profits and losses were to be shared Therese ¼; Jean-Luc ½; Frebus ¼.

Required
Prepare:

a a revaluation account
b a goodwill account
c partners' capital accounts
d a balance sheet as at 1 February 20*5.

If we consider a more detailed balance sheet, the principles for dealing with the introduction of another partner are just the same as those already used.

Do you remember that we collect all the detailed changes to assets and liabilities in the revaluation account?

WORKED EXAMPLE

Gwen and David are in partnership, sharing profits and losses in the ratio 3:2 respectively. The following information is provided:

Gwen and David
Balance sheet as at 30 June 20*4

	£	£
Fixed assets		
Premises at cost		45,000
Equipment at cost		23,000
Vehicles at cost		17,000
		85,000
Current assets		
Stock	11,000	
Trade debtors	4,500	
Bank	1,500	
	17,000	
Current liabilities		
Trade creditors	2,000	15,000
		100,000
Capital accounts – Gwen		60,000
David		40,000
		100,000

Anne was admitted to the partnership on 1 July 20*4. It was agreed that she paid £30,000 into the business bank account as her capital and share of the goodwill.

It was agreed that the assets of the business be valued at:

	£
Premises	80,000
Equipment	15,000
Vehicles	8,000
Stock	10,800
Trade debtors	4,400
Goodwill	40,000

It was further agreed that in future profits and losses be shared equally and that goodwill should not remain in the books of account.

Required

Prepare:
a a revaluation account
b a goodwill account
c partners' capital accounts
d a balance sheet as at 1 July 20*4, after the admission of Anne as a partner.

WORKED EXAMPLE *continued*

Answer

Revaluation account

	£		£
Equipment	8,000	Premises	35,000
Vehicles	9,000	Goodwill	40,000
Stock	200		
Trade Debtors	100		
Capital – Gwen	34,620		
David	23,080		
	75,000		75,000

Goodwill account

	£		£
Revaluation account	40,000	Capital – Gwen	13,334
		David	13,333
		Anne	13,333
	40,000		40,000

Capital accounts

	Gwen	David	Anne		Gwen	David	Anne
Goodwill	13,334	13,333	13,333	Balance b/d	60,000	40,000	
				Revaluation a/c	34,620	23,080	
Balances c/d	81,286	49,747	16,667	Bank			30,000
	94,620	63,080	30,000		94,620	63,080	30,000
				Balances b/d	81,286	49,747	16,667

Gwen, David and Anne
Balance sheet as at 1 July 20*4 (after the admission of Anne)

	£	£
Fixed assets		
Premises at valuation		80,000
Equipment at valuation		15,000
Vehicles at valuation		8,000
		103,000
Current assets		
Stock	10,800	
Trade debtors	4,400	
Bank balance	31,500	
	46,700	
Current liabilities		
Trade creditors	2,000	44,700
		147,700
Capital accounts – Gwen		81,286
David		49,747
Anne		16,667
		147,700

QUESTION 11

Chuck and Todd are in partnership, sharing profits and losses in the ratio 2:1 respectively. They provide the following information:

Balance sheet as at 31 March 20*4

	£	£	£
Fixed assets			
Land and buildings at cost			65,000
Equipment at cost			34,000
Vehicles			56,000
			155,000
Current assets			
Stock		4,800	
Trade debtors		6,200	
		11,000	
Current liabilities			
Trade creditors	4,570		
Bank overdraft	2,430	7,000	4,000
			159,000
Long-term liability			
Loan – Mellerby Building Society			29,000
			130,000
Capital accounts – Chuck			80,000
Todd			50,000
			130,000

On 1 April 20*4 Buzz was admitted to the partnership. The following terms were agreed.
Buzz would pay £25,000 as his capital and share of goodwill. Profits and losses in future would be shared Chuck ½; Todd ¼; and Buzz ¼.
The following asset values were agreed:

	£
Land and buildings	140,000
Equipment	10,000
Vehicles	26,000
Stock	4,100
Trade debtors	6,000
Goodwill	60,000

It was also agreed that a goodwill account would not be maintained in the books of account.

Required
Prepare:

a a revaluation account
b a goodwill account
c partners' capital accounts
d a balance sheet as at 1 April 20*4 (after the admission of Buzz as a partner).

QUESTION 12

Paddy and Mick are in partnership, sharing profits and losses in the ratio 4:1 respectively. They provide the following information:

Balance sheet at 30 November 20*4

	£	£	£
Fixed assets			
Equipment at cost			26,500
Vehicles at cost			23,500
			50,000

	£	£	£
Current assets			
Stock		4,000	
Trade debtors		3,000	
		7,000	
Current liabilities			
Trade creditors	2,600		
Bank overdraft	2,400	5,000	2,000
			52,000
Long-term liability			
Mortgage			25,000
			27,000
Capital accounts – Paddy			12,000
Mick			15,000
			27,000

On 1 December 20*4 Declan was admitted to the partnership, under the following terms. Declan would contribute £20,000 as his capital and share of goodwill. The new profit-sharing ratio would be Paddy ½; Mick ⅓ and Declan ⅙.
The following asset values were agreed:

	£
Equipment	8,000
Vehicles	12,000
Stock	3,100
Trade debtors	2,900
Goodwill	12,500

It was agreed that a goodwill account would not be maintained in the books of account.

Required
Prepare:

a   a revaluation account
b   a goodwill account
c   partners' capital accounts
d   a balance sheet as at 30 November, after Declan was admitted to the partnership.

THE RETIREMENT OF A PARTNER

We have dealt with the admission of a new partner in some detail. The same principles apply when a partner leaves a partnership. The business assets (and liabilities) need to be examined in order to determine whether they reflect the true worth of the business.

Imagine that you have been a partner in a business for many, many years and the following is the summarised balance sheet:

	£	
Fixed assets (NBV)	12,000	These fixed assets include your premises that were
Net current assets	8,000	purchased many years ago. Property prices in general
	20,000	have risen over your years of ownership and these
Capital –You	10,000	premises could now be sold for, say, £80,000!
Your partner	10,000	Would you settle for a payout of £10,000 – your worth
	20,000	(capital) shown on the balance sheet? I think not!

You would have the business assets revalued so that you could retire (or perhaps start a new business) and receive the true value of your worth represented by the net assets of the business.

As Del Boy would say: 'You know it makes sense!'

WORKED EXAMPLE

Gertie, Bertie and Jon are in partnership, sharing profits and losses in the ratio 3:2:1 respectively. They supply the following information:

Balance sheet as at 30 September 20*4

	£	£
Fixed assets (book value)		45,000
Current assets		
Stock	4,300	
Trade debtors	3,700	
Bank balance	4,000	
	12,000	
Current liabilities – trade creditors	8,000	4,000
		49,000
Capital accounts – Gertie		20,000
Bertie		15,000
Jon		14,000
		49,000

Jon has decided to retire with effect from close of business on 30 September 20*4.

The partners have agreed that:

■ fixed assets be revalued at £100,000
■ stock be valued at £4,000
■ debtors be valued at £3,000
■ goodwill be valued at £12,000 and goodwill should not appear in the business books of account
■ any amount due to Jon would be paid from the business bank account (assume that overdraft facilities have been agreed with the business bank)
■ in the future, Gertie and Bertie will share profits and losses equally.

Required
Prepare:

a a revaluation account
b a goodwill account
c partners' capital accounts
d a balance sheet as at 30 September 20*4, after the retirement of Jon.

Answer

Revaluation account

	£		£
Stock	300	Fixed assets	55,000
Debtors	700	Goodwill	12,000
Capital – Gertie	33,000		
Bertie	22,000		
Jon	11,000		
	67,000		67,000

Goodwill account

	£		£
Revaluation a/c	12,000	Capital – Gertie	6,000
		Bertie	6,000
	12,000		12,000

Capital accounts

	Gertie	Bertie	Jon		Gertie	Bertie	Jon
Bank			25,000	Bals b/d	20,000	15,000	14,000
Goodwill	6,000	6,000		Revaluation	33,000	22,000	11,000
Bals c/d	47,000	31,000					
	53,000	37,000	25,000		53,000	37,000	25,000
				Bals b/d	47,000	31,000	

Gertie and Bertie
Balance sheet as at 30 September 20*4 (after the retirement of Jon)

	£	£	£
Fixed assets at valuation			100,000
Current assets			
Stock		4,000	
Trade debtors		3,000	
		7,000	
Current liabilities			
Trade creditors	8,000		
Bank overdraft	21,000	29,000	(22,000)
			78,000
Capital accounts – Gertie			47,000
Bertie			31,000
			78,000

Note that the question is dealt with in two parts because it involves two businesses:

Up to midnight on 30 September 20*4	From a microsecond after midnight (on 1 October 20*4)
Owners were Gertie, Bertie, Jon	Owners are Gertie and Bertie

We credited the capital accounts with the increase in the value of the net assets in order that Jon can receive his just dues before his retirement. After all, he has presided over the increase in the value of the assets as well as contributing to the value of the goodwill of the business.

We debited the two capital accounts (there are only two partners – Gertie and Bertie – in this new business) with the writing-off of the asset of goodwill. Notice that when we wrote off the goodwill there were only two partners in the 'new' business – Jon is now no longer involved in the running of the business.

HOW CAN A RETIRING PARTNER BE PAID OUT WHEN HE OR SHE LEAVES THE BUSINESS?

This can pose problems to a partnership. A retiring partner could have a considerable amount standing to the credit of his or her capital (and current) account. If a large sum were to be paid out, the withdrawal could deprive the business of a great deal of liquid resources.

How can the problem be resolved?

- The retiring partner's capital account balance could be transferred to a loan account and an amount could be paid each year to the partner who had retired.
- A new partner could join the business and the payment made by the new partner could be used to pay off the 'old' partner.

- The cash to pay off the 'old' partner could be borrowed from a bank or other financial institution.
- Remaining partners could inject sufficient further capital into the business to allow the payment to be made.
- An investment could be made which, on maturity, would pay for the retirement.

QUESTION 13

Gordon, Frances and Jacqui are in partnership, sharing profits and loss in the ratio 2:2:1. They provide the following information:

Balance sheet as at 31 March 20*5

	£	£
Fixed assets		34,000
Current assets	12,000	
Current liabilities	9,000	3,000
		37,000
Capital accounts – Gordon		20,000
Frances		10,000
Jacqui		7,000
		37,000

Frances decided to retire at the close of business on 31 March 20*5.
The partners have agreed that:

- fixed assets be valued at £84,000
- goodwill be valued at £20,000
- any balance owed to Frances be temporarily transferred to a loan account
- a goodwill account should not remain in the books of account
- from 1 April 20*5 profits and losses be shared equally.

Required
Prepare:

a a revaluation account
b a goodwill account
c partners' capital accounts
d a balance sheet as at 31 March 20*4 (after Frances's retirement).

QUESTION 14

Daisy, Dot and Dora are in partnership, sharing profits and losses in the ratio 3:3:1 respectively. The following information is available:

Balance sheet as at 31 December 20*4

	£	£
Fixed assets		125,000
Current assets	65,000	
Current liabilities	50,000	15,000
		140,000
Capital accounts – Daisy		60,000
Dot		55,000
Dora		25,000
		140,000

Daisy retired at the close of business on 31 December 20*4. It was agreed that the fixed assets be valued at £200,000 and that goodwill was valued at £60,000.
Dot and Dora are to continue in business. They will share profits in the ratio of 3:2 respectively. They agree that a goodwill account would not be maintained in the business books of account. An balance due to Daisy should be transferred temporarily to a loan account.

Required
Prepare:

a a revaluation account
b a goodwill account
c partners' capital accounts
d a balance sheet as at 31 December 20*4, after Daisy's retirement.

QUESTION 15

Ruairi, Gareth and Jock were in partnership, sharing profits and losses in the ratio 3:2:1 respectively. The following information is available:

Balance sheet as at 31 August 20*4

	£	£	£
Fixed assets			
Premises			45,000
Equipment			23,000
Vehicles			34,000
			102,000
Current assets			
Stock		11,250	
Trade debtors		5,800	
Bank balance		1,480	
		18,530	
Current liabilities			
Trade creditors		6,530	12,000
			114,000
Capital accounts			
Ruairi			60,000
Gareth			40,000
Jock			14,000
			114,000

Gareth retired from the partnership with effect from the close of business on 31 August 20*4. It was agreed that the following valuations would apply on that date:

	£
Premises	110,000
Equipment	5,000
Vehicles	18,000
Stock	10,250

It was further agreed that goodwill be valued at £36,000.
Ruairi and Jock carried on in business, sharing profits and losses equally. They agreed that goodwill would not be maintained in the business books of account and that any amount due to Gareth be transferred to a loan account.

Required
Prepare:

a   a revaluation account
b   a goodwill account
c   partners' capital accounts
d   a balance sheet as at 31 August 20*4, after Gareth's retirement.

QUESTION 16

George, Mildred and Michelle were in partnership, sharing profits and losses in the ratio 4:4:1 respectively. The following information is available:

Balance sheet as at 31 December 20*4

	£	£	£
Fixed assets			
Land and buildings			68,000
Equipment			54,000
Vehicles			48,000
			170,000

	£	£	£
Current assets			
Stock		64,300	
Trade debtors		17,800	
		82,100	
Current liabilities			
Trade creditors	14,700		
Bank overdraft	7,400	22,100	60,000
			230,000
Capital accounts			
George			90,000
Mildred			90,000
Michelle			50,000
			230,000

George retired from the partnership with effect from the close of business on 31 December 20*4. It was agreed that certain assets be revalued:

	£
Land and buildings	208,000
Equipment	44,000
Vehicles	39,000
Stock	63,300

It was further agreed that goodwill be valued at £60,000.

Mildred and Michelle carried on in business, sharing profits in the ratio 3:2 respectively. They agreed that a goodwill account would not be maintained in the business books of account and that any amount due to George on his retirement be transferred to a loan account.

Required
Prepare:

a a revaluation account
b a goodwill account
c partners' capital accounts
d a balance sheet as at 31 December 20*4, after George's retirement.

A CHANGE TO THE PROFIT-SHARING RATIOS

Any change to the profit-sharing ratios must be treated in much the same way as other structural changes.

View the change as dealing with two distinct businesses.

The 'first' business must be revalued in order that the 'old' owners can be credited with any increase in the value of their business.

If goodwill is not to be maintained in the 'second' business's books of account it must be deleted and the 'new' partners debited in their profit-sharing ratios.

WORKED EXAMPLE

Jean and Sean are in partnership, sharing profits and losses in the ratio of 3:1 respectively. From 1 January 20*5 they will share profits and losses equally.

Their summarised balance sheet as at 31 December 20*4 showed:

	£	£
Fixed assets		48,000
Current assets	12,000	
Less Current liabilities	8,000	4,000
		52,000
Capital accounts – Jean		30,000
Sean		22,000
		52,000

The partners agreed that fixed assets be revalued at £70,000 and that goodwill be valued at £28,000. They further agreed that a goodwill account would not be maintained in the business books of account.

Required Prepare a balance sheet as at 31 December 20*4, after the change to the new profit-sharing ratio has been implemented.

Answer

Balance sheet as at 31 December 20*4

	£	£	
Fixed assets		70,000	
Current assets	12,000		
Less Current liabilities	8,000	4,000	
		74,000	
Capital accounts – Jean		53,500	(30,000 + 37,500 − 14,000)
Sean		20,500	(22,000 + 12,500 − 14,000)
		74,000	

PARTNERSHIP DISSOLUTION

A partnership may be dissolved, that is it may cease to be a partnership, under the following circumstances:

■ on the death of a partner
■ on the retirement of a partner
■ when a partner is declared bankrupt
■ by mutual agreement of the partners.

When a partnership is dissolved, the assets of the business are disposed of and any liabilities are then settled. The order of settling any debts (liabilities) is:

1. creditors
2. partners' loan accounts
3. partners' capital accounts.

The assets can be disposed of in a variety of ways:

■ some assets may be sold for cash
■ some assets may be sold to a limited company for shares, or debentures or a combination of cash, debentures and shares
■ some assets may be taken over by one or more partners.

The way we tackle the closing down of the partnership is by preparing a realisation account. This is rather like a combined trading and profit and loss account.

On the debit side of the account, we find the assets that are disposed of and any expenses incurred in the dissolution. On the credit side, we find what the assets have realised.

Trading and profit and loss account

What has been sold (purchases)	What has been realised (sales)
Costs of running the business (expenses)	Other incomes or benefits
Profit	Loss

Realisation account

The book value of the assets	The proceeds from the sale of the assets shown opposite
Costs of the dissolution	Other incomes or benefits
Discounts allowed	Discounts received
Profit on realisation	Loss on realisation

Unless you are told differently in a question, assume that the partnership will collect any outstanding monies from debtors and pay off outstanding creditors.

Try to think what you will be doing in the circumstances when a partnership is dissolved.

All the assets to be disposed of are entered on the debit side of the realisation account.

All the proceeds of the disposals are entered on the credit side.

> ## ● EXAMINATION TIP
>
> The most common error in examination answers is to enter the sale value of the assets in the debit side of the realisation account. Make sure that the book values of the assets are entered on the debit side of the realisation account.

Any **profit** resulting from the realisation of the assets will appear on the debit side of the realisation account. It is posted from here to the credit side of the partners' capital accounts in their profit-sharing ratios.

Any **loss** will be shown on the credit side of the realisation account and it will be posted to the debit side of the partners' capital accounts in their profit-sharing ratios.

If partners take over any of the assets, treat these as a 'sale' to the partner.

If a question states that a partner takes over the stock of the partnership, the entries would be:

Dr Partner	Cr Realisation account

with the agreed value of the stock.

So if Jim, a partner, takes a business-owned car at an agreed valuation of £4,700, this would be entered as:

Dr Capital – Jim £4,700	Cr Realisation account £4,700

WORKED EXAMPLE

Barbara and Ben are in partnership, sharing profits and losses in the ratio 2:1 respectively. They agree to dissolve their partnership on 30 November 20*4. They provide the following information:

Balance sheet as at 30 November 20*4		
	£	£
Fixed assets		80,000
Current assets	17,000	
Bank	3,000	
	20,000	
Current liabilities	14,000	6,000
		86,000
Capital – Barbara		50,000
Ben		36,000
		86,000

WORKED EXAMPLE *continued*

- The current liabilities were paid their due amounts.
- The fixed assets were sold for £100,000 cash.
- The current asset fetched £15,000.

Required
Prepare:
a a bank account
b a realisation account
c partners' capital accounts.

Answer

Realisation account

	£		£
Fixed assets	80,000	Cash	100,000
Current assets	17,000	Cash	15,000
Capital – Barbara	12,000		
Ben	6,000		
	115,000		115,000

Bank

	£		£
Balance	3,000	Creditors	14 000
Realisation – Fixed assets	100,000	Barbara – Capital	62 000
Current assets	15,000	Ben – Capital	42 000
	118,000		118,000

Capital accounts

	Barbara £	Ben £		Barbara £	Ben £
Bank	62,000	42,000	Bal b/d	50,000	36,000
			Realisation	12,000	6,000
	62,000	42,000		62,000	42,000

In order to show the sequence of entries shown above, the entries have been journalised:

Dr Creditors	14,000	
Bank a/c		14,000

Paying creditors

Realisation	80,000	
Fixed assets		80,000

Clearing the partnership books of the fixed assets

Realisation	17,000	
Current assets		17,000

Clearing the partnership books of the current assets

Bank	100,000	
Realisation		100,000

Sale of fixed asset for cash

Bank	15,000	
Realisation		15,000

Sale of current assets for cash

Realisation account	12,000	
Capital – Barbara		12,000

Barbara's share of profit on realisation

Realisation account	6,000	
Capital – Ben		6,000

Ben's share of the profit on realisation

Capital – Barbara	62,000	
Bank		62,000

Payment from business bank account to clear Barbara's capital

Capital – Ben	42,000	
Bank		42,000

Payment from business bank account to clear Ben's capital

Do not attempt to share the balance left in the bank account in any pre-determined ratio. The bank account is used to clear any outstanding balances left on the partners' capital accounts.

WORKED EXAMPLE

Dave and Dierdre are in partnership, sharing profits 3:2 respectively. They agree to dissolve their partnership on 29 February 20*4. They provide the following information:

Balance sheet as at 29 February 20*4	£	£
Fixed assets		40,000
Current assets	8,000	
Bank	2,000	
	10,000	
Current liabilities	6,000	4,000
		44,000
Capital accounts – Dave		25,000
Dierdre		19,000
		44,000

- The fixed assets were taken over by Dave at an agreed value of £36,000.
- The current assets realised cash of £7,000.
- The current liabilities were settled at book value.

Required

Prepare:

a a realisation account
b a bank account
c partners' capital accounts.

Answer

Realisation account

Fixed assets	40,000	Capital – Dave		36,000
Current assets	8,000	Cash		7,000
		Capital – Dave		3,000
		Dierdre		2,000
	48,000			48,000

Bank

Balance	2,000	Creditors	6,000
Realisation	7,000	Dierdre	17,000
Dave	14,000		
	23,000		23,000

Capital accounts

	Dave	Dierdre		Dave	Dierdre
Realisation	36,000		Balance	25,000	19,000
Realisation	3,000	2,000	Cash	14,000	
Cash		17,000			
	39,000	19,000		39,000	19,000

WORKED EXAMPLE *continued*

Again, to show the sequence of events:

Creditors	6,000	
Bank		6,000

Paying off creditors

Realisation	40,000	
Fixed assets		40,000

Closing down fixed assets accounts

Realisation	8,000	
Current assets		8,000

Closing down current assets accounts

Capital – Dave	36,000	
Realisation		36,000

Dave 'buys' fixed assets from partnership

Bank	7,000	
Realisation		7,000

Sale of current assets

Cash	14,000	
Capital – Dave		14,000

Dave pays off the deficit on his capital account

Capital – Dierdre	17,000	
Bank		17,000

Dierdre withdraws sufficient cash to clear the amount the partnership owes her.

QUESTION 17

Eliza, Sze Hang and Hazel were in partnership, sharing profits and losses equally. They agree to dissolve their partnership on 31 October 20*4. They provide the following information:

Balance sheet as at 31 October 20*4

	£	£
Fixed assets		
Premises		70,000
Equipment		30,000
Vehicles		18,000
		118,000
Current assets	16,000	
Bank	3,000	
	19,000	

	£	£
Current liabilities		
Trade creditors	7,000	12,000
		130,000
Capital accounts – Eliza		60,000
Sze Hang		40,000
Hazel		30,000
		130,000

The following assets were sold for cash:

	£
Premises	100,000
Equipment	18,000
Current assets	15,000

■ The vehicles were taken over by Hazel at an agreed valuation of £10,000.
■ Trade creditors were paid the amounts due.

Required
Prepare:

a a realisation account
b a bank account
c partners' capital accounts.

QUESTION 18

McStravich, Thomas and Henry were in partnership, sharing profits and losses 2:2:1 respectively. They agree to dissolve their partnership on 31 July 20*4. They provide the following information:

Balance sheet as at 31 July 20*4

	£	£
Fixed assets		
Land and buildings		120,000
Equipment		80,000
Vehicles		30,000
		230,000
Current assets	26,000	
Bank	4,000	
	30,000	
Current liabilities		
Trade creditors	10,000	20,000
		250,000
Capital accounts – McStravich		100,000
Thomas		70,000
Henry		80,000
		250,000

The following assets were sold for cash:

	£
Land and buildings	150,000
Equipment	37,000
Current assets	23,000

■ The vehicles were taken over by Henry at an agreed valuation of £8,000.
■ Trade creditors were paid the amounts due.

Prepare:

a a realisation account
b a bank account
c partners' capital accounts.

Clearly, there are times when the debtors do not all pay the amounts that they owed to the business when the partnership is wound up. This may be because there may be some bad debtors or because the partnership offers cash discounts in order to get the cash in quickly.
Similarly, there may be times when the partnership is able to benefit from cash discounts available from creditors.
Any discounts received from creditors and discounts allowed to debtors are entered in the realisation account (as would any debtors who proved to be bad).

WORKED EXAMPLE

Alex, Bernard and Charlie decide to dissolve their partnership on 30 April 20*4. At that date debtors owed £7,450 and creditors were owed £3,950.

Debtors paid £7,250 in settlement and creditors accepted £3,800 in settlement.

Required

Prepare the entries to record these transactions on:

a the realisation account
b the bank account
c sundry debtors account
d sundry creditors account.

Answer

Realisation account			
Sundry debtors	200	Sundry creditors	150

Bank account			
Sundry debtors	7,250	Sundry creditors	3,800

Sundry debtors account			
Balance	7,450	Bank	7,250
		Realisation	200
	7,450		7,450

Sundry creditors account			
Bank	3,800	Balance b/d	3,950
Realisation	150		
	3,950		3,950

Winding up the partnership will inevitably incur costs. These costs may be to advertise various assets to be sold; they may be to a solicitor who will tie up and formalise the legal side of the dissolution. Any costs should be:

debited to the **realisation account** ... and ... **credited** to the **bank account**.

Finally, remember to settle any partnership loans after you have dealt with debtors and creditors – very straightforward:

Dr Loan account   Cr Bank account.

WORKED EXAMPLE

Mary and Douglas were in partnership, sharing profit and losses equally. They agreed to dissolve their partnership on 31 July 20*4. They provide the following information:

Balance sheet as at 31 July 20*4

	£	£
Fixed assets		40,000
Current assets		
Stock	9,000	
Trade debtors	4,000	
Bank	2,000	
	15,000	
Current liabilities		
Trade creditors	8,000	7,000
		47,000
Less **Long-term loan** – Douglas		2,000
		45,000
Capital accounts:		
Mary		25,000
Douglas		20,000
		45,000

- The fixed assets were sold for £58,000.
- Stock was taken over by Mary at an agreed value of £7,700.
- Debtors paid £3,800 in settlement.
- Creditors were paid £7,500 in settlement.
- The costs incurred during the dissolution amounted to £3,400.

Required
Prepare:

a   a realisation account for the partnership
b   a bank account
c   capital accounts.

Answer

Realisation account

	£		£
Fixed assets	40,000	Discounts received	500
Stock	9,000	Bank	58,000
Discount allowed	200	Capital – Mary	7,700
Costs	3,400		
Profit – capitals	13,600		
	66,200		66,200

Bank account

	£		£
Balance	2,000	Loan – Douglas	2,000
Debtors	3,800	Creditors	7,500
Realisation	58,000	Costs	3,400
		Capital – Mary	24,100
		Douglas	26,800
	63,800		63,800

Capital accounts

	Mary	Douglas		Mary	Douglas
Realisation	7,700		Balance	25,000	20,000
Bank	24,100	26,800	Realisation	6,800	6,800
	31,800	26,800		31,800	26,800

QUESTION 19

Bertram, Chipperfield and Mills were in partnership, sharing profits and losses 3:2:1 respectively. They agree to wind up their partnership with effect from 31 December 20*4. The following information is available:

Balance sheet as at 31 December 20*4

	£	£
Fixed assets		
Premises		210,000
Equipment		84,000
Three vehicles		42,000
		336,000
Current assets		
Stock	12,400	
Trade debtors	8,200	
Bank	2,700	
	23,300	
Trade creditors	9,300	14,000
		350,000
Less **Long-term loan**		
Chipperfield		50,000
		300,000
Capital accounts		
Bertram		150,000
Chipperfield		100,000
Mills		50,000
		300,000

The following assets were sold for cash:

	£
Equipment	57,000
Vehicle (1)	9,000
Stock	10,800

- Premises were taken over by Bertram at an agreed value of £300,000.
- Vehicle (2) was taken over by Chipperfield at an agreed value of £5,000.
- Vehicle (3) was taken over by Mills at an agreed value of £6,000.
- Debtors paid £8,100 in settlement.
- Creditors accepted £8,900 in settlement.
- Costs incurred during the dissolution amounted to £6,450.

Required

Prepare:

a a realisation account
b a bank account
c partners' capital accounts.

Tip: Do not panic over the treatment of the vehicles. Here are the journal entries. Enter them in the appropriate account in your answer.

Dr Realisation account	£42,000	
Cr Vehicles account		£42,000
Dr Bank	£9,000	
Cr Realisation account		£9,000
Dr Capital – Chipperfield	£5,000	
Realisation account		£5,000
Dr Capital – Mills	£6,000	
Realisation account		£,6000

QUESTION 20

Jason, Robert and Samuel are in partnership, sharing profits and losses 5:9:1 respectively. They agree to dissolve their partnership on 31 January 20*5. They provide the following information:

Balance sheet as at 31 January 20*5

	£	£	£
Fixed assets			
Premises			190,000
Equipment			48,000
Vehicles (2)			33,000
			271,000
Current assets			
Stock		14,780	
Trade debtors		3,960	
		18,740	
Current liabilities			
Trade creditors	4,120		
Bank overdraft	2,620	6,740	12,000
			283,000
Long-term loan – Jason			40,000
			243,000
Capital accounts			
Jason			100,000
Robert			80,000
Samuel			63,000
			243,000

The following assets were sold for cash:

	£
Premises	350,000
Equipment	18,000
Stock	14,500

- One car was taken over by Robert at an agreed value of £15,000.
- The other was taken over by Samuel at an agreed value of £8,000.
- Trade debtors paid £3,800 in full settlements.
- Trade creditors accepted £3,750 in settlements.
- Costs of dissolution amounted to £6,560.

Required
Prepare:

a a realisation account
b a bank account
c partners' capital accounts.

So far, all assets of the business have either been taken over by a partner or have been sold for cash. We must finally consider the situation where some assets are sold to a limited company. The limited company could settle the deal by paying:

- cash or
- cash and shares or
- cash and debentures or
- any combination of the three.

Sounds daunting, doesn't it?

WORKED EXAMPLE

Karl and Betty are in partnership, sharing profits and losses in the ratio 2:1 respectively. They agreed to sell their business to Tontong Ltd. The purchase consideration was £100,000, being made up of £20,000 cash and 50,000 ordinary shares of £1 each. The partners agreed that the shares be distributed to the partners in their profit-sharing ratios. The partnership balance sheet immediately prior to the takeover was:

Net assets	82 000
Capital – Karl	50,000
Betty	32,000
	82,000

Required Prepare the account to close the books of Karl and Betty.

Answer

Realisation account

Net assets	82,000	Tontong Ltd		100,000
Capital – Karl	12,000			
Betty	6,000			
	100,000			100,000

Tontong Ltd

Realisation	100,000	Bank		20,000
		Capital – Karl		53,333
		Betty		26,667
	100,000			100,000

WORKED EXAMPLE *continued*

Bank account

Tontong Ltd	20,000	Capital – Karl	8,667
		Betty	11,333
	20,000		20,000

Capital accounts

	Karl	Betty		Karl	Betty
Ord. shares in Tontong	53,333	26,667	Balance	50,000	32,000
Cash	8,667	11,333	Realisation	12,000	6,000
	62,000	38,000		62,000	38,000

Journal entries to show the chronology of the entries:

Realisation	82,000	
Net assets		82,000

This closes down the asset accounts.

Tontong Ltd	100,000	
Realisation		100,000

Purchase consideration agreed between Tontong Ltd and the partners.

Realisation	18,000	
Capital – Karl		12,000
Betty		6,000

Profit on realisation is credited to the partners in their profit sharing ratios.

Bank	20,000	
Tontong Ltd		20,000

Cash paid by Tontong Ltd.

Capital – Karl	53,333	
Betty	26,667	
Tontong Ltd		80,000

Shares given to the partners in the agreed ratios – note that the ordinary shares are shared in value terms, not in nominal values.

Capital – Karl	8,667	
Betty	11,333	
Bank		20,000

Cash is issued to balance the capital accounts.

Talk yourself through this a couple of times. It is much easier than you think. The point at which most candidates go wrong is when the ordinary shares have to be given to the partners – simply divide the balance on the company's account by the ratios given in the question.

WORKED EXAMPLE

Ray and Rex are in partnership, sharing profits and losses in the ratio 3:2 respectively. They sell their business to Dorken Ltd for an agreed purchase consideration of £200,000. The purchase consideration being made up as follows:

	£
Cash	40,000
6% debentures	50,000
30,000 ordinary shares of £1 each	

[Remember that those £1 ordinary shares may be worth more than £1 or less than £1. Can you say how much they are worth?

£3.67 each. Did you get it right? Value £110,000/30,000.]

It was agreed that the partners would distribute the debentures in the last agreed capital account ratios and that the ordinary shares would be divided according to the profit and loss-sharing ratio.

The partnership balance sheet immediately prior to takeover was:

	£
Net assets	120,000
Capital – Ray	80,000
Rex	40,000
	120,000

Required Prepare the entries to close the partnership books of account.

Answer

Realisation account

Net assets	120,000	Dorken Ltd	200,000
Capital – Ray	48,000		
Rex	32,000		
	200,000		200,000

Dorken Ltd

Realisation	200,000	Bank	40,000
		Debentures	50,000
		Ordinary shares	110,000
	200,000		200,000

Bank

Dorken Ltd	40,000	Capital – Ray	28,667
		Rex	11,333
	40,000		40,000

WORKED EXAMPLE *continued*

Capital accounts

	Roy	Rex		Roy	Rex
Dorken (Debentures)	33,333	16,667	Balances	80,000	40,000
Dorken (Ordinary shares)	66,000	44,000	Realisation	48,000	32,000
Bank to (balance)	28,667	11,333			
	128,000	72,000		128,000	72,000

Journal entries:

Realisation	120,000	
Net assets		120,000

Dorken Ltd	200,000	
Realisation		200,000

Realisation	48,000	
Realisation	32,000	
Capital – Ray		48,000
Rex		32,000

Bank	40,000	
Dorken Ltd		40,000

Capital – Ray	33,333	
Rex	16,667	
Dorken Ltd (debentures)		50,000

Capital – Ray	66,000	
Rex	44,000	
Dorken Ltd (ordinary shares)		110,000

Capital – Ray	28,667	
Rex	11,333	
Bank		28,667
Bank		11,333

As a point of interest, the entries in the books of Dorken Ltd would show:

- bank reducing by £40,000
- debentures increasing by £50,000
- ordinary share capital increasing by £30,000 (share premium £80,000)
- net tangible assets increasing by £120,000
- and yes, you've guessed it – goodwill by £80,000.

QUESTION 21

Joan and Darby are in partnership, sharing profits and losses 4:1 respectively. They agree to sell their partnership assets to Agas Ltd for £210,000. The purchase consideration is made up of £25,000 cash and 60,000 ordinary shares of £1 each. The partners agree that the shares in Agas Ltd would be distributed according to the profit-sharing ratios.

Joan and Darby's balance sheet prior to the purchase was:

	£
Net assets	100,000
Capital – Joan	60,000
Darby	40,000
	100,000

Required Prepare entries to close the partnership books of account.

QUESTION 22

Ned and Ted are in partnership, sharing profits and losses 3:1 respectively. They agree to sell their partnership assets to Tedden plc, the purchase consideration of £200,000 being made up of £30,000 cash; 60,000 6% debentures (to be shared equally between the partners) and 400,000 ordinary shares of 10p each (to be shared in profit-sharing ratios).

Ned and Ted's balance sheet prior to the purchase was:

	£
Net assets	140,000
Capital – Ned	100,000
Ted	40,000
	140,000

Required Prepare entries to close the partnership books of account.

Occasionally, when the dissolution has been completed, a partner's capital account ends up with a debit balance, as in the case of Dave (Dave and Dierdre, earlier). Generally, the partner will pay an amount to clear the debt.

There are times when a partner may not be able to clear the balance.

In the case of *Garner v Murray*, the court ruled that such a deficiency was to be shared among the remaining partners in the ratio of the capital account balances shown in the balance sheet prepared at the end of the last financial year.

WORKED EXAMPLE

Doc, Grumpy and Bashful are in partnership, sharing profits and losses equally. At 31 December 20*4 their capital account balances were £30,000, £40,000 and £10,000 respectively. The partnership is dissolved. After closing all ledger accounts for the partnership, the following balances remain in the books of account:

	Dr	Cr
	£	£
Capital		
Doc		17,000
Grumpy		6,000
Bashful	14,000	
Bank	9,000	

Bashful is unable to meet his liability to the partnership out of his personal funds.

Required Prepare the entries to close the partnership books of account.

WORKED EXAMPLE *continued*

Answer

	Doc	Grumpy	Bashful		Doc	Grumpy	Bashful
Capital							
Balance			14,000	Balance	17,000	6,000	

Under normal circumstances, Bashful would pay £14,000 into the partnership bank account; Doc and Grumpy would receive £17,000 and £6,000 respectively; so . . .

	Doc	Grumpy	Bashful		Doc	Grumpy	Bashful
Capital							
Bank	17,000	6,000		Bank	17,000	6,000	14,000

Bashful cannot do this so the £14,000 debt to the partnership must be shared between the remaining partners in the ratio of the balance standing in the capital accounts in the balance sheet drawn up at the end of the last financial period.

Bashful's debt must be shared between the remaining two partners ⅔ to Doc and ⅓ to Grumpy.

So the closing entries are:

	Doc	Grumpy	Bashful		Doc	Grumpy	Bashful
Capital account							
Balance			14,000	Balance	17,000	6,000	
Bashful	6,000	8,000		Doc			6,000
Bank	11,000			Grumpy			8,000
				Bank		2,000	
	17,000	8,000	14,000		17,000	8,000	14,000

Bank account				
Balance b/d	9,000	Doc	11,000	
Grumpy	2,000			
	11,000		11,000	

Doc receives £11,000 while Grumpy pays £2,000 into the bank account.

QUESTION 23

Stephen, Asman and Shably are in partnership, sharing profits and losses equally. They agree to dissolve their partnership. They provide the following information:

Balance sheet as at 31 May 200*4

	£
Net assets	40,000
Bank	10,000
	50,000
Capital accounts	
Stephen	40,000
Asman	20,000
Shably	(10,000)
	50,000

The net assets were sold for £55,000 cash. Shably is unable to meet any liability to the partnership out of his personal funds.

Required
Prepare:

a a realisation account
b a bank account
c partners' capital accounts.

QUESTION 24

Kurt, Liam and Mike are in partnership, sharing profits and losses in the ratios 3:2:1 respectively. They agree to dissolve their partnership on 31 December 20*4.
They provide the following information:

Balance sheet as at 31 December 20*4

	£
Net assets	120,000
Bank overdraft	(8,000)
	112,000
Capital accounts	
Kurt	110,000
Liam	20,000
Mike	(18,000)
	112,000

The net assets were sold for £150,000 cash. Mike is unable to meet any liability in the partnership out of his personal funds.

Required
Prepare:

a a realisation account
b a bank account
c the partners' capital accounts.

Chapter summary

- When a structural change takes place in a partnership, two appropriation accounts should be prepared – one before the change and one after the change.
- When a structural change takes place the business should be revalued and a value is placed on goodwill. This value is shared among the 'old' partners (who have helped to create it) in their profit-sharing ratios.
- When writing off goodwill it is the profit-sharing ratios of the 'new' partnership that are used to debit the partners' capital accounts.
- When a partnership is wound up, assets are transferred to a realisation account and any profit or loss is calculated. The profit (or loss) is then apportioned to the partners in their profit-sharing ratios.
- Capital accounts are closed by a transfer of cash to or from the bank account.
- If a partner is insolvent the balance on the capital account is shared between the remaining partners in a ratio that reflects the balance on the capital accounts as shown on the balance sheet at the end of the last financial year.

Self-test questions

- Give an example of a structural change to a partnership.
- Explain why it is necessary to revalue assets when a structural change takes place.
- Define 'goodwill'.
- Explain one method of placing a value on goodwill.
- Goodwill is the purchase of existing customers. True or false?

- Fixed assets £30,000; current liabilities £8,000; purchase price £50,000. Calculate the value of goodwill.
- Explain the term 'inherent goodwill'.
- Explain how inherent goodwill would be shown on a balance sheet.
- Explain the circumstances under which a partnership would be dissolved.
- Explain the ruling in *Garner v Murray*.

TEST QUESTIONS

QUESTION 25

Arbuthnot and Barton were in partnership, sharing profits and losses equally. They provide the following information:

Balance sheet as at 30 June 20*4

	£	£
Fixed assets		
Premises		48,000
Equipment		23,000
Vehicles		34,000
		105,000
Current assets		
Stock	8,900	
Trade Debtors	4,600	
Bank	2,500	
	16,000	
Trade creditors	6,000	10,000
		115,000
Capital accounts – Arbuthnot		65,000
Barton		50,000
		115,000

On 1 July 20*4 Currock was admitted to the partnership under the following terms:

- Currock would contribute £40,000 as his share of capital and goodwill
- the new share ratios would be 3:2:1 respectively.

The following asset values were agreed:

	£
Premises	100,000
Equipment	15,000
Vehicles	20,000
Stock	8,500
Goodwill	60,000

It was also agreed that a goodwill account would not be maintained in the business books of account.

Required
Prepare:

a a revaluation account
b a goodwill account
c partners' capital accounts
d a balance sheet as at 1 July 20*4, immediately after Currock was admitted as a partner.

QUESTION 26

Xerxes and Yolande were in partnership, sharing profits and losses 2:1 respectively. They provide the following information:

Balance Sheet at 29 February 20*4

	£	£	£
Fixed assets			
Land and buildings			180,000
Equipment			20,000
Vehicles			40,000
			240,000
Current assets			
Stock		12,400	
Trade Debtors		7,900	
		20,300	
Current liabilities			
Trade creditors	6,800		
Bank overdraft	3,200	10,000	10,300
			250,300
Capital accounts – Xerxes			140,800
Yolande			109,500
			250,300

On 29 February 20*4 Zena was admitted to the partnership. The following terms were agreed:

■ Zena would contribute £100,000 as her share of capital and goodwill
■ the new profit-sharing ratio would be 2:2:1 respectively.

The following asset values were agreed:

	£
Land and buildings	300,000
Equipment	18,000
Vehicles	12,000
Stock	11,400
Goodwill	35,000

It was also agreed that a goodwill account would not be maintained in the business books of account.

Required
Prepare:

a a revaluation account
b a goodwill account
c partners' capital account
d a balance sheet as at 29 February, immediately after Zena was admitted as a partner.

QUESTION 27

Petteril, Eden and Calder were in partnership, sharing profits and losses 5:4:1 respectively.
The following information is available:

Balance sheet as at 30 September 20*4

	£	£
Fixed assets:		
Premises		60,000
Equipment		14,000
Vehicles		32,000
		106,000
Current assets:		
Stock	4,200	
Trade debtors	7,600	
Bank	1,200	
	13,000	
Trade creditor	3,000	10,000
		116,000

Capital accounts	£	£
Petteril		50,000
Eden		36,000
Calder		30,000
		116,000

Petteril retired from the partnership at close of business on 30 September 20*4. The following asset values were agreed on that date:

	£
Premises	100,000
Equipment	6,000
Vehicles	24,000
Goodwill	27,000

Eden and Calder carried on in business, sharing profits and losses in the ratio of 2:1 respectively, and they agreed that a goodwill account would not be maintained in the business books of account. They agreed that any amount due to Petteril would be transferred to a loan account.

Required

Prepare:

a a revaluation account
b a goodwill account
c partners' capital accounts
d a balance sheet as at 1 October 20*4, immediately after the retirement of Petteril.

QUESTION 28

Findlay, Forster and Farquar were in partnership, sharing profits and losses 3:3:1 respectively. The following information is available:

Balance sheet as at 31 January 20*5

	£	£	£
Fixed assets			
Equipment			27,000
Vehicles			18,000
			45,000
Current assets:			
Stock		21,000	
Trade debtors		9,400	
		30,400	
Current liabilities:			
Trade creditors	14,300		
Bank overdraft	9,100	23,400	7,000
			52,000
Capital accounts – Findlay			28,000
Forster			8,000
Farquar			16,000
			42,000

Findlay retired from the partnership at close of business on 31 January 20*5. The following asset values were agreed:

	£
Equipment	16,000
Vehicles	9,000
Goodwill	90,000

Forster and Farquar carried on in business, sharing profits in the ratio 3:2 respectively and they agreed that a goodwill account would not be maintained in the business books of account.

They agreed that any amount due to Findlay would be paid out of the business bank account. Their bank manager agreed to provide overdraft facilities if they were necessary.

Required

Prepare:

a a revaluation account
b a goodwill account
c partners' capital account
d a balance sheet as at 31 January 20*5, immediately after Findlay's retirement.

QUESTION 29

Stan and Ollie are in partnership, sharing profits and losses equally. Their balance sheet as at 30 April 20*4 is shown:

Balance sheet as at 30 April 20*4

	£	£
Fixed assets		
Equipment		65,000
Vehicles		25,000
		90,000
Current assets		
Stock	10,000	
Trade debtors	9,000	
Bank	1,500	
	20,500	
Current liabilities		
Trade creditors	8,500	12,000
		102,000
Capital accounts – Stan		70,000
Ollie		32,000
		102,000

They agree that from close of business on 30 April 20*4: they will share profits and losses ¾ to Stan and ¼ to Ollie. The following values have been agreed for business assets:

	£
Equipment	40,000
Vehicles	8,000
Goodwill	50,000

It has been agreed that a goodwill account will not be maintained in the business books of account.

Required Prepare a balance sheet as at 30 April 20*4, after the change to the profit-sharing ratios.

QUESTION 30

McMeel and Coary are in partnership, sharing profits and losses 2:1 respectively. The following information is available:

Balance sheet as at 30 November 20*4

	£	£
Fixed assets:		
Premises		28,000
Equipment		87,000
Vehicles		35,000
		150,000

	£	£
Current assets		
Stock	2,100	
Trade debtors	1,800	
Bank	800	
	4,700	
Trade creditors	4,200	500
		150,500
Capital accounts – McMeel		75,500
Coary		75,000
		150,500

It has been agreed that from close of business on 30 November 20*4 partners would share profits and losses in the ratio 3:2 and that the following assets would be revalued:

	£
Premises at	40,000
Equipment at	60,000
Vehicles at	20,000
Goodwill at	70,000

It was further agreed that a goodwill account would not be maintained in the business books of account.

Required Prepare a balance sheet as at 30 November 2004, after the change to the profit-sharing ratio.

QUESTION 31

Pritpal and Sukhdeep are in partnership, sharing profits and losses equally. They decide to dissolve their partnership on 28 February 20*5. Their balance sheet as at that date showed:

	£	£
Fixed assets		
Land and buildings		40,000
Equipment		30,000
Vehicle		10,000
		80,000
Current assets		
Stock	3,400	
Trade debtors	18,400	
Bank	2,700	
	24,500	
Trade creditors	6,400	18,100
		98,100
Long-term loan – Pritpal		25,000
		73,100
Capital accounts – Pritpal		48,300
Sukhdeep		24,800
		73,100

The debtors realised £18,000. Equipment was sold for £17,000 cash. The vehicle was taken over by Sukhdeep at an agreed value of £6,000. Dissolution expenses were £4,300 and discounts of £300 were received from creditors. The buildings were sold to Divya Ltd for a purchase consideration of £60,000, consisting of 40,000 ordinary shares of 50p each, to be divided between the partners in their profit-sharing ratio, and £30,000 cash.

Required
Prepare:

a a realisation account
b a bank account

c partners' capital accounts.

QUESTION 32

McTavish and McGonagle have been in partnership for many years, sharing profits and losses in the ratio 3:2 respectively. Their balance sheet as at 31 January 20*5 is as follows:

Balance sheet as at 31 January 20*5

	£	£	£
Fixed assets			38,000
Current assets			
Stock		4,800	
Trade debtors		6,000	
		10,800	
Current liabilities			
Trade creditors	4,900		
Bank overdraft	1,400	6,300	4,500
			42,500
Capital accounts – McTavish			25,000
McGonagle			17,500
			42,500

McTavish and McGonagle decide to dissolve their partnership.

- The stock was sold for £4,000 cash.
- Trade debtors were paid £5,700 in settlement.
- Trade creditors accepted £4,750 in settlement.
- Dissolution costs amounted to £5,700.
- The fixed assets were sold to Ripov Ltd for £100,000.

The purchase consideration consisted of £30,000 cash; £40,000 5% debentures, to be shared in profit-sharing ratio; and 10,000 ordinary shares of £1 each; to be shared equally between the partners.

Required
Prepare:

a a realisation account
b a bank account
c partners' capital accounts.

QUESTION 33

Jacques, Marcel and Guillaume, who share profits and losses in the ratio 3:2:1, decide to dissolve their partnership with effect from 30 June 20*4.
They provide the following information:

Balance Sheet as at 30 June 20*4

	£	£
Fixed assets		
Equipment		42,000
Current assets		
Stock	17,000	
Trade debtors	3,500	
Bank	800	
	21,300	
Current liabilities		
Trade creditors	6,400	14,900
		56,900
Long-term loan – Guillaume		30,000
		26,900
Capital accounts – Jacques		15,000
Marcel		1,900
Guillaume		10,000
		26,900

- The equipment was sold for £25,000 cash.
- Stock was taken over by Jacques at an agreed valuation of £15,000.
- Trade debtors were allowed discounts of £300 and discounts received from creditors amounted to £140.
- Costs of dissolution amounted to £8,300.
- Marcel is unable to meet any liability to the partnership out of private funds.

Required
Prepare:

a   a realisation account
b   a bank account
c   partners' capital accounts.

QUESTION 34

Tom, Dick and Mary have been in partnership for many years, sharing profits and losses 4:2:1 respectively. They decide to dissolve their partnership with effect from the close of business on 31 March 20*5. They provide the following information:

Balance Sheet as at 31 March 20*5

	£	£	£
Fixed assets			
Premises			40,000
Equipment			30,000
Vehicles (3)			20,000
			90,000
Current assets			
Stock		10,000	
Trade debtors		7,000	
		17,000	
Current liabilities			
Trade creditors	6,000		
Bank overdraft	5,000	11,000	6,000
			96,000
Long-term loan – Tom			36,000
			60,000
Capital accounts – Tom			40,000
Dick			15,000
Mary			5,000
			60,000

- Premises were sold for £50,000 cash.
- Equipment was taken over by Tom at an agreed value of £18,000.
- One vehicle was taken over by Tom at an agreed value of £8,000.
- Another vehicle was taken over by Dick at an agreed value of £6,000.
- The third vehicle was sold for scrap for £500 cash.
- Stock realised £9,500.
- Another trade debtor who owed £2,000 was written off as a bad debt; the remainder paid what they owed.
- Trade creditors allowed £400 cash discount.
- Dissolution expenses amounted to £7,450.
- Mary is unable to meet any liability to the partnership out of private funds.

Required
Prepare:

a   a realisation account
b   a bank account
c   partners' capital accounts.

CHAPTER SIX

The Accounts of Limited Companies

A **limited company** is an organisation that has a legal identity that is separate from that of its owners. The owners of a limited company are called **shareholders** (or members); their liability is limited to the amount that they have agreed to pay the company for their shares.

A limited company can be a very small business, or a giant multinational business with branches and/or subsidiary companies trading throughout the world.

The majority of businesses are sole traders or partnerships. The major drawback of these two types of business is that their owners have unlimited liability.

As we have already seen, a sole trader is responsible for all debts incurred by him or her in the course of running their business.

If Mona, a sole trader, runs up business debts of £25,000, she may have to settle these debts from her private building society account or she may have to sell her house or car to clear the debts. Mona has unlimited liability.

Similarly, if the business partnership of Clint and Dyke has debts of £30,000, both partners are 'jointly and severally responsible' for the debts of the business and between them they may have to raise the money privately to pay off the amount that is owed. Clint and Dyke have unlimited liability.

However, Blinva plc has debts of £345,000. Jemma, a shareholder in the company (she owns 500 ordinary shares of £1 each), could not be asked to contribute further funds in order to help pay off the debts of the company. She could lose her investment but that is all she would lose. Her personal possessions are safe. Jemma has limited liability.

So unlimited liability means that the owners of a business have responsibility for all the debts incurred by their business.

In the vast majority of cases unlimited liability is of little significance. However, if a business is making losses on a regular basis then the continued existence of the business may well be in doubt.

So a major drawback of being a sole trader or a partner in a business is unlimited liability for the owners.

As a consequence of unlimited liability there is another major drawback for unlimited businesses. There are fewer opportunities to find extra capital that may be necessary for an expansion programme. Prospective investors may not wish to take the risk of losing their private assets as well as their investment.

Specification coverage:
AQA 15.1; OCR 5.6.1; 5.6.2.

By the end of this chapter you should be able to:
- prepare a set of final accounts for internal use
- distinguish between different types of shares
- account for and distinguish between different types of reserves
- account for right issues and bonus issues of shares.

THE MAIN FEATURES OF PARTNERSHIPS AND PRIVATE LIMITED COMPANIES

Partnerships	Private limited companies (Ltd)
2–20 partners	1 to no maximum
Unlimited liability of partners	Limited liability of shareholders
Profits credited to partners' current accounts according to partnership agreement	Profits distributed by dividends
No tax on business profits*	Corporation tax charged on company profits
Partners run the business	Shareholders delegate running of the business to directors
*Partnerships are not taxed on their business profits. The partners pay tax on their earnings as partners.	

THE MAIN FEATURES OF PRIVATE LIMITED COMPANIES AND PUBLIC LIMITED COMPANIES

Private limited companies	Public limited companies
'Ltd' appears after company name	'plc' appears after company name
1 to the limit of authorised share capital	2 to the limit of authorised share capital
Share trading restricted	No restriction to share trading
No minimum to authorised capital	£50,000 minimum authorised capital
No stock market listing	Usually listed on recognised stock market

Private limited companies do not sell their shares to the general public at large, so if a private limited company wishes to raise additional finance through a share issue, the directors must find other people who might be willing to invest in the company.

This is why many private limited companies are often family businesses, with members of the family or close friends owning all the shares.

On the other hand, if the directors of a public limited company wish to raise additional finance, the directors may well advertise the fact in the financial sections of daily newspapers in order that the general public at large may subscribe to the offer.

The advantages of limited liability status and the ability to raise large amounts of finance are offset by certain legal obligations:

- annual accounts must be audited by professionally qualified personnel (this is not the case with partnerships or with sole traders)
- annual returns must be completed and filed with the Registrar of Companies. These filed accounts may be inspected by the general public at Companies House
- companies are regulated by the Companies Act 1985, as amended by the Companies Act 1989
- copies of the company's annual audited accounts must be sent to each shareholder and debenture holder.

All business organisations produce accounts for two main purposes.

Can you remember them? Of course you can.

■ Accounts are produced for **management** purposes. The accounts are used by management to highlight areas of good practice and to find areas within the business that could benefit from improvement.
■ Accounts are also produced for **stewardship** reasons. The accounts show the providers of finance how the funds that they provided are being used. Are the funds being used wisely or is the finance being squandered?

Under the stewardship umbrella we also find the need to provide accounts that comply with:

■ the Companies Act 1985
■ accounting standards
■ Stock Exchange regulations
■ tax legislation.

In this chapter we are going to concentrate on the first of these.

It was pointed out in *Introducing Accounting* that the final accounts prepared for all business organisations are broadly similar. A limited company may prepare a manufacturing account, a trading account and a profit and loss account.

If the heading was covered over, the set of final accounts prepared for a limited company would look the same as a set of final accounts prepared for a sole trader.

A limited company usually has more than one owner. So, rather like a set of final accounts for a partnership, we need to prepare an appropriation account in order to show users of the accounts what has happened to the profits earned by the company.

Sole trader	Partnership	Limited company
Manufacturing account	Manufacturing account	Manufacturing account
Trading account	Trading account	Trading account
Profit and loss account	Profit and loss account	Profit and loss account
	Appropriation account	Appropriation account
Balance sheet	Balance sheet	Balance sheet

Who are the users of the final accounts of a limited company?

They include:

Shareholders

Employees   Pressure groups

Customers   Suppliers

Directors   Competitors

Banks   Researchers

Students   Teachers

Customs and excise   Inland Revenue

Financial press

THE PROFIT AND LOSS ACCOUNT OF A LIMITED COMPANY

Dividends are the rewards paid to shareholders out of the profits earned by a limited company. The dividends are paid to individual shareholders in proportion to the number of shares they own. Dividends are paid annually, but most limited companies will pay an **interim dividend** half way through their financial year.

Ordinary dividends are variable in nature. The dividend will vary according to the level of profits earned by the company

Preference dividends are usually a fixed amount. Generally, half of the total dividend is paid as an interim dividend, the balance being paid at the year-end.

Debenture interest is paid to investors who have loaned money to a company. The interest is usually paid in two equal instalments during the year.
Note: These definitions will be expanded later, when shares and debentures are discussed more fully.

Here is an example of a trading and profit and loss account of a limited company:

EXAMPLE

Nedert Ltd
Trading and profit and loss and appropriation account
for the year ended 31 December 20*4

	£000	£000	
Sales		3,434	Looks similar to 'other' sets of final accounts so far, doesn't it?
Less Cost of sales			
Stock as at 1 January 20*4	632		
Purchases	1,578		
	2,210		
Stock as at 31 December 20*4	711	1,499	
Gross profit		1,935	
Less Expenses			
Wages	451		
Other general expenses	349		
Depreciation	56	856	
Profit before taxation		1,079	Here is where the changes start!
Taxation		223	
Profit after taxation		856	
Ordinary dividends	214		
Preference dividends	60	274	
Retained profit for the year		582	

⊙ EXAMINATION TIP

Learn the layout for a set of final accounts for a limited company.

You already know most of it. So concentrate on the lower third – the parts after the net profit has been calculated.

Operating profit is the profit earned by a limited company after deducting all operating expenses but before deducting any interest payable.

Why is it important to identify the operating profit? Consider this simple example.

EXAMPLE

Ken is a sole trader. His wealthy father set him up in business a number of years ago. His business earns a gross profit of £100,000 per annum.

Kath is a sole trader who is in the same business sector as Ken. Their businesses are a similar size. She has no wealthy relatives and she borrowed money from the bank to help finance her business. Her business also earns a gross profit of £100,000 per annum.

Ken's business expenses for the year are £60,000. Kath's business expenses for the year are £70,000 of which £20,000 is interest payments to the bank.

Which of the two business owners runs a more efficient business?

Ken's operating profit is £40,000 while Kath's is £50,000.

If Kath had been blessed with a rich daddy, her profits would have been the greater of the two. She appears to be running her business more efficiently than Ken.

After the deduction of interest payable from the operating profit we have ... profit before taxation.

One other point.

It is usual to group certain types of expenses together. The reason for this is that it makes the production of published accounts easier. We will consider published accounts a little later.

WORKED EXAMPLE

The directors of Treadle plc provide the following information at 31 October 20*4:

	£
Sales	956,230
Purchases	438,920
Stock as at 1 November 20*3	43,310
Stock as at 31 October 20*4	41,760
Directors' fees	106,900
Salaries – sales personnel	54,970
administrative	67,830
Depreciation – delivery vehicles	54,000
premises	20,000
Other expenses – selling and distribution	31,140
administrative	34,800
Audit fees	23,000
Debenture interest	40,000
Corporation taxation	21,000
Ordinary dividends	24,000

Required Prepare a trading and profit and loss account for the year ended 31 October 20*4.

WORKED EXAMPLE *continued*

Answer

Treadle plc
Trading and profit and loss account for the year ended 31 October 20*4

	£	£
Sales		956,230
Less Cost of sales		
Stock as at 1 November 20*3	43,310	
Purchases	438,920	
	482,230	
Stock as at 31 October 20*4	41,760	440,470
Gross profit		515,760
Selling and distribution		
Salaries	(54,970)	
Directors' fees	(106,900)	
Other expenses	(31,140)	
Depreciation – delivery vehicles	(54,000)	(247,010)
Administration		
Salaries	(67,830)	
Audit fees	(23,000)	
Other expenses	(34,800)	
Depreciation – premises	(20,000)	(145,630)
Operating profit		123,120
Interest payable		(40,000)
Profit before taxation		83,120
Corporation taxation		(21,000)
Profit after taxation		62,120
Ordinary dividends		(24,000)
Retained profit for the year		38,120

Revenue reserves are profits that are retained in the company.

Dividends are the part of the profits of a company that are paid to the shareholders (owners). Any part of the profit that is not paid out to the shareholders as dividends is retained within the company as a revenue reserve.

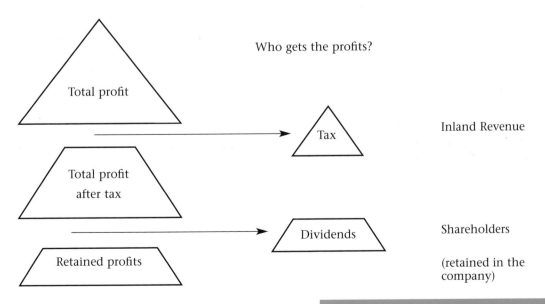

Who gets the profits?

Total profit

Tax — Inland Revenue

Total profit after tax

Dividends — Shareholders

Retained profits — (retained in the company)

The portion of the profits retained in the business is sometimes said to be 'ploughed back'. These retained profits may be described on the balance sheet as one of the following:

■ retained profits
■ retained earnings
■ profit and loss account.

All profits (after taxation and preference dividends) belong to the ordinary shareholders (owners), so the amount of profit retained within the company will, generally, have a positive effect on the price of second-hand shares in the (stock) market place.

The retained profits are a revenue reserve.

Traditionally, many companies transferred part of the retained profits into a general reserve in order to strengthen the financing of the company. These transfers do not often take place nowadays but we will transfer amounts to the general reserve since this procedure is still tested on some occasions.

WORKED EXAMPLE

The following information is available at 31 March 20*5 for Evahline plc:

Profit before taxation	746
Taxation	218
Ordinary dividends	146
Preference dividends	70

The directors recommend a transfer to general reserve of £60,000.

Required Prepare a profit and loss appropriation account for the year ended 31 March 20*5.

Answer

Evahline plc
Profit and loss appropriation account for the year ended 31 March 20*5

	£000	£000
Profit before taxation		746
Taxation		218
Profit after taxation		528
Transfer to general reserve		60
		468
Dividends – ordinary shares	146	
preference shares	70	216
Retained profit for year		252

QUESTION 1

The following information is available for Purlin plc at 30 November 20*4:

	£000
Net profit	786
Directors' fees	144
Preference dividends	35
Ordinary dividends	95
Taxation	120

The directors recommend a transfer to general reserve of £100,000.

Required Prepare a profit and loss appropriation account for the year ended November 20*4.

QUESTION 2

The following information is available for Vestov and Freaze plc at 29 February 20*4:

	£000
Net profit	409
Directors' fees	97
Preference dividends	18
Ordinary dividends	46
Taxation	88

The directors recommend a transfer to general reserve of £75,000.

Required Prepare a profit and loss appropriation account for the year ended 29 February 20*4.

WORKED EXAMPLE

The following information is provided for the year ended 31 December 20*4 for Dohoma plc:

		£000
Sales		3,160
Purchases		211
Stock:	1 January 20*4	87
	31 December 20*4	91
Salaries and general expenses		531
Directors' fees		312
Rent and rates		80
Depreciation of delivery vehicles		75
Salespersons' salaries		612
Advertising		147
Ordinary share dividend		200
Preference share dividend		180
Taxation		312
Depreciation – office equipment		28
Debenture interest		50

Required Prepare a trading, profit and loss and appropriation account.

WORKED EXAMPLE *continued*

Answer

Dohoma plc trading and profit and loss and appropriation account for the year ended 31 December 20*4

	£000	£000
Sales		3,160
Less Cost of sales		
Stock	87	
Purchases	211	
	298	
Stock	91	207
		2,953
Selling and distribution expenses		
Salaries	(612)	
Advertising	(147)	
Depreciation – delivery vehicles	(75)	(834)
Administration expenses		
Salaries and general expenses	(531)	
Directors' fees	(312)	
Rent and rates	(80)	
Depreciation – office equipment	(28)	(951)
Operating profit		1,168
Interest payable		(50)
Profit before taxation		1,118
Taxation		(312)
Profit after taxation		806
Ordinary dividend	(200)	
Preference dividend	(180)	(380)
Retained profit for year		426

Note the way that the expenses are categorised. You should be able to tell quite early which expense goes under which heading.

Make sure that you use the correct labels, eg:

- operating profit
- profit before taxation
- profit after taxation
- retained profit for year.

If you do not use these labels correctly, you could be throwing valuable marks away.

QUESTION 3

The following information is given for Sleerock plc at 31 July 20*4:

	£000
Ordinary dividends	70
Preference dividends	40
Sales	757
Purchases	312
Stock: 1 August 20*3	83
31 July 20*4	74
Selling and distribution expenses	89
Administration expenses	112
Financial charges	36
Taxation	39

Required Prepare a trading, profit and loss and appropriation account for the year ended 31 January 20*5.

QUESTION 4

The following information is available for Aromability plc at 31 January 20*5:

	£000
Ordinary dividends	210
Preference dividends	120
Sales	2,746
Purchases	1,874
Stock: 1 February 20*4	163
31 January 20*5	148
Selling and distribution costs	106
Financial charges	45
Taxation	135

Required Prepare a trading and profit and loss account and appropriation account for the year ended 31 January 20*5.

CAPITAL STRUCTURE

A limited company raises capital in order to provide finance for the purchase of the fixed assets (and initially to provide working capital). It raises capital in a variety of ways.

A company can:

- issue shares
- issue debentures
- borrow from financial institutions.

> **Liquidation** is a legal procedure applied to a limited company when it is unable to discharge its liabilities.

> **Nominal value**, also known as the par value, is the face value of shares. Once the shares have been issued, their market price can rise or fall. Any change in the market price is not reflected in the company's books of account.

Shares are divided into:

ORDINARY SHARES

Ordinary shares are the most common type of share. They are also known as equity shares. The holders of ordinary shares are part-owners of the company. At meetings in which voting is required, each share has one vote, so ordinary shareholders can appoint the directors and can influence the policies that the directors and managers wish to follow. They may receive a variable dividend in years when the company is profitable. They may receive an interim dividend during the year and a final dividend shortly after the financial year-end.

PREFERENCE SHARES

Preference shareholders are entitled to a fixed dividend (if profits and cash are available). The percentage is calculated on the nominal value of the shares. In the event of a liquidation, the preference shareholders are entitled to be repaid the nominal value of their shares before the ordinary shares are repaid.

Preference shares may be **cumulative** or **non-cumulative**. The dividends due on **cumulative** preference shares will accumulate if the company is unable to pay a dividend in any particular year, eg on 6% cumulative preference shares for three years, the holder would receive 18% dividend in Year 4 if sufficient profits were made. Most preference shares are cumulative.

If the preference shares are **non-cumulative**, any dividends not paid are forfeit.

Redeemable preference shares may be bought back by the company on a specified date. The date is shown on the balance sheet or as a note to the balance sheet.

Debentures are not shares (repeat after me: 'Debentures are not shares'!) – they are bonds recording a long-term loan to a company. The document is evidence of the loan and the holder is entitled to a fixed rate of interest each year. They may be repayable at some future date or they may be irredeemable, that is the holder will be repaid only if the company goes into liquidation.

Some debentures have the loan secured against specific assets or against all the company's assets. These are known as **mortgage debentures**.

If the company is wound up or fails to pay the interest due, the holders of mortgage debentures can sell the assets of the company and recoup any outstanding amounts.

CHARACTERISTICS OF LONG-TERM FINANCE AVAILABLE TO LIMITED COMPANIES

Ordinary shares	Preference shares	Debentures
Shares	Shares	Long-term loans (Creditor)
Part-owners of company	Not owners	Not owners
Voting rights	(Usually) no voting rights	No voting rights
Paid out last in case of liquidation	Paid out before ordinary shareholders in case of liquidation	Paid out before preference shareholders in case of liquidation
Dividends	Dividends	Interest
Variable dividend	Fixed dividend	Fixed rate of interest
Part of capital employed	Capital employed	Capital employed
Part of equity capital	Not part of equity capital	Not part of equity capital

Authorised share capital identifies the amount of share capital that a company is allowed to issue in accordance with its memorandum and articles of association.

Current syllabuses at A Level do not require a detailed knowledge of the book-keeping entries that would be used to record the issue of shares. This technique will be necessary if you continue your studies to a professional level.

Issued share capital is the amount of share capital that has actually been issued by the company. The issued share capital can never exceed the authorised share capital.

Called-up share capital is the amount of issued share capital that the shareholders have been asked to pay to date. It may be less than the value of the issued share capital.

Paid-up capital is the amount of share capital that appears on the balance sheet and is the amount of cash that the company has actually received from the shareholders.

The balance sheet of a limited company is very similar to the balance sheets that you have already prepared many times before. There are differences but if you follow the same pattern that you have previously used, you will soon master the technique again.

There are some important differences in layout and in the accounting terms used. It is very important that you start to learn these differences now.

The 'top' section of a vertical balance sheet for sole traders and partnerships looks like this:

	£	£
Fixed assets		100
Current assets	30	
Less Current liabilities	10	20
		120
Long-term liabilities		50
		70

Figures are included for illustrative purposes only.

It is only the lower part that looks different:

Sole Trader		Partnership		
	£		£	£
Capital	70	Capital account – Doe		40
		Ray		25
				65
		Current accounts – Doe	3	
		Ray	2	5
				70

The lower part of the balance sheet of a limited company might look like this:

	£
Share capital and reserves	
Ordinary shares of £1 each	35
6% Preference shares of 50p each	25
Reserves	10
	70

Let us look initially at the lower section of a company balance sheet.

The section should be headed 'Share capital and reserves'.

Examination questions often give figures for authorised share capital. This should be shown somewhere in an answer. In real life the details will generally be shown as a note to the accounts, not actually in the main 'body' of the balance sheet, although legally both methods are acceptable.

○ EXAMINATION TIP

Show the authorised share capital at the start of the lower section of the balance sheet; rule it off but do not add it to the remainder of the section.

Both the authorised and issued share capital can have preference and ordinary shares. Each should be described fully, for example:

Authorised share capital	£m
120,000,000 ordinary shares of £1 each	120
1,750,000 7% preference shares of £1 each	1.75
	121.75

Issued share capital	
Ordinary shares of £1 each	50
7% preference shares of £1 each	1

The balance sheet extract shows that the nominal value of each class of share is £1 and that the company could issue 120 million ordinary shares and 1.75 million preference shares. It further shows that 50 million ordinary shares have actually been issued and 1 million preference shares have actually been issued.

Any ordinary dividend to be paid will be expressed as a percentage of the nominal value or as an amount per share. So a dividend may be declared as 5% (ie 5% of £1 nominal value) or as an amount of, say, 6.3 pence (ie the holder of 100 shares would receive £6.30 as a dividend).

The preference shareholder will receive a dividend of 7% (ie 7 pence for every share held).

The issued share capital may be the same as the authorised share capital. If this is the case, it is acceptable to combine the headings so:

Authorised and issued share capital	£
30,000 ordinary shares of £1 each	30,000

Do be very careful when using millions and thousands – many errors are caused when candidates put decimal points in the wrong place, for example:

Correct answer	Wrong answer
£000	**£000**
30	30
1.6	1,600

Errors like this cost marks. If you are not confident, then write the figures in full, for example:

£
30,000
1,600

RESERVES

The profits earned by a sole trader or by the partners belong to them (the owners) but the profits earned by a limited company belong to the ordinary shareholders (the owners).

Some profits are taken out of the business by the owners as drawings (in the case of a sole trader or partnership) or as dividends (in the case of limited companies). The profit that remains in the business increases the capital structure of the business.

EXAMPLE

	Sole trader	Partnership	Limited company
Profit £26,000	Drawings £12,000	Drawings, say, £8,000 and £4,000	Dividends £12,000
Retained profit	£14,000	£14,000	£14,000
	Part of capital	Part of capital	Part of reserves

RETAINED PROFITS AND RESERVES

Do not say that reserves are cash. Some of the profits will already have been used to replace fixed and other assets.

There are two types of reserves:
■ **Revenue reserves** are 'normal' trading profits that have been retained in (ploughed back into) the company. They are debited to the profit and loss appropriation account, thus reducing the amount of profits available for dividend purposes.
Revenue reserves are the most flexible form of reserve. If in the future the revenue reserves are found to be excessive or are unnecessary they can be added back to current profits and used for dividend purposes.
The revenue reserves can either be set aside for a specific purpose, such as the expansion of the company or replacement of fixed assets, or generally in order to strengthen the financial postion of the company.
The main revenue reserves that you might encounter are:

- the profit and loss account (retained earnings)
- general reserve (less commonly seen in practice nowadays)
- asset replacement reserve.

■ **Capital reserves** arise from capital transactions and adjustments to the capital structure of the company. Since they do not arise through 'normal' trading activities, they are not available for the payment of cash dividends. Any distribution to shareholders of these reserves will take the form of bonus shares.

The three main capital reserves that you might encounter are:
- share premium account
- revaluation reserve and
- a capital redemption reserve.

SHARE PREMIUM ACCOUNT

A share premium account arises when a company issues shares at any price that is greater than the nominal value of the shares.

● **EXAMINATION TIP**

A share premium account only arises when the company issues the shares.

If Maggie sells her £1 shares in Placton plc to Moira for more than the nominal value (or the price that she paid for them) there is no share premium. This is a private financial transaction and will not be recorded in the company's books of account. [Maggie's name will be taken out of the company share register and Moira's name will be included.]

The book-keeping entries are fairly straightforward.

WORKED EXAMPLE

Premsha plc offers 100,000 ordinary shares of 50p each for sale at £1.50 each. All monies were received on application.

Required Prepare the ledger accounts to record the share issue.

Answer

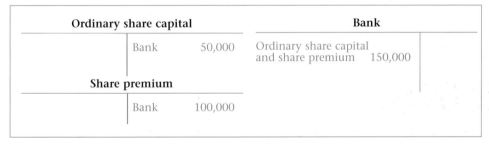

Ordinary share capital			Bank	
	Bank	50,000	Ordinary share capital and share premium	150,000
Share premium				
	Bank	100,000		

More often than not, the ledger accounts will not be required. Candidates may be asked to show the effect on the company balance sheet.

Answer

	£
Current assets	
Bank	+150,000
Share capital and reserves	
Ordinary shares of 50p each	+50,000
Share premium account	+100,000

A share premium account may be used to:

- pay up unissued shares to issue as bonus shares
- write off preliminary expenses (expenses incurred in the formation of the company)
- write off any expenses incurred in the issue of shares
- provide any premium payable on the redemption of shares or debentures.

A **revaluation reserve** is created when a fixed asset is revalued in order to reflect an increase in the value of the asset. It ensures that the balance sheet shows the permanent increase in value.

Once again, the book-keeping entries are fairly straightforward.

WORKED EXAMPLE

The summarised balance sheet of Kato plc is shown:

Kato plc
Balance sheet as at 31 December 20*4

	£000
Fixed assets at cost	40,000
Net current assets	8,000
	48,000
Share capital and reserves	
Ordinary shares	25,000
Retained earnings	23,000
	48,000

The directors of the company revalue the fixed assets on 31 December 20*4 at £51,000,000

Required Prepare a balance sheet as at 31 December 20*4, after revaluation of the fixed assets.

Answer

Kato plc
Balance sheet as at 31 December 20*4

	£000	
Fixed assets at valuation	51,000	*(increase of £11 million)*
Net current assets	8,000	
	59,000	
Share capital and reserves		
Ordinary shares	25,000	
Revaluation reserve	11,000	
Retained earnings	23,000	
	59,000	

The book-keeping entries would be:

Fixed assets

Balance	40,000,000
Revaluation reserve	11,000,000

Revaluation reserve

	Fixed assets	11,000,000

If the fixed asset to be revalued has been depreciated then any depreciation needs to be written off.

WORKED EXAMPLE

Heret plc shows the following accounts:

Premises		Provision for depreciation of premises	
Bal b/d 200,000			Bal b/d 120,000

The directors revalue the premises at £350,000.

Required

Prepare:

a book-keeping entries to record the revaluation of premises
b journal entries to record the revaluation.

Answer

a

Premises		Provision for depreciation of premises	
Bal b/d 200,000	Revaluation reserve 120,000	Bal b/d 120,000	
Revaluation reserve 150,000			

Revaluation Reserve	
	Premises 150,000
	Depreciation 120,000

b Premises	150,000	
Provision for depreciation of premises	120,000	
Revaluation reserve		270,000
Revaluation of premises to a value of £350,000.		

A revaluation reserve may be used to pay up unissued shares to issue as bonus shares.

RIGHTS ISSUES AND BONUS ISSUES OF SHARES

Rights issues and bonus issues of shares are frequently mixed up by students. They are frequently the subject of examination questions.

THE CHARACTERISTICS OF A RIGHTS ISSUE AND A BONUS ISSUE

Rights issue	Bonus issue (scrip issue)
Issue is offered to existing shareholders	Issued to existing shareholders
Issue based on present holding	Issue based on present holding
The control of the company does not change; it remains with the existing shareholders	The control of the company does not change it remains with the existing shareholders
Specified price is usually cheaper than present market price since the company saves on widely advertising the issue and preparing a full prospectus	No charge to shareholders
If shareholder does not wish to exercise his or her right it may be sold to a third party	

Bonus shares are issued when the directors of a company feel that the ordinary share capital account does not adequately reflect the net asset base of the company.

Consider the two scenarios:

Balance sheet many years ago	£
Net assets	800
Ordinary share capital	800

Balance sheet today	£
Net assets	25,000
Ordinary share capital	800
Reserves	24,200

You can see that over the years the ordinary share capital has remained unchanged whereas the asset base of the company has increased, with retained revenue reserves and capital reserves.

The directors may redress this imbalance, if the shareholders agree, by transferring some of the balances on reserve accounts to the ordinary share capital account.

Again, the process is fairly straightforward:

Dr Reserve(s) account

Cr Share capital account.

WORKED EXAMPLE

The following balance sheet is given for Blazet plc:

	£
Net assets	13,000
Ordinary share capital (£1 shares)	4,000
Share premium account	2,000
Profit and loss account	7,000

A bonus issue is made on the basis of one new share for every share already held.

It is the directors' policy to maintain reserves in their most flexible form.

Required Prepare a balance sheet after the bonus issue has been completed.

Answer

Blazet plc
Balance Sheet

	£
Net assets	13,000
Ordinary share capital	8,000
Profit and loss account	5,000

Notice that the share premium account has been fully used and the remainder of the issue has come from the profit and loss account.

The instruction re 'maintaining the reserves in their most flexible form' means that you should use capital reserves first.

QUESTION 5

The following balance sheet has been prepared for Typleat plc:

Balance sheet as at 28 February 20*5

	£000	£000
Fixed assets		1,836
Current assets	457	
Creditors: amounts falling due in less than one year	349	108
		1,944
Share capital and reserves		
Ordinary shares of £1 each		900
Share premium account		450
Profit and loss account		594
		1,944

On 28 February 20*5 Typleat plc made a rights issue of 100,000 ordinary shares at a premium of £1 each. Immediately after the rights issue a bonus issue of shares of one ordinary share for every two held was made (the rights issue of shares was eligible for the bonus issue). It is company policy to maintain reserves in their most flexible form.

Required Prepare a balance sheet as at 28 February 20*5, immediately after both share issues.

QUESTION 6

The following balance sheet for Omigosh plc is given:

Balance sheet as at 31 October 20*4

	£000	£000
Fixed assets		2,176
Current assets	377	
Creditors: amounts falling due in less than one year	283	94
		2,270
Share capital and reserves		
Ordinary shares of £1 each		1,000
Share premium account		500
Revaluation reserve		200
Profit and loss account		570
		2,270

On 31 October 20*4 Omigosh plc made a rights issue of 1 million ordinary shares at a premium of £1 each. Immediately after the rights issue the company issued one bonus share for every two ordinary shares held (the rights issue of shares was eligible for the bonus issue). It is company policy to maintain reserves in their most flexible form.

Required Prepare a balance sheet as at 31 October 20*4, immediately after the rights issue and the bonus issue.

At this point it may be as well to highlight the differences between provision, reserves and liabilities.

Provision	Reserves	Liabilities
Amounts set aside out of profits for a known expense the amount of which is uncertain.	Any other amount set aside out of profits.	Amounts owed that can be determined with substantial accuracy.

FIXED ASSETS

Fixed assets should be shown under three headings:

■ **intangible fixed assets** – these are non-physical assets such as goodwill, the ownership of a patent, a licence, a trade mark etc
■ **tangible fixed assets** – these are assets that can be seen and touched: examples would include land and buildings, plant and machinery, fixtures and fittings, vehicles etc
■ **investments** – like other assets, should be valued at cost. (Remember that these investments are long term, ie over one year. If the investment was for less than one year then it would be classified as a current asset.)

LIABILITIES

Liabilities are classified according to when payment is due.

The long-term liabilities that we encountered earlier in our studies are headed: **'Creditors: amounts falling due after more than one year'**. These would include debentures, mortgages, bank loans.

Current liabilities are headed: **'Creditors: amounts falling due within one year'**. These would include trade creditors, proposed dividends, current taxation due.

THE PUBLISHED ACCOUNTS OF LIMITED COMPANIES

The AQA Advanced level specification requires candidates to understand the contents of published accounts but candidates are not expected to be able to prepare profit and loss statements or balance sheets in a form suitable for publication.

However, the OCR specification requires candidates to be able to prepare profit and loss accounts and balance sheets according to the Companies Act 1985 format 1. Format 1 is a prescribed layout to comply with the Companies Act 1985. Before the Act became law, companies could produce their own version of published accounts, provided that they included all disclosure requirements.

There are four profit and loss formats allowed but formats 3 and 4 are rarely seen in practice because they use a horizontal layout.

Once the format has been chosen, it should be used each year unless the directors of the company decide that a change is necessary.

Format 1
1. Turnover
2. Cost of sales
3. Gross profit
4. Distribution costs
5. Administration expenses
6. Other operating income
7. Income from shares in group companies
8. Income from shares in related companies
9. Income from other fixed-asset investments
10. Other interest receivable and similar income
11. Amounts written off investments

12. Interest payable and similar charges
13. Tax on profit or loss on ordinary activities
14. Profit or loss on ordinary activities after taxation
15. Extraordinary income
16. Extraordinary charges
17. Extraordinary profit or loss
18. Tax on extraordinary profit or loss
19. Other taxes not shown under the above items
20. Profit or loss for the financial year.

The final accounts that a limited company produces have to be used by the directors and managers for decision-making purposes. They need to contain much useful detail. If those same accounts were published in this useful form, competitors might gain access to information that could be used to undermine the company.

The Companies Act 1985 requires every company to send a copy of the company's accounts to:

- every shareholder
- every debenture holder
- all other persons entitled to receive copies.

The accounts must be sent not less than 21 days before the Annual General Meeting.

So, although legally the shareholders, lenders and others must be sent a copy of the accounts, the law protects the company by allowing it to publish an 'abridged' version that contains much less detail.

The accounts that are published are incorporated into an annual report.

The annual report contains:

- profit and loss account
- balance sheet
- cash flow statement
- explanatory notes on:
  - accounting policies
  - items in the profit and loss account:
    - turnover
    - interest
    - income from investments
    - rent from land
    - amounts payable for the hire of plant and machinery
    - the amount of auditors' expenses paid
    - details of the tax charged in the accounts
    - particulars of staff
    - wages and salaries paid (including the number of high-earning employees)
    - particulars of directors' emoluments
- items in the balance sheet
- a statement from the chairman
- directors' report
- auditors' report.

You may obtain copies of company reports by writing to the registered office of the company or you may visit the company's website.

Try:

- http://www.manutd.com
- http://www.tesco.com
- http://marks-and-spencer.co.uk
- The **notes on accounting policies** will explain the accounting policies used to prepare the accounting statements. It will cover items such as: turnover, depreciation policy, treatment of goodwill etc.
- **Explanatory notes** will show details of the figures published in the profit and loss account, balance sheet and cash flow statement.
- The statement from the chairman will give a brief review of the company's progress over the past years, highlighting sales, profits, dividends etc. It may indicate future developments in the company while evaluating current developments.
- The directors' report will cover a review of the period covered by the accounts, commenting on results and dividend policies. It will outline company employment policy, paying

particular attention to equal opportunities and policies on the employment of people with disabilities. It provides a list of directors and their interest in the company, together with any share options. The report itemises political and charitable donations, sets out health and safety policy and provides an insight into future developments for the company.

■ The auditors' report is a legal requirement. The report sets out the respective responsibilities of directors and auditors. The report makes a statement on the basis of the audit opinion and then gives an opinion stating whether the financial statements present a 'true and fair view' of the company's activities over the financial period covered by the accounts.

Chapter summary

■ A limited company has a legal identity separate from that of its members.
■ Shareholders have limited liability. They may receive dividends if the company is profitable and it has sufficient cash to pay the dividend.
■ Directors of a company are not its owners. They run the company on behalf of the shareholders.
■ Companies raise capital by issuing shares and debentures. Debentures are not part of the share capital.
■ Profits are retained within the company in the form of reserves. Revenue reserves are trading profits that have been 'ploughed back' into the company and may be used to pay dividends. Capital reserves arise through capital profits and may not be used to issue dividends.
■ Companies must send a copy of the final accounts to all shareholders and debenture holders. These published accounts are produced in an abridged format in order to protect the company.

Self-test questions

■ Define limited liability.
■ A private limited company could have 35 shareholders. True or false?
■ A public limited company could have 3,500 shareholders. True or false?
■ Shareholders must own a minimum of 100 shares in order to have a vote at a company's AGM. True or false?
■ Gross profit £30,000; administration expenses £10,000; interest payable £8,000. Calculate operating profit and profit before taxation.
■ Profit after taxation £120,000; transfer to general reserve £20,000; dividends £18,000. Calculate retained profits for the year.
■ Explain the difference between revenue reserves and capital reserves.
■ Bonus shares can be issued out of revenue reserves. True or false?
■ Bonus shares can be issued out of capital reserves. True or false?
■ Name one revenue reserve.
■ Name one capital reserve.
■ Explain the main difference between a rights issue of shares and a bonus issue of shares.

TEST QUESTIONS

QUESTION 7

The directors of Pitcherdy plc provide the following information at 31 December 20*4:

	£000
Ordinary shares of £1 each fully paid	1,000
6% preference shares of £1 each fully paid	200
Gross profit	746
Administration expenses	124
Selling and distribution expenses	88
Interim dividends paid – preference shares	6
ordinary shares	14
Interest payable	36

The directors wish the following to be taken into account:

■ proposed final ordinary dividend of 2%
■ proposed final preference dividend
■ taxation of £160,000 is to be provided on the year's profit
■ a transfer of £50,000 to an asset replacement reserve is to be made.

Required Prepare a profit and loss account and appropriation account for the year ended 31 December 20*4.

QUESTION 8

The directors of Brocknam plc provide the following information at 31 August 20*4:

	£000
7% preference shares of £1 each fully paid	400
Ordinary shares of £1 each fully paid	500
Gross profit	1,347
Administration expenses	487
Selling and distribution expenses	391
Interim dividends paid – preference shares	14
ordinary shares	11
Interest paid and payable	76

The directors also wish the following to be taken into account:

■ proposed final ordinary dividend of 4.2%
■ proposed final preference dividend
■ taxation of £98,000 is to be provided on the profit for the year
■ a transfer of £40,000 is to be made to general reserve.

Required Prepare a profit and loss account for the year ended 31 August 20*4.

QUESTION 9

The following information is available for Masqik plc at 30 November 20*4:

	£000
Share capital and reserves	
Ordinary shares of £1 each	1,500
8% preference shares	400
Share premium account	412
Profit and loss account	228
	2,540

On 1 December 20*4 a bonus issue of one ordinary share for every five held was made. It is company policy to maintain reserves in their most flexible form.

Required Prepare the shareholders' funds section of the balance sheet as at 1 December 20*4, immediately after the share issue.

QUESTION 10

The following balances have been taken from the books of account of YTP plc at 31 January 20*5:

	£000
Ordinary shares of 50 pence fully paid	1,200
6% preference shares of £1 each	400
Share premium account	600
Profit and loss account	452
	2,652

On 1 February 20*5 a bonus issue of one ordinary share for every six held was made. The issue was funded by transferring equal amounts from all reserves.

Required Prepare the shareholders' funds section of a balance sheet as at 1 February 20*5, immediately after the share issue.

QUESTION 11

The following is a summarised balance sheet of Klobule plc at 30 September 20*4:

	£000
Net assets (including bank)	2,973
Share capital and reserves	
Ordinary shares of 25 pence	1,390
Share premium account	450
Profit and loss account	1,133
	2,973

On 1 October 20*4 an issue of 1,000,000 ordinary shares was made at 40 pence per share.

Required Prepare a summarised balance sheet as at 1 October 20*4, immediately after the issue of shares.

QUESTION 12

The summarised balance sheet as at 28 February 20*5 for Potyiat plc is shown:

	£000
Net assets (including bank)	2,450
Share capital and reserves	
Ordinary shares of 50 pence each	1,600
Share premium account	340
Profit and loss account	510
	2,450

On 1 March 20*5 an issue of 500,000 ordinary shares was made at 60 pence per share.

Required Prepare a summarised balance sheet as at 1 March 20*5, immediately after the share issue.

QUESTION 13

The following summarised balance sheet as at 31 July 20*4 is available for Ardbeck plc:

	£000
Net assets	2,050
Share capital and reserves	
Ordinary shares of 10 pence each	900
Share premium account	850
Profit and loss account	300
	2,050

On 1 August 20*4 the net assets were revalued at £2,500.

After the revaluation, a bonus issue of ordinary shares was made, of one new share for every one already held. The issue was funded by transferring equal amounts from all capital reserves.

Required Prepare a balance sheet as at 1 August 20*4, after all the above transactions have been taken into account.

QUESTION 14

The following summarised balance sheet as at 31 August 20*4 is available for Harmark plc:

	£000
Net assets	4,250
Share capital and reserves	
Ordinary shares of £5 each	2,000
Share premium	1,100
Profit and loss account	1,150
	4,250

On 1 September 20*4 the net assets were revalued at £5,000.

A bonus issue of one ordinary share for every four held was made. Equal amounts were transferred from all capital reserves.

Required Prepare a balance sheet as at 1 September 20*4, after the above transactions have been taken into account.

QUESTION 15

The following balance sheet extract has been prepared at 31 March 20*5 for McTavish-Jones plc:

	£000
Share capital and reserves	
Ordinary shares of £1 each	600
6% preference shares of £1 each	120
Share premium account	130
Revaluation reserve	50
Profit and loss account	238
	1,138

1. On 1 April 20*5 the company increased its ordinary share capital by an issue of bonus shares, one bonus share being issued for every three ordinary shares held. It is company policy to maintain reserves in their most flexible form.
2. On 2 April 20*3 a rights issue was made whereby all shareholders (including preference shareholders) subscribed for five ordinary shares at £2.50 for every three shares of either class held. Bonus shares were excluded from the issue. The full amount was received on 2 April 20*5.

Required An extract from the balance sheet as at 2 April 20*5, showing the share capital and reserves section.

QUESTION 16

The following is an extract taken from the balance sheet as at 31 January 20*5 for Arkwright-Thoms plc:

	£000
Share capital and reserves	
Ordinary shares of 25 pence each	200
7% preference shares of £1 each	60
Share premium account	260
Asset replacement reserve	45
Profit and loss account	345
	910

The following transactions took place on 1 February 20*5:

1. One bonus share was issued for every five ordinary shares held. It is company policy to maintain reserves in their most flexible form.
2. Both ordinary shareholders and preference shareholders subscribed for one ordinary share for every share held (excluding bonus shares). 40 pence per share was received.

Required Prepare a balance sheet extract as at 1 February 20*5, showing the share capital and reserves section of the balance sheet.

QUESTION 17

Omerdoh plc has prepared the following draft balance sheet at 31 December 20*4:

	Cost £	Depreciation £	Net £
Fixed assets			
Premises	240,000	66,000	174,000
Equipment	86,000	56,000	30,000
Vehicles	112,000	84,000	28,000
	438,000	206,000	232,000
Current assets			
Stock		64,000	
Debtors		47,000	
Bank balance		51,000	
		162,000	
Creditors: amounts falling due in less than one year			
Trade creditors		21,000	141,000
			373,000
Share capital and reserves			
Ordinary shares of £1 each			300,000
Share premium account			40,000
Profit and loss account			33,000
			373,000

No entries have been made in the final accounts for the following:

1. A bonus issue of one ordinary share for every five ordinary shares held was made in October 20*4. The share premium account was utilised for the issue.
2. On 31 December 20*4 the premises were revalued at £250,000.
3. Included in the stock held at 31 December 20*4 was obsolete stock with a cost value of £5,000. The stock can only be sold for scrap at £1,000.
4. During August a vehicle that had cost £36,000 was involved in a road accident and had to be written off. The vehicle had a net book value of £9,000. The insurance company paid £7,000 in compensation for the loss.

Required Prepare the balance sheet at 31 December 20*4 after taking notes 1 – 4 into account.

QUESTION 18

The following balance sheet has been prepared at 1 February 20*5 for Lisamarg plc:

	£000	£000
Fixed assets		
Land and buildings		650
Other fixed assets		215
		865
Current assets including bank balance	400	
Creditors: amounts falling		
due in less than one year	120	280
		1,145
Share capital and reserves		
Ordinary shares of 25 pence each		500
4% preference shares £1 each		400
Share premium account		70
Profit and loss account		175
		1,145

The following transactions took place in February 20*5:

1. On 2 February 20*5 a rights issue of one ordinary share for every five shares of any class held was made at £1 per share. All shareholders took up their rights.
2. Land and building were revalued at £750,000 on 14 February 20*5.
3. On 20 February 20*5 a bonus issue was made of one ordinary share for every four held this was made by utilising the share premium account.

No other transactions took place during February 20*5.

Required Prepare a balance sheet as at 28 February 20*5 after the transactions in notes 1–3 are taken into account.

CHAPTER
SEVEN

Accounting Standards

Limited companies must prepare their final accounts within a regulatory framework.

This framework consists of:

- the Companies Act 1985, as amended by the Companies Act 1989
- accounting standards as set out in Statements of Standard Accounting Practice (SSAPs) and Financial Reporting Standards (FRSs)
- regulations required by the Stock Exchange (these will not be discussed here since none of the major UK examinations boards examines these regulations).

The regulations regarding the conduct of limited companies have evolved over time. Before 1970, companies were regulated by various Companies Acts. In 1970 the first standards were issued by the Accounting Standards Steering Committee.

Nowadays, limited companies must adhere to the Companies Act 1985, as amended by the Companies Act 1989, as well as to accounting standards.

Why is there a need to have standards?

The standards seek to:

- iron out areas of difference in the preparation and presentation of accounting information
- recommend disclosure of accounting bases
- identify any departure from the standards
- improve existing disclosure requirements.

The Accounting Standards Committee also sought to introduce a system to aid the consultation process on setting standards.

The four major accounting bodies are expected to comply with all the standards that are currently in use. In addition, all auditors of limited companies must belong to one of the major accounting bodies.

So the standards are the 'ground rules' that apply to the preparation of the accounts of limited companies and the audit of their accounts. These ensure that the standards that are applied in Carlisle are the same as those being applied in Cheltenham.

At the moment there are 10 SSAPs in operation and 19 FRSs.

Fortunately for you, not all of the 29 standards are examined.

HEALTH WARNING!

- It is important to stress that you will not be required to have a detailed knowledge of the standards that are examinable.
- However, you should know the number, for example 'FRS 15 *Tangible fixed assets*' and the broad outline of what the standard says.
- Different examination boards examine different standards. The examination board will be identified prior to discussion of each standard.

Specification coverage:
AQA 15.4; OCR 5.6.3.

By the end of this chapter you should be able to:
- demonstrate a basic knowledge of SSAP 9; FRS 10; FRS 13 (OCR only); FRS 15; FRS 18.

Health Warning

SSAP 9 *STOCKS AND LONG-TERM CONTRACTS* (OCR; AQA)

This standard is one of the most frequently tested.

'Stocks' are defined as:

- goods or other assets purchased for resale
- consumable stores
- raw materials and components purchased for incorporation into products for sale
- products and services in intermediate stages of completion
- finished goods.

> **'Cost'** is defined as 'expenditure which has been incurred in the normal course of business in bringing the product or service to its present location and condition'.

Cost of purchase comprises purchase price including import duties, transport and handling costs and any other directly attributable costs less trade discounts, rebates and subsidies.

> **Production overheads**: overheads incurred in respect of materials, labour or services for production, based on the normal level of activity, taking one year with another.

Cost of conversion comprises:

- costs which are specifically attributable to units of production, eg direct labour, direct expenses and sub-contracted work
- production overheads
- other overheads, if any.

> **Net realisable value** is the actual or estimated selling price (net of trade discount but before cash discount) less all further costs to completion and all marketing, selling and distribution costs.

The standard states that stock should be valued at the lower of cost or net realisable value of the separate items of stock or of groups of similar items.

The stocks should be categorised in the balance sheet as raw materials, work in progress or finished goods.

The standard accepts stocks valued using:

- FIFO ('first in, first out')
- AVCO (weighted average cost)
- standard cost (if it bears a reasonable relationship to actual costs obtained during the period).

> **Base cost** is 'the calculation of the cost of stocks on the basis that a fixed unit value is ascribed to a pre-determined number of units of stock . . .'

The standard does not accept:

- LIFO ('last in, first out')
- base cost
- replacement cost (unless it provides the best measure of net realisable value and this is less than cost).

Work in progress should be valued at total cost of production.

Prime cost is not acceptable as a basis.

SSAP 13 *ACCOUNTING FOR RESEARCH AND DEVELOPMENT* (OCR)

> **Pure research** is 'experimental or theoretical work undertaken ... to acquire new scientific or technical knowledge for its own sake'. The work does not have any particular aim or objective in mind.

> **Applied research** is 'original investigation to acquire new scientific or technical knowledge and directed towards a specific aim or objective'.

> **Development** is 'the use of scientific or technical knowledge in order to produce new or substantially improved materials, devices, products, processes, systems or services prior to the commencement of commercial production'.

Any fixed assets acquired or constructed in order to facilitate research and development over a number of accounting periods should be treated like all other fixed assets. They should be capitalised and written off over their useful life.

Other expenditure on pure or applied research should be treated as revenue expenditure and written off in the year of expenditure.

Development expenditure should be treated as revenue expenditure and written off in the year of expenditure. Exceptions to this treatment are when:

■ there is a clearly defined project
■ the related expenditure is separately identifiable
■ the outcome of a project has been assessed as technically feasible and commercially viable
■ further development costs are to be incurred on the same project and the total of these costs is more than covered by future revenues from that project
■ adequate resources already exist that enable the project to be completed.

Development costs deferred to future periods should be amortised.

In such cases the expenditure may be deferred to future periods.

THE ACCOUNTING TREATMENT

■ The accounting policy on research and development expenditure should be stated and explained.
■ The total amount of research and development expenditure charged to the profit and loss account should be disclosed.
■ A distinction should be made between current year expenditure on research and development and amounts amortised from deferred expenditure.

FRS 1 *CASH FLOW STATEMENTS* (OCR; AQA)

This topic is dealt with in detail in the next chapter.

FRS 10 *GOODWILL AND INTANGIBLE ASSETS* (OCR; AQA)

This standard requires that capitalised goodwill and intangible assets are charged to the profit and loss account in the period in which they are depleted.

It also requires that users are able to determine the impact of goodwill and intangible assets on the financial position and performance of the company.

Intangible assets do not have physical substance. They are identifiable and are controlled by the company. They include licences, quotas, patents, copyrights, franchises and trademarks. The treatment of intangible assets is similar to the treatment of goodwill.

Purchased goodwill is the difference between the cost of acquiring an entity and the total of the fair values of the entity's identifiable assets and liabilities. Purchased goodwill may be positive.

For example: assets £130,000; liabilities £20,000; purchase price £200,000.
Positive goodwill   = £200,000 − (£130,000 − £20,000)
                    = £90,000

Or the purchased goodwill may be negative:

For example: assets £150,000; liabilities £30,000; purchase price £100,000
Negative goodwill   = £100,000 − (£150,000 − £30,000)
                    = £20,000

Internally generated goodwill (sometimes referred to as inherent goodwill) should not be capitalised.

Intangible assets purchased separately from a business should be capitalised at cost.

Internally developed intangible assets should be capitalised only if they have a measurable market value.

If goodwill (or an intangible asset) is regarded as having a limited useful economic life, it should be amortised systematically over its life.

If goodwill (or an intangible asset) is regarded as having an infinite life, it should not be amortised.

So in this respect goodwill and intangible assets are no different to any other asset.

The standard assumes that purchased goodwill (or intangible assets) will have a maximum economic life of 20 years, unless:

■ the business life will exceed 20 years
■ the intangible asset has a useful life in excess of 20 years
■ the goodwill (or intangible assets) is capable of being valued beyond 20 years.

The standard accepts that when a business is acquired its previous reputation will live on for a while until the new owners stamp their own 'image' on the business.

The asset should be amortised using the straight-line method (unless a different method can be proved to be more appropriate).

A residual value should be included in the calculation only if the residual value can be determined with reliability.

If the asset has a readily ascertainable market value it may be revalued to reflect this.

Once revalued, periodic revaluation should be undertaken to ensure that the reported value does not differ significantly from the market value at the balance sheet date.

Amortisation should be based on the revalued amounts and the remaining useful economic life of the asset.

The financial statements should describe:

■ the method used to value the asset
■ the method and period of amortisation of the asset
■ the reason for choosing the time period.

Negative goodwill should be shown in brackets under the heading of fixed assets on a balance sheet.

The following information should be disclosed for positive goodwill, negative goodwill and each class of intangible asset:

■ cost (or revalued amount) at the beginning of the financial period and at the balance sheet date
■ the total of the provision for amortisation
■ a reconciliation of movements, ie additions, disposals, revaluations and amortisation
■ the net carrying amount at the balance sheet date.

Any changes to the period or method of amortisation should be disclosed.

Financial statements should disclose the periods in which negative goodwill is being written back in the profit and loss account.

FRS 15 *TANGIBLE FIXED ASSETS* (OCR; AQA)

The objectives of the standard are to ensure that accounting principles regarding fixed assets, any revaluations and depreciation policies are applied consistently and the company's policies are understood by the users of the accounts.

Tangible fixed assets should be valued at cost initially. Cost can include expenditure directly attributable to bringing the assets into a usable condition. Costs could include stamp duty, import duties etc, the cost in preparing the site, delivery charges, labour costs and other installation costs. Expenditure that ensures that the fixed asset is able to continue its performance should be treated as revenue expenditure. Tangible fixed assets can be revalued when this is part of company policy. Any revaluation should reflect the value of the asset at the balance sheet date.

When a revaluation has taken place, the following details should be disclosed:

- name and qualification of the valuer
- the basis of the valuation
- the date and amount of the valuation.

The disclosure should state whether the persons carrying out the valuation are internal or external to the company.

The objective of depreciation is to reflect the cost of using a tangible fixed asset. The charge to the profit and loss account should reflect the cost of using the asset over the period under review. It should reflect the pattern in which the economic benefits derived from the asset are consumed. The depreciation charge for the period should be recorded as an expense in the profit and loss account.

The depreciation charge is calculated by reference to the asset's:

- useful economic life
- residual value
- depreciation method.

These will depend on:

- the usage of the asset
- the passage of time
- the repair and maintenance of the asset
- economic obsolescence
- technological obsolescence
- legal or similar limits on the use of the asset.

A variety of methods can be used to calculate the annual charge for depreciation, for example:

- the straight-line method
- the reducing balance method.

When the pattern of use of the asset is uncertain, the straight-line method is usually adopted.

Changing methods is permissible only where the new method gives a fairer representation of the use of the asset.

Any change to the method used must be a permanent change.

The following information should be disclosed for each class of tangible fixed asset:

- depreciation method used
- useful economic life or the rate used
- total depreciation for the year
- the effect of any change to the company's policy
- cost (or revalued amount) at the start of the financial period and at the balance sheet date
- total amount of provision for depreciation at the balance sheet date
- reconciliation of movements, ie additions, disposals, revaluations, depreciation etc.

FRS 18 *ACCOUNTING POLICIES* (OCR; AQA)

The objectives of the standard are to ensure that the company adopts accounting policies that are most appropriate to its circumstances in order to give a true and fair view of its financial position and profit or loss and that the company reviews its policies on a regular basis to ensure the appropriateness of its policies. It also helps to ensure that a company will adopt new policies if they prove to be more appropriate.

Companies should prepare their financial statements on a going concern basis unless this is clearly not the case.

Companies should prepare their financial statements on an accruals basis (clearly this cannot be the case for cash flow statements).

The company should only recognise profits that are realised at the date of the balance sheet (profits are realised when cash or another asset (usually a debt) is recognised with a reasonable certainty).

The appropriateness of accounting policies should be judged against the following objectives:

- **relevant**: appropriate accounting policies will result in presenting financial information that is relevant, ie if it is able to influence the decisions of users and if it is provided in time to influence those decisions
- **reliable**: financial information is reliable if it can be depended on to be a faithful representation of the substance of what has taken place. The information should be:
  - bias free
  - free of material errors
  - complete
  - prudently prepared
- **comparable**: financial statements should be comparable with the statements prepared in other time periods. This should be achieved through disclosure policies and the application of consistent measures. Appropriate accounting policies should be applied so that users can identify and evaluate differences and similarities
- **understandable**: information should be capable of being understood by people with a reasonable knowledge of business and accounting. This may require 'study with reasonable diligence' on behalf of the user.

The information to be disclosed:

- a description of each accounting policy
- details of changes to the accounting policies being followed in the accounts
- an explanation of why the policy was changed
- an indication of the effects of any change to policy
- the effect on the results of any prior period adjustment.

Chapter summary

- Standards provide basic 'ground rules' by which all accounting records are produced.
- Standards need not be known off by heart – just the broad outlines need to be understood.
- It is important that the number of each standard mentioned is known, together with the title.
- The broad general principles must be thoroughly understood so that you can apply them to a variety of business problems.

Self-test questions

- Why is there a need for accounting standards?
- Which standard deals with goodwill?
- What does FRS 1 deal with?
- Which standard deals with depreciation of fixed assets?
- What does SSAP 9 deal with?
- Which standard deals with research and development?
- Which standard deals with intangible fixed assets?

- Which standard says that accounts should be understandable?
- Which objective in the preparation of accounts is missing: relevant; comparable; and understandable?
- What is the over-riding principle used in valuing stock?

TEST QUESTIONS

QUESTION 1

A company has spent £25 million establishing a brand name. The finance director plans to include the brand name as an intangible asset on the next balance sheet. It will be amortised over the next five years.

Required Comment on the finance director's proposal.

QUESTION 2

On 1 January 20*5 a business was acquired by Ashish and Turner plc. Goodwill valued at £50,000 arising on the acquisition has been debited to the profit and loss account since it has an estimated economic life of only five years.

Required Comment on the treatment of the goodwill.

QUESTION 3

Gretera plc commenced trading in 1997. Since then, sales have increased by 300% and the number of customers has more than doubled. The company enjoys a very good reputation in its business sector. Because of these factors, the directors propose to introduce £100,000 goodwill into the balance sheet at 31 December 20*4.

Required Comment on the directors' proposal.

QUESTION 4

Stocks which cost £50,000 can now be replaced for £40,000. The estimated net realisable value of the stock is £37,500. The directors of Attled plc are to include the stocks in the balance sheet at £37,500.

Required Comment on the directors' proposed treatment of stock.

QUESTION 5

Ng, Tripp and Co plc purchased new premises in 1991. The market value of local properties fell for the first five years of ownership, so the directors depreciated the premises. Since 1996 property prices have risen substantially; the directors propose to revalue the premises and discontinue the practice of depreciating them.

Required Comment on the directors' proposal.

QUESTION 6

Sadleigh plc has undertaken pure research which has cost £1.3 million this year. It is proposed to capitalise the research since this is such a large amount.

Required Comment on the proposal.

QUESTION 7

Gougham and Kram plc purchased a piece of machinery costing £560,000 from Switzerland. The transportation costs from Switzerland cost £4,600 and installation costs amounted to £7,400.

The finance director wishes to capitalise £572,000: the whole amount.

The managing director wishes to capitalise £560,000 and include the £12,000 expenses on the profit and loss account.

Required Advise the board of directors as to which treatment is correct.

QUESTION 8

After preparing the final accounts of Tryodge plc, the directors are disappointed at the level of the profits revealed. They plan to rearrange the way the final accounts are presented, to disguise the poor results.

Required Comment on the directors' plan.

CHAPTER EIGHT

Cash Flow Statements – FRS 1

Throughout this chapter, reference will be made to companies. All but the smallest limited companies are required to prepare a cash flow statement.

Even though small companies, sole traders and partnerships do not have to produce a cash flow statement, they may find it in their best interests to prepare one.

FRS 1 requires that companies prepare a cash flow statement in the format described in the standard. It defines cash flows as cash in hand and deposits repayable on demand.

It provides the following standard headings:

■ operating activities
■ returns on investments and servicing of finance
■ taxation
■ capital expenditure and financial investment
■ (acquisitions and disposals – outside the scope of A Level specifications)
■ equity dividends paid
■ management of liquid resources
■ financing.

Where different categories appear under the same heading, they must be shown separately.

The standard requires two reconciliation statements that are not part of the statement:

■ between operating profit and net cash flow from operating activities
■ the movement of cash in the period and the movement of net debt. This comprises cash in hand and deposits repayable on demand less any overdrafts.

So, the cash flow statement should include all inflows and outflows involving cash. Any transactions that do not involve cash should not appear in the statement.

Specification coverage:
AQA 15.4; OCR 5.6.1.

By the end of this chapter you should be able to:
■ prepare a cash flow statement using the indirect method as per FRS 1.

USES OF CASH FLOW STATEMENTS

The trading and profit and loss accounts concentrate on the determination of profits or losses over a period of time, since profits should ensure the long-term survival of the company. The balance sheet concentrates on the position of the company at a particular moment in time.

Cash flow statements:

■ concentrate on cash inflows and cash outflows since cash is important for the short-term survival of all businesses
■ reveal information that is not disclosed in the trading and profit and loss account. This helps in financial planning
■ provide information that enables users to assess the efficiency (or inefficiency) or how cash has been used during the year
■ provide information that helps to assess the liquidity, viability and financial adaptability of the company
■ allow comparisons to be made year on year or inter-firm. This is facilitated by a prescribed format (although a cash flow statement is a historical document (ie it is prepared using the figures from the last financial year)
■ help to provide information that will assist in the projection of future cash flows.

We shall concentrate initially on the calculation of the figures to be used in a cash flow statement. We will then categorise the cash flows under the appropriate headings.

THE CALCULATIONS

Cash is money in notes and coins and deposits that are repayable on demand.

Cash equivalents are short-term investments that are convertible into cash without notice. They have less than three months to run when acquired. Overdrafts repayable in less than three months are deducted from cash equivalents.

In most examinations, information will be given in the form of two balance sheets; one prepared at the beginning of the financial year and one prepared at the end of the financial year. This is known as the **indirect method**.

The technique used to find cash flows is to compare the two sets of information.

WORKED EXAMPLE

The following balance sheets are available:

Bursil plc
Balance sheets as at 31 March

	31 March 20*4 £000		31 March 20*5 £000	
Fixed assets				
Premises at cost	7,065		11,377	
Less Depreciation	3,112	3,953	3,967	7,410
Machinery at cost	3,789		4,413	
Less Depreciation	1,351	2,438	1,736	2,677
Vehicles at cost	1,657		1,657	
Less Depreciation	763	894	1,176	481
		7,285		10,568
Current assets				
Stock	734		918	
Debtors	330		323	
Balance at bank	81		94	
Cash in hand	31		51	
	1,176		1,386	
Less **Creditors: falling due in less than one year**				
Trade creditors	312		338	
Taxation	334		358	
Dividends	275	255	294	396
	921	7,540	990	10,964
Capital and reserves				
Issued share capital		2,570		3,850
Share premium		1,735		2,375
Profit and loss account		3,235		4,739
		7,540		10,964

Note:
1. No interim dividends have been paid during the year.
2. There have been no disposals of fixed assets during the year.

WORKED EXAMPLE *continued*

Required Prepare a statement to identify the cash inflows and cash outflows.

Answer

Each calculation is done in turn, identifying the cash inflow or outflow. The summary appears at the end, when all the calculations have been completed. We are going to systematically take each item on the balance sheet and compare the opening figure with the closing figure. Any difference in the two figures will be because of a cash movement (with one notable exception!).

Premises on the first day of the financial year had cost £7,065,000; on the last day of the year the figure has risen to £11,377,000. Bursil plc must have purchased some additional premises during the year, at a cost of £4,312,000. The purchase must have entailed cash leaving the company. **Cash outflow £4,312,000.**

The next item on our way down the balance sheet is **depreciation of premises**.

Let us consider depreciation and how it affects cash. (Do you remember that in *Introducing Accounting* we said that depreciation does not have a direct influence on cash flows? – no one appears at my front door demanding that I pay the depreciation on my car or television set!)

To help clarify the situation, consider the following:

WORKED EXAMPLE

Dougie is a trader who deals only in cash.

During one particular week, Dougie drives his van to Manchester and purchases £400 worth of jeans and sells them over the next couple of days for £600.

He prepares his revenue account.
It looks like this: His bank account would also show:

	£			£
Sales	600			
Less Purchases	400	Income from sales		600
	200	*Less* Cheque for jeans		400
Petrol	35	Cheque for petrol		35
Profit	165	Balance		165

Dougie's cash and profit are the same!

However, as an A Level accounting student, you explain to Dougie that the 'matching' concept required him to include the value placed on the use of any assets used to generate his profit. He should include in his revenue account an amount for the use of his van (ie depreciation on his van). You suggest £20.

His redrafted revenue statement now shows:

	£
Sales	600
Less Purchases	400
	200
Less Petrol	35
Less Depreciation	20
Profit	145

His profit now no longer matches his cash flow.

How can we reconcile the two figures?

We can reconcile the two figures by adding the depreciation charged to the profit and loss account to the profit figure.

Profit £145 + depreciation of van £20 = £165, which agrees with the bank balance.

So, in order to calculate any cash flows for the year, depreciation charges should be added to the net profit for the year.

Depreciation on premises at the start of the year is £3,112,000; at the end of the year it is £3,967,000. Change for the year is £855,000.

Although this is not really a cash inflow, we treated it as such, as we did with Dougie.

To be added to the **cash inflows: £855,000** for depreciation of premises.

The depreciation charged to the profit and loss account for the other two fixed assets should be treated in the same way.

Add to cash inflow: ■ **£385,000** for depreciation of machinery and
■ **£413,000** for depreciation of vehicles.

Machinery purchased during the year amounted to £624,000.

Would this cause cash to flow out of the business or cash to flow into the business?

That's right, it is a cash outflow. **Cash outflow £624,000.**

There has been no change in the cost of vehicles during the year. As as far as we can tell, no purchases have been made.

During the year, **stocks** have increased by £184,000.

In order to increase stocks, a cash outflow has to take place. **Cash outflow £184,000.**

Debtors at the start of the year were £330,000. At the end of the year the amount was £323,000, so debtors have fallen by £7,000. This is because of a net cash inflow. **Cash inflow £7,000.**

The next two items, ie **balance at bank** and **cash in hand**, are overlooked at the moment. Why?

They are ignored because we are trying to amass information to explain why there is a change to these balances over the year.

Trade creditors at the start of the year were owed £312,000. One year later they were owed £338,000. They have increased by £26,000. This increase in creditors can be used to finance the company's activities and is therefore an inflow. **Cash inflow £26,000.**

We can see that at the end of the year Bursil plc owed the **Inland Revenue** £358,000. This amount has been entered in the company's profit and loss appropriation account – it has reduced the year's retained profit but it will not be paid to the tax authorities for some time yet. (This is why it appears as a creditor.) It has reduced the profit but has not yet become a cash outflow. This amount needs to be added back to the profit as a cash inflow. **Cash inflow £358,000.**

The same principle applies to the **proposed dividends** – they too have been deducted from profits but have yet to be paid (they need ratification by the shareholders at the AGM). **Cash inflow £294,000.**

In last year's cash flow statement the same adjustments were made for taxation and proposed dividends. But last year's amounts owed will have been paid in the year covered by the cash flow statement.

WORKED EXAMPLE *continued*

So:

Cash outflows for:

- taxation £334,000
- dividends £275,000.

The **issued share capital** has increased by £1,280,000. The company has made a further issue of shares during the year. **Cash inflow £1,280,000.**

The **share premium** has increased by £640,000. The new issue of shares has clearly been issued at a premium of 50% on nominal value. **Cash inflow £640,000.**

Finally, the profit and loss account (**retained earnings**) increased by £1,504,000; the amount of unappropriated profit ploughed back into the company. **Cash inflow £1,504,000.**

A summary of all the differences deduced would look like this:

Cash inflows		£	Cash outflows	£
Depreciation: premises		855	Purchase of premises	4,312
	machinery	385	Purchase of machinery	624
	vehicles	413	Increase in stocks	184
Decrease in debtors		7	Taxation paid	334
Increase in creditors		26	Dividends paid	275
Taxation owed		358		
Proposed dividend		294		
Share issue		1,280		
Premium on share issue		640		
Profits		1,504		
		5,762		5,729

So you can see that, according to our calculations, Bursil plc received £33,000 more cash than it spent during the year.

This should be reflected in the cash and cash equivalent balances held by the company at the end of the year compared with those it held at the start of the year.

	£
Cash and bank balances at the start of the year	112
Cash and bank balances at the end of the year	145
Increase in cash and bank balances during the year	33

QUESTION 1

The following information is available for Rao plc:

Rao plc
Balance sheets as at 31 January

	£000	20*4 £000	£000	£000	20*5 £000	£000
Fixed assets			962			1,546
Current assets						
Stock		146			159	
Debtors		212			198	
Bank balance		39			46	
		397			403	

	£000	£000	£000	£000	£000	£000
Creditors: amounts falling due in less than one year						
Trade creditors	162			171		
Taxation	48			53		
Proposed dividend	60	270	127	70	294	109
			1,089			1,655
Capital and reserves						
Share capital			500			600
Share premium			100			400
Profit and loss account			489			655
			1,089			1,655

Required Prepare a table showing cash inflows and cash outflows for the year ended 31 January 20*5.

QUESTION 2

The following information is given:

Rabadia plc
Balance sheets as at 30 November

		20*3			20*4	
	£000	£000	£000	£000	£000	£000
Fixed assets			1,010			830
Current assets						
Stock		486			479	
Trade debtors		318			337	
Bank		104			86	
		908			902	
Creditors: less than a year						
Trade creditors	192			189		
Taxation	86			92		
Proposed dividend	38	316	592	57	338	564
			1,602			1,394
Share capital and reserves						
Ordinary share capital			800			800
Profit and loss account			802			594
			1,602			1,394

Required Prepare a table showing cash inflows and cash outflows for the year ended 30
November 20*4.

EXAMPLE OF TRANSACTIONS THAT RESULT IN CASH INFLOWS AND OUTFLOWS

Cash inflows	Cash outflows
Profits	Losses
Interest received	Interest paid
Investment income received	
Dividends received	Dividends paid
Tax refund	Taxation paid
Sale of fixed assets	Purchase of fixed assets
Decrease in stocks	Increase in stocks
Decrease in trade debtors	Increase in trade debtors
Increase in trade creditors	Decrease in trade creditors
Increase in share capital	Redemption of share capital

Cash inflows	Cash outflows
Increase in debentures	Redemption of debentures
Increase in long-term loans	Repayment of long-term loans

The standard requires that cash flows should be analysed under the following standard headings:

- operating activities
- returns on investment and servicing of finance
- taxation
- capital expenditure and financial investment
- equity dividends paid
- management of liquid resources (the cash shown under this heading may be shown in the next section, providing that separate sub-totals are shown for each)
- financing.

Some students learn the headings by remembering the capital letters of the first words as 'ORTCEMF' or by using a mnemonic such as 'Oprah Returns Tax Cos 'Er Man is Fine'.

The standard also requires two reconciliation notes – they are not part of the cash flow statement and should be kept separate from the statement:

- a reconciliation of operating profit to net cash flow from operating activities
- a reconciliation of the movement in cash to the movement in net debt.

It is important that you memorise the headings and use them each time you prepare a cash flow statement using FRS 1.

> The **reconciliation of operating profit** to cash flows from operating activities seeks to calculate the actual cash generated through the operating activities of the company.

The operating profit is adjusted for movements in stock, trade debtors and trade creditors as well as for non-cash items included in the profit and loss account. The non-cash items are: annual provision for depreciation charges; annual provision for doubtful debts charges; and any profits or losses on the disposal of fixed assets. They should be clearly identified and shown separately.

> **Net debt** is borrowings less liquid resources.

> The **reconciliation of the movement in cash to the movement in net debt** shows all the cash flows (from the cash flow statement) that affect the net debt position. It includes changes in cash debt and liquid resources. It reconciles the net debt at the beginning of the year with the net debt at the end of the year.

The headings:

OPERATING ACTIVITIES

Cash flows from operating activities are the cash inflows and outflows resulting from operating or trading activities, normally found in the profit and loss account. This figure is arrived at by preparing the reconciliation of operating profit to cash flows from operating activities.

RETURNS ON INVESTMENTS AND SERVICING OF FINANCE

Cash flows that result from ownership of investments and payment to the providers of finance.

Cash **inflows** include interest and dividends received.

Cash **outflows** include interest paid to debenture holders and dividends paid to preference shareholders.

TAXATION

Cash flows to and from the Inland Revenue for taxation on both revenue and capital profits.

Cash **inflows** would include refunds for tax rebates and overpayments of taxes.

Cash **outflows** include payments of tax, including Advance Corporation Tax.

CAPITAL EXPENDITURE AND FINANCIAL INVESTMENT

Cash flows resulting from the disposal or acquisition of fixed assets.

Cash **inflows** include receipts from the sale or disposal of property, plant and equipment and receipts from the sale of long-term investments and the repayment of loans previously granted to other companies.

Cash **outflows** include payments to acquire property, plant and equipment, the purchase of long-term investments and loans made to other companies.

EQUITY DIVIDENDS PAID

This is a cash **outflow** of dividends paid by the company to ordinary shareholders.

MANAGEMENT OF LIQUID RESOURCES

Liquid resources are current asset investments held as readily disposable stores of value, ie short-term deposits.

Cash **inflows** include the sale or redemption of investments held as current asset/lquid resources.

Cash **outflows** include the purchase of investments to be held as current assets.

FINANCING

Cash flows resulting from receipts or payments from and to external providers of finance.

Cash **inflows** include receipts from a share issue or an issue of debentures; also receipts from other long-term borrowings (but not overdrafts).

Cash **outflows** include repayments of loans (not overdrafts) and payments to redeem shares.

Note: The heading 'Acquisitions and disposals' has not been included since it is relevant only to cash flow statements relating to group accounts.

There are a number of tricky areas involved in the preparation of the cash flow statement.

CALCULATION OF OPERATING PROFIT

Operating profit is the net profit before tax and interest.

WORKED EXAMPLE

The following information is given for Blodkins plc:

	£000
Profit before taxation	713
Debenture interest paid	40

Required Calculate the operating profit.

Answer
Operating profit = £753 (713 + 40).

WORKED EXAMPLE

The following information is given for the year ended 31 July 20*4 for Edcor plc:

	£000
Profit before tax (interest paid £60)	212
Tax	70
Transfer to general reserve	50
Proposed dividend	12

Required Prepare a profit and loss extract showing clearly operating profit, profit before taxation, profit after taxation and retained profit for the year.

Answer

Edcor plc
Profit and loss extract for the year ended 31 July 20*4

		£000
Operating profit		272
Interest paid		(60)
Profit before taxation		212
Taxation		(70)
		142
Transfer to general reserve	(50)	
Proposed dividends	(12)	(62)
Retained profit for year		80

In many questions a profit and loss extract is not given and the profit and loss account has to be reconstructed from the available information.

WORKED EXAMPLE

The following extracts are taken from the balance sheet of Ocset plc at 31 December:

	20*3 £000	20*4 £000
Creditors: amounts falling due within one year		
Taxation	168	120
Proposed dividends	140	150
Share capital and reserves		
Ordinary shares	2,500	2,500
General reserve	350	400
Profit and loss account	1,346	1,612

During the year ended 31 December 20*4 debenture interest amounting to £78,000 was paid.

Required Calculate the operating profit for the year ended 31 December 20*4.

WORKED EXAMPLE *continued*

Answer

	£000	£000
Increase in profit over year		266
Add Provision for taxation 20*4	120	
Proposed dividend	150	
Transfer to general reserve	50	
Debenture interest	78	398
Operating profit		664

An extract from the profit and loss account would have shown:

Profit and loss account extract for the year ended 31 December 20*4

		£000
Operating profit		664
Less Debenture interest		(78)
Profit before taxation		586
Taxation		(120)
Profit after taxation		466
Less Transfer to general reserves	(50)	
Proposed ordinary dividend	(150)	(200)
Retained profit for year		266

QUESTION 3

The following information is given for McGarry & Coary plc at 31 March:

	20*4 £000	20*5 £000
Creditors: amounts falling due within one year		
Taxation	130	112
Proposed dividends	60	80
Share and capital reserves		
Ordinary shares	1,000	1,200
General reserve	100	120
Profit and loss account	1,372	1,596

During the year ended 31 March 20*5 interest paid was £27,000.

Required Calculate the operating profit for the year ended 31 March 20*5.

QUESTION 4

The following information is given for Neal, Harrison & Co Ltd at 30 November:

	20*3 £000	20*4 £000
Creditors: amounts falling due within one year		
Taxation	260	245
Proposed preference dividend	40	40
Proposed ordinary dividend	120	110
Share capital and reserves		
Ordinary shares	1,700	1,700
8% preference shares	500	500
General reserve	300	400
Profit and loss account	1,783	1,849

Required Calculate the operating profit for the year ended 30 November 20*4.

CALCULATION OF THE ANNUAL PROVISION FOR DEPRECIATION OF FIXED ASSETS

In some cases, the calculation of the provision for depreciation of fixed assets is straightforward. It involves comparing the aggregate depreciation at the start of the year with the aggregate depreciation at the end of the year.

WORKED EXAMPLE

The following extracts have been taken from the balance sheets of Beta and Biga Ltd:

	31 July 20*3 £000	£000	31 July 20*4 £000	£000
Fixed assets				
Premises	2,500		2,500	
Less Depreciation	1,800	700	1,850	650
Machinery	1,830		1,830	
Less Depreciation	1,098	732	1,281	549
Office equipment	611		611	
Less Depreciation	308	303	369	242
Vehicles	1,100		1,100	
Less Depreciation	630	470	855	245

Required Calculate the provision for depreciation for the year ended 31 July 20*4 for each asset.

Answer

		£
Provision for depreciation –	Premises	50,000
	Machinery	183,000
	Office equip.	61,000
	Vehicles	225,000

Clearly, examiners may make the calculations a little more difficult (they often do!).

In other cases the calculation of the annual provision for depreciation of fixed assets is less straightforward.

CALCULATION OF CASH FLOWS RESULTING FROM THE DISPOSAL OF FIXED ASSETS

WORKED EXAMPLE

The following is an extract from the balance sheets of Neps plc at 30 April 20*5:

	20*4 £000	20*5 £000
Fixed assets at cost	2,332	2,573
Less Depreciation	1,021	1,238
	1,311	1,335

During the year ended 30 April 20*5, fixed assets which had cost £720,000 had been sold for £274,000. The assets sold had been depreciated by £433,000.

Required Identify any cash flows resulting from the sale of fixed assets.

Answer

Using 'T' accounts, we can gain a complete picture of the transactions involved in the problem.

Journal entries are given to help you with the timing of the entries:

Fixed assets

May 20*4 Balance b/d	2,332	Disposal	720
Missing figure	_____	Balance c/d	2,573
			3,293
May 20*5 Balance b/d	2,573		

Depreciation of fixed assets

Disposal	433	1 May 20*4 Balance b/d	1,021
1 May 20*5 Balance c/d	1,238	*Missing figure*	_____
	1,671		
		1 May 20*5 Balance b/d	1,238

Disposal of fixed assets

Fixed asset	720	Depreciation of fixed asset	433
		Bank	274
		Profit and loss account	13
	720		720

	Dr	Cr
Disposal of fixed assets	720,000	
Fixed assets		720,000

Fixed assets are removed from the fixed asset account and are entered in the disposal account.

Depreciation of fixed assets	433,000	
Disposal of fixed assets		433,000

WORKED EXAMPLE *continued*

Depreciation 'belonging' to the asset is taken from the depreciation account and entered in the disposal account.

Bank (not shown)	274,000	
Disposal of fixed asset		274,000

The cash inflow is entered in the disposal account.

At this point we need to insert a missing figure £13,000. So:

Profit and loss account	13,000	
Disposal		13,000

The 'profit' made on disposal is entered on the profit and loss account. It is **not** cash but it has been entered in the profit and loss account as an extra expense – it reduces profit but **no** cash has moved!

Enter the closing balances given in the question.

Enter them under the account and take them back diagonally into the account.

Add the fixed asset account and the depreciation account. They will not add unless you put in the two missing figures. The missing figure in the fixed asset account must be either a revaluation or the purchase of further fixed assets. A revaluation has not been mentioned so the missing figure must be fixed assets purchased during the year: a cash outflow of £961,000.

To make the depreciation account balance, this year's charge to the profit and loss account must be inserted, so £650,000 is the amount to be entered in the account and in the profit and loss account.

The profit is reduced by £650,000 but **no** cash has moved.

Both the profit on disposal £13,000 and the depreciation for the year of £650,000 have reduced profit but no cash has moved.

Both have to be added back on to our operating profit to arrive at the cash flow, just like the depreciation on Dougie's van in an earlier example.

QUESTION 5

The following information has been extracted from Kelly plc:

Balance sheet as at 31 August

	20*3	20*4
	£000	£000
Fixed assets at cost	2,160	2,490
Less Depreciation	830	910
	1,330	1,580

During the year ended 31 August 20*4 fixed assets costing £850,000, which had been depreciated by £610,000, had been sold for £170,000.

Required Identify all entries that should be made in a cash flow statement for the year ended 31 May 20*4.

QUESTION 6

The following information is available for Kai Hong plc:

Balance sheet extract as at	31 December 20*3	31 December 20*4
	£000	£000
Fixed assets	978	1,346
Less Depreciation	394	488
	584	858

During the year ended 31 December 20*4 fixed assets that had cost £400,000 were sold for £82,000. The assets had been depreciated by £320,000.

Required   Identify all entries that should be made in a cash flow statement for the year ended 31 August 20*4.

TREATMENT OF A REVALUATION OF FIXED ASSETS

A revaluation of fixed assets will clearly have an impact on the balance sheet of the company. However, since such a revaluation is merely a book entry, there will be no movement of cash, so there will be no entry in a cash flow statement.

TREATMENT OF A BONUS ISSUE OF SHARES

Again, such transactions will impact on the balance sheet of the company but will not cause any movement in cash balances. The book entry to record the issue of share will not be shown in a cash flow statement.

Both revaluations and bonus issues give many candidates problems. Many candidates include them in their answers to cash flow problems.

Don't be one of those candidates!

WORKED EXAMPLE

The directors of Tomkins Smyth & Co plc provide the following balance sheets as at 31 May:

	31 May 20*4		31 May 20*5	
	£000		£000	
Tangible fixed assets (Note 1)				
Land and buildings		18,215		23,970
Machinery		3,370		1,990
Vehicles		1,050		950
Investments		5,050		6,000
		27,685		32,910
Current assets				
Stock	1,730		2,000	
Trade debtors	550		950	
Cash – at bank and in hand	278		183	
	2,558		3,133	
Creditors: amounts falling due within one year				
Trade creditors	670		1,075	
Taxation	380		420	
Proposed dividend	337		400	
	1,387		1,895	
Net current assets		1,171		1,238
Total assets less current liabilities		28,856		34,148
Creditors: amounts falling due after more than one year				
8% debenture stock		1,200		1,200
		27,656		32,948
Capital and reserves				
Called-up ordinary share capital		12,100		12,600
Share Premium account		4,650		6,150
Revaluation reserve				3,200
Profit and loss account (Note 2)		10,906		10,998
		27,656		32,948

Notes to the balance sheet

Note 1 Fixed assets

	31 May 20*4 £000	31 May 20*5 £000
Land and buildings		
Cost	27,815	31,020
Revaluation		3,200
Depreciation to date	(9,600)	(10,250)
	18,215	23,970
Machinery		
Cost	6,500	?
Depreciation to date	(3,130)	?
Net book value	3,370	?
Vehicles		
Cost	1,650	1,750
Depreciation to date	(600)	(800)
Net book value	1,050	950

During the year ended 31 May 20*5 machinery which had originally cost £1,200,000 was sold for £750,000. The depreciation charge on this machinery up to 31 May 20*4 was £480,000. No additions to machinery were made during the year ended 31 May 20*5.

There were no disposals of land, buildings or vehicles during the year ended 31 May 20*5.

Note 2
The summarised profit and loss account for the year ended 31 May 20*5 was as follows:

	£000	£000
Net profit before taxation		1,112
Provision for corporation tax		420
Net profit after taxation		692
Dividends – paid	200	
proposed	400	600
Retained profit for year		92

Required Prepare a cash flow statement for the year ended 31 May 20*5, using the FRS 1 format.

Answer
Workings

Land and buildings		Depreciation		Cash flow statement	
27,815			9,600	650	(3,205)
3,200		10,250	MF 650		
MF 3,205	34,220	10,250	10,250		
34,220	34,220		10,250		
34,220					

WORKED EXAMPLE *continued*

	Revaluation reserve			Disposal of machinery	
	3,200		1,200	480	
			30	750	
			1,230	1,230	

Machinery		Depreciation		Cash flow statement	
6,500	1,200	480	3,130		
		3,310	MF 660	750	
	5,300	3,790	3,790	660	(30)
6,500	6,500		3,310		
5,300					

Net book value at end £5,300 − depreciation = £1,990.

So, balance on depreciation account at year end = £3,310.

Vehicles			Depreciation		Cash flow statement	
	1,650			600	200	(100)
MF	100	1,750	800	MF 200		
	1,750	1,750	800	800		
	1,750			800		

Investments			Cash flow statement	
	5,050			(950)
MF	950	6,000		
	6,000	6,000		
	6,000			

Increase in stock		(270)
Increase in trade debtors		(400)
Increase in trade creditors	405	
Taxation (last year's taxation paid this year)		(380)
Dividends (last year's dividends paid this year + interim paid)		(537)
Debenture interest (You might have to deduct debenture interest. The interest paid might be given in the question – or it might not be given, as in this example.) 8% of £1,200,000 = £96,000		(96)
Increase in share capital	500	
Increase in share premium	1,500	
Revaluation reserve	No movement of cash	
Operating profit (profit before tax + interest £1,112,000 + £96,000)	1,208	
All these changes should equal the change in the cash at bank and in hand balances	5,873	5,968

Change in cash balances £95,000.

Change in cash flows £5,873 − £5,968 = (£95,000)

Decrease in cash during period   95

WORKED EXAMPLE *continued*

We now have all the information needed to prepare our cash flow forecast. Take the figures from your workings and insert them under the correct headings. (Remember Oprah!)

Reconciliation of operating profit to net cash flow from operating activities

	£000	£000
Operating profit		1,208
Depreciation charges for year		
Land and buildings	650	
Machinery	660	
Vehicles	200	1,510
Profit on sale of machinery		(30)
Increase in stock		(270)
Increase in trade debtors		(400)
Increase in trade creditors		405
Net cash inflows from operating activities		2,423

Tomkins Smyth & Co plc
Cash flow statement for the year ended 31 May 20*5

	£000	£000
Operating activities		
Net cash inflow from operating activities		2,423
Returns on investments and servicing of finance		
Interest paid		(96)
Taxation		
Corporation tax paid		(380)
Capital expenditure and financial investment		
Payments to acquire tangible fixed assets	(3,305)	
Receipts from sale of machinery	750	
Payments to acquire investments	(950)	
		(3,505)
Equity dividends paid		
Dividends paid during year		(537)
Net cash outflow before financing		(2,095)
Financing		2,000
Receipts from issue of shares		(95)
Decrease in cash		
Reconciliation of net cash flow to movement in net debt		
Decrease in cash in the period		(95)
Net debt as at 1 June 20*4		(922)
Net debt as at 31 May 20*5		(1,017)

Net debt is borrowings less cash.

So debentures – cash. (1,200 − 278 = 922) and (1,200 − 183 = 1,017)

Chapter summary

- All limited companies (except small companies) must prepare a cash flow statement.
- FRS 1 requires that cash flow statements must be prepared in the standard format. Remember Oprah!
- The format requires two reconciliation statements that are not part of the cash flow statement.
- All cash movements are shown in the statement.
- Non-cash flows are not shown in the statement (ie issues of bonus shares and revaluations of fixed assets).

Self-test questions

- All businesses must prepare a cash flow statement. True or false?
- Do cash flow statements calculate the profits of a company?
- Why would a business prepare a cash flow statement?
- Why is depreciation added back to the profits of a business when calculating cash flows?
- How is a profit on disposal of fixed assets treated in a cash flow statement?
- How is a loss on disposal of fixed assets treated in a cash flow statement?
- Land and building have been revalued from £120,000 to £250,000. Under which heading of a cash flow statement would this be shown?
- Proposed ordinary dividend £31,000; interim ordinary dividend paid £12,000. Under which heading should this be shown in a cash flow statement? How much should be shown?
- How is net debt calculated?
- A company that makes losses does not have to produce a cash flow statement until it is profitable. True or false?

TEST QUESTIONS

QUESTION 7

The following information is available for Egdal plc:

	31 December 20*3 £	31 December 20*4 £	Cash inflow	Cash outflow
Premises at cost	37,000	46,000		
Stock	4,200	6,100		
Trade debtors	3,900	3,700		
Trade creditors	4,600	4,750		

Required Calculate the cash flows that have taken place during the year.

QUESTION 8

The following information is available for Docht plc:

	31 August 20*3 £	31 August 20*4 £	Cash inflow £	Cash outflow £
Machinery at cost	17,450	15,270		
Stock	8,100	7,930		
Trade debtors	5,650	6,130		
Trade creditors	4,980	5,350		

Required Calculate the cash flows that have taken place during the year.

QUESTION 9

The following balance sheets are available for Shakoor Ltd:

			At 31 March 20*4		At 31 March 20*5	
	£	£	£	£	£	£
Fixed assets at cost			416,000			548,000
Less Depreciation			118,000			156,000
			298,000			392,000
Current assets						
Stock		50,200			53,700	
Trade debtors		31,780			29,800	
Bank balance		8,400			7,600	
		90,380			91,100	
Creditors: amounts fallings due within one year						
Trade creditors	26,910			22,300		
Taxation	40,000			38,000		
Dividends	36,000	102,910	(12,530)	30,000	90,300	800
			285,470			392,800
Share capital and reserves						
Ordinary shares			200,000			300,000
Profit and loss account			85,470			92,800
			285,470			392,800

Required Prepare a detailed analysis of the changes to the bank balance during the year.

QUESTION 10

The following balance sheets are available for Tigles plc:

	At 29 February 20*4			At 28 February 20*5		
	£000	£000	£000	£000	£000	£000
Fixed assets at cost			1,378			1,462
Less Depreciation			912			936
			466			526
Current assets						
Stock		312			280	
Trade debtors		182			192	
Bank					39	
		494			511	
Creditors: amounts falling due within one year						
Trade creditors	188			204		
Bank overdraft	49					
Taxation	120			110		
Dividends	25	382	112	30	344	167
			578			693
Share capital and reserves						
Ordinary share capital			250			250
Profit and loss account			328			443
			578			693

Required Prepare a detailed analysis of the changes to the bank balance during the year.

QUESTION 11

The following information is given for Dixon-Mark & Co Ltd:

	31 May 20*3	31 May 20*4
	£	£
Premises – at cost	250,000	
at valuation		350,000
depreciation	(20,000)	(30,000)
Net book value	230,000	320,000

There were no disposals of premises during the year.

Required Calculate the changes to cash flows that have taken place during the year.

QUESTION 12

The following information is given for Hantar plc:

	31 July 20*3 £	31 July 20*4 £
Machinery at cost	312,000	370,000
Less Depreciation	(72,000)	(91,000)
Net book value	240,000	279,000

There were no disposals of machinery during the year.

Required Calculate the changes to cash flows that have taken place during the year.

QUESTION 13

The following information is given for Calclot plc:

	31 January 20*4 £	31 January 20*5 £
Plant – at cost	240,000	?
depreciation	(100,000)	?
Net book value	134,000	96,200

During the year ended 31 January 20*5 a piece of plant that had been purchased for £32,000 was sold for £13,200.

The aggregate depreciation charged on the plant to the year ended 31 January 20*4 was £20,000. No plant was purchased during the year.

Required Identify all entries to a cash flow statement for the year ended 31 January 20*5.

QUESTION 14

The following information is given for Lasopsid Ltd:

	31 October 20*3 £	31 October 20*4 £
Vehicles – at cost	380,000	?
depreciation	195,000	?
Net book value	185,000	250,000

During the year a vehicle costing £150,000 was sold for £3,000. The aggregate depreciation charged to the vehicle to the year ended 31 October 20*3 was £20,000.

No vehicles were purchased during the year.

Required Identify all entries to a cash flow statement for the year ended 31 October 20*4.

QUESTION 15

The following extracts have been taken from the balance sheets of Thomas Tinkle plc:

	31 January 20*3 £000	31 January 20*4 £000
Share capital and reserves		
Ordinary shares	2,000	3,000
6% preference shares	600	800
Share premium account	1,630	630
Profit and loss account	1,920	1,990

During the year a bonus issue of one ordinary share for every two held was made, and 200,000 6% preference shares of £1 were issued at par.

Required Identify the entries to be made in the cash flow statement for the year ended 31 January 20*4.

QUESTION 16

The following extracts have been taken from the balance sheets of Kerry Harry plc:

	31 May 20*3 £000	31 May 20*4 £000
Share capital and reserves		
Ordinary share capital	3,600	4,800
7½% preference shares	1,000	2,000
Revaluation reserve	750	
Share premium account	600	150
Profit and loss account	1,880	2,350

During the year a bonus issue of one ordinary share for every three held was made. A further 1,000,000 7½% preference shares of £1 were issued at par.

Required Identify the entries to be made in the cash flow statement for the year ended 31 May 20*4.

QUESTION 17

The following information has been extracted from the books of account of Jasper Turnip Ltd:

	28 February 20*3 £	29 February 20*4 £
Fixed assets at cost	362,000	490,000
Depreciation of fixed assets	140,000	220,000
Stock	48,000	52,000
Trade debtors	26,700	18,700
Trade creditors	23,000	18,000
Profit and loss account	136,000	196,000
Debenture interest paid	7,000	7,000

During the year ended 29 February 20*4 fixed assets which had cost £70,000 were sold for £17,000. The fixed assets had been depreciated by £60,000 up to 28 February 20*3.

Required Prepare a reconciliation of operating profit to net cash inflow from operating activities.

QUESTION 18

The following information has been extracted from the books of account of Raymondec plc:

	31 December 20*3 £	31 December 20*4 £
Fixed assets at cost	1,468	1,782
Depreciation of fixed assets	596	668
Stock	312	298
Trade debtors	172	183
Trade creditors	104	106
Profit and loss account	2,567	2,647
Debenture interest paid	32	32

During the year ended 31 December 20*4 fixed assets that had cost £110,000 were sold for £24,000. The assets had been depreciated by £95,000 up to 31 December 20*3.

Required Prepare a reconciliation of operating profit to net cash inflow from operating activities.

QUESTION 19

The following information is given for Currock and Cummersdale plc:

	At 31 August 20*3 £000	At 31 August 20*4 £000
Machinery at cost	488	531
Depreciation of machinery	236	262
Stock	84	92
Trade debtors	27	23
Trade creditors	34	37
Profit and loss account	1,384	1,443
Debenture interest paid	18	18

During the year ended 31 August 20*4 a machine that had cost £102,000 some years earlier was sold for £10,000. The machine had been depreciated by £87,000 up to 31 August 20*3.

Required Prepare a reconciliation of operating profit to net cash inflow from operating activities.

QUESTION 20

The following information is given for Denton Homes Ltd:

	At 31 July 20*3 £	At 31 July 20*4 £
Vehicles at cost	212,000	240,000
Depreciation of vehicles	88,000	97,000
Stock	57,500	53,000
Trade debtors	48,600	51,300
Trade creditors	34,720	29,420
Profit and loss account	1,972,400	1,979,000
Debenture interest paid	42,000	42,000

During the year ended 31 July 20*4 a vehicle that had cost £42,000 was sold for £1,000. The depreciation charged on the vehicle to 31 July 20*3 was £25,000.

Required Prepare a reconciliation of operating profit to net cash flow from operating activities.

QUESTION 21

The following information is given for Finnegan and McMeel plc:

	At 30 June 20*3 £000	At 30 June 20*4 £000
Bank balance	112	137
Cash in hand	16	15
Ordinary shares	2,000	2,500
7% debenture stock	1,000	1,500
Long-term loan	750	800

Required Prepare a reconciliation of net cash to movement in net debt.

QUESTION 22

The following information relates to Josoap Ltd:

	At 30 September 20*3 £000	At 30 September 20*4 £000
Bank balance	212	278
Cash in hand	36	12
Ordinary shares	1,000	1,200
6% debenture stock	600	1,000
Long-term loan	200	280

Required Prepare a reconciliation of net cash to movement in net debt.

QUESTION 23

The directors of Araby & Upperby Ltd provide the following information:

	At 30 April 20*4 £000	At 30 April 20*5 £000
Bank balance	110	
Bank overdraft		130
Cash in hand	8	13
7% debenture stock	2,000	1,300
Long-term loan	400	750

Required
Prepare a reconciliation net cash to movement in net debt.

QUESTION 24

The information given relates to Stan Wicks plc:

	At 31 October 20*3 £000	At 31 October 20*4 £000
Bank balance		137
Bank overdraft	210	
Cash in hand	24	28
6% debenture stock	1,100	500
Long-term loan	350	700

Required Prepare a reconciliation of net cash to movement in net debt.

QUESTION 25

The following information is given for McDonnel & Prince plc for the year ended 31 January 20*5:

	£000
Operating profit	2,167
Debenture interest	(40)
Profit before taxation	2,127
Taxation	(316)
Profit after taxation	1,811
Dividends – preference paid	(180)
ordinary paid	(460)
Retained profit for year	1,171

Over the year the following changes have taken place:

	£000
Purchase of fixed assets	1,400
Increase in stocks	12
Decrease in debtors	17
Decrease in creditors	23
Profit on sale of fixed assets	18
Receipts from sale of fixed assets	47
Depreciation of fixed assets	214
Receipts from issue of shares	2,000
Corporation tax paid	298

Required

Prepare:
a a cash flow statement using the FRS 1 layout
b a reconciliation of operating profit to net cash flow from operating activities.

QUESTION 26

The following information is available for Retrac plc:

Summarised profit and loss account extract for the year ended 31 December 20*4

		£000
Operating profit		1,783
Debenture interest		(130)
Profit before taxation		1,653
Corporation tax		(512)
Profit after taxation		1,141
Dividends – paid	(30)	
proposed	(90)	(120)
Retained profit for the year		1,021

Additional information
During the year the following transactions took place:

	£000
Taxation paid for year ended 31 Dec 20*3	536
Dividends paid for year ended 31 Dec 20*3	84
Purchase of fixed assets	407
Depreciation of fixed assets	215

	£000
Receipts from sales of fixed assets	80
Loss on sale of fixed assets	6
Decrease in stock	9
Increase in debtors	28
Increase in creditors	14
Receipts from share issue	642

Required

Prepare

a a cash flow statement using FRS 1 layout
b a reconciliation of operating profit to net cash flow from operating activities.

QUESTION 27

The following extracts from the profit and loss account and balance sheets of Sagoo and Simpson Ltd are given:

Sagoo and Simpson Ltd
Profit and loss account extract for the year ended 31 July 20*4

	£000	£000
Profit before taxation (Note 1)		133
Taxation		(40)
Profit after taxation		93
Dividends – paid	(14)	
proposed	(31)	(45)
Retained profit for year		48

Note 1
After adding interest received £12,000 and deducting interest paid £8,000.

Balance sheet as at 31 July

	20*3		20*4	
	£000	£000	£000	£000
Fixed assets (Note 2)				
Intangible assets		95		500
Tangible assets:				
Land and buildings at cost	540		612	
Depreciation	(280)	260	(300)	312
Total fixed assets		355		812
Current assets				
Stock	99		109	
Trade debtors	67		79	
Bank	42		32	
	208		220	
Creditors: amounts falling due within one year				
Trade creditors	(41)		(48)	
Tax	(38)		(40)	
Dividends	(29)		(31)	
Net current assets	108	100	119	101
Total assets less current liabilities		455		913
Creditors: amounts falling due after more than one year				
5% debentures		70		80
		385		833
Share capital and reserves				
Ordinary share capital		250		650
Profit and loss account		135		183
		385		833

Note 2
There were no sales of fixed assets during the year.

Required Prepare a cash flow statement for the year ended 31 July 20*4.

QUESTION 28

The following information has been extracted from the final accounts of Jaswal and Jarrett plc:

Jaswal and Jarrett plc
Extract from the profit and loss account for the year ended 31 March 20*5

	£000	£000
Profit before taxation (Note 1)		4,168
Taxation		1,198
Net profit after taxation		2,970
Dividends – paid	(412)	
proposed	(738)	(1,150)
Retained profit for year		1,820

Note 1
After adding interest received £291,000 and deducting interest paid £20,000.

Balance sheets as at 31 March

	20*4		20*5	
	£000	£000	£000	£000
Fixed assets (Note 2)				
Intangible assets		1,350		1,600
Tangible assets				
Land and buildings –				
at cost	1,512		2,732	
depreciation	(782)	730	(712)	2,020
Equipment	706		1,430	
Depreciation	(262)	444	(268)	1,162
Total fixed assets		2,524		4,782
Current assets				
Stock	415		436	
Trade debtors	42		39	
Bank	6		58	
	463		533	
Creditors: amounts falling due within one year				
Trade creditors	(51)		(39)	
Taxation	(804)		(1,198)	
Dividends	(412)		(738)	
	(1,267)		(1,975)	
		(804)		(1,442)
		1,720		3,340
Creditors: amounts falling due after more than one year				
6% debentures		(500)		(300)
		1,220		3,040
Share capital and reserves				
Ordinary share capital		850		850
Profit and loss account		370		2,190
		1,220		3,040

Note 2
There were no sales of fixed assets during the year.

QUESTION 29

The following profit and loss account for the year ended 31 August 20*4 is given together with balance sheets as at 31 August 20*3 and 31 August 20*4.

Dratas plc
Profit and loss account for the year ended 31 August 20*4

	£000
Operating profit	1,123
Interest paid	(29)
Profit before taxation	1,094
Taxation	(447)
Profit after taxation	647
Ordinary dividends	(298)
Retained profit for year	349

Balance sheets as at:	31 August 20*3		31 August 20*4	
	£000	£000	£000	£000
Intangible assets				
Patents		198		174
Fixed assets				
Premises	1,045		895	
Depreciation	(199)	846	(186)	709
Machinery	770		995	
Depreciation	(348)	422	(447)	548
		1,466		1,431
Current assets				
Stock	634		932	
Trade debtors	656		805	
Bank	77		462	
	1,367		2,199	
Creditors: amounts falling due within one year				
Trade creditors	(472)		(522)	
Taxation	(363)		(447)	
Dividends	(134)		(298)	
	(969)		(1,267)	
Net current assets		398		932
		1,864		2,363
Creditors: amounts falling due after more than one year		300		300
Share capital and reserves		1,564		2,063
Ordinary shares of £1 each		1,020		1,170
Profit and loss account		544		893
		1,564		2,063

Additional information

1. There were no disposals of machinery during the year.
2. Part of the premises were sold during the year, for £175,000. The profit on the sale was £50,000. There were no additions to premises during the year.
3. Patents originally cost £240,000 and are being amortised over 10 years.

Required   Prepare a cash flow statement for the year ended 31 August 20*4.

QUESTION 30

The following balance sheets have been prepared for Dixted and Keenan plc together with a profit and loss account for the year ended 31 December 20*4:

Dixted and Keenan plc
Profit and loss account for the year ended 31 December 20*4

	£000	£000
Operating profit		575
Interest paid		11
Profit before taxation		564
Taxation		223
Profit after taxation		341
Dividends – interim	98	
proposed	66	164
Retained profit for the year		177

Balance sheets as at:	31 December 20*3		31 December 20*4	
	£000	£000	£000	£000
Fixed assets				
Land and buildings	480		430	
Depreciation	(100)	380	(90)	340
Machinery	370		490	
Depreciation	(140)	230	(185)	305
		610		645
Investments at cost				55
Current assets				
Stock	306		370	
Trade debtors	410		448	
Bank	16		61	
	732		879	

	£000	£000	£000	£000
Creditors: amounts falling due within one year				
Trade creditors	(273)		(207)	
Taxation	(192)		(223)	
Dividends	(26)		(66)	
	(491)		(496)	
Net current assets		241		383
		851		1,083
Creditors: amounts falling due after more than one year				
10% debentures		120		100
		731		983
Share capital and reserves				
Ordinary shares of £1		535		610
Profit and loss account		196		373
		731		983

QUESTION 31

The directors of Gray and Lyons plc provide the following information:

Gray and Lyons plc

Balance sheets as at:	29 February 20*4		28 February 20*5	
	£000	£000	£000	£000
Tangible fixed assets (Note 1)				
Land and buildings		575		688
Machinery		260		188
Vehicles		104		60
Investments		80		90
		1,019		1,026
Current assets				
Stock	495		599	
Trade debtors	208		282	
Bank balance	104			
Cash in hand	26		50	
	833		931	
Creditors: amounts falling due within one year				
Trade creditors	(156)		(195)	
Bank overdraft			(27)	
Proposed ordinary dividend	(31)		(39)	
Proposed pref. dividend	(14)		(14)	
Taxation	(146)		(172)	
	(347)	486	(447)	484
		1,505		1,510
Creditors: amounts falling due after more than one year				
8% debenture 20*9 (Note 2)		(260)		(100)
		1,245		1,410
Share capital and reserves				
Ordinary shares of £1 (Note 3)		390		600
7% preference shares of £1		400		400
Share premium account		80		
Profit and loss account		375		410
		1,245		1,410

Notes to the balance sheet

Note 1

	29 February 20*4	28 February 20*5
	£000	£000
Fixed assets		
Land and buildings		
Cost	680	
Valuation		700
Depreciation	(105)	(12)
Net book value	575	688

During the year ended 28 February 20*5 the premises were revalued at £700,000.

There were no disposals of premises during the year.

Machinery

Cost	400	?
Depreciation	(140)	?
Net book value	260	188

During the year ended 28 February 20*5 a machine which had cost £65,000 was sold for £20,000. The accumulated depreciation on the machine to the year ended 29 February 20*4 was £40,000.

No machinery was acquired during the year.

Vehicles

Cost	450	550
Depreciation	(346)	(490)
Net book value	104	60

There were no disposals of vehicles during the year.

Note 2

£160,000 8% debentures were redeemed on 30 November 20*4 (no transfer to debenture redemption reserve was made).

Note 3

During the year a bonus issue of shares was made. The revaluation reserve and the share premium account had been used for the purpose. Part of the profit and loss account was also used.

Profit and loss account for the year ended 28 February 20*5

	£000	£000
Operating profit		325
Interest paid		12
Profit before taxation		313
Taxation		172
Profit after taxation		141
Dividends – preference paid	14	
preference proposed	14	
ordinary paid	34	
ordinary proposed	39	101
Retained profit for year		40

Required Prepare a cash flow statement for the year ended 28 February 20*5.

QUESTION 32

The financial statements and notes to the accounts are given for Appleby and Penrith plc:

Balance sheet at 31 December

	20*3		20*4	
	£000	£000	£000	£000
Tangible fixed assets (Note 1)		2,890		3,670
Current assets				
Stock	593		312	
Trade debtors	937		1,312	
Bank balance	1,015		1,202	
	2,545		2,826	
Creditors: amounts falling due within one year				
Trade creditors	(593)		(406)	
Taxation	(937)		(781)	
Dividends	(156)		(312)	
	(1,686)		(1,499)	
Net current assets		859		1,327
Total assets less current liabilities		3,749		4,997
Creditors: amounts falling due after more than one year				
Bank loans (20*5–20*9)		(390)		(800)
		3,359		4,197
Share capital and reserves				
Called-up capital (ordinary shares)		1,950		2,350
Profit and loss account		1,409		1,797
		3,359		4,197

Notes to the balance sheet

Note 1

Tangible fixed assets	£000
At 1 January 20*4	5,460
Additions during year	1,340
At 31 December 20*4	6,800
Accumulated depreciation	
At 1 January 20*4	2,570
Charge for year	560
At 31 December 20*4	3,130

Profit and loss account for the year ended 31 December 20*4

		£000
Operating profit		1,600
Interest paid		35
Profit before taxation		1,565
Taxation		781
Profit after taxation		784
Ordinary dividend – paid	114	
proposed	312	426
Retained profit for year		358

Required Prepare a cash flow statement for the year ended 31 December 20*4.

CHAPTER
NINE

Performance Evaluation

Financial statements are prepared to convey information to management and the other users of accounts.

The financial statements provide us with much financial information but in order to use this information we must be able to analyse and interpret it. Figures cannot be used in isolation because they can sometimes be misleading. Financial statements use absolute numbers. We need to place the figures in context.

In the days of Charles Dickens a good annual salary was probably £25 per year!

A woman earns $40,000 per year. Is this a good annual income? That depends on whether she lives in Zimbabwe, Singapore, Australia or the USA.

Absolute figures have to be placed in context.

The same is true about accounting information.

A business makes a net profit of £45,000 for the year ended 31 March 20*5. Has the business had a good year?

If the business under review was Freda's Fruit shop in the High Street, what would your answer be? I guess that it would be different if the business was Marks and Spencer plc.

Profits provide only one facet of business activity. Profits are important; they ensure the long-term survival of a business.

The other main facet of business activity is the ability to generate cash. Cash is so important for the day-to-day survival of the business. If a business has insufficient cash then it might be unable to pay staff wages; it might be unable to pay the providers of the utilities; it might be unable to pay its creditors. All of these people are likely to withdraw resources if the business does not pay its debts.

So, two key areas of performance evaluation are: profitability and liquidity.

Specification coverage:
AQA 13.1; 15.3;
OCR 5.3.2.

By the end of this chapter you should be able to:
- calculate ratios to assess profitability and liquidity
- calculate the relevant investors' ratios
- compare and contrast the results of different organisations
- analyse and interpret accounting statements using ratios.

PERFORMANCE EVALUATION

How would the users of accounting information decide whether the profitability and/or the liquidity of a business is acceptable?

In the same way that you decide whether the state of your earnings is acceptable or not:

- you compare your earnings this year with your earnings last year
- you compare your earnings with those of your friends
- you compare your earnings with the national average
- you might even compare your earnings with what you planned to earn.

Performance evaluation is about making comparisons.

Ratio analysis is about putting information in context and making comparisons.

The users of accounting information follow similar procedures to the ones that you might use. They ask:

- 'Is the business performing better (or worse) than last year?' They compare previous results with the current year's results.

- 'Is the business performing better (or worse) than similar businesses?' They compare the results of businesses in the same industrial sector.
- 'Is the business performing better (or worse) than the figures available for the UK's top 200 publicly quoted companies in the same sector?'

The manager will ask: 'Is the business performing better (or worse) than the figures produced in budgets or forecasts?'

'**Ratios**' is the term applied to calculations used to compare the results of businesses using ratio analysis. It is a generic term applied to results expressed in:

- ratios, eg the current ratio might be 2.2:1
- percentages, eg the mark-up might be 42%
- time, eg the debtor collection period might be 38 days or the rate of stock turnover might be seven times per year.

Why use ratios?

- Figures in isolation are meaningless; they need to be put into context.
- To analyse the current year's performance.
- To compare ratios over a number of years in order to identify trends.
- To extrapolate trends to try to make judgements about possible future performance.
- To compare the results with the results of other businesses in the same industrial sector.

The most common ratios may be classified into:

- profitability
- financial
- utilisation
- investment.

Although we will group ratios under these four major headings, you will not usually be asked to categorise your answers in this way.

In order to calculate and explain the ratios, we will use the following financial statement of Oyan Magenta & Co Ltd for the years 20*4 and 20*5.

Even though the figures relate to a private limited company, the principles would apply equally as well to the accounts of a sole trader or a partnership.

Ratios covered in *Introducing Accounting* will also be calculated as a revision aid.

Oyan Magenta & Co Ltd
Trading and profit and loss account for the year ended 31 March

	20*4		20*5	
	£000	£000	£000	£000
Sales		2,000		2,600
Less Cost of sales				
Stock	90		100	
Purchases	1,240		1,460	
	1,330		1,560	
Stock	110	1,220	120	1,440
Gross profit		780		1,160
Less Selling and distribution	(140)		(310)	
Administration	(180)	(320)	(340)	(650)
Operating profit		460		510
Interest payable		(16)		(40)
Profit before tax		444		470
Taxation		(129)		(145)
Profit after taxation		315		325
Preference dividend	(6)		(6)	
Ordinary dividend	(48)	(54)	(55)	(61)
Retained profit for year		261		264

Balance sheets

	at 31 March 20*4		at 31 March 20*5	
	£000	£000	£000	£000
Fixed assets at net book value		1,800		3,063
Current assets				
Stock	110		120	
Trade debtors	220		240	
Balance at bank	570		140	
	900		500	

	£000	£000	£000	£000
Creditors: amounts falling due within one year				
Trade creditors	(122)		(98)	
Taxation	(129)		(145)	
Proposed dividend	(54)		(61)	
	(305)		(304)	
Net current assets		595		196
Total assets less current liabilities		2,395		3,259
Creditors: amounts falling due after more than one year				
8% debentures		200		800
		2,195		2,459
Share capital and reserves				
Ordinary shares of £1		1,500		1,500
6% preference shares		100		100
Profit and loss account		595		859
Shareholders funds		2195		2459
Market price per share		£1.50		£1.70

PROFITABILITY RATIOS

RETURN ON CAPITAL EMPLOYED

This is often known as the **primary ratio**. It is the measure of how effectively the managers of the business are using its capital employed in the business.

Capital employed can be calculated by using:

- total assets less current liabilities or
- shareholders' funds plus long-term liabilities or
- issued share capital and reserves plus long-term loan capital.

There are a variety of ways of calculating the capital employed to be used. We could use:

- opening capital employed
- closing capital employed or
- an average of opening and closing capital employed.

It is important that you use the same method each time. Choose the method you feel most comfortable with.

To enable an examiner to check your answer, always state the formula that you use. This principle applies to all ratio calculations.

RETURN ON CAPITAL EMPLOYED (ROCE)

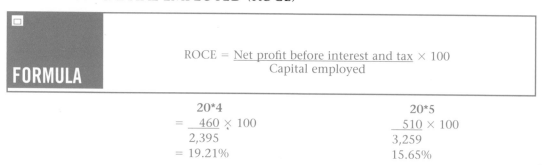

FORMULA

$$ROCE = \frac{\text{Net profit before interest and tax}}{\text{Capital employed}} \times 100$$

20*4	20*5
$= \frac{460}{2,395} \times 100$	$\frac{510}{3,259} \times 100$
$= 19.21\%$	15.65%

This tells us that for every £100 invested in the business in 20*4 the business earned £19.21; a year later the business earned £15.65 for every £100 invested – a worse result.

Could the capital be used elsewhere to earn a greater return? Compare this ratio with the return in similar businesses.

Certainly, there has been a deterioration since 20*4.

RETURN ON OWNERS' EQUITY (ROOE)

This is a refinement of the ROCE calculation. It measures the return on funds provided by the owners. In the case of a limited company this is the owners' equity, ie ordinary share capital plus all reserves.

FORMULA

$$ROOE = \frac{\text{Net profit before interest and taxation}}{\text{Owners' equity}} \times 100$$

20*4	20*5
$= \frac{454^*}{2,095} \times 100$	$\frac{504^*}{2,359} \times 100$
$= 21.67\%$	$= 21.36\%$

* operating profit less preference share dividends

Both ROCE and ROOE should be as large as possible. However, we cannot comment on whether these ratios are good or not. We would need to know individual averages or the performance of other businesses in the industry.

GROSS PROFIT PERCENTAGE (ALSO KNOWN AS THE GROSS MARGIN)

FORMULA

$$\text{Gross margin} = \frac{\text{Gross profit}}{\text{Sales}} \times 100$$

20*4	20*5	
	$= \frac{780}{2,000} \times 100$	$\frac{1,160}{2,600} \times 100$
	$= 39\%$	44.62%

This shows that for every £100 of sales, the margin was £39 in 20*4. It then improved to £44.62 in 20*5.

The margin will vary from business to business. A business with the need for a rapid turnover in stock will generally have a lower margin than a business with a slower turnover of stock.

The change identified might be caused by a decrease in the cost of goods sold while maintaining selling price or it may be caused by a slight increase in the selling price while the cost of goods sold has reduced.

MARK-UP

This is calculated as follows:

FORMULA

$$\text{Mark-up} = \frac{\text{Gross profit}}{\text{Cost of sales}} \times 100$$

20*4	20*5
$= \frac{780}{1,220} \times 100$	$= \frac{1,160}{1,440} \times 100$
$= 63.93\%$	$= 80.56\%$

This means that for every £100 of goods purchased the price has been increased to £163.93 in 20*4 and £180.56 in the following year.

Students are advised not to use both ratios in any analysis they undertake.

● EXAMINATION TIP

An increase in the volume of sales will not affect mark-up or margin. These ratios will remain constant. Changes in selling price and/or changes in purchasing price will affect mark-up or margin.

NET PROFIT PERCENTAGE (ALSO KNOWN AS THE NET MARGIN)

FORMULA

$$\text{Net margin} = \frac{\text{Net profit before interest and tax (operating profit)}}{\text{Sales}} \times 100$$

20*4	20*5
$= \frac{460}{2,000} \times 100$	$= \frac{510}{2,600} \times 100$
$= 23\%$	$= 19.62\%$

This shows that in 20*4 out of every £100 sales the business earned £23 after all operating costs and cost of sales had been covered. This amount fell to £19.62 the following year.

We can look at this from another angle; it tells us that in 20*4 the business expenses were £40.93 (£63.93 − £23.00) out of every £100 of goods sold. In 20*5 this amount spent on expenses rose to £60.94 (£80.56 − £19.62). This begs the question: is the business losing control as far as expenses are concerned?

In absolute terms, expenses have more than doubled yet sales have only increased by 600/2000, ie 30%. We can perhaps see why this has happened by examining the details of the profit and loss account expenses.

In 20*4 selling and distribution expenses accounted for £7 of each £100 of sales; in 20*5 the figure has risen to £11.92.

In 20*4 administration costs amounted to £9 in every £100 of sales; in 20*5 the figure has risen to £13.08.

Finance charges rose to £1.54 for every £100 of sales in 20*5. It had been 80p for every £100 of sales. This is an increase of 92.5%.

In all this analysis of figures we have simply considered the available information. You must try to develop this technique.

RETURN ON TOTAL ASSETS

This ratio shows how efficiently total assets are being used to generate profits.

FORMULA

$$\text{Return of total assets} = \frac{\text{Operating profit}}{\text{Fixed assets} + \text{Current assets}}$$

$$
\begin{array}{ll}
20{*}4 & 20{*}5 \\
= \dfrac{460}{2{,}700} \times 100 & = \dfrac{510}{3{,}563} \times 100 \\
= 17.04\% & = 14.31\%
\end{array}
$$

The company was using its assets more effectively in 20*4. For every £1 invested in assets the company earned just over 17p; the following year the return for every £1 invested in assets fell to 14.31p.

QUESTION 1

The following information is given for Trashott & Co Ltd:

Year ended 31 March	20*4 £000	£000	20*5 £000	£000
Sales		987		1,046
Less Cost of sales		648		667
Gross profit		339		379
Selling and distribution costs	(67)		(78)	
Administration	(48)	(115)	(58)	(136)
Operating profit		224		243
Interest payable		(38)		(40)
Profit before taxation		186		203
Taxation		(42)		(46)
Profit after tax		144		157
Dividends		(40)		(42)
Retained profit for year		104		115
Capital employed		1,388		1,516

Required

a Calculate for both years:
   i) mark-up
   ii) gross margin
   iii) net profit margin
   iv) overheads (expenses) to turnover
   v) ROCE.
b Comment on your results.

QUESTION 2

The following information is given for Prolill plc:

Year ended 31 December	20*5 £000	£000	20*4 £000	£000
Sales		1,348		1,563
Less Cost of sales		617		599
Gross profit		731		964
Selling and distribution costs	(112)		(208)	
Administration	(106)	(218)	(132)	(340)
Operating profit		513		624
Interest payable		(30)		(30)
Profit before taxation		483		594
Taxation		(133)		(152)
Profit after taxation		350		442
Dividends		(100)		(130)
Retained profit for year		250		312
Capital employed		2,460		2,830

a Calculate for both years:
   i)   mark-up
   ii) gross margin
   iii) net profit margin
   iv) overheads (expenses) to turnover
   v)   ROCE.
b Comment on your results.

FINANCIAL RATIOS

Financial ratios assess the ability of a business to pay its short-term liabilities as they fall due. Liquidity is important since a business has to pay not only its trade creditors but its employees and other providers of resources too. Although creditors are grouped on a balance sheet under headings that indicate payment within 12 months and payments due after 12 months, in reality many creditors require payment in a much shorter time.

Solvency is the ability of a business to settle its debts when they require payment.

Long-term investors are mainly interested in the solvency of the business – they require that the business will survive into the foreseeable future (or at least until their debt can be settled!).

Although solvency means an excess of assets over liabilities, many assets are difficult to dispose of and so many users of accounts are more interested in the liquidity position of the business. They wish to examine and analyse the components of working capital in detail.

CURRENT RATIO (ALSO KNOWN AS THE WORKING CAPITAL RATIO)

There is no ideal current ratio.

The ratio shows how many times the current assets are covering the current liabilities. It is usually expressed as a 'times' ratio, that is the right-hand term should be expressed as unity so the ratio should be expressed as 'something':1. Generally, the ratio should be in excess of unity (i.e. greater than 1:1), although many businesses prosper with a ratio which is less than this.

Once again, we should be looking for trends when we consider the current ratio. If a series of results shows that the current ratio has been declining over a number of years, this may mean that the business might have some difficulties in meeting its short-term obligations in the future.

If the series shows that the current ratio is increasing each year, this could be an indication that the business is tying up an increasing proportion of its resources in stock, debtors and bank balances, ie non-productive assets, instead of the resources being invested in fixed assets that will earn profit.

Many analysts consider that a reasonable current ratio should fall between 1.5:1 and 2:1 although it is dangerous to be too dogmatic about this. The ratio will depend on the type of business and the direction of any trend.

FORMULA

Current ratio = Current assets:Current liabilities

Or $\dfrac{\text{Current assets}}{\text{Current liabilities}}$:1

$$\frac{900}{305}:1 \qquad \frac{500}{304}:1$$

2.95:1   1.64:1

The working capital ratio has fallen by around 44% (1.31/2.95). It does appear that in 20*4 rather too many resources were tied up in unproductive resources and it does appear that in 20*5 this was more under control. An examination of the balance sheet reveals that the main change in current assets and current liabilities is that Oyan Magenta & Co Ltd has reduced the cash held in its bank account by £430,000.

Obviously, the greater the number of years' results that are available, the easier it is to identify and confirm a trend.

THE LIQUID RATIO (ALSO KNOWN AS THE ACID TEST RATIO OR THE QUICK RATIO)

Once again, we should be looking for trends when considering this ratio. Liquid assets are current assets and a definition of current assets is that they are assets that are cash or will be cash in the near future. The least liquid of the current assets is stock. The liquid ratio tests the ability of the business to cover its current liabilities with its current assets other than stocks.

FORMULA

Liquid ratio = Current assets − Stock:Current liabilities

Or $\dfrac{\text{Current assets} - \text{Stock}}{\text{Current liabilities}}$:1

$$\dfrac{790}{305}:1 \qquad \dfrac{380}{304}:1$$

$$2.59:1 \qquad 1.25:1$$

Year 20*4 seems rather high so rather too many resources are tied up in a liquid form, not earning profits.

The ratio has improved in 20*5, mainly because of a reduction in the bank balance from £570,000 to £140,000.

The business is still able to cover every £1 owed with £1.25 of liquid assets.

Once again, it is impossible to say what is an acceptable level of ratio – some businesses, for example some supermarkets, perform satisfactorily with a liquid ratio of less than 0.5:1.

DEBTORS' COLLECTION PERIOD (OR DEBTOR DAYS)

This calculates how long, on average, it takes a business to collect its debts.

Generally, the longer a debt is outstanding, the more likely it is that the debt will prove to be irrecoverable. It is also advisable to have a shorter debt collection period than the creditor payment period.

A question might not identify cash and credit sales; in such cases it is acceptable to use the total sales figure given. It is essential that the same basis is used when making comparisons.

FORMULA

Debtors collection period = $\dfrac{\text{Trade debtors} \times 365}{\text{(Credit) Sales}}$

$$\dfrac{220 \times 365}{2,000} \qquad \dfrac{240 \times 365}{2,600}$$

$$= 41 \text{ days} \qquad = 34 \text{ days}$$

Note the rounding of the answer. In 20*4 the actual figure calculated was 40.15 days (that is 40 days, 3 hours and 36 minutes!). We always round to the next full day.

Remember that the calculation will give us an average collection time. It uses all debtors – this may mask the fact that one significant debtor is a very poor payer while the other debtors pay promptly.

30 days' credit is a reasonable yardstick to use. So, using this measure, in 20*4 debts were

outstanding for 41 days – perhaps a little too long. There was an improvement in 20*5: debts were collected in 34 days – a week faster.

CREDITORS' PAYMENT PERIOD (OR CREDITOR DAYS)

This measures the average time a business takes to pay its creditors.

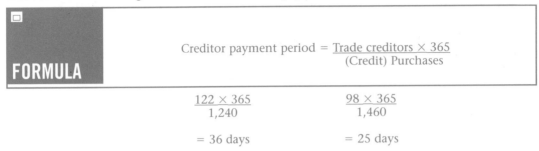

FORMULA

$$\text{Creditor payment period} = \frac{\text{Trade creditors} \times 365}{\text{(Credit) Purchases}}$$

$$\frac{122 \times 365}{1,240} \qquad \frac{98 \times 365}{1,460}$$

$$= 36 \text{ days} \qquad = 25 \text{ days}$$

In 20*4 Oyan Magenta was paying its creditors on average in 36 days; a year later it was paying in 25 days.

The shortening (efficacy) of this 11-day reduction does need investigation.

A comparison of the debtor days and creditor days shows that, in both years, creditors are on average being paid more quickly than cash is being received from debtors. This position needs to be reversed if possible. (It may be the case that one large creditor is insisting on rapid payment.)

RATE OF STOCK TURNOVER (ALSO KNOWN AS STOCK TURN OR RATE OF STOCK TURN)

In every 'bundle' of stock held by a business there is an element of profit and there is cash tied up in the stock. It is essential that this cash is released and that profits are earned as quickly as possible. So the more often stock can be 'turned over', the better it is for the business.

FORMULA

$$\text{Rate of stock turnover} = \frac{\text{Cost of sales}}{\text{Average stock held during the year}}$$

$$\frac{1,220}{100} \qquad \frac{1,440}{110}$$

$$= 12.2 \text{ times} \qquad = 13.09 \text{ times}$$

This shows that in 20*4 the company turned its stock over approximately once a month; it increased this in 20*5.

If you require the time taken to turn stock over in days, you can either divide 365 by the result of your calculation:

eg $\frac{365}{12.2}$ = 30 days and $\frac{365}{13.09}$ = 28 days

or you can use the formula: $\frac{\text{Average stock} \times 365}{\text{Cost of sales}}$

Clearly, the higher the rate of stock turn the better, since this means that stock is kept in the business for a shorter length of time.

In some industries the need to hold large quantities of stock at any one time has almost been totally eradicated with the introduction of just in time (JIT) ordering of stock.

WORKING CAPITAL CYCLE

This shows the length of time taken between making payment for goods taken into stock and the receipt of cash from customers.

The shorter the time between the business laying out cash for the purchase of stock and the collection of cash from the sales of stock, the better for the business.

The shorter the cycle, the lower the value of working capital to be financed from other sources.

The cycle can be shortened by:

■ reducing stock levels held
■ speeding up debtor collection
■ delaying payment to creditors.

FORMULA	Working capital cycle = Rate of stock turnover (days) + debtor collection period (days) − creditor payment period (days)
30 days + 41 days − 36 days = 35 days	28 days + 34 days − 25 days = 37 days

The main cause of worsening of the working capital cycle is the more rapid payment of creditors.

QUESTION 3

The following information is available for Rywicke plc:

	At 31 August 20*3 £	At 31 August 20*4 £
Sales	720,000	730,000
Purchases	346,000	361,000
Opening stock	28,000	32,000
Closing stock	32,000	34,000
Debtors	74,000	70,000
Bank	14,000	1,000
Creditors	30,000	34,000

Note: All purchases and sales were on credit.

Required
a Calculate the following ratios (show the formulae used) for both years:
   i)   current ratio
   ii)   liquid ratio
   iii) debtors' collection period
   iv)   creditors' payment period
   v)   rate of stock turnover
   vi)   working capital cycle.
b Comment on your results for debtor and creditor days.

QUESTION 4

The following information is given for Bajpan plc:

Sales (credit)	900,000	1,100,000
Purchases (credit)	537,000	524,000
Opening stock	42,000	50,000
Closing stock	50,000	52,000
Debtors	85,000	102,000
Bank	4,000	1,000
Creditors	60,000	44,500

Required
Calculate the following ratios (show the formulae used). Comment on the current and liquid ratios.
   i)   current ratio
   ii)   liquid ratio
   iii) debtors' collection period

iv)   creditors' payment period
v)   rate of stock turnover
vi)   working capital cycle.

INVESTMENT RATIOS

Equity shareholders generally have invested in a limited company in order to gain a return on their investment. They are also interested in the market value of their shares.

Before equity shareholders are able to receive any return on their investment the providers of long-term loans (debenture holders) and preference shareholders need to be rewarded.

Debenture holders must receive their interest however profitable or unprofitable the company has been.

The preference shareholders are entitled to dividends (provided there are sufficient profits) before ordinary shareholders.

The ordinary shareholders return may be at risk if the company's capital is provided mainly by debenture holders and preference shareholders.

The degree of risk is measured by the gearing ratio or the debt equity ratio.

GEARING

This is the relationship that exists between fixed cost capital and total capital.

So:

FORMULA

$$\text{Gearing} = \frac{\text{Fixed cost capital}}{\text{Total capital}} = \frac{\text{Long-term loans} + \text{Preference shares}}{\text{Long-term loans} + \text{Preference shares} + \text{issued Ordinary share capital} + \text{all reserves}}$$

$$= \frac{200 + 100}{200 + 100 + 1,500 + 595} \qquad = \frac{800 + 100}{800 + 100 + 1,500 + 859}$$

$$= \frac{300}{2,395} \qquad\qquad = \frac{900}{3,259}$$

$$= 12.5\% \qquad\qquad\qquad = 27.6\%$$

The gearing of a company is said to be :

■ **high** when the ratio is more than 50%
■ **neutral** when the ratio is 50%
■ **low** when the ratio is less than 50%.

So: high geared =

■ high borrowing
■ high debt
■ high risk.

    low geared

■ low borrowing
■ low debt
■ low risk.

In the first year 12.5% of total capital employed is provided by people other than ordinary shareholders. In the second year the company has become more highly geared: 27.6% of capital employed is provided by people other than the ordinary shareholders. The company has become more highly geared but on our measure it is still a low-geared company; 72.4% of capital employed is provided by the ordinary shareholders.

Investment in a highly geared company is more of a risk than an investment in a low-geared company because if the company is unable to service its long-term liabilities then it may be forced into liquidation by those long-term investors.

It follows that a highly geared company may find it difficult to borrow further funds because of the inherent risk. Banks may also be reluctant to lend to highly geared companies since they may feel that the ordinary shareholders should be prepared to finance their own company rather than rely on 'outsiders'.

EARNING PER SHARE

Earnings are net profit after taxation and after the deduction of preference dividends. That is, earnings that belong totally to the ordinary shareholders.

In year 20*4: Earnings are £315,000 profit after taxation

    Less £6,000 preference dividend

    £309,000 profits available for ordinary shareholders

In year 20*5: Earnings are £325,000 profit after taxation

    Less £6,000 preference dividend

    £319,000 profits available for ordinary shareholders

FORMULA

$$\text{Earnings per share} = \frac{\text{Profit after taxation and preference dividends in pence}}{\text{Number of ordinary shares}}$$

$$\frac{30,900,000}{1,500,000} \qquad \frac{31,900,000}{1,500,000}$$

$$= 20.6 \text{ pence} \qquad = 21.27 \text{ pence}$$

The earnings per share has increased in the second year. It has improved by 0.67 pence per share.

● EXAMINATION TIP

The calculation used numbers of ordinary shares issued, not the value. So £2,000,000 ordinary shares of 25 pence each would use 8,000,000 as the denominator in the calculation.

PRICE/EARNINGS RATIO

The P/E ratio relates the market price of the share to the earnings per share. It represents the number of years' earnings that investors are prepared to pay to purchase one of the company's shares.

The higher the P/E ratio, the greater the confidence investors have in the future of the company.

FORMULA

$$\text{Price/earnings ratio} = \frac{\text{Market price per ordinary share}}{\text{Earnings per ordinary share}}$$

$$= \frac{£1.50}{20.6\text{p}} \qquad = \frac{£1.70}{21.27\text{p}}$$

$$= 7.28 \qquad = 7.99$$

Investors are more confident at 31 March 20*5 than they were a year earlier. They are paying almost eight times the earnings to acquire shares in Oyan Magenta.

Since the ratio compares current market price with earnings per share, an increase in market price will increase the ratio. Demand for shares is dependent on investors' perception of the company's future performance. An increase in demand for the shares will generally cause an increase in the shares price. A high P/E ratio will indicate expected future growth (or an overvalued share). A low P/E ratio indicates expected poor performance in the future (or an undervalued share).

DIVIDEND YIELD

Shareholders invest in a company in order to gain a return (dividends) on their investment. (They also hope that the market price of the share will rise so that if they sell their holding they will make a capital profit – a capital gain.)

The dividend yield expresses the actual dividend as a percentage of the market price of the share. It shows the actual percentage return an investor can expect, based on the current market price of the shares.

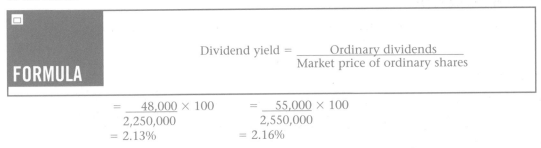

FORMULA

$$\text{Dividend yield} = \frac{\text{Ordinary dividends}}{\text{Market price of ordinary shares}}$$

$$= \frac{48,000 \times 100}{2,250,000} \qquad = \frac{55,000 \times 100}{2,550,000}$$
$$= 2.13\% \qquad\qquad = 2.16\%$$

The dividend yield is still low but has increased by over 20% in the second year.

Another version of the formula is:

$$\text{Declared rate of dividend} \times \frac{\text{nominal value of ordinary shares}}{\text{market price of ordinary shares}}$$

DIVIDEND COVER

This ratio indicates how likely it is that the company can continue to pay its current rate of ordinary share dividend in the future.

A high figure is good since it suggests that the company should be able to maintain dividends to ordinary shareholders at the current level even if profits fall. It may indicate that the directors operate a conservative dividend policy and that much of the profit is being reinvested in the company.

Low dividend cover may indicate a reckless dividend policy and a small reduction in company profits may have an adverse effect on dividends in future.

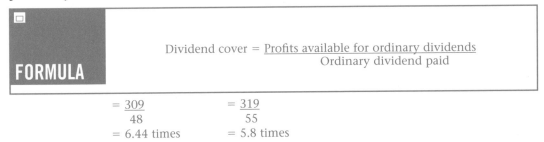

FORMULA

$$\text{Dividend cover} = \frac{\text{Profits available for ordinary dividends}}{\text{Ordinary dividend paid}}$$

$$= \frac{309}{48} \qquad\qquad = \frac{319}{55}$$
$$= 6.44 \text{ times} \qquad = 5.8 \text{ times}$$

Both are quite high but there has been deterioration over the two years. Although profits have increased (3.2%), the dividend paid has increased by a greater percentage (14.6%). Is this a sign of a change in dividend policy?

DIVIDEND PAID PER SHARE

This indicates how much each ordinary share received as a dividend.

FORMULA

$$\text{Dividend paid per share} = \frac{\text{Ordinary dividend paid}}{\text{Number of issued ordinary shares}}$$

$$= \frac{48,000}{1,500,000}$$ $$= \frac{55,000}{1,500,000}$$
= 3.2 pence   = 3.67 pence

The amount received by each ordinary shareholder has improved by 14.7% to 3.67 pence per share held.

○ **EXAMINATION TIP**

Always indicate whether the answer to your calculations is a percentage (%) or numbers of days, pence or times etc; if you do not, you will throw marks away.

INTEREST COVER

This shows how many times profits are able to cover current interest payments. It is generally thought that profits before interest and taxation should cover interest payments by at least three times. The ratio shows how secure the interests of the debenture holders are. It also indicates how secure the shareholders' interests are.

FORMULA

$$\text{Interest cover} = \frac{\text{Operating profit}}{\text{Interest charges}}$$

$$= \frac{460,000}{16,000}$$ $$= \frac{510,000}{40,000}$$
= 28.75 times   = 12.75 times

Both ratios are high. In the second year the interest cover has reduced by more than half because of the increased debenture interest. Debentures have risen from £200,000 to £800,000 so a full year's interest next year will be £64,000, which could reduce the cover even more.

LIMITATIONS ON USING RATIOS

■ The results are based on the use of historic cost because it is objective. However, some results may be misleading if results are compared over a long period. For example, the value of assets shown on a balance sheet from a number of years ago is unlikely to be the same as the market value today. When your great-grandfather first started to work, he may have earned just £2 per week. If he had been given a huge 20% pay rise, this wage would have risen to £2.40. If you or I received a 20% pay rise it would be substantially more than 40p per week.

■ Emphasis is placed on past results. Past results are not a totally reliable indicator of future results. If your football team has won its past six matches in the Premiership, there is no guarantee that it will win its seventh game.

■ Published accounts give only an overview – perhaps disguising inefficient sections of a business. The return on capital employed may be 27% – however, on closer scrutiny we might find that one section of the business is earning a return on capital of 50% and the other section earns a return of just 4%.

■ Final accounts show only the monetary aspects of the business. They do not show the strengths and weaknesses of individual managers or members of staff. They do not show staff welfare. Some businesses are very successful and pay top wages but have workers who hate going to work each day.

■ It is extremely difficult to compare like with like between two businesses; they have:
  ■ different sites
  ■ different management teams
  ■ different staff
  ■ different customers etc.

■ The external environment faced by the business may change. The changes may have an immediate effect or the result of the changes may be felt only after a time lag. A devaluation of the currency may cause imported materials to rise in price, but if the business carries large stocks and issues those stocks using the FIFO method of issue, increased costs may not be incorporated into product costs for some time.

■ Different organisations have different structures; different methods of financing their operation; different expense and revenue patterns. They may use different accounting policies, techniques, methods of measuring and apply different conventions. No matter how similar businesses appear to be from the outside, all businesses are different.

    ■ The final accounts of a business are prepared on a particular date. The balance sheet on that date may well be unrepresentative of the usual position of the business. A fancy goods business may well have low stocks at 31 December, after the Christmas rush. During the rest of the year it may carry large stocks of goods.

    ■ Ratios show only the results of business activity. They do not indicate the causes of good or bad results. Coughs, sneezes and a running nose are the results of having a cold. These symptoms do not indicate how the cold was contracted.

● EXAMINATION TIP

When comparing 'like with like' there may be a need to make adjustments to the figures given. Notional rents and management salaries may need to be included in one set of comparative figures.

EXAMPLE

Business renting premises	Business owning premises – Include notional rent of premises
Business employing management team	Business run by owner – Include notional manager's salary

QUESTIONS 5 AND 6

The following information is given for two companies for the year ended 31 May 20*4:

	Been & Pole plc £000		Ebyam plc £000	
Profit and loss accounts				
Operating profit		313		630
Debenture interest		(70)		
Profit before taxation		243		630
Taxation		(93)		(250)
Profit after taxation		150		380
Dividends – Preference	(14)		(42)	
Ordinary	(80)	(94)	(100)	(142)
Retained profit for year		56		238
Balance sheet extracts				
Share capital and reserves				
Ordinary shares £1		250		
Ordinary shares 50p				250
7% preference shares		200		600
Share premium		62		
Revaluation reserve		120		
Profit and loss account		95		1,077
		727		1,927
7% debentures		1,000		
		1,727		1,927
Market price per ordinary share		£6.80		£4.10

QUESTION 5

Calculate the following investment ratios for Been & Pole plc at 31 December:
i)   interest cover
ii) EPS
iii) ordinary dividend cover

iv) dividend yield
v) P/E ratio
vi) dividend paid per share
vii) gearing ratio.

QUESTION 6

Calculate the following investment ratios for Ebyam plc for the year ended 31 January 20*5:
i)   interest cover
ii) EPS
iii) ordinary dividend cover
iv) dividend yield
v) P/E ratio
vi) dividend paid per share
vii) gearing ratio.

QUESTION 7

The following information is provided for Apacolo plc as at 31 March 20*5:

	£000
Ordinary shares of £1 each	3,486
6% preference shares of £10 each	1,400
7% debenture stock 2025/2026	1,000
Reserves	2,114
Operating profit	1,250
Provision for corporation tax	380
Dividend cover	6 times
Market price of ordinary shares	£5.50

	Formula	31 March 20*3	31 March 20*4	31 March 20*5
Interest cover		16.4 times	17.1 times	
EPS		17.8 pence	18.74 pence	
Ordinary dividend paid per share		3.1 pence	3.3 pence	
P/E ratio		24.5	25.7	
Dividend yield		0.6%	0.6%	
Gearing		23%	18.62%	

Required
a Calculate the ratios shown as at 31 March 20*5.
b Complete the table and comment on the trends shown over the three years.

QUESTION 8

The following information is given for Rowlerby plc as at 31 December 20*4:

	£000
Ordinary shares of 50p each	540
7% preference shares of £1 each	300
6% debenture stock 2018/2019	150
Reserves	410
Operating profit	303
Provision for corporation tax	49
Dividend cover	7 times
Market price of ordinary shares	£1.30

	Formula	31 December 20*2	31 December 20*3	31 December 20*4
Interest cover		24.6 times	30.8 times	
EPS		16.46 pence	18.59 pence	
Ordinary dividend paid per share		2.04pence	2.38 pence	
P/E ratio		4.86	5.9	
Dividend yield		2.55%	2.16%	
Gearing		26.4%	29.2%	

a Calculate the ratios shown as at 31 December 20*4.

b Complete the table and comment on the trends shown over the three years.

QUESTION 9

The following information is given for two companies for the year ended 31 December 20*4:

	Baliaba plc £000	Firty Leaves plc £000
Operating profit	260	330
Debenture interest		(63)
Profit before taxation	260	267
Taxation	(57)	(71)
Profit after taxation	203	196
Dividends – preference	(16)	(32)
ordinary	(38)	(42)
Retained profit for year	149	122
Share capital and reserves		
Ordinary shares of £1 each	195	
Ordinary shares of 25p each		200
8% preference shares	200	400
Share premium	50	130
Revaluation reserve	100	60
Profit and loss account	425	550
	970	1,340
7% debentures		900
	970	2,240
Market price per share	£4.20	£1.40

Required

a Calculate the following investment ratios for the two companies:
   i)   gearing ratio
   ii) interest cover
   iii) EPS
   iv) dividend paid per share
   v)   dividend yield
   vi   P/E ratio.

b Comment on the information gained from each of the ratio calculations.

QUESTION 10

The following information is available for two companies for the year ended 28 February 20*5:

	Becktom plc £000	Mirtimax plc £000
Operating profit	2,458	1,276
Debenture interest		(300)
Profit before taxation	2,458	976
Taxation	(983)	(382)
Profit after taxation	1,475	594
Dividends – preference	(240)	(60)
ordinary	(393)	(320)
Retained profit for year	842	214
Share capital and reserves		
Ordinary shares of 50p each	3,960	
Ordinary shares of £1 each		3,500
6% preference shares	4,000	1,000
10% debentures		3,000
Share premium	1,320	1,980
Revaluation reserve	500	–
Profit and loss account	1,840	638
	11,620	10,118
Market price per share	£1.10	£2.10

Required

a Calculate the following investment ratios for the two companies:
   i)   gearing ratio
   ii)   interest cover
   iii) EPS
   iv)   dividend paid per share
   v)   dividend yield
   vi)   P/E ratio.
b Comment on the information gained from each of the ratios calculated.

● EXAMINATION TIP

Avoid making assumptions where there is no evidence in the question. Do tell the examiner if you do make an assumption. The instruction on the front of the examination paper tells you to do so.

● EXAMINATION TIP

Always state the formulae used. The examiner may have based his or her result on one formula; you may have obtained your results by using an alternative (equally correct) formula. The examiner will not know this if you do not state the formula used.

Chapter summary

■ Ratios are used as a method of performance evaluation. 'Ratios' is the generic term used for true ratios, percentages and other measures.
■ Ratios are only useful if comparisons are made either with other businesses in the same line of business or with previous years' results – ie trend analysis.
■ Ratios can be divided into profitability ratios, liquidity ratios and investment ratios.
■ It is necessary to learn the formulae for ratios and produce these before calculating the figures.

Self-test questions

- Why are results converted into ratios?
- What do profitability ratios tell us?
- Give an example of a profitability ratio.
- What do liquidity ratios tell us?
- Give an example of a liquidity ratio.
- Give the formula for calculating the net margin.
- Give the formula for calculating the rate of stock turnover.
- How is average stock calculated?
- Mary makes a gross margin of 54%. Is this good or bad?
- Mary's debtors pay, on average, in 42 days; she pays her creditors in 19 days. Is this a good or a bad policy? Consider why.
- Give an example of one investor ratio.
- What does the price/earnings ratio tell us?
- Identify two limitations of using ratios as an evaluation of performance.

TEST QUESTIONS

QUESTION 11

The following final accounts for Gerard Guillaume are given:

Trading and profit and loss account for the year ended 31 March 20*5

	£	£	£
Sales			148,120
Cost of sales			88,872
Gross profit			59,248
Expenses			45,811
Net profit			13,437

Balance sheet as at 31 March 20*5

	£	£	£
Fixed assets			
Vehicle		8,500	
Less depreciation		2,000	6,500
Fixtures		8,000	
Less depreciation		1,600	6,400
Current assets			
Stock		4,650	
Trade debtors		6,348	
		10,998	
Current liabilities			
Bank overdraft	5,078		
Trade creditors	4,020	9,098	1,900
			14,800
Capital			14,800

The following ratios are available:

Year ended 31 March	20*4	20*3	20*2	20*1
Gross profit margin	38.2%	37.1%	39.7%	35.2%
Net margin	8.8%	7.7%	10.1%	7.1%
ROCE	89%	87%	89%	82%
Current ratio	1.5:1	1.7:1	2.1:1	2.3:1
Liquid ratio	0.8:1	0.9:1	1.1:1	1.2:1

Required

a Calculate the following ratios for the year ended 31 March 20*5:
   i)   gross profit margin
   ii) net profit margin
   iii) return on capital employed
   iv) current ratio
   v)   liquid (Acid test) ratio.
b Comment on your results.

QUESTION 12

The following final accounts for Antoine Ltd at 31 March are provided:

Trading and profit and loss account for the year ended 31 March

	20*4 £000	20*4 £000	20*5 £000	20*5 £000
Sales		12,460		16,620
Less Cost of sales		(8,720)		(12,630)
Gross profit		3,740		3,990
Less Expenses		(2,350)		(2,520)
Net profit		1,390		1,470
Taxation	(750)		(800)	
Dividends	(580)	(1,330)	(640)	(1,440)
Retained profit for year		60		30

Balance sheet at 31 March 20*4

	20*4 £000	20*4 £000	20*4 £000	20*5 £000	20*5 £000	20*5 £000
Fixed assets at NBV			12,900			14,200
Current assets						
Stock		2,160			4,120	
Debtors		2,100			4,070	
Bank		890			–	
		5,150			8,190	
Creditors: amounts falling due in less than one year						
Trade creditors	2,130			3,850		
Tax and dividend	1,330	3,460		1,440		
Bank overdraft				2,480	7,770	
Net current assets			1,690			420
			14,590			14,620
Creditors: amounts falling due in more than one year			3,800			3,800
			10,790			10,820
Share capital and reserves						
Ordinary shares of £1 each			8,300			8,300
Reserves			2,490			2,520
			10,790			10,820

Required

a Calculate for both years:
   i)   gross profit margin
   ii) net profit margin
   iii) return on capital employed
   iv) current ratio
   v)   liquid (acid test) ratio.
b Calculate for 20*5 only:
   i)   stock turn
   ii) debtors ratio
   iii) creditors ratio.
c (**Note:** transfer price is the price for which shares in a private limited company change hands; this is the equivalent to the market price paid for ordinary shares in a public (plc) limited company.)
   Assuming that the transfer price per share was £1.30 at 31 March 20*5, calculate:
   i)   earnings per share (EPS)
   ii) price/earnings ratio (P/E)
   iii) dividend cover.

QUESTION 13

The following accounts are provided for the year ended 31 January for Vincent and Varsha Ltd:

Trading and profit and loss account for the year ended 31 January

	20*4 £000	20*5 £000
Turnover	15,600	16,550
Cost of sales	(7,900)	(8,380)
Gross profit	7,700	8,170
Selling and distribution costs	(3,200)	(3,525)
Administration expenses	(1,500)	(1,800)
Operating profit	3,000	2,845
Interest payable	(80)	(88)
Profit before taxation	2,920	2,757
Taxation	(900)	(850)
Profit after taxation	2,020	1,907
Dividends	(790)	(650)
Retained profit for year	1,230	1,257

Balance sheet as at 31 January

	20*4 £000	20*5 £000
Tangible fixed assets	16,500	18,000
Stocks	680	706
Debtors	3,800	4,800
Bank balance	1,050	81
	22,030	23,587
Less **Creditors: due within one year**	(6,400)	(6,600)
Total assets less current liabilities	15,630	16,987
Less **Creditors: due after more than one year**	(1,000)	(1,100)
	14,630	15,887
Share capital and reserves		
Ordinary shares of 50p each	8,000	8,000
Reserves	6,630	7,887
	14,630	15,887
Transfer price of ordinary shares	£0.90	£1.10

Required
a Calculate for both years:
   i)   gross margin
   ii)   net margin
   iii)   operating expense/sales
   iv)   return on capital employed
   v)   current ratio
   vi)   liquid ratio
   vii)   interest cover
   viii) dividend cover
   ix)   earnings per share
   x)   price/earnings ratio
   xi)   gearing ratio
   xii)   dividend yield
   xiii) rate of stock turn
   xiv)   debtors ratio.
b Comment on ratios (vii)–(xi).

QUESTION 14

The following final accounts are provided to the year ended 31 August for Catas and Trofy Ltd:

	20*3 £000	20*3 £000	20*3 £000	20*4 £000	20*4 £000	20*4 £000
Sales (credit)			2,773			3,390
Less Cost of sales						
Stock		166			184	
Purchases (credit)		1,970			2,250	
		2,136			2,434	
Stock		184	1,952		198	2,236
Gross profit			821			1,154
Less:						
Admin, selling and distribution expenses			(455)			(584)
Operating profit			366			570
Interest payable			(11)			(33)
Profit before taxation			355			537
Taxation			(120)			(190)
Profit after tax			235			347
Preference dividend		(9)			(9)	
Ordinary dividend		(70)	(79)		(130)	(139)
Retained profits for year			156			208

Balance sheet as at 31 August

	20*3 £000	20*3 £000	20*3 £000	20*4 £000	20*4 £000	20*4 £000
Fixed assets						
Net book value			870			1,450
Current assets						
Stock		184			198	
Debtors		380			510	
Balance at bank		266			210	
		830			918	
Creditors: falling due in less than one year						
Trade creditors	(220)			(330)		
Taxation	(120)			(190)		
Dividends	(79)	(419)	411	(139)	(659)	259
			1,281			1,709
Creditors: falling due in more than one year						
10% debentures			(110)			(330)
			1,171			1,379
Share capital and reserves						
Ordinary shares of £1 each			700			700
6% preference shares			150			150
Share premium			70			70
Profit and loss account			251			459
			1,171			1,379
Market price per share			£1.40			£2.10

Required

a   Calculate for both years (state the formulae used):
  i)   gross margin
  ii)   net margin
  iii)   operating expenses to sales
  iv)   return on capital employed
  v)   current ratio
  vi)   liquid ratio
  vii)   interest cover
  viii) dividend cover
  ix)   earnings per share
  x)   price/earnings ratio
  xi)   gearing ratio
  xii)   dividend yield.
b   Calculate for the year ended 31 August 20*4:
  xiii) rate of stock turn
  xiv)   debtors ratio
  xv)   creditors ratio.

QUESTION 15

The following final accounts are provided for the year ended 30 November for two businesses:
Del Tipper (a sole trader) and Tanka Continental Traders Ltd:

Profit and loss accounts for the year ended 30 November 20*4

| | Del Tipper | | Tanka Continental Traders Ltd | |
	£	£	£000	£000
Sales		136,000		1,030
Less Cost of sales:				
Stock	2,900		140	
Purchases (credit)	60,000		460	
	62,900		600	
Stock	1,100	61,800	160	440
Gross profit		74,200		590
Operating expenses		(34,000)		(280)
Net profit		40,200		310

Balance sheets as at 30 November 20*4

| | Del Tipper | | Tanka Continental Traders Ltd | |
	£	£	£000	£000
Fixed assets		110,000		700
Current assets				
Stock	1,100		160	
Trade debtors	5,500		120	
Bank balance	8,000		85	
	14,600		365	
Current liabilities				
Trade creditors	(1,250)	13,350	(250)	115
		123,350		815
Capital		123,350	**Share capital and reserves**	
			Ordinary shares	500
			Profit and loss account	315
				815

Additional information

Both Del and Tanka Continental Traders Ltd are in the same line of business. Both businesses purchase and sell all goods on credit.

Del manages his own business. If he were to work outside the business he would have to employ a manager to run his business. The manager would have to be paid £18,000 per annum.

If Del sold his business he could earn 8% on any capital invested.

Required

a Calculate for both businesses:
 i)   gross margin
 ii) net margin
 iii) expenses/sales ratio
 iv) return on capital employed
 v)   current ratio
 vi) liquid ratio
 vii) debtors ratio
 viii) creditors ratio
 ix) rate of stock turn.
b Comment on your results.
c Advise Del on the best way of maximising his income in the future.

QUESTION 16

The following balance sheets as at 31 August are given for Pawar Ltd:

	20*4 £000	20*4 £000	20*4 £000	20*5 £000	20*5 £000	20*5 £000
Fixed assets						
Freehold property at valuation			3,600			4,000
Plant and machinery at cost	2,820			4,925		
Less Provision for depreciation	1,160	1,660		2,040	2,885	
Vehicles at cost	1,450			2,890		
Less Provision for depreciation	670	780		850	2,040	
Office equipment at cost	220			660		
Less Provision for depreciation	110	110		140	520	
			6,150			9,445
Current assets						
Stock		905			1,160	
Debtors		370			520	
Bank		1,280			1,250	
		2,555			2,930	
Creditors: amounts due within one year						
Trade creditors	(160)			(325)		
Tax	(505)			(412)		
Proposed dividend	(430)	(1,095)	1,460	(480)	(1,217)	1,713
Total assets less current liabilities			7,610			11,158
Creditors: amounts falling due after more than one year						
7% debenture stock			(700)			(1,600)
			6,910			9,558
Capital and reserves						
Ordinary shares of £1 each			2,600			2,600
6% preference shares of £1 each			1,000			3,000
Share premium			110			110
Revaluation reserve			550			950
Asset replacement reserve			900			900
Profit and loss account			1,750			1,998
			6,910			9,558
Market price per share			£2.50			£3.00

Profit and loss account extract for the year ended 31 August 20*5

	£000	£000
Operating profit		1,562
Interest payable		(112)
Profit before taxation		1,450
Taxation		(412)
Profit after taxation		1,038
Dividends – preference – paid	(90)	
proposed	(90)	
ordinary – paid	(220)	
proposed	(390)	(790)
Retained profit for year		248

Required

a Calculate for both years:
  i)   current ratio
  ii) liquid ratio
  iii) gearing ratio.
b Calculate for year ended 31 August 20*5 only:
  i)   interest cover
  ii) dividend cover
  iii) earnings per share
  iv) price /earnings raio
  v)   dividend yield.
c Explain what is meant by:
  i)   earnings per share
  ii) price/earnings ratio
  iii) dividend yield.

Business Ownership

Business activity takes place within organisations with varied legal structures. The status of ownership of a business will determine what financial records must be kept and how they must be presented. For example, there is no legal requirement for a sole trader or a partnership to produce a set of final accounts. However, it has long been accepted that it is in the best interests of sole traders and partnerships to produce a full set of accounts in order to be able to provide the information that might be required by the Inland Revenue and/or Customs and Excise. This would be a good idea because of the functions of accounting (remember the stewardship and management functions).

Sole traders and partnerships might also want to produce a set of accounts in order to make it easier for them to review their performance in financial terms and perhaps to help them to predict the impact of any suggested changes in their business strategy. In the event of a sole trader or a partnership approaching a bank manager to ask for a loan, they might be asked to present a set of accounts so that the bank manager can make a judgement about whether or not the business is secure enough for them to agree a loan safely.

Many businesses in the United Kingdom are formed as sole traders and although this type of ownership is usually associated with small businesses, that need not necessarily be the case.

The status of sole trader simply means that one person retains total ownership and control of the business.

Specification coverage:
AQA 14.5; OCR 5.2.6.

By the end of this chapter you should be able to:
- distinguish between different types of business ownership
- identify the advantages and disadvantages of the different types of ownership.

ADVANTAGES OF BEING A SOLE TRADER

1. The owner retains total control of business decisions.
2. Decision-making might be faster because only one person makes all key decisions.
3. The owner will receive all the profits generated by the business.
4. It is easy to set up, as starting a business as a sole trader does not involve many complicated procedures and/or documentation. The individual must notify the Inland Revenue that they intend to be self-employed.

DISADVANTAGES OF BEING A SOLE TRADER

1. Although decision-making might be faster, the sole trader might lose out on the benefit of discussion before decisions are made.
2. Just as the owner might receive all the profits, they must also bear all the losses of the business.
3. Sole traders have unlimited liability. This means that in the event of the business having debts that cannot be met from the resources within the business, the owner remains liable for the outstanding debt, even if this means selling personal possessions in order to settle it.
4. Sole traders experience limited access to finance. This is often restricted to what can be raised from personal savings and contacts and from bank loans.
5. However, this disadvantage has been partially offset in recent years as a result of the government and European Union grants that have been made available to small businesses.
6. Lack of continuity. If the owner dies or retires, the business ceases to exist.

It is the lack of access to finance that has led many sole traders to take in a partner, or partners, who might not only introduce more ideas to the business but often bring in crucial additional finance. It is extremely rare for any individual to give financial support to a business without requiring something in return. So, what would someone putting money into a business expect?

Obviously, they hope for a return on their investment and in order to give some peace of mind regarding the security of their investment, they will usually want a 'say' in the running of the business, ie some control over business decisions, so meaning that they acquire part-ownership of the business. They become a partner in the business.

The status of the business has now become that of a partnership.

ADVANTAGES OF A PARTNERSHIP

1. Access to additional finance.
2. The introduction of more ideas into the business.
3. The opportunity for discussion to take place before any key decisions are made. This might make decisions more informed.
4. Partnerships can allow for more continuity of business activity, for example when one partner is on holiday or perhaps ill, the remaining partner(s) can ensure that the business continues to function as normal.
5. The introduction of a partner(s) might allow some specialisation to take place, as perhaps each of the partners can specialise in the aspect of the business in which they are most competent.
6. Relatively easy to set up. Setting up a partnership does not require lots of documentation and legal processes to be completed.

DISADVANTAGES OF A PARTNERSHIP

1. Finance is still only mainly available from the partners' personal sources and contacts together with bank loans and any grants that might be available.
2. Agreement might be more difficult to arrive at when decisions need to be made. The more people that are involved in making a decision, the more views there are likely to be and therefore reaching a concensus might slow the decision-making process down.
3. Profits now need to be shared between the partners. This is done in agreed profit-sharing ratios.
4. Partnerships still have unlimited liability, which leaves the personal possessions of all the partners at risk if the business were to be declared insolvent. There is the possibility of forming a limited partnership (see later).
5. Lack of continuity of the business entity. If a partner retires or dies, the partnership (and therefore the business) ceases to exist in its previous form and a new business must be formed if trading is to continue. (See Dissolution of partnerships in Chapter Five.)
6. All partners are liable for the actions of others. They are jointly and severally liable. This means that if the actions of one partner result in debts for the business, all the partners are liable to repay that debt even though they might not have been consulted about the action that had caused the debt.

   For example, you set up a business in partnership with a friend who then, unknown to you, takes out a large bank loan on behalf of the business. However, the money is never used for the business; instead your 'friend' disappears to live in the sun, using the bank loan to buy a house and to finance a rich lifestyle. What happens to the bank loan in a case like this? If your partner cannot be found and the money retrieved, then you, as the remaining partner in the business, will be held liable to repay the whole of the debt to the bank. It is then not surprising that people will tell you that you should not consider going into business with anyone, unless you would trust them with your last penny: that is exactly what they might take, if the situation above occurred – and occasionally it does!

Many partnerships draw up a legally binding document known as a **deed of partnership** that outlines the key terms that have been agreed with regard to such things as how profits are to be shared and perhaps the terms of loans to the business from the partners. It might also include details of the valuation of goodwill and other assets in the case of any structural change.

It should be noted that in cases where a deed of partnership has not been drawn up and a dispute occurs that cannot be resolved by the partners, the dispute will be resolved by recourse to law, ie the Partnership Act 1890. The terms of this Act would then over-rule any verbal agreements that might have been made by the partners. For example, two partners might have verbally agreed a profit-sharing ratio of 3:1 but the Partnership Act 1890 would impose equal sharing of profits unless there was sufficient evidence to prove that the ratio of 3:1 had been the usual practice over a number of years. Therefore, if any partnership wants to agree terms that are not consistent with the Partnership Act then it is advisable that the partners outline all such terms in a deed of partnership that would then be binding on them all.

The situation of partners being 'jointly and severally liable' might be just the kind of eventuality that partners would want to protect themselves from. This might be easier for partners who are fully involved in the business on a day-to-day basis. What about partners who have put money into a business but who are not involved in the everyday activity of the business? How do they protect themselves? One way is for the partnership to give them **limited liability** covered under the Limited Partnerships Act of 1907. This Act provides for the personal possessions of partners to be protected in the event of insolvency. However, it also states that at least one partner must have unlimited liability. Limited partnerships are usually formed when someone is willing to inject money into the business, but they do not want, or are not able, to take any part in the running of the business. In the case of a limited partnership, the liability for the debts of the business is limited, to the amount invested, for those partners with limited liability. This offers some security to people who are willing to invest in a partnership but who want to protect themselves from situations similar to the one outlined above. It is often the case that the only partner(s) afforded limited liability are those who put money into the business without actively participating in the business. They are sometimes known as 'sleeping partners'.

Many partnerships can suffer from the same financial starvation as some sole traders because of the limited sources of finance to which they have access. It is for this reason that sometimes people who do not intend to have any involvement in the day-to-day running of the business are approached for financial support – more partners with limited liability.

A change from a partnership into a limited company can meet the needs of those who do not wish to put their personal assets at risk by involvement in a business venture. A change to a limited company gives all the owners limited liability. There are two types of limited companies:

■ private limited company
■ public limited company.

The process of establishing a limited company, whether private or public, requires the submission of specified documents to the Registrar of Companies. Each company must produce a memorandum of association and articles of association.

A **memorandum of association** is a document that must be filed with the Registrar of Companies before the company can become incorporated. It defines the external relationship of the company to the outside world.

The details filed include:

■ the company's name, address and registered office
■ details of the share capital
■ the company's objectives.

Articles of association state the company's rules which will govern the internal organisation of the company. Details include:

■ organisation and control
■ shareholders' voting rights
■ conduct of directors' meetings
■ conduct of shareholders' annual general meeting
■ directors' powers
■ rights attached to different types of shares.

In the case of a private limited company once these documents have been accepted by the Registrar of Companies, a certificate of incorporation will be issued. Once this formality is completed, a private limited company can begin to trade. However, in the case of a public limited company a prospectus will have to be prepared before shares can be issued for sale to the public.

At this point we need to remind ourselves of the key features and differences between a private limited company and a public limited company by referring to Chapter Six.

Chapter summary

- Businesses differ in their legal structure sometimes according to the number of people involved, eg a sole trader involves only one person whereas a partnership involves between two and 20 people (20 being the maximum for a normal business). This raises issues regarding the ownership and control of a business.
- Businesses can also differ with regard to whether or not they have limited or unlimited liability.

Self-test questions

- State two advantages of being a sole trader.
- State two disadvantages of being a sole trader.
- State two advantages of being in partnership.
- State two disadvantages of being in partnership.
- When did the Partnership Act become law?
- When did the Limited Partnership Act become law?
- Sole traders have limited liability. True or false?
- Partners have unlimited liability. True or false?
- What does the term 'jointly and severally liable' mean?
- State how profits are to be shared if there is no partnership deed drawn up by partners.
- The owners of a limited company are known as partners. True or false?
- Identify two items stated in a company's memorandum of association.
- Identify two items stated in a company's articles of association.
- The owners of a limited company have limited liability. True or false?

CHAPTER
ELEVEN

Sources of Finance

Finding initial or additional finance is the concern of many businesses at some time or other in their existence.

There are many different sources of finance available but not all of them are accessible to all businesses. Accessibility of finance can depend on the legal status of the business and the amount of security that the business can offer to the potential lender.

Specification coverage:
AQA 14.5; OCR 5.2.6.

By the end of this chapter you should be able to:
- assess different types of business finance
- appreciate the relevance of the various sources of finance for different forms of business ownership.

PERSONAL FINANCE

Personal savings are often used to provide the first injection of money into a business, however, this is usually a very limited source and there is sometimes a need for finance to be acquired from additional sources. This is often the only source of finance when a person is establishing a business as a sole trader. It is important to recognise that the amount of money made available to a business can often be determined by the degree of risk involved in the investment. The element of risk is reduced for the investor in a company, as business ownership provides for limited liability in the event of the business becoming insolvent. However, in the case of a sole trader, using personal savings to start up or expand a business, their liability in the case of insolvency is unlimited.

FUNDS FROM FRIENDS AND FAMILY

In the early stages of establishing a business, owners frequently seek the help of family and friends to provide some of the required finance. While such contacts might be willing to show their confidence in the business, they might want some security for their investment. This is often the cause of a business that was established as a sole trader transforming its legal status into that of a partnership. By making the providers of finance partners in the business they will now have some control over its day-to-day running and so can, to some extent, protect their investment. However, there is still the possibility that investors might lose all of the money invested because partnerships have unlimited liability and so their personal possessions might also be under threat in the event of the business becoming insolvent. (See Chapter Nine for limited partnerships.)

OVERDRAFT

This is a short-term source of finance obtained from banks. Most businesses will have agreed an overdraft limit prior to any need to use it arising. It is in the interest of businesses to agree an overdraft limit with their bank just in case they find it necessary to use this source of finance. This is because the interest charged on an authorised (agreed) overdraft is usually less than if they had not agreed (unauthorised) an overdraft facility in advance.

It is advisable for businesses to try to negotiate an overdraft limit that is slightly greater than any amount that they feel they might need. This is in order to prevent them going beyond the authorised overdraft limit and so incurring higher charges.

The rate of interest charged on overdrafts tends to be higher than that charged on long-term borrowing, so for this reason a business is only likely to want to use an overdraft in the short term. Although an overdraft could conceivably be maintained in the longer term, it would be an expensive way of raising finance when compared with say, a bank loan. Providers of overdrafts do not require the level of security that they would require when granting a bank loan and therefore the level of risk is much higher for them. The rate of interest charged on overdrafts reflects this higher degree of risk. An overdraft is often used when the amount of additional finance required can only be calculated approximately and the period for which it is required is estimated to be short. If the circumstances of the business are such that the owners feel that they might need additional finance for a longer period of time than would be advisable when using an overdraft, they might then apply to their bank for a loan.

BANK LOANS (SHORT-TERM AND LONG-TERM)

The benefits of arranging a bank loan rather than using an overdraft are that the bank usually charges a lower rate of interest on the amount borrowed. The loan is taken out for an agreed period of time and the repayments are usually for an agreed amount at specified intervals during the loan. The most common arrangement is for equal monthly repayments over the duration of the loan. However, varied arrangements can be made with the lender. For example, some banks might agree to smaller payments being made in the first two or three years of a 15-year loan, with the repayments gradually increasing towards the end of the term. This can allow time for an investment to begin to produce a return before the larger payments need to be paid.

Banks will usually require some collateral (security) for their loan and so loans are often secured by the business's buildings (or homes in the case of sole traders and partnerships). In the event of the loan not being repaid, the bank would seize the item on which the loan had been secured. It is not uncommon for a bank to require the deeds to property to be handed over to it until the loan is repaid in full. This reduces the risk to the lender because if the business does not repay the loan then they can sell the business property (or the owner's house) if necessary to get their money back. While many loans are for a five- or 10-year period, the length of a business loan is dependent on the amount being borrowed and the length of time for which a lender is willing to lend. Banks usually lend to businesses at approximately 3–4% above their base rate but this again varies with the amount of risk and the length of the loan.

Even though a bank might hold the deeds to the business's property, the loan does not give it any say in the day-to-day running of the business. Therefore, by using a bank loan to raise additional finance, a business is not sacrificing any ownership or control of the business to the outside providers of finance.

ISSUE OF SHARES

When a business raises additional finance through the issue of shares it is actually selling off part of the business. The ownership of the business passes to the shareholders. (If you buy some shares in a business this means that you have bought a 'share' or a 'part' of that business.) For this reason, businesses who choose to raise additional finance through the issue of shares are very careful not to sell too many shares and thus to allow the overall ownership and control of the business to be taken by investors. Theoretically, if the original owners of a business retain 50% plus one share, they would have the deciding vote of key issues because they would always have one more vote than all of the other shareholders put together (assuming that one share equals one vote).

The way in which shares can be sold differs depending on whether the business is a private limited company or a public limited company.

■ Private limited company

In a private limited company shares can be purchased only through private agreements. They cannot be offered for sale to the general public through the Stock Exchange. This can limit the amount of finance that can be made available through the sale of shares.

■ Public limited company

A public limited company can extend the range of people to whom it can offer its shares for sale. Once it has satisfied all the requirements of the Stock Exchange, its shares can be bought and sold by the general public through the stock market.

Note: When shares are issued by a company for the first time, all monies paid for those shares will go to the business in question. However, if the original purchasers decide to sell their shares, the money paid by the next owner of the shares does not go into the company but to the seller of the shares (usually a stock broker). It is similar to Ford selling a car to a Ford garage. When the garage first purchases the car from Ford, the company, Ford, will receive the money. The garage then sells the car to a customer. The garage keeps the money paid for the car, together with any profit that it has made on the deal – just as if it had bought shares in Ford and later sold them for a profit. Many years later, that same car might have changed ownership four or five times. Each time a sale is made, the seller of the car receives the amount paid for the car – none of the money ever goes to the Ford company after that first sale of the car to the garage (the first owner).

This is a common area of misunderstanding for students, particularly when they discuss a fall in share prices; comments are often made by students about the business losing money if the share price falls or that a rise in share prices means more money going into the business. From the example above, I hope that you can see that this is not the case.

DEBENTURES

Debentures are long-term loans made to companies. The loans are made at an agreed rate of interest. The holders of debentures will receive interest payments, usually annually, on the amount loaned. At the end of the agreed period of the loan, the capital sum will be repaid to the lender. This is an efficient way of raising finance for a business as only the interest has to be paid until the time when the repayment is due. For the lender, debentures carry less risk than buying ordinary shares because, in the event of bankruptcy, they will be paid out of the company's assets before any monies are paid to shareholders. However, the downside to this is that if the business begins to gain large profits, that allow it to make bigger dividend payments to shareholders, the debenture holders will continue to receive the same amount of interest that they agreed at the start and they will not gain any additional return as a result of increasing profitability. This is the sacrifice they make for having more security.

VENTURE CAPITAL

This is finance made available by individuals who are looking for return on their money, perhaps from investing in more risky ventures.

GOVERNMENT GRANTS

In a bid to encourage the survival and growth of different sectors of the economy, the Government has, at times, made various grants available to businesses. Such grants have varied with regard to the reason for their being given. Some grants have been given specifically for the purchase of new capital equipment while others have been made available for training the workforce. The type of grant available to a business can depend on what the Government sees as a priority in the economy at that time and also which part of the country the business is in. Some parts of the country are seen to need more help than others when it comes to support for businesses. For example, an area of high unemployment is likely to attract more Government funds than an affluent area that has little or no unemployment.

Grants for various businesses have also been made available through the European Union, again perhaps depending on the factors outlined above.

It is important to realise that the same grants are not always available, as their availability can vary with the economic status of the area in which the business is situated and the needs of other areas either within the United Kingdom or within Europe in the case of a grant from the EU.

TAX ALLOWANCES

The Inland Revenue allows businesses to offset certain of their expenses against their tax liability. For example, businesses can claim a percentage allowance against capital equipment being used in the business or an allowance for contributions made to the pension funds of their employees.

These allowances are implemented by the Inland Revenue and can vary according to what the Government hopes to achieve in the economy at the time. At times, the Government seeks to encourage the introduction of automated production processes or the increased use of information technology in all aspects of business. At such times the Inland Revenue is likely to be allowing a greater percentage of the cost of such investments to be offset (treated as an expense) against any tax that the business is deemed liable to pay. As such allowances are deducted from net profit, this reduces the amount of profit on which the business must pay tax and therefore leaves more money in the business as retained profits.

HIRE PURCHASE

Hire purchase is a means by which a business can acquire assets without paying the full amount at the time of acquisition. Although it is not a source of additional finance for a business, it does allow businesses to conserve any funds that they might have for use elsewhere. When assets are purchased using this method the purchaser would usually pay a deposit followed by regular payments until the full amount has been paid. Until the final purchase is made, the purchaser is legally only 'hiring' the equipment, hence the name 'hire purchase'. When the final payment is made, ownership passes from the vendor to the purchaser. This method of purchasing assets also usually involves the payment of interest on the amount due.

MORTGAGE

A mortgage is usually used to acquire high-value assets whose cost is greater than the current finance available within the business. It is a long-term loan most frequently used for the purchase of the business's buildings. The provider of the mortgage uses the building being purchased as collateral to secure the loan. In the event of a business being unable to finance the regular payments required, the lender would have the right to sell the building in order to recoup their money.

LEASING

This is a means of having the use of assets without ever having to own them. They can be leased (borrowed) from a leasing company. Again, regular payments will need to be made by the business in order to secure the continued use of the asset.

Hire purchase, mortgage and leasing allow businesses to budget because these methods are supported by regular payments being made on the part of the business.

Note: Although assets that are being leased and those that are being purchased on hire purchase technically do not belong to the business, they should nevertheless be included on the business balance sheet since they are being used to generate profits. This is an application of the principle of 'substance over form'. (This is when the person who gains the benefit from the use of an asset is not the legal owner of that asset.)

SALE AND LEASEBACK

Times of cash shortage can sometimes be alleviated by the sale of assets bringing in a lump sum of money realised by their sale. Such assets can then be acquired through a lease company for use in the business. In this way the business gets the money released by the sale of assets and then makes regular (usually monthly) payments for use of the required assets on a lease basis.

One point to remember here is that if a business sells off assets in order, for example, to resolve a cash flow problem, that problem might be solved in the short term but that it can prove to be more expensive to the business in the longer term. This is because previously the business owned the asset but now it must make payments for as long as use of the asset is required. In the short term cash flows in but in the longer term money flows out on a regular basis and for as long as the business wants to use the asset. There is also a danger that when the lease expires the new owner may not renew it, perhaps leaving a business needing to find alternative accommodation and/or equipment.

RETAINED PROFIT

This is probably the most important source of finance for a business because it is this source that ensures that the business is self-financing. If a business constantly has to rely on injections of external finance (from relatives, banks, shares issue, issues of debentures etc) then this source might eventually dry up and if the business is not profitable the result might be its liquidation.

Charles Dickens said many years ago in one of his books that an income of £20 per year(!) with expenditure of £19.99 per year would result in happiness. However, an income of £20 per year with expenditure of £20.01 would result in misery!

If you earn £100 per week from a job and you are spending £120 on a regular basis you will become reliant on external finance to fund your lifestyle. There will come a time when parents and friends are no longer willing to subsidise your activities. The same principle applies in the case of a business.

Note: When finance is raised from a source that incurs an interest charge, the interest should be charged to the profit and loss account and any capital repayments reduce the amount owed as shown on the balance sheet.

For example, Tom makes a payment of £21,000 to his business mortgage provider. The payment is made up of £1,000 of interest and the remainder is a repayment of part of the capital sum. The financial recording of this transaction would be that £1,000 is charged to the profit and loss account and his long-term liability on the balance sheet would be reduced by £20,000.

● EXAMINATION TIP

When a question asks you to identify sources of finance for a business, take careful note of the legal status of the business in question. The source of finance that you suggest must be one that is available to that particular type of business. Do not suggest that a sole trader raises additional capital by issuing shares, for example, as this source of finance is not available to them unless they change the legal structure of the business and form a limited company.

Chapter summary

- There are many ways in which businesses can raise capital.
- Some are available only to limited companies, eg finance raised from the issue of shares and debentures.
- Other forms of finance are available to all types of business.
- You will have noticed that many of the sources of capital are external to the business but that businesses can also be funded internally by using retained profits.
- Funds can be retained within a business by financing certain activities by using hire purchase, leases etc.

Self-test questions

- Name two sources of finance that are available to a sole trader.
- Why might someone worry about putting money into a partnership if they were not going to take any part in the day-to-day running of the business?
- What type of business is allowed to issue shares for sale to the general public?
- To whom can a private limited company sell shares?
- Which form of finance is likely to carry a lower rate of interest: a five-year bank loan or an overdraft?
- Explain why using hire purchase is regarded as a source of finance.
- Outline one benefit of using sale and leaseback.
- Identify one advantage that a government grant has over a long-term bank loan.
- Name one disadvantage of acquiring finance from a relative.
- Explain why a sole trader cannot issue ordinary shares to the general public.
- Why might a Government give a tax allowance to businesses in the northeast of England and not to businesses in the south of England?
- Explain how interest to service a long-term bank loan and capital repayments of the bank loan are treated in a set of final accounts.

CHAPTER
TWELVE

The Valuation of Stock

In *Introducing Accounting* we considered the valuation of the current asset of stock. We said that the over-riding principle that should be used at all times is that stock should be valued at the lower of cost or net realisable value.

Since this principle causes so many problems to students it is worth a moment's revision.

SSAP 9 *Stocks and long-term contracts* defines cost as 'the expenditure which has been incurred in the normal course of business in bringing the product or service to its present location and condition'.

The standard defines net realisable value as 'the estimated proceeds from the sale of items of stock less all further costs to completion and less all costs to be incurred in marketing, selling and distributing . . . the items'.

Specification coverage:
AQA 14.4; OCR 5.2.3.

By the end of this chapter you should be able to:
- understand the main methods of valuing stock using LIFO, FIFO and AVCO methods
- calculate the effect of different methods of stock valuation on profit
- calculate the value of closing stock when stock-taking takes place after the financial year-end.

WORKED EXAMPLE

Daphne Baird sells one type of vacuum cleaner. They cost £80 each to purchase. At 31 March 20*5 she has 14 cleaners in stock. The cleaners usually sell for £120 each.

Daphne has one cleaner in stock that is damaged. She intends to have the cleaner repaired at a cost of £35. It can then be sold for £100.

REQUIRED
Calculate the value of Daphne's closing stock as at 31 March 20*5.

ANSWER
Daphne's stock should be valued at £1,105.

Workings	£	£
13 cleaners at £80 each		1,040
1 damaged cleaner		
Selling price	100	
Less Repair costs	35	65
		1,105

Up to now we have valued most stocks at cost and net realisable value.

Fairly straightforward – or is it?

Consider the following example.

Jitesh sells only one product: a 'sedrit'. He provides the following information:

Purchases of sedrits		Sales of sedrits	
January	2 at £10 each	May	4 at £30 each
April	3 at £15 each	December	3 at £35 each
November	4 at £20 each		

You can see that Jitesh has two sedrits remaining in stock at 31 December.

How should he value the two sedrits remaining in stock?

He should value them at cost!

Should he choose to value them at £10 each; or £15 each; or £20 each; or one at £10 the other at £15; or ...?

You can see that there are many combinations that we could choose when valuing Jitesh's closing stock.

So valuing stock at cost is not quite so simple as it first seems. The total purchases figure for the year is £145 and the total sales revenue for the year is £225. We could prepare a trading account if we could decide on a method by which we could value the closing stock.

In the example used above it might be fairly straightforward to identify the actual units of sedrits that had been sold and hence identify the two remaining in the business. However, if we had many hundreds of items available for sale this would be well-nigh impossible.

Most businesses will be unable to identify with any precision the actual items that they have remaining in stock at the end of their financial year, and even if they could it would be a mammoth task to go back through purchase invoices to determine the price paid for each item of stock.

The valuation of stock is therefore a matter of expediency rather than strict accuracy.

So in the valuation of closing stocks we do not trace through the actual units that have been sold; rather, we identify certain items of stock that are deemed to be sold and therefore certain items of stock are deemed to remain in stock.

The following methods are most frequently used to identify the goods deemed to have been issued to either a final customer or another department within the same business.

'FIRST IN, FIRST OUT' METHOD OF VALUING STOCK (FIFO)

As the name suggests, this method **assumes** that the **first** goods received by the business will be the **first** ones to be delivered to the final customer or the department requisitioning the goods. It assumes that goods have been used in the order in which they were purchased. Therefore any remaining stock will be valued as if it were the latest stock purchased.

Remember that this is only an assumption.

This is a method of valuing stock – it is not necessarily the way that goods are actually issued. Goods may be issued in any way that best suits a particular business regardless of when stocks were received.

EXAMPLE

A garage mechanic requires a set of spark plugs to fit into the car he is working on. The store keeper in the parts department will issue the first set of plugs he can lay his hands on; he will not waste time seeking out the first set of plugs bought in to give to the mechanic.

'LAST IN, FIRST OUT' METHOD OF ISSUING STOCK (LIFO)

This method assumes that the **last** goods to be purchased are the **first** ones to be issued to the final customer or requisitioning department. This means that the valuation of stock will begin by using the value of the earliest stock purchased.

WEIGHTED AVERAGE COST METHOD OF ISSUING STOCK (AVCO)

The average cost of goods held is recalculated each time a new delivery of goods is received. Issues are then priced out at a weighted average cost.

METHODS OF VALUING CLOSING STOCKS

Some businesses keep extremely detailed records of the stocks that they hold.

Every transaction affecting the purchase and sale of stock is recorded in great detail.

The value of stock is then recalculated after each transaction. (The stock records look rather like a bank statement.)

The method of recalculating the value of stock held after each transaction is known as the **perpetual** method.

This method is used by businesses that need to cost their work out to customers very carefully. It is also used in the major supermarkets. Each time a transaction is 'swiped' at the check-outs the bar code is read and the stock records are updated electronically to record the sale (stock issue). Each time a delivery arrives in the warehouse the goods received will be 'swiped' and the stock records will be updated with the receipt of stock.

Other less sophisticated businesses may simply value their stock once, at the financial year-end. The owner of your local newsagents or take-away will probably take stock at close of business at their year-end. They will list all items remaining unsold on the last day of the financial year; they will then assign a value to each category of goods in stock and the total of all goods in stock will give the closing stock figure to be used in the final accounts.

This is known as a **periodic** method of stock valuation.

Let us examine the results given when we use a perpetual method of stock valuation.

WORKED EXAMPLE

During the month of February the following receipts and issues of the component SMH/19 took place:

	Receipts of SMH/19	Issues of SMH/19
2 February	8 @ £10	
7 February		6
9 February	9 @ £11	
16 February		10
24 February	7 @ £12	
27 February		6

Required Calculate the value of closing stock of component SMH/19, using the 'first in, first out' method of valuing stock (FIFO).

Answer
The value of closing stock using the FIFO method of issue is £24.00.

Date	Receipts	Issues	Balance
2 February	8 @ £10		£80.00 (8 @ £10)
7 February		6	£20.00 (2 @ £10)
9 February	9 @ £11		£119.00 (2 @ £10; 9 @ £11)
16 February		10	£11.00 (1 @ £11)
24 February	7 @ £12		£~~194.00~~ 95 00 (1 @ £11; 7 @ £12)
27 February		6	£24.00 (2 @ £12)

WORKED EXAMPLE

Using the same data for February shown above:

Required Calculate the value of closing stock of component SMH/19, using the
'last in, first out' method of valuing stock (LIFO).

Answer
The value of valuing closing stock using the LIFO method of issue is £22.00

Date	Receipts	Issues	Balance
2 February	8 @ £10		£80.00 (8 @ £10)
7 February		6	£20.00 (2 @ £10)
9 February	9 @ £11		£119.00 (2 @ £10; 9 @ £11)
16 February		10	£10.00 (1 @ £10)
24 February	7 @ £12		£94.00 (1 @ £10; 7 @ £12)
27 February		6	£22.00 (1 @ £10; 1 @ £12)

WORKED EXAMPLE

Using the same data for February shown above:

Required Calculate the value of closing stock of component SMH/19, using the
weighted average cost method of valuing stock (AVCO).

Answer
The value of closing stock of component SMH/19 using the weighted average cost
(AVCO) method of issuing stock is £23.70.

Date	Receipts	Issues	Balance
2 February	8 @ £10		£80.00 (8 @ £10)
7 February		6	£20.00 (2 @ £10)
9 February	9 @ £11		£119.00 (Average cost £119.00/11 = £10.82)
16 February		10	£10.82 (£10.82 × 1)
24 February	7 @ £12		£94.82 (Average cost £94.82/8 = £11.85)
27 February		6	£23.70 (£11.85 × 2)

Check each of the methods shown above. They are regularly examined at Advanced Level.

Since each method gives a different closing stock figure, it follows that different gross profits will
be revealed by using different methods of valuing stocks to the customer.

Imagine that component SMH/19 has been sold for £20 per unit.

What would be the gross profit be for each method of issue?

	FIFO		LIFO		AVCO	
	£	£	£	£	£	£
Sales		440.00		440.00		440.00
Less Cost of sales						
Opening stock	0		0		0	
Purchases	263.00		263.00		263.00	
	263.00		263.00		263.00	
Less Closing stock	24.00	239.00	22.00	241.00	23.70	239.30
Gross profit		201.00		199.00		200.70

The level of profits revealed in a set of final accounts always depends on the way the stock has
been valued.

● EXAMINATION TIP

If you alter the value of closing stock, you will alter reported profits.

- If you **increase** the value of closing stock . . . you will **increase** reported profit.

- If you **decrease** the value of closing stock . . . you will **decrease** reported profit.

Notice that FIFO reveals the highest profits; LIFO reveals the lowest profits; while AVCO gives a profit figure
between the two extremes. (However, do note that this is the case only where purchase prices are rising over
the period under review.)

Now we will calculate the closing stock using the **periodic** method.

Remember that this method uses only one valuation – at the end of the period being considered.

In the example used above, we consider February as one complete time period (usually the trader will value stock at the end of a full financial year).

USING FIFO

24 SMH/19 components were purchased during February and 22 were issued, so at the end of the month there were two remaining in stock. Using FIFO, we assume that the first components were the first ones to be issued. The two components that are remaining in stock are deemed to be from the last ones purchased. Closing stock is therefore deemed to consist of two from the last batch purchased. Closing stock is valued at £24.00 (2 × £12).

We have arrived at the same figure that we calculated using the perpetual method – coincidence? No: FIFO will give the same result whether you use the perpetual or the periodic method.

USING LIFO

The last components are deemed to be the first ones sold, so any remaining in stock are assumed to be from the first purchases made. The closing stock of components is valued at £20.00 (2 × £10.00).

You will notice that this is a different value to that calculated using the perpetual method.

USING AVCO

Sorry – there is no shorter version of calculating closing stock when an average price is taken for issuing stock.

Should you use the periodic method or the perpetual method when answering an examination question? Always use the method you find easiest. Use the method you are most comfortable using. Since the periodic method is, I think, easier, I would use it every time for FIFO and LIFO calculations, **unless** the question specifically requires the perpetual method.

QUESTION 1

The following information is available for the purchases and sales of 'pomsels' during October. At 30 September one 'pomsel' costing £100 remained in stock.

Date	Purchases	Sales
4 October	6 at £100	
7 October		4
12 October	5 at £110	
23 October		6
24 October	7 at £120	
30 October		6

During October the selling price for 'pomsels' was £200.

Required
a Calculate the value of 'pomsels' in stock, using:
   (i) the 'first in, first out' (FIFO) method of valuing stock
   (ii) the 'last in, first out' (LIFO) method of valuing stock
   (iii) the weighted average stock (AVCO) method of valuing stock.
   Use a perpetual method for each calculation.
b Prepare a trading account for each method, using your results from (a).

QUESTION 2

The following information relates to the purchases and issues of 'giottas' during December. At 30 November there were three 'giottas' in stock; they had each cost £6 when purchased.

Date	Purchases	Issues
2 December	4 at £6	
13 December		6
15 December	5 at £8	
17 December		4
20 December	8 at £10	
30 December		7

During December the selling price of 'giottas' was £25 each.

Required
a Calculate the value of the stock of 'giottas' at 31 December, using:
    (i)   the 'first in, first out' (FIFO) method of valuing stock
    (ii) the 'last in, first out' (LIFO) method of valuing stock
    (iii) the weighted average cost (AVCO) method of valuing stock.
    Use the perpetual method of calculation.
b Prepare a trading account for the month ending 31 December for each method, using your calculations from (a).

QUESTION 3

The following information relates to the purchases and issues of 'velspore' during August. At 31 July there were no stocks of 'velspore'.

Date	Purchases	Issues
5 August	2 at £16	
15 August		1
17 August	4 at £17	
21 August		3
27 August	7 at £18	
31 August		6

The selling price of a 'velspore' during August was £40.

Required
a Calculate the value of closing stock of 'velspores' at 31 August, using:
    (i)   the 'first in, first out' (FIFO) method of valuing stock
    (ii) the 'last in, first out' (LIFO) method of valuing stock.
    Use a periodic calculation for each method.
b Prepare a trading account for the month ending 31 August for each method, using your results from (a).

QUESTION 4

Gwladys Voisin started trading in January 20*4. She purchases and sells canal long boats. Her transactions during 20*4 are shown:

Month	Purchases	Sales
January	1 at £23,000	
February	1 at £24,000	
March	2 at £25,000	
June		1
August		2
October	2 at £26,000	
November		2
December	1 at £27,000	

The selling price of a canal long boat during 20*4 was a uniform £40,000.

Required
(a) Calculate the value of stock of long boats at 31 December 20*4, using:
    (i) the 'first in, first out' (FIFO) method of valuing stock
    (ii) the 'last in, first out' (LIFO) method of valuing stock.
    Use a periodic calculation for each method.
(b) Prepare a trading account for the year ended 31 December 20*4, using your results from (a).

ADVANTAGES OF USING FIFO

- Most people feel that this is intuitively the right method to use, since it seems to follow the natural way that stocks are generally issued, ie in the order in which they are received.
- Stock values are easily calculated.
- Issue prices are based on prices actually paid for stock purchases.
- Closing stocks are based on prices most recently paid.
- It is a method that is acceptable to the Inland Revenue for tax purposes. It is also acceptable for the purposes of the Companies Act 1985 and SSAP 9.

DISADVANTAGES OF USING FIFO

- Because it feels right intuitively, many people feel that this is the way stocks are issued.
- Issues from stock are not at the most recent prices and this may have an adverse effect on pricing policy.
- In times of rising prices FIFO values stocks at higher prices than other methods. This lowers the value of cost of sales and thus increases reported profits. This can be regarded as being contrary to the concept of prudence.

ADVANTAGES OF USING LIFO

- Value of closing stock is based on prices actually paid for the stock.
- Valuation of closing stocks is easy to calculate.
- Issues are valued at most recent prices.
- In times of rising prices LIFO values stocks at lower prices than other methods. This decreases reported profits.

DISADVANTAGES OF USING LIFO

- It is less realistic than FIFO since it assumes that most recently acquired stock will be issued before older stock.

- The most recent prices are not used for stock valuation purposes.
- LIFO is not accepted by the Inland Revenue or by accounting standards (SSAP 9).

ADVANTAGES OF USING AVCO

- Issues of stock are made at a weighted average price. This recognises that all issues from stock have equal value an equal importance to the business.
- Variations in issue prices are minimised.
- It allows the comparison of reported profits to be made on a more realistic basis, since any marked changes in the price of stock issues are ironed out.
- Because the average price used for issues is weighted towards the most recent purchases, the value of closing stock will be fairly close to the latest prices paid for purchases.
- AVCO is acceptable to the Inland Revenue, the Companies Act 1985 and under SSAP 9.

DISADVANTAGES OF USING AVCO

- It requires a new calculation each time purchases of stock are made. This makes it rather more difficult to calculate than the other two methods.
- The prices charged for issues of stock will not generally agree with the prices paid to purchase the stock.

ACCOUNTING CONCEPTS AND STOCK VALUATION

Examiners are quite fond of asking which concepts are used when valuing stock.

Clearly, the **cost concept** is adhered to.

The principle of **consistency** is important since results obtained from the final accounts must be able to be used for comparative purposes.

The **concept of prudence** should be adhered to so that profits are not overstated – this means that the lower of cost and net realisable value should be applied when valuing stock.

The **accruals concept** is used when considering repair costs or delivery charges etc to be deducted from selling price to determine net realisable value.

● EXAMINATION TIP

FIFO, LIFO and AVCO are methods of valuing stock: they do not necessarily reflect the way actual issues are made.

SSAP 9 states that stocks (and work in progress) should be valued at the total of the lower of cost and net realisable value of the separate items of stock or work in progress. (It allows the grouping of similar items.)

It also states that FIFO and AVCO are acceptable bases for valuing stocks. LIFO and replacement cost are not acceptable

STOCK RECONCILIATIONS

Goods sent on sale or return remain the property of the 'sender' until the customer indicates that a sale has taken place.

The value of stock that appears as a current asset on the balance sheet of a business is the result of a physical stock count and valuation. Although many businesses use a perpetual method of valuing their stock by the use of bar code technology, the computerised valuation that results from this is invariably incorrect.

How can this be? I hear you shout. Computers never make errors! They are much more efficient than people!

It is true that computers can be much faster than we are. They can be more accurate than some of us. So why use a physical means of checking closing stock?

The computer relies on accurate inputs by receiving departments of a business – no problem. It also relies on accurate records for issues, and this is where the problem arises.

Consider your local supermarket. Most goods sold in the store do get scanned and the stock records are immediately updated, but what of the goods:

■ stolen by local shop-lifters
■ broken by your unruly young brother
■ eaten by the local mouse population.

None of these 'issues' will be recognised by the computer. This is why a physical stock count is important to gain an accurate closing stock figure to complete the final accounts.

One final problem. Sometimes it is not possible to make a stock count immediately after the close of business on the final day of the financial year. Staff may be absent on the day. It may be too big a job to complete in that one day. No doubt you can think of other reasons why the physical stock count cannot be made at the right time.

Examination questions based on the stock count not being completed at the financial year-end are also popular with examiners.

Adjustments need to be made to the figures arrived at if the stock count and valuation were made after the financial year end in order to determine the actual stock figure at the appropriate date.

WORKED EXAMPLE

Albert was unable to conduct his annual stock-take on 31 March 20*5, his financial year-end. However, he was able to complete it on 6 April 20*5. The stock had a value of £8,430 on that date.

Albert provides the following information of transactions that took place between 1 April and 6 April 20*5.

A gross profit margin of 20% is earned by Albert on all his sales.

(i)   Goods purchased £450.
(ii) Sales made £600.
(iii) Goods returned by Albert to suppliers £90.
(iv) Faulty goods returned by customers £120.

Required Calculate the value of Albert's stock at as 31 March 20*5.

Answer

Calculation of stock as at 31 March 20*5

	£	
Stock as at 6 April 20*5	8,430	
Less net purchases	360	(£450 − £90)
Add Net sales	400	(£600 − £120 = £480 ÷ 1.2)
Stock as at 31 March 20*5	8,470	

Note: The purchases and sales figures are net of returns.

Stock is always valued at cost (or net realisable value) so the profit margin included in the net sales figure must be eradicated.

Purchases are taken off the stock as at 6 April since they were not with Albert as at 31 March. Sales have been added back since Albert did have this stock at the end of March.

QUESTION 5

Krishna was unable to undertake her annual stock-take at her financial year-end on 31 December 20*4. However, she was able to complete it on 5 January 20*5 at which date stock was valued at cost as £26,870.

The following information is available:

Krishna has a uniform mark-up of 33⅓% on all the goods she sells.

In the period 1 January to 5 January 20*5 the following transactions took place:

1. Purchases of goods for resale £1,940.
2. Sales of goods on credit amounted to £3,500.
3. Cash sales amounted to £480.
4. Sales returns were £40.
5. Purchase returns were £72.

Required Calculate Krishna's closing stock as at 31 December 20*4.

QUESTION 6

Vera was unable to take stock at her year-end on 31 October 20*4.

When she did take stock on 9 November 20*4 she valued her stock at £32,840.

The following information is available:

Vera marks up her stock for resale at a uniform 50%.

The following transactions took place in the period 1 November to 9 November 20*4:

1. Cash sales were £2,890.
2. Credit sales amounted to £6,780.
3. Cash purchases amounted to £1,430.
4. Credit purchases were £8,510.
5. Goods returned by customers £290.
6. Goods returned to suppliers £450.

Required Calculate the value of Vera's closing stock as at 31 October 20*4.

Chapter summary

- FIFO, LIFO and AVCO are methods of valuing stock. All three methods are regularly examined at A2 Level.
- They are methods of valuing stock, they do not necessarily determine the order in which stocks are actually issued.
- FIFO and LIFO may be calculated using either a perpetual method or a periodic method. If a question does not stipulate the method to be used then use the periodic method it is quicker easier and you are less likely to make an error.
- There is no right or wrong method of valuing stock but some methods are more acceptable than others to the Inland Revenue.
- The method chosen will determine the level of reported profit.
- If stock is taken some time after the financial year-end a statement showing the necessary adjustments to the stock-take figure must be prepared.

Self-test questions

- Which methods used to value stock are acceptable to the Inland Revenue?
- Which methods are acceptable for the purposes of the Companies Act 1985?
- A greengrocer must always use FIFO as a method of valuing his stock. True or false?
- Which accounting standard deals with stocks and work in progress?
- Which method values closing stocks at the most recent prices paid to purchase the stock?
- In times of rising prices which method reveals profits later than other methods?
- The closing stock figure shown on the balance sheet of a business is always determined by a physical count/computer print-out. Delete the incorrect answer.
- Financial year-end 31 May. The stock-take is conducted on 10 June.
  - How should goods purchased on 7 June be treated?
  - How should sales returns received on 5 June be treated?
- Bill sends Mary some goods on sale or return. Who includes these goods as part of their stock?
- If stock has been overvalued what effect has this had on reported profits?
- If stock has been undervalued this will ....reported profits. Fill the gap.

TEST QUESTIONS

QUESTION 7

Ray Galpin provides the following information for March. Ray purchases and sells 'ingac'. There were no stocks in hand on 1 March. The purchases and sales of 'ingac' are shown:

Date	Purchases	Sales
2 March	5 at £4	
7 March		4
12 March	17 at £5	
21 March		15
24 March	10 at £6	
30 March		7

Required

Calculate the value of closing stock at 31 March, using:
a   the 'first in, first out' method (FIFO)
b   the 'last in, first out' method (LIFO)
c   the weighted average cost method (AVCO).

Ray uses a perpetual calculation when valuing his stock.

QUESTION 8

Marion Lycett provides the following information for November. She purchases and sells 'ilins'. She had no stocks in hand on 1 November. The following transaction are given for 'ilins':

Date	Purchases	Sales
3 November	6 at £12	
7 November	9 at £15	
10 November		8
18 November	7 at £18	
23 November		3
25 November		9

Required
Calculate, using a perpetual calculation, the value of closing stock at 30 November using:
a the 'first in, first out' method (FIFO)
b the 'last in, first out' method (LIFO)
c the weighted average cost method (AVCO).

QUESTION 9

Jackie Bryan provides the following information for January. Jackie purchases and sells 'glomfos'. Jackie had four 'glomfos' in stock at 1 January: they cost £200 each. The transactions for January are shown:

Date	Purchases	Sales
6 January		3
8 January	5 at £210	
13 January		4
17 January	12 at £220	
26 January		10
30 January		3

Jackie uses a periodic calculation to determine closing stock.

Required
Calculate the value of closing stock, using:
a the 'first in, first out' method (FIFO)
b the 'last in, first out' method (LIFO).

QUESTION 10

Tamsin Fretwell provides the following information for September. She purchases and sells 'retyos'. Tamsin had one 'retyo' in stock at 1 September: it had cost £22. The transactions for September are given:

Date	Purchases	Sales
1 September	40 at £22	
7 September	30 at £23	
12 September		65
18 September	50 at £25	
28 September		51

Tamsin uses a periodic calculation to determine closing stock.

Required

Calculate the value of closing stock at 30 September, using:
a the 'first in, first out' method (FIFO)
b the 'last in, first out' method (LIFO).

QUESTION 11

Anil Patel purchases and sells 'derits'. He provides the following information for August. He had 8 'derits' in stock at 1 August: they cost £12 each. He calculates stock using a perpetual method. The following transactions are for August:

Date	Purchases	Sales
4 August	10 at £12	
9 August		15
15 August	12 at £8	
21 August	15 at £7	
26 August		28

'Derits' are sold for £15 each.

Required

a Calculate the closing stock of 'derits' as at 31 August, using the 'last in, first out' (LIFO) method of valuing stock.
b Prepare a trading account for the month of August.

QUESTION 12

Gao Feng purchases and sells 'loits'. He provides the following information for April. He had four 'loits' in stock at 31 March, valued at cost £30 each. The following information is given:

Date	Purchases	Sales
6 April	4 at £9	
9 April		6
18 April	8 at £6	
23 April		7
29 April	4 at £5	
30 April		5

'Loits' are sold at £20 each.

Required
a Calculate the closing stock as at 30 April, using the 'first in, first out' (FIFO) method of valuing stock.
b Prepare a trading account for the month ended 30 April.

QUESTION 13

Olivia Oyle purchases and sells 'greftas'. She provides the following information for September.

Date	Purchases	Sales
3 September	8 at £15	
7 September		6
11 September	12 at £16	
14 September		10
23 September	8 at £17	
27 September		6

She had one 'grefta' in stock on 1 September: it had cost £15. The following information is given:

Greftas are sold for £40 each.

Required
a Calculate the value of closing stock, using the weighted average cost (AVCO) method of valuing stock.
b Prepare a trading account for the month of September.

QUESTION 14

Barney Rumble purchases and sells 'ciarfs'. They sell for £110 each. He provides the following information for December:

At 1 December Barney had seven 'ciarfs' in stock: they cost £40 each.

Date	Purchases	Sales
4 December	4 at £42	
7 December		10
9 December	12 at £45	
14 December		11
20 December	10 at £50	
27 December		9

Required

a Calculate the closing stock of 'ciarfs' as at 31 December, using the 'last in, first out' (LIFO) method of valuing stock using a perpetual calculation.

b Prepare a trading account for the month of December.

QUESTION 15

Gwen Davies was unable to take stock at her financial year-end on 30 April 20*5. When she did take stock on 7 May, she valued her stock at £2,940. The following information is available:

■ Gwen marks up all her stock by 25% on cost to achieve her selling price.
■ the following transactions took place between 1 April and 7 May 20*5:

1. sales amounted to £1,200
2. purchases amounted to £420

Required

Calculate Gwen's closing stock as at 30 April 20*5.

QUESTION 16

John Blunt was unable to take stock at his financial year-end on 30 October 20*4.

When he did take stock on 6 November, he valued his stock at £3,670.

He was able to give the following additional information:

■ stocks are marked up at a uniform rate of 40% on cost to obtain his selling price
■ the following transactions took place took place between 1 November and 6 November 20*4:

1. purchases amounted to £2,560
2. sales amounted to £4,060.

Required

Calculate John's closing stock as at 30 October 20*4.

QUESTION 17

Siobhan O'Malley was unable to take stock at her year-end on 31 May 20*4. When she did take stock on 4 June, she valued her stock at £14,880.

Using her 4 June valuation for stock, her draft accounts revealed a net profit of £185,750.

The following information is available:

■ she marks up her stock at 20% on cost to achieve selling price
■ the following transactions took place between 1 June and 4 June 20*4:

1. sales amounted to £2,400
2. purchases amounted to £850
3. sales returns amounted to £36
4. purchase returns amounted to £84.

a Calculate the value of closing stock as at 31 May 20*4.
b Calculate Siobhan's corrected net profit for the year ended 31 May 20*4.

QUESTION 18

Jennie McGonagle took stock on 8 January 20*5 and valued it at £1,720. She had been unable to take stock at her financial year-end on 31 December 20*4. She used this figure in her draft final accounts and calculated her net profit to be £56,900.

Jennie marks up all her goods by a uniform 60% to achieve her selling price.

The following transactions took place between 1 January and 8 January 20*5:

1. sales amounted to £1,024
2. purchases amounted to £540
3. purchase returns amounted to £17
4. sales returns amounted to £96.

a Calculate the value of closing stock as at 31 December 20*4.
b Calculate the corrected net profit for the year ended 31 December 20*4.

QUESTION 19

David Parker was unable to take stock at his financial year end on 31 July 20*4.

However, he was able to take stock on 9 August 20*4 when he valued it at £2,000.

Using this figure he obtained a draft net profit of £42,870. David marks all goods up by 70% on cost to obtain selling price.

The following transactions took place between 1 August and 9 August 20*4:

1. sales amounted to £1,904
2. purchases amounted to £1,560
3. sales returns amounted to £170
4. purchase returns amounted to £40
5. goods sent on sale or return during July amounted to £510 at selling price.

a Calculate the value of closing stock as at 31 July 20*4.
b Calculate the corrected net profit for the year ended 31 July 20*4.

QUESTION 20

Pat Nicholson was unable to take stock at her financial year-end on 30 June 20*4. When she did take stock on 5 July she valued her stock at £3,565. Using this figure, she was able to determine her draft profit as £180,564.

Pat works on a gross margin of 50% on all goods sold.

The following transactions took place between 1 July and 5 July 20*4:

1. sales amounted to £2,360
2. purchases amounted to £980
3. sales returns amounted to £130
4. purchase returns amounted to £58
5. goods dispatched on sale or return during June amounted to £1,420 at selling price.

a Calculate the closing stock as at 30 June 20*4.
b Calculate the corrected net profits for the year ended 30 June 20*4.

Absorption Costing

It is of vital importance that a manufacturing business is able to calculate what each product (or group of products) has cost to make. This is necessary so that the business can fix a selling price in order to recover the costs incurred in operating the business and provide profits to ensure the survival of the business.

Specification coverage:
AQA 16.1.

Direct costs are those costs that can clearly be attributable as part of the product being produced.

CIMA (the Chartered Institute of Management Accountants) defines 'direct costs' as 'expenditure which can be economically identified with a specific saleable cost unit'.

Indirect costs cannot be identified easily with the product being produced.

CIMA's definition is 'expenditure ... which cannot be economically identified with a specific saleable unit'.

By the end of this chapter you should be able to:
- understand the uses and limitations of absorption costing
- allocate and apportion costs
- apportion costs for service departments using the elimination method
- calculate overhead absorption rates
- cost a simple project.

QUESTIONS

- Identify a direct cost incurred in the manufacture of the jeans you wear.
- Identify an indirect cost incurred in their manufacture.
- Identify a direct cost incurred in the manufacture of the burger you ate yesterday.
- Identify an indirect cost incurred in its manufacture.
- Your answers for direct costs could have included denim, threads, designer labels, zips etc as the directs costs incurred in the production of your jeans. The indirect costs could have included the rent of the factory, business rates for the factory, factory power etc.
- Beef, buns, relish etc would be direct costs incurred in the production of the burger, while any factory overhead would be included in your answer for indirect costs incurred in production.

You have probably noticed the constituent parts of a manufacturing account already.

A cost centre may be a department, a machine, a person to whom costs can be associated.

Cost centre is defined by CIMA as 'a production or service location, function, activity or item of equipment whose costs may be attributed to cost units'.

Cost centres are usually determined by the type of business being considered. In a college or a large retailer the primary cost centre might be each department. In a garage the cost centres might be the repair department, the sales department or parts department.

Cost unit is a unit of production which absorbs the cost centre's overhead costs.

Cost units in a college might be students while in the garage repairs department the cost unit might be each car being worked on.

For example, the cost of the paper that this book is printed on is a direct cost. The denim in your jeans is a direct cost.

> **Direct labour** costs can be specifically identified with the finished product (or service).

For example, the wages of the hairdresser styling your hair are a direct cost.

> **Direct expenses** are any other costs that can be specifically identified with the finished product.

For example, royalties payable to the inventor of a process or design of a product; another example might be the costs of hiring equipment needed for a specific job.

> **Prime cost** is the total of all the direct costs.

Prime cost = Direct material costs + Direct labour costs + Direct expenses

Absorption costing determines the total cost of production. (In fact it is sometimes called total costing.)

This means that all costs incurred in the production of the product are absorbed into the cost of production.

WORKED EXAMPLE

The following information is available for the month of January 20*5 for Chaudhry and Son, a manufacturing business. They produce one product: a 'higle'.

Production for January 20*5 was 1,000 units and the costs involved were:

	£
Direct labour costs	78,000
Direct material costs	56,000
Indirect labour costs	34,000
Indirect material costs	17,000
Other indirect costs	26,000
Selling and distribution costs	46,000
Administration expenses	62,000
Royalties	2,000
Depreciation of factory machinery	14,000

Required
a Prepare an absorption costing statement for the month of January 20*5.
b Calculate the cost of producing one unit, using an absorption costing basis.

Answer
a **Absorption costing statement for January 20*5**

	£
Direct materials	56,000
Direct labour	78,000
Royalties	2,000
Prime cost	136,000
Indirect materials	17,000
Indirect labour	34,000

	£
Other indirect costs	26,000
Depreciation	14,000
Total production cost	227,000
Selling and distribution costs	46,000
Administration costs	62,000
Total cost	335,000

b On an absorption costing basis, each 'higle' has cost £335 (£335,000 /1,000).

USES OF ABSORPTION COSTING

- Calculation of profit or loss when selling price is fixed.
- Setting selling price in order to achieve a pre-determined level of profit.

CALCULATION OF PROFIT WHEN SELLING PRICE IS FIXED.

If the selling price of higles is fixed at £500 per unit.

The profit on the sale of each higle is £165 (£500 − £335).

CALCULATING THE SELLING PRICE WHEN A PRE-DETERMINED LEVEL OF PROFIT IS REQUIRED.

If Chaudhry and Son wish to achieve a profit of £70 on the sale of each 'higle', the selling price has to be £405 per unit (£335 + £70).

If Chaudhry and Son require a net profit margin of 25%:

Net profit on sales = 25% is the same as 33⅓% on cost of sales.

Cost of sales = £335,000

33⅓% of £335,000 = £111,667

So the net margin is £111,667.

Total cost of producing 'higles'	£335,000
Net profit	£111,667
Selling price	£446,667 or £446.67 per unit (£446,667/1,000)

QUESTION 1

Tucon Ltd manufactures one product, a 'sepyt'. The management provides the following information:

	£000
Material costs – direct indirect	938 463
Labour costs – direct indirect	461 726
Manufacturing royalties	20
Selling and distribution costs	612
Administration costs	300
Other indirect costs	84
Depreciation – factory machiney office equipment	100 48

4 million units of 'sepyt' will be produced in August 20*4.

a Prepare an absorption costing statement for the month of August 20*4.
b Calculate the total cost of producing one unit of sepyt.

QUESTION 2

Llandfferon plc manufactures 'dortees'. The following information is given for January 20*5:

Production for the month is 42,000 units.

	£
Direct labour	210,000
Indirect labour	130,000
Direct materials	67,000
Indirect materials	38,000
Other direct expenses	17,000
Other indirect expenses	42,000
Selling expenses	58,000
Administration expenses	36,000
Depreciation of factory machinery	34,000
Depreciation of office equipment	16,000
Depreciation of delivery vehicles	20,000

Required
a Prepare an absorption costing statement for the month of January 20*5.
b Calculate the total cost of producing one unit of 'dortee'.

QUESTION 3

Cardeter Ltd manufactures one product called a 'dible'. The total cost of producing 20,000 'dibles' is £127,000.

The directors wish to make a profit of £2.18 per 'dible'.

Required Calculate the selling price of one 'dible'.

QUESTION 4

Transburn Ltd manufactures 'vuiten'. The total cost of producing 40,000 kilograms of 'vuiten' is £312,000. The directors wish to make a profit of £0.50 per kilogram of 'vuiten'.

Required Calculate the selling price of one kilogram of 'vuiten'.

QUESTION 5

ADTE Ltd manufactures 'treamils'. The total cost of producing 45,000 'treamils' is £159,000. The directors wish to make a net profit margin of 25% on sales of 'treamils'.

Required Calculate the selling price of one 'treamil'.

QUESTION 6

Froddy Ltd manufactures DT/34, a component for the electronics industry. The total cost of producing 54,000 units of DT/34 is £448,200. The directors wish to make a net profit margin of 33⅓%.

Required Calculate the selling price of one DT/34.

Well, there does not seem to be much to worry about with regard to absorption costing!

> **Allocation of costs** is the term used to describe the process of charging whole items of expenditure to a cost centre or a cost unit. The costs are easily identified as deriving from the cost centre.

> **Apportionment of overheads** is the process by which some overhead costs are charged to cost centres on some rational basis because they cannot be directly attributed to a particular cost centre.

When all overhead costs have been apportioned to a cost centre the total has to be charged to specific units of production. This process is known as **absorption**.

The examples that we have considered so far have only considered one product. So all overheads have simply been added to the prime cost of the product to arrive at the total cost. The overheads have been absorbed into total cost of the product.

In the 'real world' (and generally in examination questions) things are rarely so simple.

Consider the following scenarios.

Ivor Fillin sets up in business, manufacturing toothbrushes. He employs Harry Sheen to help in the manufacturing process. Ivor rent two units on a local industrial estate.

Ivor can very easily prepare an absorption costing statement since all the costs go towards manufacturing the toothbrushes. He can use the statement to calculate his profits and he can even use it to work out his pricing strategy.

After a couple of successful years, Harry, by now a skilled brush maker, suggests that they should diversify into also producing hairbrushes. Ivor agrees that this would be an excellent idea. In the smaller of the two rented units Ivor continues to produce toothbrushes, while in the larger unit Harry produces hairbrushes.

How would they determine the costs involved in producing the two different types of brushes?

They can very easily allocate the direct costs to each product, since labour costs and material costs are unique to each product.

The problem arises when rent, business rates, electricity charges and other overheads have to be charged to the two products.

These are costs which apply to the business as a whole.

They need to be apportioned on some equitable basis.

BASES OF APPORTIONMENT APPLIED TO INDIRECT EXPENSES

Overhead	Basis of apportionment to cost centres
Rent	Floor area of cost centre
Rates	Floor area of cost centre
Insurance	Value of items being insured
Heating and lighting	Volume of cost centre (if this is not available then floor area may be used)
Depreciation	Cost or book value of the asset in cost centre
Canteen	Numbers of personnel in each cost centre
Personnel	Numbers of personnel in each cost centre

WORKED EXAMPLE

The directors of the Beckmond Engineering Company provide the following budgeted information for the month of February.

The following budgeted overheads cannot be allocated to the two departments run by the company:

	£
Rent	375,000
Rates	90,000
Power	300,000
Supervisory wages	96,000
Depreciation of factory machinery	150,000

Additional information

Total factory area is 240,000 m^2	Department A occupies 60,000 m^2 Department B occupies 180,000 m^2
Power used in each department	Department A 60,000 Kwh Department B 40,000 Kwh
Cost of machinery in each department	Department A £300,000 Department B £600,000
Staff employed in each department	Department A 30 workers Department B 10 workers

Required
Prepare an overhead analysis sheet for February.

WORKED EXAMPLE *continued*

Answer

Overhead	Total cost £	Basis of apportionment	Dept A £	Dept B £
Rent	375,000	Floor area	93,750	281,250
Rates	90,000	Floor area	22,500	67,500
Power	300,000	Kwh	180,000	120,000
Supervisory wages	96,000	Number of workers	72,000	24,000
Depreciation of machinery	150,000	Cost of machinery	50,000	100,000
	1,011,000		418,250	592,750

QUESTION 7

Bhunit Ltd has the following budgeted costs for October. They cannot be allocated to its three departments.

	£
Rent	36,000
Depreciation of premises	6,000
Depreciation of machinery	210,000
Heating and light	9,000
Supervisors' wages	160,000

The following additional information is also available:

Floor area	Dept 1	2,000 m²
	Dept 2	4,000 m²
	Dept 3	6,000 m²
Number of workers	Dept 1	40
	Dept 2	90
	Dept 3	70
Cost of machinery	Dept 1	£150,000
	Dept 2	£300,000
	Dept 3	£600,000

Required Prepare a statement showing the aportionment of overheads for October.

QUESTION 8

The directors of Hoolihan Ltd provide the following budgeted overhead costs for March. The overheads cannot be allocated to any of the four departments.

	£
Rent	61,200
Rates	21,240
Canteen costs	3,780
Insurance of machinery	36,000
Power	20,160
Supervisory wages	70,000
Depreciation of machinery	75,000

The following additional information is also available:

Total factory area is 540,000m² of which:	
Department M occupies	30,000m²
Department N occupies	750,000 m²
Department O occupies	210,000 m²
Department P occupies	120,000 m²
Staff employed in each department:	
Department M	14 workers
Department N	17 workers
Department O	28 workers
Department P	11 workers
Power used in each department:	
Department M	25,200 Kwh
Department N	28,800 Kwh
Department O	7,200 Kwh
Department P	10,800 Kwh
Cost of machinery used in each department:	
Department M	£65,000
Department N	£72,000
Department O	£37,000
Department P	£26,000

Required Prepare a statement showing the apportionment of overheads for March.

TRANSFER OF SERVICE DEPARTMENT COSTS

Departments that provide services for the production department, and hence other cost centres, clearly are not involved directly in production of finished products. They cannot recoup their costs by incorporating them into the selling price of their product. Yet their costs must be recovered by the business.

The estimated costs of service departments must be apportioned to each production department. This means that each production department will recover its own overheads and some of the overheads incurred by the service department.

Service departments in effect charge the other cost centres in the business for the services that they provide for them.

Sometimes service departments keep detailed records of work completed in each department in such cases these costs can be allocated to the appropriate department.

This often the case in a reprographics department of a college or school. Each department will be charged for the photocopying for which they are responsible.

Examples of service departments would include:

- canteen
- stores
- maintenance
- personnel.

WORKED EXAMPLE

Thierity Ltd has three production departments. The company operates a staff canteen for all staff. The following budgeted cost information is given *after* all costs have been allocated or apportioned to the appropriate department.

	£
Department D	412,000
Department E	346,000
Department F	110,000
Canteen	63,000

Required Prepare a table showing the apportionment of canteen overheads to the production departments.

Overhead	Total	Basis of apportionment	Dept D	Dept E	Dept F	Canteen
Total	931,000		416,000	346,000	110,000	63,000
Canteen		?	30,000	24,000	9,000	(63,000)
			<u>446,000</u>	<u>370,000</u>	<u>119,000</u>	

Answer

Statement showing apportionment of canteen costs between production departments.

Can you guess how the canteen costs have been apportioned?

What information was missing in the question?

The information that was missing was the numbers of people working in each department. There were 10 workers in department D; eight in department E; three in department F. This information was deliberately omitted. Would you have used people working in each department?

Don't worry – the information will be given in examination questions.

QUESTION 9

The Cafcal company has four production departments.

The maintenance department services all four production departments.

The following budgeted cost information is given *after* all costs have been allocated or apportioned to the departments.

Department	Total costs £
Z1	386,100
Y2	227,300
X3	180,400
W4	110,500
Maintenance	69,900

The number of machines in each production department is:

Department	Number of machines
Z1	14
Y2	9
X3	5
W4	2

Required Prepare a statement showing the apportionment of maintenance costs between production departments.

QUESTION 10

The Teafoo company has three production departments.

The maintenance department services the three departments.

The following budgeted cost information is given *after* all costs have been allocated or apportioned between the departments.

Department	Total costs £
P/15	1,279,800
Q/17	326,400
R/19	807,040
Maintenance	126,000

The number of machines in each production department is:

Department	Number of machines
P/15	35
Q/17	7
R/19	18

Required Prepare a statement showing the apportionment of maintenance costs between production departments.

> **Reciprocal services** is the term used when a department provides a service for another department and receives a service from the same department.

The picture becomes a little more complicated when reciprocal services are provided.

For example, the canteen provides a service for all the departments including the maintenance engineers; the maintenance engineers keep the canteen equipment in good working order as well as servicing equipment and machinery in all other departments.

The power generating section will provide heating for all departments, as will personnel.

Examination questions will usually have only two service departments as a maximum.

There are three main methods of dealing with inter-departmental transfers of overheads.

Fortunately, for us, examinations at A Level only examine the elimination method.

The elimination method is sometimes referred to as the simplified method, since it does not actually reflect the reciprocity of the service departments to each other.

WORKED EXAMPLE

The cost accountant of Oxian Ltd provides the following information on budgeted total departmental costs after all costs have been allocated or apportioned:

	Production departments			Service departments	
	M	**N**	**P**	**Q**	**R**
	£	£	£	£	£
Total costs	45,000	60,000	24,000	10,000	12,000

The service departments' costs are to be apportioned as follows:

Department Q	40%	30%	20%		10%
Department R	20%	10%	30%	40%	

Required Prepare a statement to show how the costs of the service departments are re-apportioned between the production departments.

WORKED EXAMPLE *continued*

Answer

	Production departments		Service departments		
	M £	N £	P £	Q £	R £
Total costs	45,000	60,000	20,000	10,000	12,000
Apportionment of Dept R costs	2,400	1,200	3,600	4,800	(12,000)
	47,400	61,200	23,600	14,800	

Note: Department R has now been eliminated.

Always start with the service department with the greater costs

From above:	47,400	61,200	23,600	14,800	
Apportionment of Dept Q costs	5,920	4,440	2,960	(14,800)	1,480
	53,320	65,640	26,560		1,480

This method ignores the amount left over for Department R.

Strictly speaking, this method is slightly inaccurate, but the estimated overheads themselves might be inaccurate since they are after all 'estimates'. Also the method of apportioning overheads is only a matter of convention and none of the methods that could have been used can claim to be perfectly accurate. In most cases the figure remaining when the process is completed will be insignificant.

QUESTION 11

The managers of the Philysiac Company provide the following information, based on budgeted total departmental costs *after* all costs have been allocated or apportioned:

	Production departments			Service departments	
	11/R £	12/S £	13/T £	UV £	WX £
Total costs	60,000	120,000	45,000	30,000	20,000

The service department's costs are to be apportioned as follows:

Department UV	25%	50%	20%	–	5%
Department WX	20%	30%	40%	10%	–

Required Prepare a statement showing how the costs of the service departments are re-apportioned between the production departments.

QUESTION 12

The mangers of Caspen Ltd provide the following information based on budgeted departmental costs *after* all costs have been allocated or apportioned:

	Production departments			Service departments	
	P/3/Q	**R/5/S**	**T/7/U**	**BZ**	**CW**
	£	**£**	**£**	**£**	**£**
Total costs	430,000	1,725,000	938,000	125,000	80,000

The service department's costs are to be apportioned as follows:

Departments BZ	50%	15%	20%	–	15%
Department CW	42%	30%	20%	8%	–

Required Prepare a statement showing how the costs of the service departments are re-apportioned between production departments.

THE ABSORPTION OF OVERHEADS

After the overheads have been apportioned to the appropriate cost centres we need to calculate the amount of the overhead to be included into the cost of each unit passing through the cost centre.

The amount of each cost centres overheads that needs to be absorbed (added) to each unit of production is termed the **overhead absorption rate** (OAR).

There are a number of different methods of calculating the overhead absorption rate.

DIRECT LABOUR HOUR RATE

When a particular department is labour intensive and there is little machinery used or machine costs are low the overhead absorption rate may be calculated using the man hours required to complete each unit of production.

Direct labour hours per unit is the number of hours (or part of an hour) that a worker would take to produce one unit of output.

WORKED EXAMPLE

Stemods Ltd manufactures two products – 'culas' and 'ginars'.

The budgeted production for each product for October is shown:

	Units	Direct labour hours per unit
Cula	10,000	2
Ginar	8,000	1.5

Budgeted overheads for October are expected to be £75,840.

Required
Calculate:

a the overhead absorption rate for each product, using the direct labour hour method
b the total amount of overheads absorbed by each product if budgets are met.

Answer

Total direct labour hours = 20,000 + 12,000 = 32,000

Labour hour overhead absorption rate = $\frac{£75,840}{32,000}$ = £2.37 per hour

a) Overhead absorption rate for each unit = Cula = £4.74 (2 hours × £2.37)
  Ginar = £3.56 (1½ hours × £2.37)

b) If the budgets are met then the total overheads will be absorbed as follows:

	£	
10,000 units of cula will absorb	47,400	(10,000 × £4.74)
8,000 units of ginar will absorb	28,440	(8,000 × £3.555)
Total overheads absorbed	75,840	

You may find that the two sub-totals calculated above are referred to as the **overhead recovery rates**. So, in the month of October the total overheads £75,840 will be recovered by culas £47,400 and by ginars £28,440.

QUESTION 13

Bonivace Ltd manufactures two products – 'feltos' and 'hevos'.

The budgeted production for each product is shown for July.

	Units	Direct labour hours per unit
Felto	15,000	0.2
Hevo	6,000	1.4

Budgeted overheads for July are expected to be £72,732.

Required
Calculate:

a the overhead absorption rate for each product, using the direct labour hour method
b the total amount of overheads absorbed by each product if budgets are met.

QUESTION 14

Jacobski Ltd manufactures 'supnil' and 'quotanil'.

The budgeted production for each product is shown for October:

	Units	Direct labour hours per unit
Sepnil	3,750	1.2
Quotanil	18,000	0.3

Budgeted overheads for October are expected to be £134,739.

Required
Calculate:

a the overhead absorption rate for each product, using the direct labour hour method
b the total amount of overheads absorbed by each product if budgets are met.

MACHINE HOUR RATE

This method is appropriate when production methods are capital intensive or machine costs are relatively high. The overhead absorption rate will take into account the number of machine hours required to produce each unit of output.

WORKED EXAMPLE

Tryndra Ltd manufactures 'dertins' and 'ghilos'.

The budgeted production for each product for February is shown:

	Units	Machine hours per unit
Dertin	4,000	0.5
Ghilo	20,000	0.25

Budgeted overheads for February are expected to be £66,780.

Required
Calculate:

a the overhead absorption rate using the direct machine hour method
b the total amount of overheads absorbed by each product if budgets are met.

Answer
Total machine hours 2,000 + 5,000 = 7,000

Machine hour overhead absorption rate = $\frac{£66,780}{7,000}$ = £9.54 per hour

a Overhead absorption rate = dertin = 0.5 × £9.54 = £4.77

ghilo = 0.25 × £9.54 = £2.39

b If the budgets are met the total overheads will be absorbed as follows:

	£	
4,000 units of dertin will absorb	19,080	(4,000 × £4.77)
20,000 units of ghilo will absorb	47,700	(20,000 × £2.385)
	66,780	

The total overheads in February will be recovered partly by sales of dertin (£19,080) and partly by sales of ghilos (£47,700).

QUESTION 15

Khuka Ltd manufactures 'klakas' and 'klovas'.

The budgeted production for each product is shown for May:

	Units	Machine hours per unit
Klaka	20,000	2.4
Klova	140,000	0.6

Budgeted overheads for May are expected to be £166,320.

Required
Calculate:

a the overhead absorption rate for each product, using the direct machine hour method
b the total amount of overheads absorbed by each product if budgets are met.

QUESTION 16

Limbachia Ltd manufactures 'peepar' and 'peekar'.

The budgeted production for each product is shown for December:

	Units	Machine hours per unit
Peppar	2,000	4.5
Peekar	5,000	3.2

Budgeted overheads for December are expected to be £240,000.

Required
Calculate:

a the overhead absorption rate for each product, using the direct machine hour method
b the total amount of overheads absorbed by each product if budgets are met.

There are four other possible ways of calculating the overhead recovery rate.

● EXAMINATION TIP

Do check the specification issued by the examination board to determine which methods of overhead absorption it might include in your examination paper.

AQA examines only direct labour hour rate and machine hour rate methods.

DIRECT LABOUR COST RATE

The estimated overheads are expressed as a proportion of the estimated cost of direct wages. The weakness of this method is that overheads will in the main accrue on a time basis whereas wages often accrue in a more complex way depending on the method of rewarding labour. For example, payment may be based on some kind of piecework or a premium bonus method.

WORKED EXAMPLE

Total overheads for April are estimated to be £283,992.

Total direct labour costs are estimated to be £151,060.

Required Calculate the overhead recovery rate for April, using the direct labour cost method.

Answer
Overhead recovery rate = $\dfrac{£283,992}{£151,060}$ = £1.88 per £1 of direct labour cost.

DIRECT MATERIAL COST RATE

This is a similar method to the direct labour cost method. The total cost of materials is used as the denominator in the calculation. The method's main weakness is that it assumes that time taken to process materials bears some kind of relationship to its cost. So high-value materials will attract more overheads than cheaper materials, regardless of the time taken to process them.

WORKED EXAMPLE

Total overheads for December are estimated to be £1,954,170.

Total material costs are estimated to be £502,350.

Required Calculate the overhead recovery rate for December, using the direct material cost method.

Answer
Overhead recovery rate = $\dfrac{£1,954,170}{£502,350}$ = £3.89 per £1 of direct materials used.

PRIME COST RATE

This method uses prime cost as the denominator. The method has the same weaknesses as the direct labour cost method and the direct material cost method.

WORKED EXAMPLE

Total overheads for July are estimated to be £1,355,500.

Prime cost is estimated to be £412,000.

Required Calculate the overhead recovery rate for July, using the prime cost method.

Answer
Overhead recovery rate = $\dfrac{£1,355,500}{£412,000}$ = £3.29 per £1 of prime cost.

UNIT PRODUCED RATE (COST UNIT RATE)

The total overheads allocated and apportioned to production are divided by the estimated number of units produced. So the overheads are spread over the goods produced. The method can only realistically be used if the business manufactures only one type of product.

> ## WORKED EXAMPLE
>
> Total overheads for May are estimated to be £15,500.
>
> The total number of units produced is estimated to be 14,500.
>
> **Required** Calculate the overhead recovery rate for May, using the cost unit method.
>
> **Answer**
> Overhead recovery rate = $\dfrac{£15,500}{14,500}$ = £1.07 per unit

So far, we have considered products that are produced in one department only. Some jobs pass through several departments before completion. As a job passes through a department it attracts a proportion of the overheads of that department. When it passes to the next department, it will attract a proportion of the overheads of the second department and so on until it is complete.

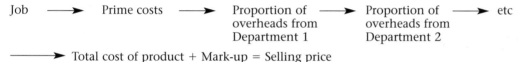

Job ⟶ Prime costs ⟶ Proportion of overheads from Department 1 ⟶ Proportion of overheads from Department 2 ⟶ etc

⟶ Total cost of product + Mark-up = Selling price

> ## WORKED EXAMPLE
>
> Yves Pichot manufactures 'desirs'. A 'desir' passes through two departments on its path to completion.
>
> Information for each department is given:
>
> | | Department 1 | Department 2 |
> |---|---|---|
> | Budgeted total overheads | £40,320 | £18,864 |
> | Budgeted total labour hours worked | 4,800 | 900 |
> | Budgeted total machine hours worked | 300 | 3,600 |
>
> A 'desir' spends four hours passing through Department 1 and three hours passing through Department 2 before completion.
>
> **Required**
>
> *a* Calculate the overhead absorption rate for a 'desir' for each department, using:
>   i) labour hours
>   ii) machine hours.
> *b* State which method of overhead recovery should be used in the two departments. Give reasons for your answer.

WORKED EXAMPLE *continued*

c   Calculate the total overheads to be absorbed by one unit of 'desir' if budgets are met.

Answer

a   Department 1   OAR using labour hours = £8.40 (£40,320/4800)
                    OAR using machine hours = £134.40 (£40,320/300)
    Department 2   OAR using labour hours = £20.96 (£18,864/900)
                    OAR using machine hours = £5.24 (£18,864/3600)
b   Since Department 1 is labour intensive; labour hours should be chosen as the method of overhead recovery.
    Machine hours should be chosen for Department 2 since it is capital intensive.
c   A 'desir' takes four hours in Department 1 so £33.60 needs to be absorbed.
                 three hours in Department 2 so £15.72 needs to be absorbed.
    Total overheads to be absorbed by a 'desir' £49.32 if budgets are met.

QUESTION 17

Alex McTavish manufactures 'sporidge'. Sporidge passes through two departments before completion.

Information for each department is given:

	Dept P	Dept N
Budgeted total overheads	£182,466	£262,145
Budgeted total labour hours worked	5,232	28,340
Budgeted total machine hours worked	40,548	2,180

A sporidge spends 9.3 hours in Department P and 6.5 hours in Department N before completion.

Required

a   Calculate the overhead absorption rate for 'sporidge' for each department, using:
    i) labour hours
    ii) machine hours.
b   State which method of overhead recovery should be used in the two departments. Give reasons for your answer.
c   Calculate the total overheads to be absorbed by one unit of 'sporidge' if budgets are met.

QUESTION 18

Daphne Cherry manufactures 'frutic'. 'Frutic' is manufactured in two departments before completion.

The information for each department is given:

	Dept I	Dept II
Budgeted total overheads	£668,670	£120,792
Budgeted total labour hours worked	107,850	14,380
Budgeted total machine hours worked	21,570	35,950

A 'Frutic' spends 15 hours in Department I and 5 hours in Department II before completion.

a Calculate the overhead absorption rate for 'Frutic' for each department, using:
 i) labour hours
 ii) machine hours.
b State which method of overhead recovery should be used in the two departments. Give reasons for your answer.
c Calculate the total overheads to be absorbed by one unit of 'Frutic' if budgets are met.

OVERABSORPTION AND UNDERABSORPTION OF OVERHEADS

Overhead recovery rates are based on predictions of future levels of activity and predicted (budgeted) levels of overhead expenditure.

If the actual level of activity is equal to that budgeted and actual expenditure on overheads is equal to budgeted expenditure then the expenditure on overheads will be recovered exactly.

If the actual level of activity is less than the budgeted level and spending on overheads is equal to the predicted level then the actual overheads will not be recovered. There will be an **under-recovery of overheads**.

If the actual level of activity is equal to the level that was budgeted but the actual spending on overheads is greater than the budgeted amount then this too will mean an **under-recovery of overheads**.

If the actual level of activity is higher than the budgeted level and actual spending on overheads is equal to that budgeted then the overheads will be more than recovered There will be an **over-recovery of overheads**.

If activity levels are the same as those budgeted but actual spending is less than that budgeted then this too will mean less spending on overheads. There will be an **over-recovery of overheads**.

■ Any under-recovery of overheads is debited to the costing profit and loss account.
■ An over-recovery of overheads is credited to the costing profit and loss account.

WORKED EXAMPLE

Bartasil Ltd manufactures kityos. The directors budget for overhead expenditure of £25,000 each month. This figure is based on an output of 5,000 kityos. The overhead absorption rate is £5 per unit.

The following information is given:

	Actual output Units	Actual expenditure on overheads £
January	5,000	24,000
February	4,900	25,000
March	5,100	25,000
April	5,000	25,100
May	5,100	28,050
June	5,100	26,000

Required Calculate the over- or under-recovery rate for each of the six months.

WORKED EXAMPLE *continued*

Answer

	Actual expenditure on overheads £	Overheads recovered £	Over-/under-recovery £
January	24,000	25,000	1,000 over-recovery
February	25,000	24,500	500 under-recovery
March	25,000	25,500	500 over-recovery
April	25,100	25,000	100 under-recovery
May	28,050	25,500	2,550 under-recovery
June	26,000	25,500	500 under-recovery

OTHER OVERHEADS

The other costs incurred by a business must also be recovered if the business is to survive in the long term.

Selling and distribution costs must be recovered.

Administration costs must be recovered and interest charges must be recovered.

These costs are recovered through the mark-up added to the goods before they are sold to the final customer.

These costs are treated as period costs and as such are debited to the profit and loss account as we have done on numerous occasions earlier in the book.

USES OF ABSORPTION COSTING

The total cost of producing goods is necessary when calculating a selling price.

The total cost of producing goods is necessary for long-term planning, since total revenue must cover direct costs as well as overheads.

PROBLEMS ASSOCIATED WITH THE USE OF ABSORPTION COSTING

Overhead absorption rates must be updated on a regular basis. They are derived from budgeted information and are therefore subject to change.

Management decision-making relies heavily on the provision of accurate information; the information provided by absorption costing may be inaccurate since it relies on budgeted information.

ABSORPTION COSTING AND SSAP 9

SSAP 9 *Stocks and long-term contracts* requires that the value of stocks, reported in the final published accounts of limited companies, includes the costs of converting the raw materials used into finished goods.

All 'normal' production costs will be included in the total cost of the product.

Occasionally there may be 'unusual' items of expenditure incurred during production; these might include idle time losses or exceptional wastage because of unforeseen circumstances. These should be excluded in the valuation.

Other overheads may be included if management deems it prudent to do so. Examples might include the accounts department or the personnel department if either has a direct input into the running of the production department.

Managers can use whatever basis they like when producing internal management accounts since SSAP 9 does not apply.

Chapter summary

- Allocation of expenditure is used when the cost is incurred for a specific cost centre.
- Expenditure that cannot be allocated is apportioned to the cost centres using some equitable basis.
- Service costs are apportioned to production cost centres.
- In the case of reciprocal service costs are apportioned by a number of methods: the elimination method is the only one examined at A Level.
- The overheads of cost centres are charged to cost units by using calculated overhead absorption rates.
- At A Level overhead absorption rates are based on direct labour hours if the operation is labour intensive, or on direct machine hours if the operation is capital intensive.
- Higher than budgeted activity and/or lower than budgeted overhead expenditure will result in an over-recovery of overheads.
- Lower than budgeted activity and/or higher than budgeted overhead expenditure will result in an under-recovery of overheads.

Self-test questions

- Give an alternative name for absorption costing.
- Identify one use of absorption costing.
- Identify one example of a cost centre.
- Identify one example of a cost unit.
- Tick the appropriate box to indicate whether the expense should be allocated or apportioned to the appropriate cost centre:

Overhead	Allocate	Apportion
Direct wages	✓	
Heating and lighting		
Direct materials		
Insurances		
Cost of running the canteen		

- What does the abbreviation 'OAR' stand for?
- Explain what is meant by the term 'reciprocal service departments'.
- Identify two methods of calculating an overhead absorption rate other than by using a direct labour hour method.
- Budgeted overheads are £23,600 and actual overheads are £24,000 and actual activity is equal to budgeted activity. Does this result in an over- or under-absorption of overheads?
- Budgeted overheads are equal to actual overheads and actual activity is 23,000 units of

production compared to budgeted activity of 25,000 units. Does this result in an over- or under-absorption of overheads?

TEST QUESTIONS

QUESTION 19

Magreta Ltd is a manufacturing company with four departments. The following information is provided:

Department	B	C	D	E
Floor area (m²)	4000	3000	2000	1000
Machinery cost (£000)	270	90	60	30
Machinery replacement cost (£000)	300	200	150	150

The following budgeted costs for October have not been apportioned to a department:

	£
Factory rent	90,000
Factory rates	15,000
Factory insurance	21,000
Factory depreciation	7,000
Heating	18,000
Machinery insurance	24,000
Machinery depreciation	27,000

Required Prepare a statement showing the apportionment of overheads for October.

QUESTION 20

Lethar Ltd is a manufacturing accompany with four departments.

The following information is provided:

Department	12	14	16	18
Floor area (m²)	2,700	4,800	6,200	1,300
Staff employed	18	46	28	8
Power units (Kwh)	1,200	1,000	900	1,400
Cost of machinery (£)	78,000	32,000	40,000	50,000
Replacement cost of machinery (£)	150,000	56,000	100,000	64,000

The following budgeted overheads for February cannot be allocated to any of the four departments:

	£
Canteen costs	68,000
Rent	14,700
Rates	9,600
Supervisory wages	56,000
Insurance – of premises	4,800
of machinery	22,570
Power	36,900
Depreciation of machinery	20,000

Required Prepare a statement showing the apportionment of overheads for February.

QUESTION 21

The Janu company has three production departments and a canteen that services the three production departments.

The following information is given:

Department	D	E	F	Canteen
Floor area (m²)	4,000	3,500	1,500	1,000
Staff employed	31	35	28	6
Power used (Kwh)	800	500	600	100
Cost of machinery (£)	4,250	1,130	1,110	10

The following budgeted costs for November have not been apportioned to a department:

	£
Rent and rates	19,350
Insurance of machinery	35,100
Heat and light	11,460
Supervisory wages	29,000
Power	28,400
Depreciation of machinery	14,950

Required

a Prepare a statement showing the apportionment of overheads for November.
b Prepare a statement showing the apportionment of canteen costs to production departments.

QUESTION 22

The Hedold company has three departments and a maintenance department that services the three production departments.

The following information is available:

Department	G	H	J	Maintenance
Floor area (m²)	5,000	12,000	11,000	2,000
Staff employed	26	40	16	8
Power used (Kwh)	450	600	300	150
Cost of machinery (number of machine in brackets)	£80,000 (8)	£150,000 (12)	£70,000 (5)	100,000

The following budgeted costs for February have not been apportioned to any department:

	£
Supervisory wages	112,500
Power	35,700
Depreciation of machinery	142,400
Rent and rates	38,100
Insurance of – premises	16,530
machinery	9,240

Required

a Prepare a statement showing the apportionment of overheads for February.
b Prepare a statement showing the apportionment of maintenance costs to production departments.

QUESTION 23

The Vilcern Company has three production departments.

The production departments are serviced by a canteen and a maintenance department.

The following information is given:

Department	XY	ZA	BC	Canteen	Maintenance
Floor area (m²)	3,000	1,000	2,000	500	1,500
Cost of machinery (£)	120,000	250,000	150,000	80,000	200,000
Number of machines	14	6	4	2	4
Number of workers	19	6	15	4	6
Power used (Kwh)	450	210	180	20	40

The following budgeted costs for April have not been apportioned to any department:

	£
Rent and rates	21,120
Heat and light	17,040
Supervisory wages	220,000
Power	29,610
Depreciation of – machinery	24,000
premises	16,800
Insurance of – machinery	21,720
premises	14,112

a Prepare a statement showing the apportioned overheads for April.
b Prepare a statement showing the apportionment of canteen costs and maintenance costs to the production departments.

QUESTION 24

The Ousrow Company has three production departments that are serviced by a maintenance department and a canteen.

The following information is available:

Department	D/3	E/2	F/1	Maintenance	Canteen
Floor area (m²)	4,500	3,000	3,500	1,000	500
Cost of machinery (£)	400,000	300,000	150,000	100,000	50,000
Number of machines	18	16	10	4	2
Number of workers	120	60	70	7	3
Power used (Kwh)	650	200	450	100	10

The following budgeted costs for September have not been apportioned to any department:

	£
Rent and rates	45,000
Heat and light	18,875
Supervisors' wages	494,000
Power	37,224
Depreciation of – machinery	270,000
premises	25,000
Insurance – machinery	15,000
premises	28,750

Required

a Prepare a statement showing the apportionment of overheads for April.

b Prepare a statement showing the apportionment of maintenance costs and canteen costs to the production departments.

QUESTION 25

The Plumet Company has two production departments that are serviced by a maintenance department and a canteen.

The following information is given:

Department	AZ	BY	Maintenance	Canteen
Area (m²)	3,000	5,000	1,000	200
Book value of machinery	£65,000	£25,000	£12,000	£8,000
Number of employees	20	40	10	5

The following budgeted information is given for June:

Department	AZ	BY	Canteen
Direct labour hours	800	4,800	
Direct machine hours	8,310	1,160	
Maintenance hours	800	300	100

The budgeted costs for June not yet apportioned to any department are expected to be:

	£
Rent and rates	47,840
Supervisory wages	172,500
Depreciation of machinery	55,000

Management has been asked to cost job PR/72. The job would require:

■ 5 kilos of materials at £9.50 per kilo
■ four hours of direct labour at £8.50 per hour.

It would spend two hours in Department AZ and three hours in Department BY.

The job would be marked up by 70% to achieve selling price.

Required

a Prepare a statement showing the apportionment of overheads for June.
b Calculate an overhead absorption rate for each department, using the most appropriate method.
c Calculate the selling price of job PR/72.

QUESTION 26

The Trinkwet Company has two production departments that are serviced by a maintenance department and a canteen.

The following information is given:

	Machining	Assembly	Maintenance	Canteen
Area (m²)	7,000	1,500	200	300
Book value of machinery	£84,000	£10,000	£5,000	£1,000
Number of employees	17	23	6	4

The following information is given for December:

Department	Machining	Assembly	Canteen
Direct labour hours	400	2,400	
Direct machine hours	1,200	300	
Maintenance hours	700	120	80

The budgeted costs for December not yet apportioned to any department are expected to be:

	£
Rent and rates	44,100
Supervisory wages	271,000
Depreciation of machinery	180,000

Job XR 471 would require 9 kilograms of material at £4.30 and three hours of direct labour at £10.40 per hour.

It would spend four hours in the machinery department and one hour in assembly.

The job would be marked up by 120% to achieve selling price.

Required

a Prepare a statement showing the apportionment of overheads for December.
b Calculate an overhead absorption for each department, using the most appropriate method.
c Calculate the selling price for job XR 471.

FOURTEEN

Marginal Costing

Variable costs vary with levels of activity within the business.

Fixed costs do not vary with levels of business activity.

Semi-variable costs cannot be classified as either fixed costs or variable costs since they contain an element of both.

We have seen in the previous chapter that a business must cover all costs in order to be profitable; it must recover all the costs it has incurred by absorbing them into the selling price charged to the final customer.

Absorption costing is the method employed in an attempt to ensure that each product does receive a proportion of the overall costs of running the whole business.

Absorption costing does have weaknesses:

■ calculations are based on predicted levels of output, so variations in levels of output are not taken into account and this can lead to overabsorption and underabsorption of overheads
■ apportion methods cannot be 100% accurate
■ calculations do not take into account differences in cost patterns exhibited by fixed costs, variable costs or semi-variable costs.

MARGINAL COSTING

Marginal costing makes a clear distinction between fixed and variable costs. When using marginal costing no attempt is made to allocate or apportion any fixed costs incurred by cost centres or cost units.

Marginal costs are the costs that are incurred when one extra unit is produced above the planned level.

Marginal revenues are the revenues earned by the sale of one extra unit.

Marginal costs usually comprise extra materials, extra direct wages, extra direct expenditure, other extra variable costs in selling and distributing the product and any extra administration costs that arise when there is an increase in the level of production.

By definition an increase in production (that is an increase in business activity) will not increase fixed costs – they will remain unchanged.

Specification coverage:
AQA 16.1.

By the end of this chapter you should be able to:
■ use marginal costing for decision-making in respect of 'make or buy' decisions, acceptance or rejection of additional work, price-setting, optimum use of scarce resources
■ calculate break-even.

Output in units	Fixed costs	Variable costs	Total costs	Marginal costs per unit
	£	£	£	£
1,000	5,000	1,000	6,000	1
1,001	5,000	1,001	6,001	1
1,002	5,000	1,002	6,002	1
1,003	5,000	1,003	6,003	

Note the variable costs change in line with the level of production.

The fixed costs have not changed with the increase in the level of production.

The variable costs are the marginal costs (in this simple example).

Contribution is the difference between selling price and variable costs.

Contribution should more properly be termed 'contribution towards fixed costs and profit' since once fixed costs are all covered contribution becomes profit.

WORKED EXAMPLE

	£
The selling price of a unit of VX/32 is	100
Variable costs per unit – direct materials	27
direct labour	32
royalties	8
Fixed costs	17

Required Calculate the contribution made by the sale of one unit of VX/32.

Answer
Contribution per unit = Selling price per unit − Variable costs per unit

Contribution per unit = £100 − £67 (£27 + £32 + £8)

Contribution per unit = £33

WORKED EXAMPLE

Emam produces a single product. The following information relates to the production and sales of the product in October:

Costs and revenues per unit	£
Sales revenue	70
Costs – direct materials	15
direct labour	12
royalties	5
fixed costs	20

Production and sales 1,000 units.

Required Prepare an income statement for October, showing the total contribution and profit.

Answer

Income statement

	£	£
Sales		70,000
Less Direct materials	15,000	
Direct labour	12,000	
Royalties	5,000	
		32,000
Contribution		38,000
Less Fixed costs		20,000
Profit		18,000

WORKED EXAMPLE

Data the same as the above worked example but 1,001 units produced and sold.

Required Prepare an income statement for October, showing the total contribution and profit.

Answer

Income statement

	£	£
Sales		70,070
Less Direct materials	15,015	
Direct labour	12,012	
Royalties	5,005	
		32,032
Contribution		38,038
Less Fixed costs		20,000
Profit		18,038

Note: The profit has risen by the contribution of the extra unit produced and sold. The fixed costs have not risen even though the activity rate has risen.

THE USES OF MARGINAL COSTING

Marginal costing is used in the following circumstances. When a business is:

- costing 'special' or one-off opportunities
- deciding whether to make or buy the product
- choosing between competing alternative actions
- employing a penetration or destroyer pricing strategy
- calculating the break-even level of output.

All of these circumstances tend to be short-term decisions.

SPECIAL OR ONE-OFF BUSINESS OPPORTUNITIES

WORKED EXAMPLE

The Troncell Manufacturing Company manufactures one product: 'troncells'. The following information is available for a production level of 5,000 'troncells':

Costs and revenues per unit	£
Selling price	45
Direct materials	12
Direct labour	19
Royalties	1
Fixed costs	8

There is spare capacity in the factory. A Malaysian retailer has indicated that she would be willing to purchase 200 troncells but only if the price to her was £35 each.

Required Advise the management of the Troncell company whether they should accept the order.

Answer
The order should be accepted. The order will make a positive contribution of £600 (£3 per unit).

Workings   Contribution = *Selling price per unit − marginal costs per unit*
                Contribution = *£35 − £32*
                Contribution = *£3 per troncell*

Note: The special order has no need to cover the fixed costs since they have already been absorbed into the 'normal' selling price.

WORKED EXAMPLE *continued*

The Malaysian contract has no need to cover the fixed costs again.

The contract is providing the manufacturer with an extra (marginal) contribution.

We can check to see if the acceptance of the Malaysian contract does make the business more profitable by preparing marginal cost statements.

	Non-acceptance of the order			Accepting the order	
	£	£		£	£
Sales		225,000	Sales		232,000
Direct materials	60,000		Direct materials	62,400	
Direct labour	95,000		Direct labour	98,800	
Royalties	5,000	160,000	Royalties	5,200	166,400
Contribution		65,000			65,600
Fixed costs		40,000	Fixed costs		40,000
Profit		25,000	Profit		25,600

Note: The fixed costs have not changed with the increased level of production.

The profit has increased by the amount of the total contribution earned by accepting the order from Malaysia.

CONDITIONS THAT MUST APPLY IF AN ORDER PRICED ON MARGINAL COSTING TECHNIQUES IS TO BE ACCEPTED

Care must be taken when accepting an order based on marginal costing principles.

- There must be spare production capacity in the business.
- The order must not displace other business (if it does then the revenue lost also becomes a marginal cost).
- There must be clear separation of existing customers from customers receiving the order priced at marginal cost (existing customers must be unaware of the cheaper price charged to the customer receiving the goods at the lower price).
- The customer receiving the goods should not be in a position to sell the goods to other customers at a price lower than the regular price.
- The customer receiving the order priced using marginal costing must be aware that the price quoted is for that one order only – the price charged should not set a precedent so that the 'cheaper price' is demanded for future orders.
- Care must be taken to ensure that competitors do not match the price for their regular customers, thus starting a price war where all producers will suffer from lower prices.

A manufacturing business must cover all costs incurred in running the business. A business cannot survive by costing all its production at marginal cost. If it did then none of the fixed costs would be covered (absorbed).

So, generally, any 'special' order which results in a positive contribution should be accepted.

ACCEPTANCE OF AN ORDER THAT WILL RESULT IN A NEGATIVE CONTRIBUTION

A special order that yields a negative contribution may be accepted under the following conditions:

- in order to retain a highly skilled workforce
- in order to maintain machinery in good condition, ie if failure to use the machinery would result in its deterioration
- in order to stimulate further orders at the 'normal price' in the future
- for altruistic reasons, ie because it is a worthwhile thing to do, eg providing a product at less than full cost, for disabled children.

QUESTION 1

The following information is given for T. Cupp, a manufacturer of pottery dinner services:

	£
Direct materials costs	4.50 per unit
Direct labour costs	7.70 per unit
Fixed costs	1.80 per unit

The dinner service sells to retailers at £30. Hallods, a large department store, wishes to purchase 3,000 dinner services at a price of £15 per service to include in its annual January sale.

Required Advise T. Cupp whether she should accept Hallods' order.

QUESTION 2

The following information is given for Isa Wally, a manufacturer of one type of sports shoe:

	£
Direct material costs	0.80 per unit
Direct labour costs	1.20 per unit
Fixed costs	7.00 per unit

The shoes are sold to retailers at £14.

BBJ sports shops wish to purchase 40,000 pairs at a price of £5 per pair to include in their summer sale as a special purchase.

Required Advise Isa whether she should accept BBJ's offer.

QUESTION 3

George Thomas manufactures scented candles – they sell for £2 each. The following information is given:

	£
Direct material costs	0.10 per unit
Direct labour costs	0.80 per unit
Fixed costs	0.50 per unit

A retailer in France wishes to purchase 1,000 candles for sale in Marseilles; he will pay £1 per candle.

Required Advise George whether to accept the order for France.

QUESTION 4

Betty Wong manufactures hand-painted greetings cards. The cards are sold to retailers at £10 each.

The following costs relate to the production of 750 cards:

	£
Direct material costs	0.08 per unit
Direct labour costs	2.42 per unit
Fixed costs	4.00 per unit

A retailer in the USA wishes to purchase 200 cards. She is prepared to pay £2.60 per card.

Required Advise Betty whether to accept the order from the USA.

QUESTION 5

The Shuttles Bowling Club rents out a room in its clubhouse at £40 per hour.

The costs involved in opening the room are:

Caretaker's wages	£8 per hour
Electricity charge	£1 per hour
Cleaner's wages	£3 per hour

None of these costs will be incurred if the room is not used. The treasurer adds £16 per hour to cover fixed costs incurred by the club.

A local bridge club wishes to use the room for a meeting lasting three hours but are only prepared to pay £50 for the use of the clubhouse.

Required Advise the club treasurer whether the room should be let to the bridge club.

QUESTION 6

The Towers Hotel owns a sports ground adjacent to the hotel. The hotel accountant provides the following information for the rent of the ground.

Cost that are only incurred when the ground is used.

	£
Groundsman's wage	8 per hour
Petrol etc for the mower	6 per hour
Cleaner's wage for changing rooms	1 per hour
	15

Other costs:

Mark up to cover fixed costs and profit	20
Charge per hour of use	35

Tiddlers Street Junior School wishes to hire the sports ground for its sports day. It will use the ground for three hours but the school budget can only afford to pay £50 for the three hours let.

Required Advise the hotel accountant whether the sports ground should be let to the school.

'MAKE OR BUY' DECISIONS

A business may have the opportunity to purchase the product that it currently manufactures itself.

In order to arrive at a decision the managers should consider the marginal costs and revenues.

WORKED EXAMPLE

Alex Droblin manufactures sweatshirts for sports retailers. The estimated costs and revenues for the next financial year are given:

Costs and revenues per unit, based on production and sales of 140,000 sweatshirts		
	£	
Selling price	12	
Direct materials	2	
Direct labour	3	
Fixed costs	4	
Total production cost	9	
Profit per sweatshirt	3	Total profit £420,000

A manufacturer in India has indicated that the sweatshirts could be supplied to Alex at a total cost of only £7 each.

Alex has calculated that if existing selling price is maintained then profits will rise to £5 per sweatshirt and total profits will rise to £700,000 next year – an increase in profits of £280,000.

Required Advise Alex whether, on financial grounds, he should accept the offer from India.

Answer

Alex should not accept the offer. If he did he would be worse off next year than if he continued to manufacture the sweatshirts himself. Profits would fall to only £140,000.

Contribution if he continues to manufacture himself = £7
(Selling price £12 − Marginal (variable costs) £5 (£2 + £3))
Contribution if he purchases from India = £5
(Selling price £12 − Marginal (variable cost) £7).

	Make			Buy		
	£	£			£	
Sales		1,680,000	Sales		1,680,000	
Direct materials	280,000					
Direct labour	420,000	700,000	Purchase price		980,000	
Contribution		980,000	Contribution		700,000	
Less Fixed costs		560,000	*Less* Fixed costs		560,000	
Profit		420,000	Profit		240,000	

Marginal costing statements show the positions clearly:

Note:

It has been assumed that any resources releases by accepting the offer from India could not be used elsewhere by Alex.

It has also been assumed that the fixed costs are in fact fixed and will have to be met whatever decision Alex arrives at.

If the manufacturing space could be sub-let to another manufacturer the income received would be a source of marginal revenue and should be added to the sales revenue as extra income.

If extra costs had to be incurred in transporting the goods to England this would have represented a further marginal cost.

If extra costs were incurred keeping the manufacturing area safe and/or secure, these costs would also represent marginal costs and would have to be included in Alex's calculations.

WORKED EXAMPLE

Alex is faced with the same details given above, however he can sub-let his manufacturing area at a rental of £200,000.

Required Advise Alex whether, on financial grounds, he should accept the offer from India.

Answer
He should accept the offer.

With the rental income, the total contribution would rise to £900,000 (original contribution £700,000 + rental income £200,000). Profit would also rise to £440,000 (compared with £420,000).

WORKED EXAMPLE

Alex is faced with the same details as given in the original example. But he has to employ a security firm to keep the factory premises secure from vandals. This will cost £120,000 per year and additional maintenance costs of £100,000.

Required Advise Alex whether, on financial grounds, he should accept the offer from India.

Answer
Alex should not accept the Indian order.

The contribution would only be £480,000 compared with the original contribution of £980,000.

Although in each case the contribution is positive, the new contribution should be compared with the contribution earned if Alex continued to manufacture the sweatshirts.

QUESTION 7

Pierre Dennis manufactures one type of high-quality marble fireplace. The following information is given for each fireplace. The figures are based on production of 80 fireplaces per year.

	£
Direct material costs	40 per unit
Direct labour costs	170 per unit
Distribution costs	30 per unit
Fixed costs	400 per unit
Total costs per unit	640
Profit	360
Selling price	1,000

Pierre has been approached by Angelo, an Italian manufacturer. Angelo can supply a similar fireplace of the same high quality for only £200. This price does not include delivery from Italy. Delivery charges will be £180 per fireplace. The prices are guaranteed for three years. Pierre says 'If I continue to sell fireplaces for £1,000, I will increase my profit to £620 for each fireplace sold'.

Required Advise Pierre whether he should purchase the fireplaces from Angelo.

QUESTION 8

Fleetfoot manufactures one type of running shoe, the 'Rapide'. The shoe sells to sports shops for £20 per pair.

The manufacturing costs per pair of shoes is:

	£
Leather	2.00
Other materials	1.20
Direct labour	5.10
Selling and distribution costs	0.60
Administration costs	0.10
Fixed costs	4.00
Total costs	13.00
Profit	7.00

Fleetfoot has been approached by a manufacturer based in China who can supply a similar shoe of the same specification and quality for £10.50 per pair. Delivery charges will be £0.40 per pair. Prices are guaranteed for two years.

Required Advise the managers of Fleetfoot whether to buy their shoes from the Chinese supplier.

MAKING A CHOICE BETWEEN COMPETING COURSES OF ACTION

The managers of a business may have to consider a choice between two or more competing strategies that would incur the same level of fixed costs. If this is the case then only the marginal costs need to be considered. The strategy that provides the greatest contribution should be the one adopted.

WORKED EXAMPLE

Marsha Knit starts a small furniture-manufacturing business. She is only able to produce one type of product. She needs to choose whether to produce tables, chairs or sideboards.

She provides the following predicted information:

Predicted production and sales	Tables 500 £	Chairs 500 £	Sideboards 500 £
Selling price per unit	400	120	380
Direct material costs per unit	80	13	70
Direct labour costs per unit	70	67	110
Total fixed costs	50,000	50,000	50,000

Required Advise Marsha which product she should manufacture.

Answer
Marsha should produce tables.

Each table produced will give a positive contribution of £250, compared with a contribution of £40 per chair and £200 per sideboard.

Check your answer by preparing marginal cost statements for each type of furniture.

QUESTION 9

The managers of Snuggles have costed the manufacture of two styles of slipper – the 'Comfy' and the 'Warmy'. However, only one type can be manufactured. They provide the following information for the production of one pair of slippers:

	Comfy £	Warmy £
Direct materials	6	5
Direct labour	3	2
Variable costs	4	4
Fixed costs	7	7
Selling price	28	25

Required Advise the managers of Snuggles which type of slipper should be manufactured.

QUESTION 10

Etomer is an electronics business manufacturing video recorders and DVD player/recorders. In their first year of this venture they will only be able to manufacture one type of machine. The costs of manufacture are expected to be:

	Video players (20,000 units) £	DVD players (15,000 units) £
Direct materials	18	20
Direct labour costs	4	4
Other variable costs	5	9
Fixed costs	15	20
Total costs	42	53
Selling price	49	65

Required Advise the managers of Etomer which product should be manufactured.

WHEN ONLY A LIMITED AMOUNT OF A FACTOR OF PRODUCTION IS AVAILABLE

A business may be faced by a short-term shortage of one or more factors of production necessary to continue the manufacturing process. There could be a temporary shortage of skilled labour;

there could be a temporary shortage of direct materials; or a temporary shortage of storage space. Any shortage of a particular resource will limit the business's ability to maximise profits.

A scarce resource is sometimes referred to as a **key factor**.

It is essential that the managers of a business utilise the scarce resources available in a way that will yield the maximum return to the business.

WORKED EXAMPLE

The Laville Company manufactures four products. The products use the same type of materials and skilled labour.

The following information is given:

Product	P	Q	R	S
Selling price per unit (£)	200	300	100	400
Maximum demand for product (units)	1,000	800	1,200	900
Material usage per unit (kg)	7	12	4	15
Labour hours per unit	3	4	2	6

Materials cost £10.00 per kilogram; labour costs £15.00 per hour.

Required A statement showing the level of production for each product that would maximise the profits for the Laville Company if:

a only 25,000 kilograms of materials are available
b only 10,000 labour hours are available.

Answer

Contribution earned by each product	P £	Q £	R £	S £
Selling price per unit	200	300	100	400
Marginal costs per unit	115	180	70	240
Contribution per unit	85	120	30	160

a

	P	Q	R	S
Contribution per kilogram of material used	£12.14	£10.00	£7.50	£10.67
Ranking	1	3	4	2

You can see that the Laville Company should produce as many of product P as possible; if there are still materials available they should produce as many of product S as possible, then product Q and finally product R.

WORKED EXAMPLE *continued*

If Laville could produce all products

they would produce	1,000	800	12,000	900
this would use	7,000 kg	9,600 kg	4,800 kg	13,500 kg

since this is not possible

they should produce	1,000	375	nil	900
this would use	7,000 kg	4,500 kg	nil	13,500 kg

This combination will maximise profits while using only 25,000 kilograms of materials.

b

Contribution per hour of labour used	£28.33	£30.00	£15.00	£26.67
Ranking	2	1	4	3

You can see that the Laville Company should produce as many unit of product Q as possible; then produce as many units of product P as possible, then product S and finally product R.

If Laville could produce all products

they would produce	1,000	800	1,200	900
this would use	3,000 hrs	3,200 hrs	2,400 hrs	5,400 hrs

since this is not possible

they should produce	1,000	800	nil	633
this would use	3,000 hrs	3,200 hrs	nil	3,798 hrs

This production pattern would maximise profits while using only 9,998 hours of scarce labour. (They have to produce only 633 of product S since the next unit would be only one-third complete!)

QUESTION 11

Seok Chin plc manufactures tables, chairs and bed headboards in Scunbridge. The same woodworking skills are used by the manufacturing labour.

Annual demand Costs per unit	Tables 300 £	Chairs 1,000 £	Headboards 400 £
Direct materials	23	8	10
Direct labour	80	32	16
Other variable costs	7	4	2
Fixed costs	20	6	8
Selling price	230	88	44

Direct labour costs £8 per hour.

In Scunbridge there is a shortage of skilled woodworker labour. There are only 5,000 hours available.

Required
a Calculate the rank order in which the products should be made in order to maximise profits.
b Calculate the number of each product that should be made in order to maximise profits.

QUESTION 12

Jock McTavish manufactures plastic goods. He produces three products; the cost patterns are given below:

Maximum demand Costs per unit	Boxes 5,000 £	Tool boxes 2,000 £	Packing cases 2,000 £
Direct materials	4	6	8
Direct labour	3	4	2
Other variable costs	2	1	3
Fixed costs	7	9	6
Total costs	16	20	19
Selling price	29	53	61

Materials cost £2 per kilogram.

There is a world shortage of the plastic needed to produce the products. Jock can obtain only 10,000 kilograms this year.

Required
a Calculate the rank order in which the products must be made in order to maximise profits.
b Calculate the number of each type of product that should be made in order to maximise profits.

QUESTION 13

Ivor Puddle makes wellington boots. Costing for the three types are given below:

Maximum demand Costs per unit	Gents 10,000 £	Ladies 8,000 £	Childrens 6,000 £
Direct materials	6	5.50	4
Direct labour	3	2.50	1
Other variable costs	2	2	2
Fixed costs	7	6	3
Total costs	18	16	10
Selling price	32	24	15

Materials cost 50p per ounce.

There is a shortage of the materials used to make the wellingtons and Ivor is able to acquire only 210,000 ounces for his production this year.

a Calculate the rank order in which the types of wellingtons must be made in order to maximise profits.

b Calculate the numbers of each type of wellington that should be made in order to maximise profits.

QUESTION 14

B. Ristle manufactures three types of brush. The following information is available:

Maximum demand Costs per unit	Toothbrush 100,000 £	Hair brush 40,000 £	Paint brush 30,000 £
Direct materials	0.50	1.00	1.50
Direct labour	1.00	1.00	1.50
Other variable costs	0.50	0.50	1.00
Fixed costs	0.50	0.75	1.00
Selling price	4.00	7.50	11.65

The brushes are made with hogs' hair which costs 50p per ounce.

There is a world shortage of hogs hair. Ristle is able to purchase only 200,000 ounces.

Required

a Calculate the rank order of production necessary in order to maximise profits.

b Calculate the number of each type of brush to be manufactured in order to maximise profits.

PENETRATION OR DESTROYER PRICING

This strategy may be employed by the managers of a business when they wish to gain a foothold in a market in which a number of firms are already well established. They decide to cost their product using only marginal costs.

They can do this because their existing customers will already be covering (absorbing) the fixed costs incurred by the business.

EXAMPLE

A UK business manufactures electrical generators. The generators retail in the UK at £273 per unit. The cost of producing one generator is:

	£
Components	56
Labour costs	112
Fixed costs	32
Total costs	200
Profit	73
Selling price in UK	273

The managers wish to penetrate the Scandinavian market.

The business could sell its generator at £168; this would cover the marginal costs incurred. The company could use this to establish the product in the Scandinavian market at this price and be no worse off. If consumer loyalty can be established in Scandinavia the business may be able to increase prices, so making a contribution towards fixed costs and profits. It might also mean that other products with the same brand name might have an advantage.

BREAK-EVEN

The break-even point is the level of sales revenue and units sold at which a business makes neither a profit nor a loss. It is a popular examination topic so it is worth spending some time mastering the three methods of determining the break-even point.

This topic has been covered in *Introducing Accounting* pages 366–381; you are recommended to revisit this chapter as a revision of this topic.

Here is an example of each method of determining the break-even point.

THE UNIT CONTRIBUTION METHOD
Can you remember the formula? Of course you can – it is:

$$\text{Break-even point} = \frac{\text{Total fixed costs}}{\text{Contribution per unit}} = \text{Number of units required to be sold}$$

WORKED EXAMPLE

The following information is given for the production and sales of 50,000 pimkles.

	£
Selling price per unit	30
Direct material costs per unit	8
Direct labour costs per unit	9
Fixed costs per unit	5

Required
a Calculate the break-even point for pimkles.
b Calculate the break-even sales revenue necessary to break even.
c Calculate the margin of safety.

Answer
a Break-even point = $\dfrac{\text{Total fixed costs}}{\text{Contribution per unit}}$ = $\dfrac{£250,000}{£13}$ = 19,231 pimkles.
b Break-even sales revenue = 19,231 × £30 = £576,930.
c Margin of safety = 30,769 pimkles (50,000 − 19,231).

THE CONTRIBUTION/SALES METHOD (ALSO CALLED THE PROFIT/VOLUME METHOD)
This method is used when:

■ there are a number of products being manufactured and sold
■ a marginal costing statement is given.

WORKED EXAMPLE

Ben Chan plc
Marginal cost statement

	£
Sales	358,700
Variable costs	126,300
Contribution	232,400
Fixed costs	150,000
Profit	82,400

$$\frac{\text{Contribution}}{\text{Sales}} = \frac{£232,400}{£358,700} = 0.648$$

$$\text{Break-even point} = \frac{\text{Total fixed costs}}{\text{Contribution/sales ratio}} = \frac{£150,000}{0.648} = £231,482 \text{ sales revenue.}$$

This method gives the break-even level of sales revenue.

GRAPHICAL MEANS

Remember: do not use this method unless a question asks specifically for a graph.

Drawing a graph is very time-consuming and can be less accurate than the other methods.

Chapter summary

- Marginal means 'one extra'.
- Contribution is an important concept in using marginal costing techniques.
- Marginal costing is a decision-making technique.
- You should be able to calculate contribution and use it in arriving at decisions.
- Most examination questions deal with acceptance or rejection of a special order at less than the price charged to 'regular' customers.

Self-test questions

- Define 'variable costs'.
- Identify two types of variable costs.
- Define 'semi-variable costs'.
- Identify one type of semi-variable cost.
- A business produces 2,000 units of a product. Variable costs are £4,000; fixed costs are £2,000. Calculate total cost if 3,000 units of the product is manufactured.
- Explain the term 'contribution'.
- Calculate the contribution from the following information: selling price £43 per unit; variable costs per unit £27; fixed costs per unit £10.
- Identify two uses of marginal costing.
- State the formula used to calculate the break-even point using the unit/contribution method.
- Explain the term 'key factor'.

TEST QUESTIONS

QUESTION 15

The following information is available for the production and sales of 10,000 units of ZQ/461, a component used in the electronics industry:

	£ per unit
Direct materials	8
Direct labour	2
Other variable costs	1
Fixed costs	4
Profit	5
Selling price	20

Required
Calculate:
a   the break-even point in units
b   the break-even point in sales revenue
c   the margin of safety.

QUESTION 16

The following information is given for the production and sales of 25,000 'slofastas', a component used in the motor industry:

	£ per unit
Direct materials	8
Direct labour	9
Other variable costs	2
Fixed costs	6
Profit	7
Selling price	32

Required
Calculate:
a   the break-even point in units
b   the break-even point in sales revenue
c   the margin of safety.

QUESTION 17

Aled Griffiths provides the following information for his engineering business for the year ended 31 March 20*5:

	£
Sales revenue	356,000
Variable costs	112,000
Fixed costs	150,000

Calculate:

a c/v ratio
b break-even level of sales revenue.

QUESTION 18

Tee Way provides the following information for his restaurant for the year ended 28 February 20*5:

	£
Sales revenue	412,300
Variable costs	197,200
Fixed costs	100,000

Required Calculate the level of sales revenue at which Way's restaurant will break even.

QUESTION 19

Morris Curry produces a hand-made savoury sausage that is sold to retailers for 70p per kilogram.

The following information is available for the production and sale of 100,000 kg:

	£
Ingredients	0.28 per kg
Direct wages	0.13 per kg
Other variable costs	0.04 per kg
Fixed costs	0.08 per kg
Total cost per kilo	0.53

Required
a Draw a graph for savoury sausages.

From your graph determine:

b Break-even point.
c Margin of safety.
d The profit or loss at 20,000 kilograms of production and sale.
e The profit or loss at 40,000 kilograms of production and sale.

QUESTION 20

Wallie McDuff manufactures wooden pallets for the canned food industry. The pallets are sold for £5 each. He provides the following information for the production and sale of 200,000 pallets:

	£
Timber	1.42 per pallet
Direct labour	1.00 per pallet
Other direct costs	0.08 per pallet
Total cost per pallet	3.30

Required

a Draw a graph for the production of pallets.

From your graph, determine:

b The break-even point.
c The margin of safety.
d The profit or loss at 50,000 output of pallets and sales.
e The profit or loss at 150,000 output of pallets and sales.

QUESTION 21

Muriel Sphinx owns and runs a small café serving a meal deal comprising a portion of fries, a burger and a cold drink. She charges £2.99. She provides the following information on costs for a meal deal, based on 10,000 meals:

	£
Fries	0.20
Burger	0.40
Bun	0.05
Drink	0.14
Fixed costs	1.00
Total cost	1.79

Akela Thomas, a local cub leader, approaches Muriel regarding a meeting of several cub packs from throughout the county. Akela requires 300 meal deals but can only afford to pay £1.50 per meal. She requires the meals at the café on 15 February, a Tuesday, the day when the café will normally be closed.

Required Advise Muriel whether she should, on financial grounds, accept Akela's booking.

QUESTION 22

Peta Burgess owns and runs a small hotel in Worksop. She has costed out the hourly use of her meeting room from the following information:

The following hourly costs are only incurred when the room is in use:

	£
Direct labour	5
Heating	2
Lighting	1

The following hourly costs are charged whether the room is used or not:

	£
Repairs	3
Maintenance	2
Fixed costs i.e. rent, rates, insurances etc.	7
Profit loading	25
Hourly charge for use of room	45

A group of senior citizens requires a room for meeting in once each month. The 12 meetings will last for two hours and each would take place at a time when the room would not normally be used. The club treasurer has approached Peta and has offered £250 for one year's meetings.

Required Advise Peta whether she should allow the senior citizens to use the room.

QUESTION 23

Fatima Grolsch manufactures four products. Each requires the use of a component called a 'grymbil' which is imported from Romania at a cost of £2 each.

The following information relates to the manufacture of each product:

	AP/7 £	BR/9 £	CQ/4 £	DS/8 £
Direct materials	9	13	11	14
Components – grymbil	2	10	6	8
Direct labour	6	12	7	9
Fixed costs	7	8	7	10
Selling price	30	85	64.50	81
Maximum demand	5,000	6,000	1,000	4,000

Following a series of strikes in the Romania factory that manufactures grymbils, Fatima can import only 10,000 units this year.

Required
Calculate:
a   the rank order of production necessary in order to maximise profits
b   the number of each type of product to be manufactured in order to maximise profits.

QUESTION 24

Uxtrim Ltd manufactures four products. Each product uses the Qong component. Qongs are imported from Taiwan and cost £14 each.

Maximum demand	Muna 5,000 £	Naxa 9,000 £	Ofza 2,300 £	Polan 4,400 £
Direct materials	16	8	30	32
Qong component	70	28	126	112
Direct labour	10	13	26	11
Fixed costs	26	18	46	38
Selling price	127.55	65.50	254	221.40

The manufacturers have told Uxtrim Ltd that only 90,000 Qongs will be available this year.

Required
Calculate:
a   the rank order of production necessary in order to maximise profits
b   the number of each type of product to be manufactured in order to maximise profits
c   the maximum profit that can be made.

QUESTION 25

Afur Moah manufactures 'critulators'. The following information relates to the costs and revenues associated with the production of 14,000 units:

	£
Direct materials	7
Direct labour	12
Semi-variable costs	5
Fixed costs	6
Profit	10
Selling price	40

On examination, Afur has determined that the semi-variable costs are 50% variable and 50% fixed.

Required

Calculate:

a the break-even level of production and sales

b the margin of safety.

QUESTION 26

Edna Silling manufactures 'durelos'. The following information relates to the costs and revenues associated with the production of 10,000 units:

	£
Direct materials	3
Direct labour	18
Semi-variable costs	9
Fixed costs	4
Profit	26
Selling price	60

Semi-variable costs are 70% fixed and 30% variable.

Required

Calculate:

a the break-even level of production and sales

b the margin of safety.

QUESTION 27

The following information is given for the production and sales of Gurizmos, a new kitchen appliance:

Costs per Gurizmo:	£
Raw materials	9
Components	1
Direct labour	5
Royalties	2
Fixed costs	3
Selling price	25

This data is based on an output of 2,000 Gurizmos.

Required
a Draw a graph based on the information given for the production and sales of Gurizmos.
b The break-even point in units.
c The break-even point in sales revenue.
d The margin of safety in units.
e The profit/loss made when 400 units are produced and sold.
f The profit/loss made when 600 units are produced and sold.
g The profit/loss made when 800 units are produced and sold.

QUESTION 28

The following information is available for the production and sales of one unit of 'Staip'. The data is based on the production and sale of 500 units.

	£
Direct materials	32
Direct labour	18
Royalties	5
Fixed costs	20
Selling price	100

Required
a Draw a graph based on the information available for production and sales of Staip.

From your graph, determine:

b The break-even point in units produced and sold.
c The break-even level of sales revenue.
d The margin of safety in units.
e The profit/loss made when 200 units are produced and sold.

QUESTION 29

The following information is given for Gwenaelle Voisin, a manufacturer, for April 20*5:

	£
Direct materials	20,000
Direct labour	30,000
Royalties	2,000
Fixed costs	7,000
Sales revenue	80,000

Required

a   Prepare a marginal cost statement for the month of April 20*5.
b   Calculate the level of sales revenue that will ensure that Gwenaelle reaches a break-even level or sales revenue.

QUESTION 30

The following information is given for the month of March 20*5:

	Units used	Price per unit £
Direct materials	7,500	2.50
Direct labour	16,000	6.00
Other direct costs	4,000	3.00

Royalties to be paid total £9,000.
Fixed costs for the month will amount to £36,000.
During the month it is estimated that sales revenue will be £20,800.

Required

a   Prepare a marginal cost statement for the month of March 20*5.
b   Calculate the break-even level of sales revenue.

Standard costing sets levels of costs and revenues that ought to be achievable when reasonable levels of performance are attained, together with efficient working practices to manufacture a product.

Variance is the difference between budgeted (standard) revenue and costs and actual revenue and costs. They arise when actual results do not correspond to predicted results.

Sub-variance is a constituent part of a total variance. Sub-variances added together give the total variance.

Adverse variances reduce predicted profits.

Favourable variances increase predicted profits.

A **budget** is a financial plan prepared in advance of a defined time period. It is based on the objectives of the business.

Specification coverage:
AQA 16.2; OCR 5.4.2.

By the end of this chapter you should be able to:
- explain the uses of a system of standard costing
- calculate and interpret sales variances, material variances and labour variances
- understand the inter-relationship of variances
- appreciate the usefulness of variance analysis to management.

We all set standards in our everyday lives. Standards are goals – things that we hope to achieve.

- I may try to save £5,000 to add to the trade-in value of my car in order that I may be able to purchase a more up-to-date model.
- You may wish to save a certain sum of money in order that you can purchase a more sophisticated games console.
- You may wish to run 400 metres in a time of 1 minute 10 seconds or less.

All the examples are realistic targets that we believe are achievable.

The same idea is widespread in manufacturing businesses. In order to achieve an efficient production process, a budget will be prepared. The details will set the targets that the business hopes to achieve – standards are set for future performance.

If I fail to save sufficient money to replace my car, then, as a rational person (in my opinion!), I would consider the reason(s) why I was unable to save the £5,000.

If you failed to accumulate sufficient funds to allow the purchase of the games console, I guess you would investigate the reasons why. In both cases it could have been because the target (standard) was unrealistic:

- because income was less than expected or
- other financial priorities took precedence.

If the desired time for completion of the 400 metres was not achieved this could be because of:

- an unrealistic target
- poor training regime
- poor athletic diet etc.

If a business does not achieve the standards set, the managers will also wish to find out why.

MATERIALS VARIANCES

> **Total direct material variance** identifies the difference between the amount that managers thought would be spent on direct materials (the standard set – the budgeted amount) and the amount that was actually spent on the direct materials.

WORKED EXAMPLE

Geoff Whyz has budgeted to use £72,000 direct materials in October. When confirmation is available in November, Geoff discovers that the actual expenditure was £75,000.

Required Calculate the total direct materials variance for October.

Answer
Total direct materials variance = £3,000 adverse (£75,000 − £72,000).

WORKED EXAMPLE

Ethel Bigome has budgeted to use direct materials costing £36,000 in January. In February Ethel was able to determine that actual direct materials cost £34,800.

Required Calculate the total direct materials variance.

Answer
Total direct materials variance = £1,200 Favourable (36,000 − £34,800).

Note: The adverse total material variance cost the business more than anticipated and will thus reduce profits (affect profits adversely). The favourable total material variance cost the business less than anticipated and therefore would increase profits (thus having a favourable effect on profits).

It is fine that we can determine whether the price actually paid has cost us more or less than was anticipated but from a management point of view it would be much more useful if we could discover why the variance from budgeted figures had arisen.

The difference in the cost of direct materials used could be because of:

- more materials being used than was expected (adverse variance)
- fewer materials being used than was expected (favourable variance)
- an increase in the prices of materials since the budget was prepared (adverse variance)
- a decrease in the prices of materials since the budget was prepared (favourable variance)
- a combination of a change in the use of materials and a change in prices.

We can identify differences in budgeted and actual expenditure caused by the above factors by calculating **sub-variances**.

Material usage sub-variance will calculate any changes in the total expenditure caused by changes in the quantity of materials used in the process. An adverse variance will indicate that the production process used more materials than was anticipated. Once identified, remedial action can be taken.

A favourable variance will indicate that the production process used fewer materials than was anticipated. If the reasons can be identified, any good efficient practices may be able to be replicated in other cost centres of the business.

WORKED EXAMPLE

R. G. Bahgi provides the following information for raw materials:

	Budgeted	Actual
Materials used	2,000 kgs	2,100 kgs
Materials cost per kg	£8	£8

Required Calculate the direct material usage variance.

Answer
Materials usage variance £800 adverse caused by using more materials than were budgeted for.

WORKED EXAMPLE

T. Cupp provides the following information for raw materials to be used in production during September:

	Budgeted	Actual
Materials used	830 m²	810 m²
Material cost per m²	£4	£4

Required Calculate the raw materials usage variance for September.

Answer
£80 favourable variance caused by fewer materials being used than budgeted for.

A **direct material price variance** calculates any differences between budgeted and actual costs caused by sub-variances that arise because of a change in the prices of the raw materials being used.

WORKED EXAMPLE

J. Gwock provides the following information for raw materials to be used in her production process for December:

	Budgeted data
Materials to be used	1,200 litres
Cost per litre	£9.60

In January, the following information became available:

	Actual
Materials used	1,200 litres
Cost per litre	£9.80

Required Calculate the material cost variance for January.

Answer
Material cost variance £240 adverse caused by an increase in the cost of acquiring each litre of the material used.

As you can see, the calculation to determine the variance is relatively straightforward if there is only one variable to consider. But what if there are differences in both the materials used and the price paid to acquire those materials from the amount and price budgeted for?

The simple way to calculate and differentiate between the two types of sub-variances is to use the following grid:

$$Sq \times Sp$$
$$Aq \times Sp$$
$$Aq \times Ap$$

Where: S = the standard (or budgeted) figure
q = the quantity
p = the price
A = the actual figure

So: Sq = the standard quantity
Sp = the standard price
Aq = the actual quantity used
Ap = the actual price of the materials used.

$Sq \times Sp = $ ⎤
⎥
⎥
$Aq \times Sp = $ ⎦ ⎤
⎥
⎥
$Aq = Ap = $ ⎦

Any difference (variance) between these two totals must be due to differences in the budgeted usage and the actual usage since the standard price remains the same on both lines.

Any difference (variance) between these two totals must be due to differences in the budgeted price as the actual quantities remain the same.

The two differences combined will amount to the total variance.

WORKED EXAMPLE

The following information is given for the use of materials used to produce 'befures':

	Budgeted	Actual
Direct materials	720 metres	730 metres
Direct material costs per metre	£3.00	£3.50

Calculate:

a the material usage sub-variance
b the material price sub-variance
c the total material variance.

Sq × Sp

720 × £3 = £2,160

Aq × Sp

730 × £3 = £2,190

Aq × Ap

730 × £3.50 = £2,555

£30

£365

To gain full marks, we need to identify whether these variances are adverse or favourable.

The first line tells us that total materials would cost £2,160.

The second line tells us that total materials actually cost £2,190.

Materials in the second line cost £30 more than the budgeted costs on line 1. An increase in costs would have an adverse effect on profits, so £30 is an adverse usage variance.

The second line tells us that materials would cost £2,190.

The third line tells us that materials actually cost £2,555.

Materials on the third line cost £365 more than the cost on the second line. An increase in costs would have an adverse effect on profits so £365 is an adverse price variance.

The material usage sub-variance and the materials price sub-variance together will give the total material variance. So:

Sq × Sp

720 × £3 = £2,160

Aq × Sp

730 × £3 = £2,190

Aq × Ap

730 × £3.50 = £2,555

£30 adverse material usage variance

£365 adverse material price variance

£395 adverse total material variance

We have successfully identified the three variances asked for in the question.

WORKED EXAMPLE

The following information is given for the use of materials in the manufacturing of 'trusmedas':

	Budgeted	Actual
Direct materials	2,400 gallons	2,250 gallons
Direct materials cost per gallon	£8	£10

Required
Calculate:

a the material usage sub-variance
b the material price sub-variance
c the total direct material variance.

Answer

Sq × Sp

2,400 × 8 = £19,200

Aq × Sp   £1,200 favourable material usage variance

2,250 × 8 = £18,000

Aq × Ap   £2,560 adverse material price variance

2,250 × 10 = £22,560   £1,360 adverse total material variance

Materials cost £1,360 more than budgeted for. This was because there was a price increase of £2,560 and a saving of £1,200 because of more efficient use of materials.

QUESTION 1

T. Ravian provides the following information for materials for August:

	Budgeted	Actual
Direct materials	7,000 litres	6,900 litres
Direct material cost per litre	£2.50	£2.40

Required
Calculate:
a the direct material usage sub-variance
b the direct material price sub-variance
c the total direct material variance.

QUESTION 2

Bimson Ltd provides the following information for materials for January:

	Budgeted	Actual
Direct materials	600 kg	530 kg
Direct materials price per kg	£4	£3.75

Required
Calculate:

a the direct material usage sub-variance
b the direct material price sub-variance
c the total direct material variance.

QUESTION 3

Bampa Ltd provides the following information for materials for July:

	Budgeted	Actual
Direct materials	2,900 tonnes	3,100 tonnes
Direct material price per tonne	£200	£220

Required
Calculate:

a the direct material usage sub-variance
b the direct material price sub-variance
c the total direct material variance.

QUESTION 4

Carmichael Ltd provides the following information for direct materials for February:

	Budgeted	Actual
Direct materials	2,130 m^2	2,600 m^2
Direct material price per m^2	£0.50	£0.60

Required
Calculate:

a the direct material usage sub-variance
b the direct material price sub-variance
c the direct material total variance.

QUESTION 5

McThrift Ltd provides the following information for materials for November:

	Budgeted	Actual
Direct materials	9,000 litres	9,100 litres
Direct material price per litre	£1.60	£1.40

Required
Calculate:

a the direct material usage sub-variance
b the direct material price sub-variance
c the direct material total variance.

QUESTION 6

Chang Ltd provides the following information for materials:

	Budgeted	Actual
Direct materials	2,400 metres	2,250 metres
Direct material price per metre	£6.50	£6.70

Required
Calculate:

a the direct material usage sub-variance
b the direct material price sub-variance
c the total direct material variance.

DIRECT LABOUR VARIANCE

Total direct labour variances identify the difference between the amount that managers thought that they would spend on direct labour costs (the standard set – the budgeted amount) and the amount that they actually spent.

WORKED EXAMPLE

Tony has budgeted that direct labour costs for March would be £172,000. The actual amount spent was £178,000.

Required Calculate the total direct labour variance for March.

Answer
Total direct labour variance = £6,000 adverse (£178,000 − £172,000).

WORKED EXAMPLE

Magdelaine budgeted to use £83,000 of direct labour in May.

In early June she discovered that she had actually spent £82,500.

Required Calculate the total direct labour variance.

Answer
The total direct labour variance = £500 favourable (£83,000 − £82,500).

Note: In the first example above, labour cost more than was budgeted – this had an adverse effect on profits.

In the second example £500 was saved on the budgeted amount – this would have a favourable effect on profit.

It would be useful for managers of a business to determine whether the total variance was caused by:

■ workers being more efficient (favourable variance)
■ workers being less efficient (adverse variance)
■ workers being paid more (adverse variance)
■ workers being paid less (favourable variance)
■ or some combination of or a change in efficiency and a change in wage rates.

We can use the same technique already used to determine direct material sub-variances to calculate sub-variances in the budgeted amount and actual amounts spent on direct labour.

In order to calculate the sub-variances that make up the total direct labour variances we can refer to our grid:

$$Sq \times Sp$$

$$Aq \times Sp$$

$$Aq \times Ap$$

However, we do need to make a couple of changes to our descriptions of the sub-variances:

■ labour 'usage' is referred to as 'labour efficiency'

■ labour 'price' is referred to as 'wage rate' or 'labour rate'.

Labour is used more or less efficiently than budgeted for.

The price of labour, as you might know from your part-time job, is the 'wage rate' that you are paid.

$$Sq \times Sp$$

$$Aq \times Sp$$

$$Aq \times Ap$$

S = the standard (or budgeted) figure

q = the number of labour hours

p = the rate at which direct labour is paid

A = the actual figure

So:

Sq is the standard number of hours thought to be necessary

Sp is the standard wage rate

Aq is the actual number of hours that were worked

Ap is the actual rate paid to the employees.

$Sq \times Sp$
$Aq \times Sp$ Any difference between these two totals must be because of the hours that managers thought would be worked by direct labour and the hours that were in fact worked.

$Aq \times Ap$ Any difference between these two totals must be because of any difference in the wage rate that had been budgeted and the wage rate actually paid.

The two differences combined will amount to the total variance.

WORKED EXAMPLE

Katap Ltd provides the following information for direct labour for November:

	Budgeted	Actual
Direct labour	37,000 hours	39,000 hours
Direct labour wage rate per hour	£7	£7.20

Calculate:

a the direct labour efficiency sub-variance
b the direct labour wage rate sub-variance
c the total direct labour variance.

Answer

$$Sq \times Sp$$
$$37,000 \times £7 = £259,000$$

$$Aq \times Sp$$

£14,000

$$39,000 \times £7 = £273,000$$

$$Aq \times Ap$$

£7,800

$$39,000 \times £7.20 = £280,800$$

To gain full marks we need to identify whether these sub-variances are adverse or favourable.

The first line tells us that the managers of Katap Ltd thought that £259,000 would be spent on direct labour wages.

The second line indicates the change caused by budgeted hours not being achieved. There was an overspend of £14,000; this would affect profits adversely.

When the second line is compared with what actually happened, we can see that another overspend occurred. The profits would be adversely affected by £7,800.

Both sub-variances are adverse.

■ The direct labour efficiency sub-variance is   £14,000 adverse
■ The direct labour rate sub-variance is   £7,800 adverse
■ The total labour variance is   £21,800 adverse

The three variances asked for have been identified.

WORKED EXAMPLE

Bash Ltd provides the following information for direct labour for April:

	Budgeted	Actual
Direct labour	6,200 hours	6,250 hours
Direct labour rate per hour	£9.50	£9.30

Required
Calculate:

a the direct labour efficiency variance
b the direct labour wage rate variance
c the total labour variance.

Answer

$$Sq \times Sp$$

$$6,200 \times £9.50 = £58,900$$

$$Aq \times Sp \qquad\qquad £475 \qquad\qquad \text{Adverse direct labour efficiency sub-variance}$$

$$6,250 \times £9.50 = £59,375$$

$$Aq \times Ap \qquad\qquad £1,250 \qquad\qquad \text{Favourable direct labour rate sub-variance}$$

$$6,250 \times £9.30 = £58,125 \qquad\qquad \underline{£775} \qquad\qquad \text{Favourable total direct labour variance}$$

The workers took longer to complete their tasks – this cost Bash Ltd £475 more than the budgeted figure but workers were paid a lower hourly rate so Bash Ltd saved £1,250.

Note: The term 'standard' will be used in place of 'budgeted' in questions, now that you have got used to the detailed calculations required.

QUESTION 7

The managers of Sheddacc provide the following information for direct labour costs for May:

	Standard	Actual
Direct labour	1,400 hours	1,350 hours
Direct labour rate per hour	£9.50	£9.60

Required
Calculate:

a the direct labour efficiency sub-variance
b the direct labour rate sub-variance
c the total direct labour variance.

QUESTION 8

The manager of Typlea plc provides the following information for direct labour costs for September:

	Standard	Actual
Direct labour	24,500 hours	24,750 hours
Direct labour rate per hour	£12.40	£12.25

Calculate:

a the direct labour efficiency sub-variance
b the direct labour rate sub-variance
c the total direct labour variance.

Many examination questions (and indeed real life) give information for both direct materials and direct labour and require the calculation of all seven variances.

WORKED EXAMPLE

The managers of Hasbec Ltd provide the following information for December:

Standard costs:
Direct materials: 430 kg costing £18 per kg
Direct labour: 170 hours at £7.50 per hour.
The **actual costs** incurred in the manufacturing process were:
Direct materials: 425 kg costing £18.10 per kg
Direct labour: 172 hours at £7.40 per hour.

Required
Calculate:

a the direct material usage sub-variance
b the direct material price sub-variance
c the total direct material variance
d the direct labour efficiency sub-variance
e the direct labour rate sub-variance
f the total direct labour variance
g the total direct expenses variance.

Answer

Direct materials: Sq × Sp

    430 × £18 = £7,740.00

    Aq × Sp

    425 × £18 = £7,650.00

£90 favourable direct material usage sub-variance (a)

    Aq × Ap

    425 × £18.10 = £7,692.50

£42.50 adverse direct material price sub-variance (b)

£47.50 favourable direct material variance (c)

Direct labour: Sq × Sp

    170 × £7.50 = £1,275.00

    Aq × Sp

    172 × £7.50 = £1,290.00

£15 adverse direct labour efficiency sub-variance (d)

    Aq × Ap

    172 × £7.40 = £1,272.80

£17.20 favourable direct labour rate sub-variance (e)

£2.20 favourable total labour variance (f)

Total direct expenses variance = £49.70 favourable (g)

QUESTION 9

The managers of Lesmark Ltd provide the following information for December:

Standard costs:

Direct materials: 1,720 litres costing £1.80 per litre

Direct labour: 810 hours at £8.40 per hour.

The **actual costs** in manufacturing were:

Direct materials: 1,735 litres costing £1.75 per litre

Direct labour: 834 hours at £8.50 per hour.

Required
Calculate:

a the direct material usage sub-variance
b the direct material price sub-variance
c the total direct material variance
d the direct labour efficiency sub-variance
e the direct labour rate sub-variance
f the total direct labour variance
g the total direct expenses variance.

QUESTION 10

The managers of Slaura Ltd provide the following information for February:

Standard costs:

Direct materials: 1,120 m^2 costing 48 pence per m^2

Direct labour: 310 hours at £16.30 per hour.

The **actual costs** incurred in manufacture were:

Direct materials: 1,110m^2 costing 50 pence per m^2

Direct labour: 320 hours at £16.20 per hour.

Required
Calculate:

a the direct material usage sub-variance
b the direct material price sub-variance
c the total direct material variance
d the direct labour efficiency sub-variance
e the direct labour rate sub-variance
f the total direct labour variance
g the total direct expenses variance.

THE FLEXED BUDGET

One of the purposes of using a standard costing system is that problem areas in production are highlighted and so remedial action can be taken. The system will also identify areas of cost saving and therefore good practice which may be emulated in other areas of the business.

The system identifies variances by making comparisons between standard (budgeted) costs and the costs that have actually been incurred.

One of the over-riding principles involved in making comparisons is that we should try, as far as is possible, to compare like with like.

This principle should be applied when comparing standard costs with actual costs. So if actual activity differs from budgeted activity, the budget must be flexed to produce a budget which reflects actual levels of activity.

EXAMPLE

The manager of Bloo Jeans plc has budgeted to produce 100,000 pairs of denim jeans in August. She budgets for the use of 140,000 m² of denim in the production process. The actual figures available in September show that only 120,000 m² of denim was used and total production was 90,000 pairs of jeans.

Clearly, the production has used less denim than had been anticipated but fewer jeans were manufactured so one would expect less materials to be used.

The comparison is 140,000 m² with 120,000 m².

However, we are not comparing like with like.

- 140,000 m² should have made 100,000 pairs of jeans
- 120,000 m² actually made 90,000 pairs of jeans.

In order to make a valid comparison to see if the materials have been used efficiently or not, we need to adjust our budget – the adjustment is called **flexing**.

If we had known earlier, when the standard was set, that only 90,000 pairs of jeans would be made, the budgeted figures for materials to be used would have been:

126,000 m² (ie 90,000/100,000 or 9/10 of 140,000m²)

and the figures to be used would be:

Standard costs:

90,000 pairs of jeans would require 126,000m² of denim.

So a comparison can now be made quite easily:

Standard materials usage:

90,000 pairs of jeans will require 126,000m² of denim.

Actual material usage:

90,000 pairs of jeans have required 120,000m² of denim.

We can then see quite clearly that less material has been used than anticipated – thus giving rise to a favourable material usage sub-variance.

WORKED EXAMPLE

The managers of Getang Ltd provide the following information for the production of 'Selvings' during March:

Budgeted output	Actual output
80,000 Selvings	70,000 Selvings
Budgeted use of direct materials	**Actual use of direct materials**
240,000 litres	220,000 litres

Required Calculate the amount of direct materials saved or wasted during March.

WORKED EXAMPLE *continued*

Answer

Flexed budget	Budgeted use of direct materials
70,000 Selvings	210,000 litres (7/8 × 240,000)
Actual usage	**Actual use of direct materials**
70,000 Selvings	220,000 litres

So 10,000 litres of direct materials were used that had not been budgeted for. The reasons for this 'wastage' should be investigated and if possible a remedy sought.

It will also be necessary to flex the standards set for the use of direct labour.

WORKED EXAMPLE

The following information is given for direct labour hours for July for the production of 'Lingts':

	Standard	Actual
Production	250,000 units	225,000 units
Direct labour hours	70,000 hours	65,000 hours

Required Calculate the direct labour hours to be used in a flexed budget for July.

Answer
225,000 Lingts should use 63,000 hours of direct labour

(225,000/250,000 × 70,000 hours). In fact, 2,000 further hours have been used. An investigation should be undertaken to determine why this has happened and remedial action taken if possible.

● EXAMINATION TIP

Only flex the **standard** quantity of direct materials and/or the **standard** hours of direct labour to be used in your grid.

WORKED EXAMPLE

The following information is given for the production of trapeds:

Standard costs for 1,000 trapeds:	
Direct materials:	220 kg at £5 per kg
Direct labour:	60 hours at £9.50 per hour.
Actual costs for the production of 950 trapeds:	
Direct materials:	204 kg at £5.75 per kg
Direct labour:	58 hours at £9.30 per hour.

Required
Calculate:

a the direct material usage sub-variance
b the direct material price sub-variance
c the total direct material variance
d the direct labour efficiency sub-variance
e the direct labour rate sub-variance
f the total direct material variance.

Answer
The budget must first be flexed. Only 95% of the budgeted trapeds have been produced so the standard usage of direct materials and direct labour should be calculated to construct an amended budget – a flexed budget.

Remember, only the standard (budgeted) quantities will be changed.

Standard costs for 950 trapeds should use (950/1,000 = 0.95)

■ 95% of budgeted materials so 0.95 × 220 = 209 kg

Standard costs for 950 trapeds should use (950/1,000 = 0.95)

■ 95% of budgeted labour hours so 0.95 × 60 = 57 hours.

Re-working the standard costs:

Standard costs for 950 trapeds:

    Direct materials: 209 kg at £5 per kg

    Direct labour: 57 hours at £9.30 per hour.

These figures are used in the 'grid'.

Direct materials: $Sq \times Sp$

            209 × £5   = £1,045

            $Aq \times Sp$ £25 favourable direct material usage sub-variance

            204 × £5   = £1,020

            $Aq \times Ap$ £153 adverse direct material price sub-variance

            204 × £5.75 = £1,173

                       £128   adverse total direct material variance

WORKED EXAMPLE *continued*

Direct labour:
$$Sq \times Sp$$
$$57 \times £9.50 = £541.50$$

£9.50 adverse direct labour efficiency sub-variance

$$Aq \times Sp$$
$$58 \times £9.50 = £551.00$$

£11.60 favourable direct labour rate sub-variance

$$Aq \times Ap$$
$$58 \times £9.30 = £539.40$$

£2.10 favourable total direct labour variance

QUESTION 11

Agripals Ltd manufacture one component for the motor industry. The following information is available for 20*4:

Standard costs for production of 7,200 components:

Direct materials:	10,800 units at £4.00 per unit
Direct labour:	720 hours at £13.50 per hour.

Actual production was 7,000 components and actual costs were:

Direct materials:	10,600 at £3.85 per unit
Direct labour:	705 hours at £13.40 per hour.

Required
Calculate:

a the direct material usage sub-variance
b the direct material price sub-variance
c the total direct material variance
d the direct labour efficiency sub-variance
e the direct labour labour rate sub-variance
f the total direct labour variance.

QUESTION 12

Diners Ltd manufactures tables. The following information is available for 20*4:

Standard costs for production of 2,400 tables:

Direct materials – timber:	3,600 m² at £14.00 per m²
Direct labour:	6,480 hours at £16.00 per hour.

Actual production was 2,200 tables and actual costs were:

Direct materials – timber:	3,450 m² at £14.50 per m²
Direct labour:	5,900 hours at £15.90 per hour.

Required
Calculate:

a the direct material usage sub-variance
b the direct material price sub-variance
c the total direct material variance
d the direct labour efficiency sub-variance
e the direct labour rate sub-variance
f the total direct labour variance.

You might find that some questions may refer to sub-variances as just 'variances'. So a direct labour efficiency variance is in fact a sub-variance.

SALES VARIANCES

Sales variances are not flexed and can be calculated in a similar way to the variances considered earlier – by using our grid. Do be careful when labelling 'adverse' and 'favourable'. Ask yourself: is the business better off (favourable variance) or worse off (adverse variance)?

WORKED EXAMPLE

The budgeted sales of tripox was 7,800 units at a selling price of £3.85. The actual sales were 8,000 units sold at £3.80.

Required
Calculate:

a the sales volume sub-variance
b the sales price sub-variance
c the total sales variance.

Answer

$$Sq \times Sp$$

$$7,800 \times £3.85 = £30,030$$

$$Aq \times Sp$$

$$8,000 \times £3.85 = £30,800$$

£770 favourable (a favourable impact on profit) sales volume sub-variance

$$Aq \times Ap$$

$$8,000 \times £3.80 = £30,400$$

£400 adverse (an adverse effect on profits) sales price sub-variance

£370 total sales variance

● **EXAMINATION TIP**

The most common type of question relates to calculation of total and sub-variances for direct materials and direct labour. So learn the grid!

QUESTION 13

Budgeted sales for 'graftoos' were 29,300 units at a selling price of £7.96 each. The actual sales were 29,250 units at a selling price of £8.03.

Calculate:

a the sales volume sub-variance
b the sales price sub-variance
c the total sales variance.

QUESTION 14

Budgeted sales for 'chukennies' were 154,000 units at a selling price of 30p each. The actual sales were 150,000 at 28p each.

Calculate:

a the sales volume sub-variance
b the sales price sub-variance
c the total sales variance.

You must learn the grid and how to use it.

You must also be able to tell quickly whether a variance that you have calculated is favourable or adverse.

Calculating variances is only part of the process; with practice, the calculations can be mastered and you should be able to gain accurate results.

However, more important than merely calculating the variances is gaining information from your calculations.

Business managers introduce a system of standard costing because it can highlight variances between the predicted costs and the actual costs.

Variances lead to investigation into the causes of the differences.

Standard costing is the natural extension of budgetary control.

Budgetary control seeks to make sections and departments more efficient and hence improve the performance of the business as a whole.

Standard costing goes into much greater detail than budgeting. It examines in detail the costs of all the constituent parts of the production process for each product.

When variances are identified, action can be implemented to correct adverse variances.

Managers must know the cause of any deviation from standard in order to take remedial action.

You will probably be asked to comment upon or make observations about the variances you have calculated in an examination question.

Variance analysis highlights areas of concern and areas of good practice and you may be asked to explain possible reasons for the variances.

You may also be asked to identify some inter-relationship between different sub-variances.

Many of the comments you may make could be speculative because you will have a limited picture or scenario from the question and thus may lack the detail necessary to arrive at a definitive conclusion. Your answer will require a lot of thought and the application of common sense.

CAUSES OF SUB-VARIANCES

The actual results may differ from the standards because there have been errors in the standards set. These errors could be caused by:

■ using incorrect data
■ setting unrealistic targets
■ managers deliberately setting low standards.

When answering an examination question, show the examiners that you are aware of possible causes of deviations from standard figures, but do not labour the point; rather, make it as a general comment that will apply to all sub-variances.

Direct material usage sub-variances	
Favourable sub-variance:	Adverse sub-variance:
Use of better-quality materials	Use of poorer materials
Use of highly skilled workers	Use of less skilled workers
Use of 'state of the art' capital equipment	Use of poor capital equipment
	Theft of materials
	Deterioration of materials

Note that the first three factors in both columns refer to wastage of materials.

Direct material price sub-variance	
Favourable sub-variance:	Adverse sub-variance:
Deflation – either general or specific to the materials being purchased.	Inflation – either general or specific to the materials being purchased
Supplier reducing price	Supplier increasing price
Use of a cheaper alternative material or less good quality of the same material	Use of more expensive alternative material or better quality of the same materials
Increase in quantity purchased so better trade discount obtained	Decrease in quantity purchased so loss of trade discount
Increase in value of the pound against the value of the euro or the dollar, making imported materials less expensive	Decrease in value of the pound against the value of the euro or the dollar, making imported materials more expensive

Direct labour efficiency sub-variance	
Favourable sub-variance:	Adverse sub-variance:
Use of workers with higher skills	Use of workers with lower skills
Workers using better machinery	Workers using poor machinery
Good working conditions	Poor working conditions
High staff morale – highly motivated	Poor staff morale – poor motivation
Good levels of quality control	Poor levels of quality control

Direct labour rate sub-variance	
Favourable sub-variance:	Adverse sub-variance:
Use of lower-grade workers earning lower rates of pay	Use of higher-grade workers earning higher rates of pay
Wage deflation	Wage inflation – general or specific to workers being used
Reduction in overtime or premium rates being paid	Increase in overtime or premium rates being paid

Sales volume sub-variance	
Favourable sub-variance:	Adverse sub-variance:
More aggressive marketing strategy	Less aggressive marketing strategy
Increased seasonal sales	Decrease in seasonal sales
Less competition in sector: ■ fewer sales by competitors ■ higher market share	More competition in sector: ■ more sales going to competitors ■ lower market share
Change in consumer tastes	Change in consumer tastes
	Defective product

Sales price sub-variance	
Favourable sub-variance:	Adverse sub-variance:
Increase in price to compensate for increased costs	Reduction in selling price for bulk sales
Increase in price after use of 'penetration' (marginal cost) pricing	Reduction in price – to attract new customers; by using marginal cost pricing; to penetrate a new market; to sell off stock quickly etc.

There are inter-connections between sub-variances and generally, in an examination, identification of these inter-relationships will perhaps gain extra development marks.

Here are a few inter-relating sub-variances:

■ <u>Favourable material usage sub-variance and Adverse labour rate sub-variance</u>
  Fewer materials being used   **because**   A higher skilled workforce is being used
                                                and has to be paid more

■ <u>Adverse labour efficiency sub-variance and Adverse material usage sub-variance</u>
  Workers taking longer to make goods   **this results in**   The machinery spoiling much of the
  because of faulty machinery   materials being used.

QUESTION 15

Chan Ltd is a manufacturer. The following is information provided:

■ favourable direct labour rate sub-variance
■ adverse direct labour efficiency sub-variance.

Required Explain a possible inter-relationship between the two sub-variances.

QUESTION 16

Davmark Ltd is a manufacturer. The following information is available:

■ favourable direct material usage sub-variance
■ adverse direct labour rate sub-variance.

Required Explain a possible inter-relationship between the two sub-variances.

QUESTION 17

Reayt Ltd is a manufacturer. The following information is available:

■ direct material usage sub-variance is adverse
■ direct labour rate sub-variance is adverse.

Required Explain any possible inter-relationship between the two sub-variances.

QUESTION 18

Dumy Ltd is a manufacturer. The following information is available:

■ favourable direct labour rate sub-variance
■ adverse sales volume sub-variance.

Required Explain a possible inter-relationship between the two sub-variances.

Chapter summary

■ Standard costs are pre-determined and reflect possible levels of costs and revenues that ought to be achieved under conditions of acceptable levels of efficiency.
■ Standard costs are used to prepare budgets and may be used in pricing policies.
■ Variances identify differences between standards set and actual performance. They are composed of sub-variances.
■ If actual performance is different from standard performance, the budget may have to be flexed.
■ Analysis of sub-variances is necessary in order to eradicate problem areas in production or to copy good practice.
■ A sub-variance in one area may cause a sub-variance in another connected area.

Self-test questions

■ Total variance = Standard cost less ....
■ Copy out the 'grid' used to calculate sub-variances.
■ Usage is applied to direct materials. What is the word that replaces 'usage' in 'direct labour..............sub-variance'?
■ We say 'material price'. What word do we use for the price of labour?
■ Standard quantity direct materials information: 40 units; standard price £10; actual quantity 50 units; actual price £10. Calculate the direct material usage sub-variance.
■ X is a manufacturing business. Budgeted production is 1,000 units; budgeted materials used 500 tonnes; actual materials used 550 tonnes. Which figure should be used in the grid for Sq?
■ Why is a budget sometimes flexed?
■ Explain a possible factor that would result in an adverse material usage sub-variance.
■ Explain a possible factor that would result in a favourable labour rate sub-variance.
■ Explain how the use of poor machinery might affect a direct material usage sub-variance and a labour efficiency sub-variance.

TEST QUESTIONS

QUESTION 19

The managers of Kambog Ltd provide the following information for direct materials for August:

	Budgeted	Actual
Direct materials	4,200 m²	4,150 m²
Direct materials – price per m²	£3.40	£3.50

Required
Calculate:

a the direct material usage sub-variance
b the direct material price sub-variance
c the total direct material variance.

QUESTION 20

The managers of O'Donnal provide the following information for direct materials for July:

	Budgeted	Actual
Direct materials	7,150 litres	7,300 litres
Direct materials – price per litre	£1.20	£1.15

Required
Calculate:

a the direct material usage sub-variance
b the direct material price sub-variance
c the total direct material variance.

QUESTION 21

The managers of Thomas Ltd provide the following information for direct labour for February:

	Budgeted	Actual
Direct labour	1,200 hours	1,400 hours
Direct labour rate per hour	£8.50	£8.60

Required
Calculate:

a the direct labour efficiency sub-variance
b the direct labour rate sub-variance
c the total direct labour variance.

QUESTION 22

The managers of McStravick Ltd supply the following information for direct labour for October:

	Budgeted	Actual
Direct labour	42,000 hours	41,950 hours
Direct labour rate per hour	£16.40	£16.35

Required
Calculate:

a the direct labour efficiency sub-variance
b the direct labour rate sub-variance
c the total direct labour variance.

QUESTION 23

The managers of Nathwani and Co Ltd provide the following information for May:

Standard costs:

Direct materials: 17,300 kg costing £1.82 per kg

Direct labour: 410 hours at £9.40 per hour.

Actual costs were:

Direct materials: 17,250 kg costing £1.80 per kg

Direct labour: 440 hours at £9.50 per hour.

a Calculate the direct material usage sub-variance.
b Calculate the direct material price sub-variance.
c Calculate the total direct material variance.
d Calculate the direct labour efficiency sub-variance.
e Calculate the direct labour rate sub-variance.
f Calculate the total direct labour variance.
g Calculate the total direct expenses variance.
h Explain one possible reason for the direct material usage sub-variance.
i Explain one possible reason for the direct labour rate sub-variance.

QUESTION 24

The managers of Dactor Ltd provide the following information for January:

Standard costs:

Direct materials:	2,870 litres at £12.00 per litre
Direct labour:	610 hours at £8.45 per hour

Actual costs were:

Direct materials:	2,910 litres at £11.98 per litre
Direct labour:	640 hours at £8.40 per hour

Required
a Calculate the direct material usage sub-variance.
b Calculate the direct material price sub-variance.
c Calculate the total direct material variance.
d Calculate the direct labour efficiency sub-variance.
e Calculate the direct labour rate sub-variance.
f Calculate the total direct labour variance.
g Calculate the total direct expenses variance.
h Explain one possible reason for the direct material usage sub-variance.
i Explain one possible reason for the direct material price sub-variance.
j Explain one possible reason for the direct labour efficiency sub-variance.
k Explain one possible reason for the direct labour rate sub-variance.

QUESTION 25

The managers of Sibi Ltd planned to sell 400,000 units of 'epco' at a price of 87p each in April. When the actual figures were available it was found that 450,000 units had been sold at 85p.

Required
Calculate:

a the sales volume sub-variance
b the sales price sub-variance
c the total sales variance.

QUESTION 26

The managers at Ybsu Ltd planned to sell 56 units of 'Krylo' at £1,940 per unit in November. The actual sales were 58 units at £2,000 per unit.

Required
Calculate:

a the sales volume sub-variance
b the sales price sub-variance
c the total sales variance.

QUESTION 27

The managers of Kopabot have budgeted to produce 30,000 hand-crafted pans in March. They provide the following information:

Standard costs for the production of 30,000 pans:

Direct materials: 16,000 m^2 at £6.10 per m^2

Direct labour: 42,000 hours at £6.80 per hour.

Actual production was 27,000 pans:

Direct materials: 14,500m^2 at £6.00 per m^2

Direct labour: 37,500 hours at £6.75 per hour.

Required
a   Calculate the direct material usage sub-variance.
b   Calculate the direct material price sub-variance.
c   Calculate the total direct material variance.
d   Calculate the direct labour efficiency sub-variance.
e   Calculate the direct labour rate sub-variance.
f   Calculate the total direct labour variance.
g   Explain one possible reason for each of the sub-variances calculated.

QUESTION 28

The managers of Osac have planned to produce 360,000 pencil cases in March. The following information is available:

Standard costs for production of 360,000 pencil cases:

Direct materials: 153,000m^2 at £1.10 per m^2

Direct labour: 162,000 hours at £5.30 per hour.

Actual production was 320,000 pencil cases:

Direct materials: 134,000m^2 at £1.10 per m^2

Direct labour: 143,000 hours at £5.40 per hour.

Required
a   Calculate the direct material usage sub-variance.
b   Calculate the direct material price sub-variance.
c   Calculate the total direct material variance.
d   Calculate the direct labour efficiency sub-variance.
e   Calculate the direct labour rate sub-variance.
f   Calculate the total direct labour variance.
g   Explain one possible reason for each of the sub-variances calculated.

QUESTION 29

The managers of Efax have planned to manufacture 1,400 handbags in October. The following information is available:

Standard costs for production of 1,400 handbags:

Direct materials – leather: 700 m^2 at £16.40 per m^2

Direct labour: 1,050 hours at £8.35 per hour.

Actual production was 1,450 handbags:

Direct materials – leather: 732 m^2 at £18.30 per m^2

Direct labour: 1,090 hours at £8.20 per hour.

Required
a   Calculate the direct material usage sub-variance.
b   Calculate the direct material price sub-variance.
c   Calculate the total direct material variance.
d   Calculate the direct labour efficiency sub-variance.

e Calculate the direct labour rate sub-variance.
f Calculate the total direct labour variance.
g Explain one possible reason for each of the sub-variances calculated.

QUESTION 30

The managers of Adod Ltd have planned to manufacture 240,000 bottles of fruit juice in November. The following information is available:

Standard costs for production of 240,000 bottles of juice:

Direct materials: 245,000 litres at £0.70 per litre

Direct labour: 1,200 hours at £6.17 per hour.

Actual production was 200,000 bottles of juice:

Direct materials: 247,000 litres at £0.75 per litre

Direct labour: 940 hours at £6.25 per hour.

Required
a Calculate the direct material usage sub-variance.
b Calculate the direct material price sub-variance.
c Calculate the total direct material variance.
d Calculate the direct labour efficiency sub-variance.
e Calculate the direct labour rate sub-variance.
f Calculate the total direct labour variance.
g Explain one possible reason for each of the sub-variances calculated.

CHAPTER
SIXTEEN

Capital Investment Appraisal

We said in *Introducing Accounting* that fixed assets are the wealth generators of a business. They are purchased with the intention that they will generate profits for the business for some years into the future.

The fixed assets used in the business usually consist of:

- land
- buildings
- machinery
- plant
- vehicles
- office equipment etc.

They are used in the business for more than one financial time period.

The managers of a business are always looking for good value when they purchase fixed assets, just as you do when buying clothes, CDs etc.

Like you, the managers of a business do not have unlimited resources; like you, available cash is a scarce resource; and like you, they must plan their capital expenditure very carefully so that they get the best value for their money. They want to ensure that they earn maximum benefits from their purchase, just like you.

Capital projects are appraised (evaluated) according to potential earning power.

Care must be taken when making a capital investment decision because:

- large sums of money are generally involved
- the money may well be 'tied up' for a considerable length of time
- the decisions cannot generally be reversed easily
- the money committed is usually non-returnable.

Consider the family commitment to the purchase of the largest item of capital expenditure – a house:

- a large sum of money is involved
- the money is often tied up for many years
- it might be difficult to resell the house
- once purchased, the house cannot be returned to the previous owners.

It is very important that care must be taken when making a capital investment appraisal. Much detailed information should be obtained from all sources that may be affected by the decision, or that may affect the decision.

Some sources of information:

Specification coverage:
AQA 16.3; OCR 5.4.3.

By the end of this chapter you should be able to:
- understand the payback and net present value methods
- OCR only – accounting rate of return method
- analyse and evaluate capital investment proposals.

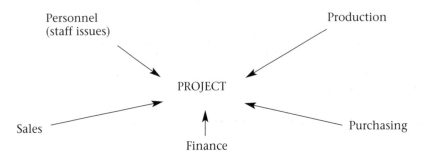

Personnel (staff issues)　　　　Production

PROJECT

Sales　　Finance　　Purchasing

Capital projects are evaluated (appraised) in terms of their potential earning power. If the managers of a business need to replace an obsolete piece of machinery or purchase further pieces of machinery to complete a new project, they must decide **which** new machine to purchase. There would be no choice to be made if there was only one type of machine on the market that would do the job; they would not have to make a choice (other than to buy or not to buy!). In the real world there are usually alternative options from which to choose.

Machines might:

- have different prices
- have different qualities
- produce different quantities of goods
- produce different quality goods
- have different life spans
- have different rates of obsolescence.

These differences apply to most capital purchases in both the business world and other machines in the world outside of business, for example TV sets, DVD machines etc.

There are four main methods of evaluating a capital project. They are:

- the **payback method** – examined by AQA and OCR
- the **accounting rate of return** (ARR) – examined by OCR
- the **net present value method** (NPV) – examined by AQA and OCR
- the **internal rate of return** (IRR) – examined by AQA and OCR.

Check with your teacher or specification which methods you could expect to find in your examination paper. All of the methods require predictions about future flows or either cash or profits.

If the predictions are inaccurate, there could be serious problems for the business because of:

- large sums of cash being involved
- long-term commitment of cash and other resources
- the effect on profits.

Note: From this point, reference will be made only to 'projects' but the text does apply to machines also.

So, managers will often use more than one method of appraising a project that could affect the business for many years.

Opportunity cost is the benefit from the alternative use of resources that is forgone when a new project is undertaken.

Sunk costs are unrecoverable expenditures already incurred before a project is undertaken.

Capital expenditure appraisal only considers incremental revenue and incremental expenditure. (The incremental expenditure may include opportunity costs.) That is any additional revenue generated by the project and any additional expenditure that may be incurred by the project.

Existing revenue and expenditure that has no influence on the new project is disregarded.

THE PAYBACK METHOD

The payback period is the length of time required for the total cash flows to equal the initial capital investment, ie: how long will it take the project to pay for itself?

Risk is an important factor to be taken into account when considering a project lasting a few years. The sooner the capital expenditure is recouped, the better – this is the essence of the payback method.

The method is used widely in practice since most businesses are concerned with short time horizons.

Also, the longer the time horizon involved, the less reliable are the predicted inflows of cash. The earlier the receipts are, the earlier further investments can be made. A long payback period increases the possibility that the initial outlay will not be recouped at all.

The payback period is measured in years.

● EXAMINATION TIP

Payback uses cash flows so non-cash items, eg depreciation, accruals and pre-payments, are ignored.

WORKED EXAMPLE

Olive Branch is considering the purchase of a new machine. Two different machines will suit her purpose.

The cash flows are given:

	Machine Argo Machine A Cost £210,000 Estimated cash flows	Machine Binko Machine B Cost £180,000 Estimated cash flows
	£	£
Year 1	70,000	70,000
Year 2	80,000	70,000
Year 3	90,000	80,000
Year 4	90,000	80,000

Required Calculate the payback period for each of the two machines.

Answer
Machine A – the initial outlay will be paid back part-way through Year 3
(£70,000 Year 1 + £80,000 Year 2 + £60,000 part-way through Year 3).
More precisely, 60,000/90,000ths through the third year.
Machine A payback is 2 and 60/90th years = **2.67 years**.
Machine B – the initial outlay will also be paid back part-way through Year 3 (£70,000 + £70,000 + £40,000 part-way through Year 3).
More precisely 40,000/80,000ths through Year 3.
Machine B payback is 2 and 40/80th years = **2.5 years**.

If Olive is only concerned with cash flows generated then she should buy machine Binko.

Note the layout below:

■ the date of initial purchase is labelled 'Year 0'
■ all cash outflows and inflows are deemed to accrue evenly throughout each year.

QUESTION 1

The managers of Patel Ltd are considering two projects. The information regarding the two projects is given:

	Project 24/JJ Cash inflows/outflows	Project 25/SM Cash inflows/outflows
	£	£
Year 0	(100,000)	(140,000)
Year 1	40,000	60,000
Year 2	50,000	80,000
Year 3	50,000	100,000
Year 4	50,000	110,000

Required

a Calculate the payback periods for both projects.
b State which project should be undertaken and why.

QUESTION 2

The managers of Glenmurray Ltd are considering two projects. The following information is supplied:

	Project RM/416 Cash inflows/outflows	Project RM/417 Cash inflows/outflows
	£	£
Year 0	(400,000)	(500,000)
Year 1	100,000	200,000
Year 2	150,000	300,000
Year 3	200,000	300,000
Year 4	250,000	300,000
Year 5	300,000	300,000

Required

a Calculate the payback period for both projects.
b State which project should be undertaken.

Some questions require that you calculate the projected cash flows to include in your calculations.

There are two types of question:

TYPE 1

When profits are given in the question. Remember that payback uses cash flows, not profits.

WORKED EXAMPLE

The following information is available for two proposed projects:

	Project 2178 £000	Project 2179 £000
Initial costs	(14,000)	(12,000)
Expected profits generated:		
Year 1	3,500	3,500
Year 2	5,000	4,000
Year 3	8,000	5,500
Year 4	10,000	6,500

Note:

The annual profit for each project has been calculated after providing for depreciation as follows:

	1,500	1,200

Required

a Calculate the payback period for both projects.
b State which project should be undertaken.

Answer

Cash flows	Project 2178 £	Project 2179 £
Year 0	(14,000)	(12,000)
Year 1	5,000	4,700
Year 2	6,500	5,200
Year 3	9,500	6,700
(a) payback	2 years 2,500/9,500 2.26 years	2 years 2,100/6,700 2.31 years

(b) Select project 2178 it has a slightly shorter payback period.

QUESTION 3

The managers of Dextok Ltd provide the following projected information for two projects:

	Project Minor	Project Nixto
	£000	£000
Initial costs	(8,800)	(7,400)
Expected profits generated:		
Year 1	3,000	1,500
Year 2	4,000	2,000
Year 3	5,000	2,500
Year 4	5,000	3,000
Year 5	5,000	2,500

The annual profit for each project has been calculated after providing for depreciation as follows:

600	200

Required

a Calculate the payback period for both projects.
b State which project should be undertaken.

QUESTION 4

The managers of Vingard Ltd provide the following information for two projects:

	Project 5432	Project 5433
	£000	£000
Initial costs	(18,000)	(8,600)
Expected profit generated:		
Year 1	3,750	2,150
Year 2	5,250	2,850
Year 3	6,000	3,150
Year 4	6,000	4,000
Year 5	6,500	4,500

The annual profit for each project has been calculated after allowing for depreciation as follows:

750	150

Required

a Calculate the payback period for both projects.
b State which project should be undertaken.

TYPE 2

When annual cash inflows and annual cash outflows are given separately.

In this type of question, simply deduct the annual cash outflows (expenses) from the annual cash inflows (receipts) to obtain the net cash flows.

- **Year 1** Cash receipts £100,000; cash expenditure £20,000; net cash flow £80,000.
- **Year 2** Cash receipts £120,000; cash expenditure £25,000; net cash flow £95,000.
- **Year 3** Cash receipts £130,000; cash expenditure £25,000; net cash flow £105,000.

QUESTION 5

The managers of Row Engineering Ltd are considering two capital expenditure proposals. The following information is available:

	Proposal 1		Proposal 2	
	£			£
Initial investment	100,000			110,000
	Annual expenditure	Annual income	Annual expenditure	Annual income
	£	£	£	£
Year 1	10,000	50,000	12,000	50,000
Year 2	12,000	55,000	13,000	57,000
Year 3	15,000	60,000	15,000	62,000
Year 4	18,000	65,000	17,000	67,000
Year 5	20,000	70,000	21,000	65,000

Required

a Calculate the payback period for both proposals.
b Advise the managers which proposal they should accept.

QUESTION 6

The managers of Townhead Ltd are considering two projects. The following information is available:

	Project PQ/712		Project RS/29	
	£			£
Initial investment	220,000			270,000
	Annual expenditure	Annual income	Annual expenditure	Annual income
	£	£	£	£
Year 1	23,000	75,000	45,000	100,000
Year 2	16,000	80,000	50,000	110,000
Year 3	18,000	90,000	50,000	120,000
Year 4	22,000	100,000	48,000	130,000
Year 5	25,000	95,000	50,000	120,000

a Calculate the payback period for both projects.
b Advise the managers which project should be chosen.

In the examples used and in the questions, we have merely considered the financial aspects of deciding on a project. Clearly, the managers of a business would consider all the ways in which a decision might impinge on the business. They would also consider, for example, how a decision might affect:

■ the **workforce** – does the decision require more workers?
                     – does the decision mean that some workers will lose their jobs?
■ the **environment** – pollution
■ the **locality** – expansion using more space.

ADVANTAGES OF USING THE PAYBACK METHOD

■ It is relatively simple to calculate.
■ It is fairly easy for non-accountants to understand.
■ The use of cash is more objective than using profits that are dependent on the accounting policies decided by managers.
■ Since all future predictions carry an element of risk, it shows the project that involves the least risk because it recognises that cash received earlier in the project life cycle is preferable to cash received later.
■ It shows the project that benefits a firm's liquidity.

DISADVANTAGES OF USING THE PAYBACK METHOD

■ It ignores the time-value of money (but see later).
■ It ignores the life expectancy of the project; it does not consider cash flows that take place after the payback period.
■ Projects may have different patterns of cash inflows.

For example, consider:

■ Project 1 has a payback period of 1 year.
■ Project 2 has a payback period of 2.2 years.

	Project 1	Project 2
	£	£
Year 0	(10,000)	(10,000)
Year 1	10,000	1
Year 2	1	1
Year 3	1	50,000
Year 4	1	50,000

If a machine has a scrap or trade-in value, this will be treated as an income in the year the machine is disposed of.

THE ACCOUNTING RATE OF RETURN METHOD (ARR)

This method of appraisal has some similarities to the approach to the calculation of ROCE. It shows the return on the investment expressed as a percentage of the average investment over the period.

Average capital seems rather complicated to calculate – have a look at the way it is calculated and then learn the formula.

WORKED EXAMPLE

A machine is purchased for £100,000. It will be used for two years and will then be traded in for £20,000.

Required Calculate the average investment on the machine over the two years.

Answer
The machine will incur depreciation using the straight-line method of £40,000 per annum.

(£100,000 − £20,000 = £80,000 ÷ 2 years = £40,000 per annum)

	Start of year	End of year	Average investment over year
Investment Year 1	£100,000	£60,000	£80,000 (160,000 ÷ 2)
Investment Year 2	£60,000	£20,000	£40,000 (80,000 ÷ 2)

So:

- in Year 1 average investment   £80,000
- in Year 2 average investment   £40,000
                                                      £120,000

Average investment over two years = $\dfrac{£120,000}{2}$ = £60,000.

WORKED EXAMPLE

A machine is purchased for £350,000. It will be used for five years after which it will have a scrap value of £50,000.

Required Calculate the average investment in the machine over the five years.

Answer
Average investment = £200,000

Annual depreciation = £300,000 ÷ 5 = £60,000

	Start of year	End of year	Average investment over year
	£	£	£
Investment Year 1	350,000	290,000	320,000
Year 2	290,000	230,000	260,000
Year 3	230,000	170.000	200,000
Year 4	170,000	110,000	140,000
Year 5	110,000	50,000	80,000
		Total	1,000,000

WORKED EXAMPLE *continued*

Average investment over five years = £1,000,000 ÷ 5 years = £200,000 per year.

There is an arithmetic short-cut which gives the correct answer without the long complicated explanation shown in the two worked examples given above.

FORMULA

$$\text{Average investment} = \frac{\text{Initial investment} + \text{Scrap value}}{2}$$

It does seem improbable that the scrap value is added but it does work – trust me, I'm an accountant!

Check the two examples above:

Purchase price £100,000 + Scrap value £20,000 = £120,000

$$\frac{£120,000}{2} = \text{Average investment } £60,000$$

Purchase price £350,000 + Scrap value £50,000 = £400,000

$$\frac{£400,000}{2} = \text{Average investment } £200,000$$

This shorter method works! It always works!

FORMULA

$$\text{Average rate of return} = \frac{\text{Average profits}}{\text{Average investment}} \times 100$$

● EXAMINATION TIP

The calculation of ARR uses profits, not cash flows.

WORKED EXAMPLE

Nancy Betts is considering the purchase of a machine. There are two models that will suit her needs. All cash flows are assumed to occur on the last day of the year

	Machine Ara Cost £160,000 Estimated cash flows	Machine Bibi Cost £210,000 Estimated cash flows
	£	£
Year 1	50,000	70,000
Year 2	60,000	90,000
Year 3	70,000	110,500
Year 4	80,000	88,000
Year 5	60,000	84,000
Year 5 Scrap value	10,000	40,000

Required

a Calculate the accounting rate of return for both machines.
b Advise Nancy which machine she should purchase.

Answer

	Machine Ara	**Machine Bibi**
Average profit:	$\dfrac{£320,000}{5 \text{ years}} = £64,000$	$\dfrac{£442,500}{5 \text{ years}} = £88,500$
Average investment:	$\dfrac{£160,000 + £10,000}{2}$	$\dfrac{£210,000 + £40,000}{2}$
	$= £85,000$	$= £125,000$

a **Machine Ara**: accounting rate of return $= \dfrac{64,000}{85,000} \times 100 = 75.3\%$

   Machine Bibi: accounting rate of return $= \dfrac{88,500}{125,000} \times 100 = 70.8\%$

b Nancy should choose Machine Ara because this gives her a higher rate of return than Machine Bibi.

QUESTION 7

Sanvision Ltd presently earns a return on capital of 25%. The directors propose to produce and market a new product. This will require the purchase of a new machine at a cost of £90,000. The machine will last for four years after which it will be traded in for £10,000. The average profits earned by the machine are expected to be £11,400 per annum. Assume that all cash flows occur on the last day of the year.

Required

a Calculate the accounting rate of return for the new product.
b Advise the directors whether they should proceed with production of the new product.

QUESTION 8

Nasirah Ltd presently earns a return on capital of 35%. The directors propose to produce and sell

'Judles', a new product. This will require the purchase of a new machine at a cost of £212,000. The machine will last for five years after which it will be scrapped. Scrap value is expected to be £8,000.

The average annual profits are expected to be £46,200.

Assume that all cash flows occur on the last day of the year.

Required

a Calculate the accounting rate of return for the production of Judles.
b Advise the directors whether they should produce and sell Judles.

> **Mutually exclusive**. The pursuit of one course of action will preclude the pursuit of any other action, for example, I can either go to a friend's party or I can go to listen to my favourite band. I cannot do both.

QUESTION 9

A company is considering in investment in one of two projects. The projects are mutually exclusive (that is, only one project can be undertaken).

Each project will entail an initial outlay of £300,000.

Assume that all cash flows occur on the last day of the year.

Forecast profits are:

	Project 321	Project 322
	£	£
Year 1	30,000	16,000
Year 2	30,000	24,000
Year 3	30,000	40,000
Year 4	30,000	60,000

Required

a Calculate the accounting rate of return for each project.
b Advise the finance director which project should the directors invest in.

QUESTION 10

The managers of Absic Ltd are considering investing in one of three projects. The projects are mutually exclusive. Each project will entail an initial outlay of £500,000.

All cash flows are received on the last year of the relevant year.

Forecast profits are:

	Project 72/GH	Project 73/GH	Project 74/GH
	£	£	£
Year 1	70,000	70,000	60,000
Year 2	72,000	75,000	75,000
Year 3	75,000	80,000	85,000
Year 4	80,000	85,000	75,000
Year 5	82,000	90,000	65,000

Required

a Calculate the accounting rate of return for each project.
b Advise the managers which project should be chosen.

ADVANTAGES OF USING THE ACCOUNTING RATE OF RETURN

- ARR is fairly easy to calculate.
- Results can be compared with present profitability.
- It takes into account the aggregate earnings of the project(s).

DISADVANTAGES OF USING THE ACCOUNTING RATE OF RETURN

- ARR does not take into account the time-value of money.
- It does not recognise the timing of cash flows (see same disadvantage for payback).

THE NET PRESENT VALUE METHOD

Which of the following would give you the better value for money?

- Spending £100 today.
- Spending £100 in 10 years' time?

I think that most people would say that £100 spent today would give them the better value. Why?

The future is uncertain – there is an element of risk involved. Also, as time goes on, there is a tendency for money to become less valuable.

When your grandparents bought a house many years ago, they may have spent £20,000. Would that buy the same house today? I don't think so!

The **time-value of money** recognises that £1 received today is worth more than £1 in one year's time or in five years' time.

If £1 were received and invested at 5% per annum, it would be worth £1.05 in one year's time; if it were left to accumulate interest it would be worth just over £1.10 (£1.102) in two years' time and just under £1.16 (£1.158) in three years' time.

Looked at from another perspective:

- If 86.4 pence was invested today at 5% for three years, this would yield £1.
- If 90.7 pence was invested today at 5% for two years, this would yield £1.
- If 95.2 pence was invested at 5% for one year, this would yield £1.

> **Cost of capital** is based on the weighted average cost of capital available to a business.

> The **net present value method of investment appraisal** of a project is calculated by taking the present-day (discounted) value of all future net cash flows based on the business's cost of capital and subtracting the initial cost of the investment.

> A **discounting factor** allows the value of future cash flows to be calculated in terms of their value if they were received today.

Managers of a business invest in capital projects to provide security for the future through profits and cash flows.

As individuals we invest to provide for the future, and we hope that the monetary rewards in the future will be worth waiting for.

In giving up the money today, we expect a reward. The reward is the interest that we will earn on our investment.

In the same way that we may invest in, say, a building society account to get a return on our investment, managers of a business will also invest in projects that will pay a return on their investment.

Managers evaluate a project by comparing the capital investment with the return that the investment will bring in the future.

In order to make a meaningful comparison between the amount originally invested and the income generated in the future by that investment, there is a need to discount the cash flows so that they are the equivalent of cash flows now. Thus, we can compare like with like.

We can compare the initial investment at today's price with future cash inflows discounted to give their values in today's world.

The discounting factor used in net present value (NPV) calculations is generally based on a weighted average cost of capital available to the business.

Schiffe Ltd has the following capital structure:

	£
Ordinary shares (currently paying a dividend of 9% per annum)	1,000,000
6% preference shares	500,000
7% debenture stock	200,000
Bank loan (current interest rate payable 8%)	300,000

The weighted average cost of capital for Schiffe Ltd is:

	Nominal value £	Rate paid	Cost of capital per annum £
Ordinary shares	1,000,000	9%	90,000
Preference shares	500,000	6%	30,000
Debenture stock	200,000	7%	14,000
Bank loan	300, 000	8%	24,000
Totals	2,000,000		158,000

$$\text{Average cost of capital} = \frac{\text{Cost of capital per annum}}{\text{Nominal value of capital}}$$

$$= \frac{158,000}{2,000,000} = 7.9\%$$

This shows that the average cost of Schiffe Ltd raising further capital would be 7.9%.

Note: The example is correct in principle. However, the interest on debenture stock and the bank loan are revenue expenditure – they reduce profits – they would reduce the amount of tax payable by Schiffe Ltd. So in reality the two figures should be shown in the calculation net of taxation.

More important note: You will be given the discount factor (ie the cost of capital) in a question – 'Thank goodness', I hear you say!

If you are given a number of discounting factors to choose from, select the one identified in the question as the cost of capital.

There is a misconception that a discounting factor is used to take into account the effects of inflation on future cash flows – this is not so. The effects that inflation have on results are self-correcting.

The discounting factor is based on the business's cost of capital, which has been explained earlier.

Generally, what we consider is what would happen if we were fortunate enough to be able to invest, say, £1,000, in a building society account or a business project for, say, four years. We calculate how much our investment would be worth each year if the investment was earning, say, 5% per annum.

At the end of:

Year 1	£1,050
Year 2	£1,102
Year 3	£1,158
Year 4	£1,216

Discounting uses the same principle but in reverse.

If I require £1,000 in four years' time and the interest rate, or rate of return, was 5%, how much would I have to invest today? I would have to invest £823.

The present value gives the value of a future sum of money at today's values.

If you wish to have £100 in four years' time and the interest rates were 7%, you should invest £76.30 today.

Working this in reverse, we can say that £100 received in four years' time is equivalent to receiving £76.30 today.

(£76.30 placed on deposit today and receiving interest of 7% per annum would produce a deposit of £100 in four years' time.)

How did I work these figures out? I used a set of present value tables!

These tables will be given in any examination question requiring the use of net present value.

WORKED EXAMPLE

Calculate the value of:

a £120
b £196
c £42

if the amount were invested for three years at 3% per annum.

The following figures give the value of £1 at a compound interest rate of 3%:

Year 1	1.030
Year 2	1.061
Year 3	1.093
Year 4	1.126

Answer

a £1 invested today would yield £1.09 (£1.093) in three years' time, so £120 invested would yield £131.16 (£120 × 1.093).
b £214.23.
c £45.91.

WORKED EXAMPLE

Calculate the present value of:

a £926
b £62
c £1,380

received in four years' time if the current cost of capital is 9% per annum.

The following figures give the present value of £1 at 9%:

Year 1	0.917
Year 2	0.842
Year 3	0.772
Year 4	0.650

Answer

a £1 received in four years' time would have a value of 65 pence if received today so £926 received in four years' time has a value of £601.90 today.
b £40.30.
c £897.

The net present value method of capital investment appraisal compares the investment (at today's prices) with future net cash flows (discounted to give the values at today's prices).

Here is a table showing the present value of £1 at a number of different discount rates:

	4%	5%	6%	7%	8%	9%	10%
Period 1	0.961	0.952	0.943	0.935	0.926	0.917	0.909
2	0.925	0.907	0.890	0.873	0.857	0.842	0.826
3	0.889	0.864	0.840	0.816	0.794	0.772	0.751
4	0.855	0.823	0.792	0.763	0.735	0.708	0.683
5	0.822	0.784	0.747	0.713	0.681	0.650	0.621

WORKED EXAMPLE

James Squirrel is considering whether to purchase a new lathe for his workshop. The machine will cost £12,000 and be used for five years after which time it will be scrapped. The following cash flows relate to the lathe.

	Revenue receipts £	Revenue expenditure £
Year 1	8,000	4,000
Year 2	8,500	5,000
Year 3	7,000	4,000
Year 4	5,000	3,000
Year 5	3,000	1,000

WORKED EXAMPLE *continued*

The current cost of capital is 10%. All costs are paid and incomes received on the last day of each financial year.

The following extract is taken from the present value tables for £1:

	10%
Year 1	0.909
Year 2	0.826
Year 3	0.751
Year 4	0.683
Year 5	0.621

Required

a Calculate the net present value of purchasing the new lathe.
b Advise James whether he should invest in the new lathe.

Answer

Year	Cash flows £	Discount factor	Net present value £
0 (now)	(12,000)	1	(12,000)
1	4,000	0.909	3,636
2	3,500	0.826	2,891
3	3,000	0.751	2,253
4	2,000	0.683	1,366
5	2,000	0.621	1,242
		Net present value	(612)

James should not invest in the new lathe as it will yield a negative net present value.

Note: The cash inflows are calculated from the revenue receipts less revenue expenditure. Any project that yields a positive net present value should be considered.

Projects that yield negative net present values should be rejected on financial grounds but may be considered on other grounds, for example to keep a good customer happy; to keep a good, skilled workforce within the business; perhaps to get further orders in the near future.

WORKED EXAMPLE

The managers of Dvorak Ltd wish to purchase a new machine. They will use the machine for four years. There are three machines that are capable of producing the quality of goods that is desired. The current cost of capital for Dvorak Ltd is 9%. The following is an extract from the present value tables for £1.

Year 1	0.917
2	0.842
3	0.772
4	0.708

The following information is available for the three machines. All cash flows arise at the end of the relevant year.

Machine	78/BA	92/DC	36/FE
	£	£	£
Purchase price	88,000	99,000	115,000
Forecast net cash flows:			
Year 1	44,000	47,000	50,000
2	44,000	47,000	49,000
3	40,000	47,000	48,000
4	40,000	45,000	44,000

Required

a Calculate the NPV of each machine.
b Advise the managers of Dvorak Ltd which of the three machines they should purchase.

Answer

a

Machine	78/BA	92/DC	36/FE
Present values	£	£	£
Year 0	(88,000)	(99,000)	(115,000)
1	40,348	43,099	45,850
2	37,048	39,574	41,258
3	30,880	36,284	37,056
4	28,320	31,860	31,152
Net present values	48,596	51,817	40,316

b The managers should purchase machine 92/DC because it yields the highest positive net present value.

Note: When a selection has to be made, the machine that yields the highest net present value should be chosen.

If all the machines yielded a negative net present value then no machine should be purchased.

ADVANTAGES OF USING THE NET PRESENT VALUE METHOD

- The time-value of money is taken into account as adjustments are made to take account of the present value of future cash flows.
- It is relatively easily understood.
- Greater importance is given to earlier cash flows.

DISADVANTAGES OF USING THE NET PRESENT VALUE METHOD

Because the figures are projections, then all of the figures are of a speculative nature:

- inflows are difficult to predict; outflows are equally difficult to predict
- the current cost of capital may change over the life of the project
- the life of the project is difficult to predict.

When the net cash flows to be discounted are the same amounts, time can be saved by totalling the discount factors for the appropriate years and multiplying the amount by this total.

WORKED EXAMPLE

The following net cash inflows are given for a machine:

Year 1	40,000
2	40,000
3	40,000
4	40,000

The present cost of capital is 4%.

All cash flows arise at the end of the relevant year.

Required Calculate the net present value of the cash flows.

Answer

	Cash flows £	Discount factor	NPV £
Year 1	40,000	0.961	38,440
2	40,000	0.925	37,000
3	40,000	0,889	35,560
4	40,000	0.855	34,200
		NPV	145,200

The same results would be given if 3.63 (0.961 + 0.925 + 0.889 + 0.855) is multiplied by the (constant) £40,000.

Note: This technique can only be used if the net cash flows are the same amount.

We said earlier that a major drawback in using the payback method was that it did not take into account the time-value of money. We can take the current cost of capital into account by using discounting techniques.

DISCOUNTED PAYBACK METHOD

This method is widely used as a method of selecting a machine or project.

WORKED EXAMPLE

Yvonne Durrant is considering the purchase of a new machine at a cost of £120,000. The estimated net cash flows generated by the machine over the next five years are provided. It is assumed that all cash flows arise at the end of the relevant year.

Year 1	30,000
Year 2	45,000
Year 3	50,000
Year 4	55,000
Year 5	45,000

The current cost of capital is 6%.

Assume that cash flows accrue evenly throughout the year.

Extracts from the present value table for £1 at 5%, 6% and 7% are given:

	5%	6%	7%
Year 1	0.952	0.943	0.935
Year 2	0.907	0.890	0.873
Year 3	0.864	0.840	0.816
Year 4	0.823	0.792	0.763
Year 5	0.784	0.747	0.713

Required Calculate the discounted payback period for the machine.

Answer
The three tables are given because in some questions a number of tables are provided. If this is the case, choose the table that corresponds with the current cost of capital. In this case the 6% table should be chosen.

	Cash flow £	Discounting factor	Net present value £
Year 1	30,000	0.943	28,290
Year 2	45,000	0.890	40,050
Year 3	50,000	0.840	42,000
Year 4	55,000	0.792	43,560
Year 5	45,000	0.747	33,615

QUESTION 11

The managers of Berg & Co are considering the purchase of a new machine costing £80,000. The machine will produce goods for four years. The following information on estimated net cash flows is available:

	£
Year 1	25,000
Year 2	30,000
Year 3	27,000
Year 4	26,000

The current cost of capital is 8%.

An extract for the present value table for £1 at 8% per annum is given.

All cash flows are assumed to arise at the end of the relevant year.

Year	8%
1	0.926
2	0.857
3	0.794
4	0.735

Required

a Calculate the NPV of the new machine.
b Advise the managers of Berg & Co whether or not they should purchase the new machine.

QUESTION 12

The managers of Catalane Ltd are considering the purchase of a new machine costing £250,000. The machine will produce goods for five years. The net cash flows are given as:

	£
Year 1	60,000
Year 2	62,000
Year 3	64,000
Year 4	63,000
Year 5	61,000

The current cost of capital is 10%.

An extract from the present value table for £1 at 10% per annum is given.

All cash flows arise at the end of the relevant year.

Year	10%
1	0.909
2	0.826
3	0.751
4	0.683
5	0.621

Required

a Calculate the NPV of the new machine.
b Advise the managers of Catalane Ltd whether or not to purchase the new machine.

QUESTION 13

The managers of Ardnas Ltd are considering the installation of a new processing plant. The two plants being considered are:

■ plant PAQ/731 costing £6.0m
■ plant BAX/482 costing £11.5m.

Forecast information for each plant is available:

	Plant PAQ/731		Plant BAX/482	
	Revenue receipts	Revenue expenditure	Revenue receipts	Revenue expenditure
	£m	£m	£m	£m
Year 1	2.9	2.0	6.1	3.1
Year 2	5.4	2.5	7.4	3.4
Year 3	6.5	3.1	8.3	4.6
Year 4	6.9	3.4	8.7	5.1
Year 5	8.3	3.9	9.8	5.8

The current cost of capital is 9%.

All cash flows arise at the end of the relevant year.

An extract from the present value table for £1 at 9% per annum is given:

Year	9%
1	0.917
2	0.842
3	0.772
4	0.708
5	0.650

a Calculate the NPV for Plant PAQ/731 and BAX/482.
b Advise the managers which plant should be purchased.

QUESTION 14

The managers of Broodihen Ltd have the opportunity to undertake one new project. The following information is provided for two possible alternative projects:

	Project A	Project B
	£000	£000
Year 1	210	412
Year 2	240	516
Year 3	300	540
Year 4	270	500

Capital cost of each project:

	600	1,500

Assumption: All cash flows arise at the end of the relevant year.

The current cost of capital is 5%.

An extract from the present value table for £1 at 5% is given:

Year	5%
1	0.952
2	0.907
3	0.864
4	0.823

a Calculate the NPV of each project.
b Advise the managers which project to pursue.

QUESTION 15

The following information relates to the purchase of machine XTP/R2:

	£000
Cost of machine	400
Net cash flows – **Year 1**	250
2	260
3	270
4	280

The current cost of capital is 7%.

All cash flows arise evenly throughout the year.

An extract from the present value table for £1 at 7% is given:

Year	7%
1	0.935
2	0.873
3	0.816
4	0.763

Calculate the discounted payback period for machine XTP/R2.

QUESTION 16

The following information relates to project 'Helom':

	£000
Cost of project	1,850
Net cash inflows – **Year 1**	400
2	700
3	600
4	500
5	400

The current cost of capital is 10%.

All cash flows accrue evenly throughout the year.

An extract from the present value table for £1 at 10% is given:

Year	10%
1	0.909
2	0.826
3	0.751
4	0.683
5	0.621

Required Calculate the discounted payback period for project 'Helom'.

Two further points to be considered:

■ Many discounted cash flow question are linked with social accounting issues, for example pollution issues, unemployment etc.
  You may have to discuss these issues once you have reached a decision about the project (or machine) that is recommended by the financial aspects of your decision.
■ At the end of a project's life there may be some residual or scrap value to be considered. This should simply be treated as further income in the year in which it occurs.

WORKED EXAMPLE

The following cash inflows are generated by a machine:

	£000
Year 1	240
Year 2	320
Year 3	650

At the end of Year 3 the machine will be sold. It is estimated that it well sell for £60,000.

WORKED EXAMPLE *continued*

Required Prepare a schedule of cash inflows generated by the machine.

Answer

Schedule of cash inflows	£000
Year 1	240
Year 2	320
Year 3	710 (£650,000 + £60,000)

Chapter summary

- There are four main methods of capital investment appraisal:
  - payback
  - accounting rate of return
  - net present value
  - internal rate of return.
- Only two are examined by AQA – payback and NPV. If you are studying for the OCR examinations then you also need to cover the accounting rate of return.
- The main disadvantage of payback is overcome by using discounted payback.
- All methods are used to appraise single investment opportunities and they are used to decide between competing strategies.

Self-test questions

- Identify two reasons why it is important to appraise capital investment decisions.
- Identify one method of capital investment appraisal that uses cash flows in the calculations.
- Identify one method of capital investment appraisal that uses profits in the calculation.
- A machine is purchased for £600. The net cash inflows are: Year 1 £250; Year 2 £250; Year 3 £250. In which year will the machine pay for itself?
- Identify one advantage of using payback as a method of investment appraisal.
- Identify one disadvantage of using NPV as a method of capital investment appraisal.
- The discounting factor used in NPV is based on the average inflation rate over the period of investment. True or false?
- NPV of Machine A (£4,760); NPV of Machine B (£1,920). Identify the machine that should be purchased.
- £1,000 received in two years' time is worth more/less than £1,000 received today? Delete the incorrect response.
- NPV is an abbreviation for 'new proven value'. True or false?

QUESTION 17

The following information is given for machine X7/5RT:

	£000
Initial cost	35
Net cash inflows –**Year 1**	8
Year 2	9
Year 3	10
Year 4	11
Year 5	12

The current cost of capital is 5% per annum.

Assume that all cash flows arise at the end of the relevant year when calculating NPV and that they arise evenly throughout the year when calculating the payback periods.

An extract from the present value table for £1 at 5% is given:

Year	5%
1	0.952
2	0.907
3	0.864
4	0.823
5	0.784

Required Calculate for machine X7/5RT:

a the payback period
b the net present value
c the discounted payback period.

QUESTION 18

The following information is given for project 'Rebtom':

	£000
Initial investment	600
Net cash inflows – **Year 1**	180
2	270
3	290
4	300
5	420

At the end of Year 5 the project will be sold for £30,000.

The current cost of capital is 10% per annum.

Assume that all cash flows arise at the end of the relevant year when calculating NPV and that they accrue evenly throughout the year when calculating the payback periods.

An extract from the present value table for £1 at 10% is shown:

Year	10%
1	0.909
2	0.826
3	0.751
4	0.683
5	0.621

Required Calculate for project 'Rebtom':

a the payback period
b the net present value
c the discounted payback period.

QUESTION 19

The Kapakian government is considering the installation of a new electricity generating facility. The following information is available:

	Type R facility		Type S facility		Type T facility	
	£m		£m		£m	
Initial cost	2,000		800		3,000	
Estimated cash flows:						
	Inflows	Outflows	Inflows	Outflows	Inflows	Outflows
	£m	£m	£m	£m	£m	£m
Year 1	830	620	460	520	1,530	1,240
Year 2	920	415	500	120	1,760	840
Year 3	1,070	540	600	150	2,000	910
Year 4	1,100	600	700	210	2,050	950
Year 5	1,100	580	700	200	2,100	900
Next 15 years	1,100	580	800	250	2,200	900

The current cost of capital is 15%.

Assume that all cash flows arise at the end of the relevant year when calculating NPV and that they accrue evenly throughout the year when calculating the payback periods.

An extract from the present value table for £1 at 15% is shown:

Year	15%
1	0.870
2	0.756
3	0.658
4	0.572
5	0.497

Required
a Calculate for each facility:
    i)   the payback period
    ii)   the net present value to the end of Year 5

iii) the discounted payback.

b Advise the Kapakian government which facility it should implement.

QUESTION 20

The managers of Aspar Ltd need to replace an obsolete machine. They are considering two alternative machines as a replacement:

■ a 'Yetty', manufactured in Outer Mongolia (a Far Eastern country) and
■ a 'Bonbon', manufactured in the EU.

The following information is available for the two machines being considered:

| | Yetty | | Bonbon | |
	£		£	
Capital cost	45,000		80,000	
Cash flows:	Revenues	Operating expenses	Revenues	Operating expenses
Year 1	35,000	7,000	44,000	9,000
Year 2	36,500	7,200	46,000	10,000
Year 3	40,500	7,800	50,000	10,500
Year 4	42,000	8,000	52,000	11,000

In addition to the above operating expenses, the Yetty will require a major overhaul costing £2,000 in Years 2 and 4.

The Bonbon will require a major overhaul in Year 4 and this will cost £5,000.

The press has reported that the Yetty pollutes the environment.

Aspar's cost of capital is currently 13% per annum.

Assume that all cash flows arise evenly throughout the year when calculating the payback periods and that they arise at the end of the relevant year when calculating NPV.

An extract from the present value table for £1 at 13% shows:

Year	13%
1	0.885
2	0.783
3	0.693
4	0.613

Required

a Calculate for each machine:
    i)   the payback period
    ii) the net present value to the end of Year 4
    iii) the discounted payback period.
b Advise the managers which machine should be purchased.

QUESTION 21

The managers of Agorc Ltd are unsure which one of the following projects should be undertaken. Each will require an initial investment of £68,000. At the end of the project, there would be a scrap value of £8,000.

The following information is available:

Net cash flows:	YP/32	WQ/43	XR/17
	£	£	£
Year 1	12,000	25,000	18,000
Year 2	10,000	25,000	18,000
Year 3	15,000	25,000	18,000
Year 4	18,000		19,000
Year 5	20,000		

Depreciation is calculated using the straight-line method.

Assume that cash flows arise at the end of the relevant year when calculating ARR and NPV and that they arise evenly throughout the year when calculating the payback periods.

Current cost of capital is 8%.

Extract from the present value table for £1 at 8%:

Year	8%
1	0.926
2	0.857
3	0.794
4	0.735
5	0.681

Required

a   Calculate for each project:
   i)   payback period
   ii)   accounting rate of return
   iii)   net present value
   iv)   discounted payback period.
b   Advise the managers which project should be chosen.

QUESTION 22

The managers of Bancard Ltd are considering selling two new products. The following information is given:

	Product JK		Product MN	
	£	£	£	£
Annual sales revenue		220,000		400,000
Cost of sales	110,000		200,000	
Administration costs	80,000		40,000	
Depreciation	8,000	198,000	87,000	327,000
Net profit		22,000		73,000

It is expected that the above results will continue for each year of each product's life.

The capital cost of Product JK is £50,000 and Product MN is £350,000.

Depreciation has been calculated on a straight-line basis and assumes a scrap value of £2,000 for both projects.

The expected demand for each product is expected to last for six years and four years respectively.

Assume that cash flows arise at the end of the relevant year when calculating ARR and NPV and that they arise evenly throughout the year when calculating the payback periods.

Bancard Ltd has a current cost of capital of 7%.

An extract from the present value table for £1 at 7% is given:

Year	7%
1	0.935
2	0.873
3	0.816
4	0.763
5	0.713
6	0.666

Required

a Calculate for each project:
 i) the payback period
 ii) the accounting rate of return
 iii) the net present value
 iv) the discounted payback period.
b Advise the managers which product should be sold.

SEVENTEEN

Examination Techniques

Remember what was said at the start of the book about examination technique.

The examination is the final chance that you will have to prove to yourself (and to others) how capable you are. This is what you have been training for over the past couple of years – this is your Cup Final! This is what could gain you entry into the Champions' League! (ie a good job or university)!

The key to success is planning and timing.

Read this section carefully: it may make the difference between gaining an A or a B (or an E and a U). Remember – the difference between one grade and another grade is only one mark – that's right, one single, teeny weeny mark!

Read the front sheet of your examination booklet.

Quickly read through the question paper.

TIMING

In AQA A2 Level examinations three-quarters of a minute is allocated to each mark. Make sure that you work out how long you should spend on each question. If you have not finished a 20-mark question in 15 minutes, then move on to the next question (unless you are within two minutes of completing it). Not timing yourself is the surest way of ensuring that you get a lesser grade than you deserve.

In **OCR** A2 Level examinations there is slightly longer time available for each mark (0.9 minutes per mark). Look at the number of marks allocated to each question and allow yourself slightly less time in minutes than the number of marks available. In a 20-mark question you should allow yourself 18 minutes to answer the question. If there are 27 marks allocated to a question then spend about 25 minutes on it (the actual calculation is 24 minutes 18 seconds!); a 32-mark question should be completed in approximately 28 minutes. Allow yourself 9 minutes for every 10 marks available.

If you run out of time on any question – **move on to the next question**. You might have some time left at the end of the examination to return and complete it. **Keep moving on**!

Many candidates fail to do justice to themselves because they spend too much time on one or two questions early in the examination, so they fail to complete the paper, or later questions, as fully as they could.

To obtain top grades, you **must** attempt all questions and all parts of questions.

MARKS

Look carefully at the number of marks allocated to each written question (you should have done this already in order to allocate your time effectively). The number of marks for a question will give you an idea of how much you should write.

For example, if a written question has been allocated two marks then a two-page answer will not be expected. The answer is likely to be two lines long or perhaps two sentences long.

A recent question asked candidates to identify the method that a trader would use to verify the bank columns in her cash book. It had been allocated one mark. A number of candidates wrote half a side of one page to answer this. Of course, the answer was 'She should prepare a bank reconciliation statement'.

The candidate who wrote a thesis as their answer had not taken heed of:

a the one-mark allocation and
b the word 'identify' in the instruction.

ABBREVIATIONS

As a rule, do not use abbreviations in your answers. 'T & P & L a/c for y/e 31/12/*4' is not acceptable.

If you are short of space then 'Bal b/d' and 'Depn' **may** be acceptable. The acceptance of the use of abbreviations is the remit of the chief examiner. Don't take the chance of dropping a mark. (This mark might be the one mark that makes a difference to your final grade. It might be the one mark needed to get you to the university of your choice.)

Do not use text language in your written sections – this will certainly lose a mark for 'quality of written communication'.

CROSSING OUT

If you have to change a figure, cross it out neatly and show the correct figure clearly. Do not go over the figure you wish to change. The examiner may not be able to tell which figure you want to be considered.

If you cross out a figure that then affects several other figures, do not cross out all subsequent figures, as:

a this will be extremely messy
b you could make many mistakes in any of the sub-totals.

Cross out the major incorrect figure and make a note at the side of how it will affect the final figure.

For example, you prepare a trading and profit and loss account (not a TPL a/c!) and include £2,340 as your opening stock figure. Just as you finish the whole account, you notice that it should be £3,240. Cross out £2,340 (neatly) and put in £3,240 clearly alongside. Put an asterisk (*) alongside the £3,240, cross out the incorrect net profit and write the corrected net profit alongside together with another asterisk and an indication of why you have made the change.

Do not use correction fluid anywhere on your script.

HEADINGS

Always use a heading for every question and every subsection. Tell the examiner what it is that you are preparing. These are easy marks to gain (every mark is precious. The difference between a grade A and a grade B . . . yes, you've heard it before – but remember this fact – it is vital).

Headings for accounting statements should include the proprietor's name and the statement heading, for example:

R. Lander
Bank reconciliation statement at 31 December 20*4.

WORKINGS

Examiners are not only interested in the actual answer that you produce and submit for marking; they are also interested in the method you used to arrive at your conclusion. This is especially true if you do not arrive at the correct conclusion.

If an examiner sees that you have used an incorrect figure in your answer he or she is interested in your reasoning to reach the incorrect answer. You will have reached your answer by using some logical (to you) thought process; let the examiner see this thought process through workings. In 99% of cases these workings result in part-marks for a partly correct process.

For example:

- The trial balance shows £79,000 for wages.
- The notes tell us that £1,000 is still owing at the trial balance date.
- Vanessa does not show workings and answers £80,000, worth 2 marks.
- Ellie shows workings 79,000 (1) + 1,000 (1) and answers £80,000 which is worth 2 marks.

So there is no advantage gained if the answer is correct. **But** and this is a very big **but**, if you make an error in your calculation and don't show workings, you will not gain any marks at all.

- Francesca does not show workings and answers £78,000, worth 0 marks.
- Albert shows workings 79,000 (1) – 1,000 and answers £78,000 and is awarded 1 mark.

You will make unforced errors in your examination answer booklet. Things that you have answered correctly 100 times in class you may answer incorrectly in the examination hall.

What is £6 + £2? Easy! I recently marked a very good script (the candidate probably gained an A grade) in which the answer appeared as £9!

Please, please, please show workings; if you do not, you may be throwing marks away.

(Remember that every mark is precious. The difference between . . .)

Identify your workings so that the examiner can trace the workings to the appropriate part of your answer. Use either a heading:

Purchases
26,000
 4,000
30,000

or an instruction **W¹**
26,000
 4,000
30,000

WRITTEN SECTIONS

Write your answers legibly (remember: do not go over incorrect words – cross them out neatly and insert the correct word). If an examiner cannot read your answer then he or she cannot award marks. Remember that this will be the first time the examiner has seen your writing; they cannot translate it from untidy scribble into English as easily as your class teacher can – they have seen your writing on numerous occasions so they are more used to translating it!

Make marking as easy as possible for the examiner.

Make a plan of what you are going to write – it need only be made using individual words or initial letters; rearrange these into a logical sequence, then, answer the question. This plan, even for very short answers, will help your answer to flow, it will stop you repeating yourself and it will save time.

When answering questions requiring written explanations, pretend that the examiner is a non-accountant and explain things in the most minute detail. Do not assume that the examiner has any prior knowledge of accounting.

Apply the mnemonic **IDA**:

- Identify the key factor(s) of your answer.
- Develop your answer in general terms showing that you understand the concept that you are writing about.
- Apply your answer to the question set by the examiner.

QUESTION

Jock is thinking about changing the rate of depreciation charged on his fixed assets from 10% to 25% per annum. Which accounting concept must he consider and why?

Answer
Consistency (**I**) this means that the same depreciation policy should be applied over the lifetime of the asset (**D**) so he should continue to use 10% as his annual charge for depreciation (**A**).

State the obvious.

QUESTION

How can Glenn improve his profitability?

A student answered along these lines: 'He can conduct a capital investment appraisal to determine which new machine he should purchase. This new machine may produce goods more efficiently at a lower cost so . . .'. This may be worth 1 mark.

'He can put up his selling price. If his cost of sales is maintained, or reduced, his profits will increase'. This is also probably worth 1 mark.

When confronted recently with this example, a student replied: 'But everyone knows that!' An examiner does not know what you know unless you tell him or her.

Examiners are trying to find out what you **know**, not what you do **not** know.

Tell the examiner – even the obvious!

Everyone wants you to pass the examinations you take:

■ **your relatives** want you to pass
■ **your teachers** want you to pass
■ **you** want to pass
■ **the examiner** wants you to pass.

If an examiner wanted you to fail he or she could guarantee this by asking questions that you would find almost impossible to answer.

Trust your teachers – they will give you all the tools necessary to pass the examination you will take.

Trust yourself during the examination.

In the words of the BBC children's radio programme, 'Go For It!'

IDENTIFY KEY WORDS IN THE QUESTIONS

There will be a clear instruction in the question that tells you how you are required to respond, for example should you give a detailed answer or are you only required to state one or two facts without explanation?

STATE/IDENTIFY

Requires a very short answer – no explanation or development is necessary.

Example:

Q. Identify a source document used to write up the sales day book.
A. Copy sales invoice.

No development is necessary – you will not impress an examiner by extending your answer to cover two sides of A4 paper. It will cost you marks that could have been gained on later questions. You do not have time to do more than is required of you.

LIST

Requires a few short answers (the number will be given.) Again, no explanation or development is required.

Example:

Q. List two items that a trader may not have included in the bank columns of his cash book that are shown in his bank statement.
A. Standing orders; bank charges. (No development required or given.)

DISCUSS

Requires arguments for a particular line of action and arguments against such actions. A conclusion should be drawn from your discussion.

Example:

Q. Discuss an issue of ordinary shares as a means of raising capital.
A. Your response would identify benefits to the company then develop these benefits in terms of

their implications for the business. Similarly, disadvantages would be identified and developed. Your answer would end with a conclusion as to whether or not this action is likely to be beneficial. Your conclusion should be drawn from (be based on) the arguments that you presented in your answer.

ANALYSE

Looks at reasons why a particular action took place or looks at the likely consequences of taking an action.

Example:

Q. Analyse the effect that a price increase would have on the profitability of a business.
A. The beneficial effects that a price increase would have and the drawbacks of an increase in price should be fully explained.

EVALUATE

This requires a conclusion to be drawn from the arguments presented in your answer (the same as 'Discuss'). Make sure that your judgements are based on the issues raised in your analysis.

Example:

Q. Advise Chetan whether to purchase Machine A or Machine B.
A. You would present the evidence for and against the purchase of each machine. Your final judgement would be to advise which machine should be purchased and why. Your judgement should be supported by the evidence that you have presented.
In answer to this type of question it is important that conflicting advice is not given, ie 'Machine A should be purchased but I think that Machine B is better'.

SOME ADDITIONAL POINTERS!

Do not repeat the question in your answer!

A significant number of candidates start written answers by saying 'I am going to discuss the many advantages and disadvantages of . . . I will list three advantages; I will then list disadvantages. After this I will then go on to . . .' and on and on. This wastes so much time – time that could be gaining valuable marks – and remember that time = marks!

Answer the question set by the examiner – not the question you wish had been asked!

Read the question carefully – if the answer requires action that will affect employees, remember this and don't give your answer from the shareholders' viewpoint or the viewpoint of the managers.

SYNOPTICITY

This means that the examiners must test your ability to incorporate knowledge gained in other units as well as the knowledge specific to the particular unit being examined.

So:

■ journal entries
■ double-entry transactions
■ manufacturing accounts etc

may also be examined at A2 Level even though they appear as AS units. A2 relies heavily on what you learned earlier. As you go through A2 topics, try to visualise how an A2 examiner might bring topics that you learned last year into the question.

Some areas will be incorporated without much effort, for example:

■ double-entry: basic to all accounting, whatever the level
■ control accounts: used automatically in incomplete record questions.

FINAL, FINAL WORD!

As I said earlier, one should not wish you 'good luck' – I wish that you 'fulfil your potential'.

My only word of advice to my own daughters before they embarked on their A Level courses was: 'Don't get into the situation in mid-August where you have to say "If only …".' 'If only I had done a bit more revision.' 'If only I had done all my homework.'

This is criminal – you are doing examinations for:

YOU – not parents; not teachers; not friends; not … **only for you!**

DO WELL!

CHAPTER ONE

QUESTION 1
Jan

Departmental trading accounts for the year ended 31 December 20*4

	Kitchen goods £	Kitchen goods £	DIY goods £	DIY goods £	Leisure goods £	Leisure goods £
Sales		97,876		73,752		102,653
Less Cost of sales						
Stock as at 1 Jan 20*4	6,980		4,870		8,820	
Purchases	42,631		30,884		38,005	
	49,611		35,754		46,825	
Stock as at 31 Dec 20*4	7,450	42,161	5,090	30,664	7,690	39,135
Gross profit		55,715		43,088		63,518

QUESTION 3
Maurice Duvall

Departmental trading and profit and loss account for the year ended 31 October 20*4

	Cheeses £	Cheeses £	Meats £	Meats £
Sales		88,630		125,330
Less Cost of sales				
Stock as at 1 Nov 20*3	2,860		1,540	
Purchases	29,960		43,750	
	32,820		45,290	
Stock as at 31 Oct 20*4	1,790	31,030	1,680	43,610
Gross profit		57,600		81,720
Wages	12,660		21,110	
Admin salaries	4,280		4,280	
Insurances	2,400		2,400	
Repairs	1,800		840	
Electricity			600	
Rent and rates	4,800		2,400	
Lighting and heating	1,120		560	
General expenses	4,275		4,275	
Motor expenses	2,300	33,635	9,200	45,665
Net profit		23,965		36,055

QUESTION 5
Calculation of total debtors as at 31 May 20*4

	£
Original total of debtors	4,775
Less Transposition error	(270)
Add Entry for C. Oyne	718
Less Bad debt written off	(316)
Corrected total of debtors	4,907

Note 2 will affect the control account. Ledger accounts will not be affected.

QUESTION 7
(a) **Corrected total creditors as per control account at 31 January 20*5:**

	£
Original balance as at 31 January 20*5	4,361
Add Clax & Co	301
Discounts received	(126)
Balance at 1 January 20*5 not used	2,717
B. Cluck	261
Corrected balance as at 31 January 20*5	7,514

(b) **Corrected total of debtors as at 31 January 20*5:**

	£
Correct balance as at 31 January 20*5	7,514
Less – Clax & Co	(301)
J. Fitzwilliam	(991)
B. Cluck	(261)
Incorrect balance at 1 January 20*5	5,961

Note 2. Discounts received are entered in the purchase ledger.
Note 5. Cash sales are not entered in the sales ledger.

QUESTION 9
(a) **Journal**

		£	£
Suspense account	Dr	100	
Advertising account			100
Purchase ledger control account	Dr	1,440	
Suspense account			1,440
Suspense account	Dr	120	
Sales account			120
Drawings account	Dr	240	
Suspense account			240
Machinery repairs account	Dr	1,600	
Machinery account			1,600

(b) **Suspense account**

	£		£
Trial balance difference		Sales account	120
(missing figure)	1,580	Drawing account	120
Advertising account	100	Ralph Simpson	1,440
	1,680		1,680

Note: The descriptions tell where the other entry can be found.
The debit for £1,440 is to the integrated purchase ledger control account – this is the double entry. £1,440 will also be debited in Ralph's account in the purchase ledger although this is not part of the double-entry system; we need to make a note in our own memorandum records that £720 has been paid.

QUESTION 11
(a) **Journal**

		£	£
Sales account	Dr	5,000	
Capital account			5,000
Commission receivable account	Dr	1,200	
Commission payable account	Dr	2,100	
Suspense Account			3,300
Suspense account	Dr	110	
Shirley Knott			73
Andy Knott			37

(b) Suspense account

	£		£
Trial balance difference (*missing figure*)	3,190	Commission receivable account	1,200
S Knott	73	Commission payable account	2,100
A Knott	37		
	3,300		3,300

No entries are required in the double-entry system for errors 3, 4 and 5. However, the following adjustments are necessary in the memorandum accounts maintained in the sales ledger:

	Dr	
	£	£
Pippa Bramley	650	
Pippin Cox		650
Shirley Knott		73
Andy Knott		37
D. County account	140	
S. County account		140

These are tricky entries – the changes need to be shown in the personal accounts but as far as the double-entry system is concerned, all the correct entries will be shown in the control account since they are all correctly entered in the subsidiary books, ie the sales day book, the cash book and the purchase returns day book respectively. The subsidiary books 'feed' the control account which is part of the double-entry system. The personal accounts need to be adjusted but these are only memorandum accounts.

CHAPTER TWO

QUESTION 1

	£
Net assets (capital) as at 30 November 20*4	50,000
Net assets (capital) as at 1 December 20*3	49,590
Retained profits for year	410
Add Drawings for year	13,500
Net profit for year ended 30 November 20*4	13,910

QUESTION 3

	£
Net assets (capital) as at 31 December 20*4	70,540
Net assets (capital) as at 1 January 20*3	69,300
Retained profits for year	1,240
Add Drawings for year	24,500
	25,740
Less Capital introduced	12,500
Net profit for year ended 31 December 20*4	13,240

QUESTION 5

Debtors

	£		£
Bal b/d	1,792	Cash	121,367
Sales (*missing figure*)	122,043	Bal c/d	2,468
	123,835		123,835
Bal b/d	2,468		

Creditors

	£		£
Cash	59,846	Bal b/d	815
Bal b/d	1,067	Purchases (*missing figure*)	60,098
	60,913		60,913
		Bal b/d	1,067

Tamsin Rook
Trading account for the year ended 31 August 20*4

	£	£
Sales		122,043
Less Cost of sales		
Stock	8,467	
Purchases	60,098	
	68,565	
Stock	9,566	
		58,999
Gross profit		63,044

QUESTION 7

Motor expenses

	£		£
Cash	8,166	Bal b/d	78
Bal c/d	461	P & L a/c (*missing figure*)	8,549
	8,627		8,627
		Bal b/d	461

Rates

	£		£
Bal b/d	120	P & L a/c (*missing figure*)	1,509
Cash	1,534	Bal a/c	145
	1,654		1,654
Bal b/d	145		

QUESTION 9

	£
Net assets as at 30 April 20*4	37,901
Net assets as at 1 May 20*3	47,682
Retained profit (loss) for year	(9,781)
Add Drawings	18,298
Net profit for year ended 30 April 20*4	8,517

QUESTION 11

	£
Net assets as at 31 August 20*4	103,413
Net assets as at 1 September 20*3	104,629
Retained profit (loss) for year	(1,216)
Add Drawings	20,548
	19,332
Less Capital introduced	21,000
Net loss for the year ended 31 August 20*4	(1,668)

QUESTION 13

Debtors

	£		£
Bal b/d	840	Cash	73,498
Sales	73,170	Bal c/d	512
	74,010		74,010
Bal b/d	512		

Creditors

	£		£
Cash	38,910	Bal b/d	3,461
Bal c/d	3,790	Purchases	39,239
	42,700		42,700
		Bal b/d	3,790

Jack Hay
Trading account for the year ended 30 June 20*4

	£	£
Sales		73,170
Less Cost of sales		
Stock	1,791	
Purchases	39,239	
	41,030	
Stock	2,348	
		38,682
Gross profit		34,488

QUESTION 15

Debtors

	£		£
Bal b/d	146	Cash	62,254
Sales	62,254	Discount allowed	310
		Bal c/d	287
	62,400		62,400
Bal b/d	287		

Creditors

	£		£
Cash	28,718	Bal b/d	1,999
Bal c/d	1,871	Purchases	28,590
	30,589		30,589
		Bal b/d	1,871

Alice Band
Trading account for the year ended 31 December 20*4

	£	£
Sales		62,254
Less Cost of sales		
Stock	982	
Purchases	28,590	
	29,572	
Stock	1,271	
		28,301
Gross profit		33,953

QUESTION 17
1. Opening statement of affairs:

	£	
Premises	65,000	
Equipment	14,000	
Stock	2,519	
Debtors	1,339	
Balance at bank	2,347	(Don't forget)
	85,205	
Creditors	(2,910)	
Accrual	(145)	
Capital (assets) as at 1 January 20*4	82,150	

2. Already done in question.
3. Adjustments accounts:

Equipment

	£		£
Balance b/d	14,000	P & L a/c	3,500
Purchases	4,500	Bal c/d	15,000
	18,500		18,500
Bal b/d	15,000		

Debtors

	£		£
Bal b/d	1,339	Cash	16,409
Credit sales	16,640	Bal c/d	1,570
	17,979		17,979
Bal b/d	1,570		

4. Final accounts:

Creditors

	£		£
Cash	23,457	Bal b/d	2,910
Bal c/d	2,341	Purchases	22,888
	25,798		25,798
		Bal b/d	2,341

Dai Johns
Trading and profit and loss account for the year ended 31 December 20*4

	£	£
Sales		81,174
Less Cost of sales		
Stock	2,519	
Purchases	22,888	
	25,407	
Stock	2,331	
		23,076
Gross profit		58,098
Less Expenses	34,692	
Dep'n of equipment	3,500	
		38,192
Net profit		19,906

Balance sheet at 31 December 20*4

	£	£
Fixed assets		
Premises at cost		65,000
Equipment at valuation		15,000
		80,000
Current assets		
Stock	2,331	
Debtors	1,570	
Bank	2,872	
	6,773	
Current liabilities		
Creditors	(2,341)	
Accrued expenses	(276)	
		4,156
		84,156
Capital		82,150
Add Net profit		19,906
		102,056
Less Drawings		17,900
		84,156

QUESTION 19

1. Opening statement of affairs:

	£
Premises	56,000
Fixtures	18,000
Vehicle	8,000
Stock	1,638
Debtors	1,649
Rent in advance	600
	85,887
Bank overdraft	(452)
Creditors	(2,225)
General expenses accrued	(127)
Capital (net assets)	83,083

2. Cash book (given in question).
3. Adjustment accounts:

Fixtures

	£		£
Bal b/d	18,000	P & L a/c	2,800
Purchases	4,800	Bal c/d	20,000
	22,800		22,800
Bal b/d	20,000		

Debtors

	£		£
Bal b/d	1,649	Cash	46,880
Sales	45,690	Bal c/d	459
	47,339		47,339
Bal b/d	459		

Creditors

	£		£
Cash	34,872	Bal b/d	2,225
Bal c/d	2,619	Purchases	35,266
	37,491		37,491
		Bal b/d	2,619

Rent

	£		£
Bal b/d	600	P & L a/c	5,000
Cash	6,600	Bal c/d	2,200
	7,200		7,200
Bal b/d	2,200		

General expenses

	£		£
Cash	13,743	Bal b/d	127
Bal c/d	981	P & L a/c	14,597
	14,724		14,724
		Bal b/d	981

Commission receivable

	£		£
P & L a/c	3,000	Cash	2,000
		Bal c/d	1,000
	3,000		3,000
Bal b/d	1,000		

4. Andre Lefevre

Trading and profit and loss account for the year ended 31 March 20*5

	£	£
Sales		89,424
Less Cost of sales		
Stock	1,638	
Purchases	41,027	
	42,665	
Stock	1,744	
		40,921
Gross profit		48,503
Commission receivable		3,000
		51,503
Less Expenses		
General	14,597	
Wages	24,797	
Rent	5,000	
Depreciation –		
Premises	2,000	
Fixtures	2,800	
Vehicles	4,000	
		53,194
Net loss		1,691

Balance sheet as at 31 March 20*5

Fixed assets at valuation		£
Premises		54,000
Fixtures		20,000
Vehicle		4,000
		78,000
Current assets		
Stock	1,744	
Debtors	459	
Rent in advance	2 200	
Commission receivable owed	1,000	
	5,403	
Current liabilities		
Creditors	(2,619)	
Bank overdraft	(21,971)	
General expenses accrued	(981)	
		20,168
		57,832
Capital		83,083
Less Loss		1,691
		81,392
Less Drawings		23,560
		57,832

QUESTION 21

Joe Duff

Trading account for year ended 31 December 20*4

	£	£
Sales		240,000
Less Cost of sales		
Stock	17,993	
Purchases	188,483	
	206,476	
Stock stolen	7,975	
Stock	18,501	
		180,000
Gross profit		60,000

Stolen stock was £7,975.

(Mark-up 33⅓%)

355

QUESTION 23

1. Opening statement of affairs:

	£
Equipment	9,700
Vehicle	3,000
Stock	984
Debtors	126
Bank balance	1,764
Cash in hand	238
	15,812
Creditors	(1,477)
Capital (Net assets)	14,335

2.

Cash account

	£		£
Bal b/d	238	Wages	4,380
Takings	120,698	Rent	2,400
		Drawings	8,460
		Banked	102,250
		Stolen	3,120
		Bal c/d	326
	120,936		120,936
Bal b/d	326		

3.

Debtors

	£		£
Bal b/d	126	Cash	6,479
Sales	6,564	Bal c/d	211
	6,690		6,690
Bal b/d	211		

Creditors

	£		£
Cash	34,107	Bal b/d	1,477
Bal c/d	1,086	Purchases	33,716
	35,193		35,193
		Bal b/d	1,086

Equipment account

	£		£
Bal b/d	9,700	P & L a/c	1,300
Purchases	2,600	Bal c/d	11,000
	12,300		12,300
Bal b/d	11,000		

4. Akit Patel

Trading and profit and loss account for the year ended 30 September 20*4

	£	£
Sales		127,262
Less Cost of sales		
Stock	984	
Purchases	35,044	
	36,028	
Stock	1,358	34,670
Gross profit		92,592
Less Expenses		
General expenses	37,328	
Wages	28,141	
Rent	2,400	
Depreciation –		
equipment	1,300	
vehicles	2,000	
Stolen cash	120	71,289
Net profit		21,303

Balance sheet as at 30 September 20*4

	£	£
Fixed assets at valuation		
Equipment		11,000
Vehicle		1,000
		12,000
Current assets	£	
Stock	1,358	
Debtors	211	
Bank balance	899	
Cash in hand	326	
Insurance claim	3,000	
	5,794	
Current liabilities		
Creditors	(1,086)	4,708
		16,708
Capital		14,335
Add Profit		21,303
		35,638
Less Drawings		18,930
		16,708

CHAPTER THREE

QUESTION 1

Rent account

	£		£
Bal b/d	200	I & E a/c	700
Cash	600	Bal c/d	100
	800		800
Bal b/d	100		

QUESTION 3

Hire of halls account

	£		£
Cash	2,467	Bal b/d	183
Bal c/d	206	I & E a/c	2,490
	2,673		2,673
		Bal b/d	206

QUESTION 5

Subscriptions account

	£		£
Bal b/d	50	Cash	875
I & E a/c	900	Bal c/d	75
	950		950
Bal b/d	75		

QUESTION 7

Subscriptions account

	£		£
Bal b/d	30	Bal b/d	1,240
I & E a/c	1,210	Cash	20
Bal c/d	60	Bal c/d	40
	1,300		1,300

QUESTION 9

Life membership fund

	£		£
I & E a/c	1,250	Bal b/d	7,600
Bal c/d	8,750	Cash	2,400
	10,000		10,000
		Bal b/d	8,750

QUESTION 11
Netters Angling Club
Income and expenditure account for the year ended 30 September 20*4

	£
Subscriptions	7,650
Donations	235
	7,885
Less Expenses	
Photocopying	372
Coach hire	2,770
Loss on competition	715
Fuel	342
Secretary's honorarium	120
Depreciation – boat	530
	4,849
Surplus	3,036

Balance sheet as at 30 September 20*4

	£
Boat at valuation	1,590
Bank balance	1,899
	3,489
Accumulated fund	453
Add Surplus	3,036
	3,489

QUESTION 13
Buliov Hockey Club
Income and expenditure account for the year ended 31 March 20*5

	£
Subscriptions	2,650
Interest	124
	2,774
Less Expenses	
General expenses	3,657
Travel costs	348
Depreciation – equipment	146
	4,151
Deficit	1,377

QUESTION 15
Scrimmage Rugby Club
Bar trading account for the year ended 31 July 20*4

	£	£
Takings		103,671
Less Cost of sales		
Stock	2,518	
Purchases	52,936	
	55,454	
Stock	2,661	
		52,793
Bar profit		50,878

QUESTION 17
Fretters Sports Club
Bar trading account for the year ended 30 November 20*4

	£	£
Takings		61,385
Less Cost of sales		
Stock	1,789	
Purchases	27,676	
	29,465	
Stock	1,904	
		27,561
Bar profit		33,824

Income and expenditure account for the year ended 30 November 20*4

	£	£
Bar profit		33,824
Subscriptions		2,730
Other income		270
		36,824
Less Expenses		
General	26,742	
Rent	3,600	
		30,342
Surplus		6,482

QUESTION 19

1. Opening statement of affairs:

	£
Land and buildings	120,000
Equipment	21,000
Stock	2,750
Rates pre-paid	342
Bank balance	1,456
	145,548
Bar creditors	(219)
Subscriptions	(160)
Net assets (Accumulated fund)	145,169

2. Receipts and payment account (given).
3. Adjustment accounts:

Equipment

	£		£
Bal b/d	21,000	I & E a/c	2,560
Purchases	4,560	Bal c/d	23,000
	25,560		25,560
Bal b/d	23,000		

4. Green Lane Bowling Club

Bar creditors

	£		£
Cash	21,761	Bal b/d	219
Bal c/d	473	Purchases	22,015
	22,234		22,234
		Bal b/d	473

Subscriptions

	£		£
I & E a/c	8,560	Bal b/d	160
Bal c/d	80	Cash	8,480
	8,640		8,640
		Bal b/d	80

Rates

	£		£
Bal b/d	342	I & E a/c	1,654
Cash	1,764	Bal c/d	452
	2,106		2,106
Bal b/d	452		

4. Green Lane Bowling Club

Bar trading account for the year ended 31 October 20*4

	£	£
Takings		34,879
Less Cost of sales		
Stock	2,750	
Purchases	22,015	
	24,765	
Stock	2,451	22,314
Bar profit		12,565

Income and expenditure account for the year ended 31 October 20*4

	£	£
Bar profit		12,565
Subscriptions		8,560
Profit on competition		222
		21,347
Less Expenses		
General expenses	16,843	
Rates	1,654	
Depreciation-equipment	2,560	21,057
Surplus		290

Balance sheet as at 31 October 20*4

	£	£
Fixed assets at valuation		
Land and buildings		120,000
Equipment		23,000
		143,000
Current assets		
Stock	2,451	
Balance at bank	109	
Rates in advance	452	
	3,012	
Current liabilities		
Creditors	(473)	
Subscriptions	(80)	
		2,459
		145,459

	£
Accumulated fund	145,169
Add Surplus	290
	145,459

QUESTION 21

1. Opening statement of affairs:

	£
Land and buildings	245,000
Equipment	3,470
Stocks	3,249
Subscriptions – arrears	1,260
Bank balance	2,447
	255,426
Life membership fund	(13,600)
Creditors	(2,165)
Subscriptions – advance	(180)
General expenses	(387)
Net assets (accumulated fund)	239,094

2. Receipts and payment account (given).
3. Adjustment accounts:

Equipment

	£		£
Bal b/d	3,470	I & E a/c	1,690
Cash	4,220	Bal c/d	6,000
	7,690		7,690
Bal b/d	6,000		

Subscriptions

	£		£
Bal b/d	1,260	Bal b/d	180
I & E a/c	47,880	Cash	48,720
Bal c/d	300	Bal c/d	540
	49,440		49,440
Bal b/d	540	Bal b/d	300

Life membership fund

	£		£
I & E a/c	1,710	Bal b/d	13,600
Bal c/d	15,390	Cash	3,500
	17,100		17,100
		Bal b/d	15,390

Bar Creditors

	£		£
Cash	23,002	Bal b/d	2,165
Bal c/d	1,908	Purchases	22,745
	24,910		24,910
		Bal b/d	1,908

General expenses

	£		£
Cash	38,011	Bal b/d	387
Bal c/d	672	I & E a/c	38,296
	38,683		38,683
		Bal b/d	672

4. Cloggers Rugby Club

Bar trading account for the year ended 31 December 20*4

	£	£
Takings		34,759
Less Cost of sales		
Stock	3,249	
Purchases	22,745	
	25,994	
Stock	4,032	21,962
		12,797
Less Bar steward's wages		7,452
Bar profit		5,345

Income and expenditure account for the year ended 31 December 20*4

	£	£
Bar profits		5,345
Subscriptions – annual	47,880	
life	1,710	
Profit on dinner dance	1,047	
Profit on discos	218	
		56,200
Less Expenses		
Wages	8,661	
General expenses	38,296	
Depreciation – equipment	1,690	48,647
Surplus		7,553

Balance sheet as at 31 December 20*4

	£
Fixed assets at valuation	
Land and buildings	245,000
Equipment	6,000
	251,000
Current assets	
Stock	4,032
Balance at bank	9,345
Subscription – arrears	540
	13,917
Current liabilities	
Creditors	(1,908)
Subscriptions – in advance	(300)
General expenses	(672)
	11,037
	262,037
Accumulated fund	239,094
Surplus	7,553
	246,647
Life membership fund	15,390
	262,037

CHAPTER FOUR

QUESTION 1
Ian and Jenny
Profit and loss appropriation account for the year ended 31 January 20*5

	£	£
Net profit		26,900
Salary – Ian		5,000
		21,900
Share of residual profits – Ian	14,600	
Jenny	7,300	21,900

QUESTION 3
Maria and Nelly
Profit and loss appropriation account for the year ended 31 March 20*5

	£	£
Net profit		74,868
Salary – Maria		4,800
		70,068
Interest on capital – Maria	3,200	
Nelly	4,800	8,000
		62,068
Share of residual profits – Maria	46,551	
Nelly	15,517	62,068

QUESTION 5
Queenie and Rusty
Profit and loss appropriation account for the year ended 29 February 20*4

	£	£
Net profit		63,842
Salary – Rusty		5,000
		58,842
Interest on capital – Queenie	1,800	
Rusty	1,200	3,000
		55,842
Share of residual profits – Queenie	27,921	
Rusty	27,921	55,842

QUESTION 7
Ursula and Vincent
Profit and loss appropriation account for the year ended 31 December 20*4

	£	£
Net profit		8,400
Salary – Ursula		6,000
		2,400
Interest on capital – Ursula	500	
Vincent	3,000	3,500
		(900)
Share of residual loss – Ursula	(540)	
Vincent	(360)	(900)

QUESTION 9
Gareth and Darius
Profit and loss appropriation account for the year ended 31 January 20*5

	£	£
Net profit		27,362
Add Interest on drawings – Gareth	146	
Darius	238	384
		27,746
Share of residual profits – Gareth	13,873	
Darius	13,873	27,746

QUESTION 11
Tramp and Hobo
Profit and loss appropriation account for the year ended 30 June 20*4

	£	£
Net profit		25,570
Add Interest on drawings – Tramp	267	
Hobo	303	570
		26,140
Salary – Hobo		2,000
		24,140
Share of residual profits – Tramp	14,484	
Hobo	9,656	
		24,140

QUESTION 13
Mark, Noreen and Oswald
Profit and loss appropriation account for the year ended 31 March 20*5

	£	£
Net loss for the year		818
Add Interest on drawings – Mark	261	
Noreen	38	
Oswald	279	578
		240
Share of residual loss – Mark	120	
Noreen	80	
Oswald	40	
		240

QUESTION 15
Rooney and Timms
Profit and loss appropriation account for the year ended 31 May 20*4

	£	£
Net profit		27,967
Add Interest on drawings– Rooney	82	
Timms	179	261
		28,228
Salary – Rooney		3,000
		25,228
Interest on capital – Rooney	1,200	
Timms	1,000	2,200
		23,028
Share of residual profits – Rooney	11,514	
Timms	11,514	
		23,028

QUESTION 17
Gray and Pink
Profit and loss appropriation account for the year ended 30 November 20*4

	£	£
Net profit		37,951
Interest on drawings – Gray	171	
Pink	298	469
		38,420
Salary – Gray		4,000
		34,420
Interest on capital – Gray	2,400	
Pink	5,600	8,000
		26,420
Share of residual profits – Gray	21,136	
Pink	5,284	
		26,420

QUESTION 19
Naylor, Niall and Norbert
Profit and loss appropriation account for the year ended 31 December 20*4

	£	£
Net profit for year		71,560
Interest on drawings – Naylor	460	
Niall	320	
Norbert	411	1,191
		72,751
Salary – Niall		7,500
		65,251
Interest on capital – Naylor	3,000	
Niall	2,100	
Norbert	2,400	7,500
		57,751
Share of residual profits – Naylor	24,750	
Niall	16,501	
Norbert	16,500	57,751

Current accounts

	Naylor	Niall	Norbert		Naylor	Niall	Norbert
Balance		162		Balance	85	7,500	131
Drawings	27,200	17,450	19,350	Salary			
Interest on drawings	460	320	411	Interest on capital	3,000	2,100	2,400
Bal c/d	175	8,169		Share of profits	24,750	16,501	16,500
				Bal c/d			730
	27,835	26,101	19,761		27,835	26,101	19,761
	175		730	Bal b/d	175	8,169	

CHAPTER FIVE

QUESTION 1
Pat, Danny and Janice
Balance sheet as at 1 January 20*5

	£	£
Fixed assets		155,000
Current assets	40,000	
Current liabilities	10,000	30,000
		185,000
Capital accounts – Pat		90,000
Danny		70,000
Janice		25,000
		185,000

QUESTION 3
Umair, Tim and Eddie
Balance sheet as at 1 October 20*4

	£	£
Fixed assets at valuation		
Premises		100,000
Equipment		1,400
Vehicles		12,000
		113,400
Current assets		
Stock	4,200	
Trade debtors	6,400	
Bank	8,700	
	19,300	
Current liabilities		
Trade creditors	2,700	
		16,600
		130,000
Capital accounts – Umair		66,000
Tim		54,000
Eddie		10,000
		130,000

QUESTION 5
Mo, Doug and Tracey
Balance sheet as at 1 April 20*4

	£
Fixed asset	
Goodwill	12,000
Current asset	
Bank	4,760
	16,760
Capital accounts – Mo	9,010
Doug	4,750
Tracey	3,000
	16,760

QUESTION 7
Victor, Ffiona and Eric
Balance sheet as at 1 October 20*4

	£
Bank balance	9,000
Capital accounts – Victor	4,300
Ffiona	(800)
Eric	5,500
	9,000

QUESTION 9
(a) Revaluation account

	£			£
Capital – Shubratha	32,000		Fixed assets	16,000
Ciaran	8,000		Goodwill	24,000
	40,000			40,000

(b) Goodwill account

	£			£
Revaluation account	24,000		Capital accounts – Shubrathra	8,000
			Ciaran	8,000
			Jim	8,000

(c) Capital accounts

	Shubratha £	Ciaran £	Jim £			Shubratha £	Ciaran £	Jim £
Goodwill	8,000	8,000	8,000		Balances b/d	20,000	15,000	15,000
Balances c/d	44,000	15,000	7,000		Cash		8,000	
					Revaluation	32,000		
	52,000	23,000	15,000			52,000	23,000	15,000
					Balances c/d	44,000	15,000	7,000

(d) Shubratha, Ciaran and Jim
Balance sheet as at 1 January 20*5

	£
Fixed assets at valuation	50,000
Current assets	26,000
Current liabilities	10,000
	16,000
	66,000
Capital accounts – Shubratha	44,000
Ciaran	15,000
Jim	7,000
	66,000

QUESTION 11
(a) Revaluation account

	£			£
Equipment	24,000		Land and buildings	75,000
Vehicles	30,000		Goodwill	60,000
Stock	700			
Debtors	200			
Capital – Chuck	53,400			
Todd	26,700			
	135,000			135,000

(b) Goodwill account

	£			£
Capital – Chuck	30,000		Revaluation	60,000
Todd	15,000			
Buzz	15,000			
	60,000			60,000

(c) Capital accounts

	Chuck £	Todd £	Buzz £			Chuck £	Todd £	Buzz £
Goodwill	30,000	15,000	15,000		Balances b/d	80,000	50,000	
Balances c/d	103,400	61,700	10,000		Revaluation	53,400	26,700	
					Cash			25,000
	133,400	76,700	25,000			133,400	76,700	25,000
					Balance b/d	103,400	61,700	10,000

(d) Chuck, Todd and Buzz
Balance sheet as at 1 April 20*4

	£
Fixed assets at valuation	
Land and buildings	140,000
Equipment	10,000
Vehicles	26,000
	176,000

(Ruari, Gareth, Jock)

Capital accounts – Ruari 33,000
Gareth 22,000
Bank balance 11,000
101,000

	Ruari £	Gareth £	Jock £
Balances b/d	60	40	14
Revaluation	33	22	11
	93	62	25
Balance b/d	75		7

(b) Goodwill account

	£		£
Revaluation	36,000	Capital – Ruari	18,000
		Jock	18,000
	36,000		36,000

(c) Capital accounts (£000)

	Ruari £	Gareth £	Jock £
Goodwill	18		18
Loan a/c		62	
Balance c/d	75		7
	93	62	25

(d) Ruari and Jock
Balance sheet as at 31 August 20*4

	£	£
Fixed assets at valuation		
Premises		110,000
Equipment		5,000
Vehicles		18,000
		133,000
Current assets		
Stock	10,250	
Trade debtors	5,800	
Bank balance	1,480	
	17,530	
Current liabilities		
Trade creditors	(6,530)	11,000
		144,000
Capital accounts – Ruari	75,000	
Jock	7,000	
		82,000
Loan account – Gareth		62,000
		144,000

QUESTION 17

(a) Realisation account

	£		£
Premises	70,000	Bank	133,000
Equipment	30,000	Hazel (vehicles)	10,000
Vehicles	18,000		
Current assets	16,000		
Profit on realisation – Eliza	3,000		
Sze Hang	3,000		
Hazel	3,000		
	143,000		143,000

	£	£
Current assets		
Stock	4,100	
Trade debtors	6,000	
Bank balance	22,570	
	32,670	
Current liabilities		
Trade creditors	(4,570)	28,100
		204,100
Long-term liability		29,000
		175,100
Capital accounts – Chuck		103,400
Todd		61,700
Buzz		10,000
		175,100

QUESTION 13
(a)

Revaluation account

	£		£
Capital accounts – Gordon	28,000	Fixed assets	50,000
Frances	28,000	Goodwill	20,000
Jacqui	14,000		
	70,000		70,000

(b) Goodwill account

	£		£
Revaluation	20,000	Capital	20,000
		Gordon	10,000
		Jacqui	10,000
			10,000

(c) Capital accounts (£000)

	Gordon £	Frances £	Jacqui £
Goodwill	10	10	7
Loan a/c		38	14
Balance c/d	38		
	48	38	21

	Gordon £	Jacqui £
Balance b/d	20	
Revaluation	28	
	48	38
Balance b/d	38	11
		21

(d) Gordon and Jacqui
Balance sheet as at 31 March 20*5

	£
Fixed assets	84,000
Current assets	12,000
Current liabilities	9,000
	3,000
	87,000
Capital accounts – Gordon	38,000
Jacqui	11,000
	49,000
Loan account – Frances	38,000
	87,000

QUESTION 15
(a)

Revaluation account

	£		£
Equipment	18,000	Premises	65,000
Vehicles	16,000	Goodwill	36,000
Stock	1,000		

(b)

Bank account

	£		£
Balance b/d	3,000	Creditors	7,000
Realisation: (assets)	133,000	Capital – Eliza	63,000
		Sze Hang	43,000
		Hazel	23,000
	136,000		136,000

Capital accounts (£000)

	Eliza £	Sze Hang £	Hazel £		Eliza £	Sze Hang £	Hazel £
Realisation (vehicle)			10	Balances b/d	60	40	30
Bank	63	43	23	Realisation	3	3	3
	63	43	33		63	43	33

QUESTION 19

(a)

Realisation account

	£		£
Premises	210,000	Discount received	400
Equipment	84,000	Bertram (premises)	300,000
Vehicles	42,000	Chipperfield (vehicle)	5,000
Stock	12,400	Mills (vehicle)	6,000
Discount allowed	100	Bank (vehicle)	9,000
Costs	6,450	Bank (equipment)	57,000
Capital – Bertram	16,625	Bank (stock)	10,800
Chipperfield	11,083		
Mills	5,542		
	388,200		388,200

(b)

Bank account

	£		£
Balance	2,700	Loan – Chipperfield	50,000
Debtors	8,100	Creditors	8,900
Realisation (vehicle)	9,000	Costs	6,450
Realisation (equipment)	57,000	Capital – Chipperfield	106,083
Realisation (stock)	10,800	Mills	49,542
Capital – Bertram	133,375		
	220,975		220,975

(c)

Capital accounts

	Bertram £	Ch'field £	Mills £		Bertram £	Ch'field £	Mills £
Realisation (premises)	300,000			Balance b/d	150,000	100,000	50,000
Realisation (vehicles)		5,000	6,000	Realisation	16,625	11,083	5,542
Bank		106,083	49,542	Bank	133,375		
	300,000	111,083	55,542		300,000	111,083	55,542

QUESTION 21

Realisation account

	£		£
Net assets	100,000	Agas Ltd	210,000
Capital – Joan	88,000		
Derby	22,000		
	210,000		210,000

Agas Ltd

	£		£
Realisation	210,000	Cash	25,000
		Capital (shares)	185,000
	210,000		210,000

Capital accounts

	Joan £	Derby £		Joan £	Derby £
Ordinary shares in Agas Ltd	148,000	37,000	Balances b/d	60,000	40,000
Cash		25,000	Realisation	88,000	22,000
	148,000	62,000		148,000	62,000

QUESTION 23

(a)

Realisation account

	£		£
Net assets	40,000	Cash	55,000
Capital – Stephen	5,000		
Asman	5,000		
Shably	5,000		
	55,000		55,000

(b)

Bank account

	£		£
Balance b/d	10,000	Capital – Stephen	41,667
Realisation	55,000	Asman	23,333
	65,000		65,000

(c)

Capital accounts

	Stephen £	Asman £	Shably £		Stephen £	Asman £	Shably £
Shably	3,333	1,667		Balance b/d	40,000	20,000	5,000
Bank	41,667	23,333		Realisation	5,000	5,000	5,000
				Balance b/d			10,000
				Capital – Stephen			
				Asman			
	45,000	25,000	10,000		45,000	25,000	10,000

QUESTION 25

(a)

Revaluation account

	£		£
Equipment	8,000	Premises	52,000
Vehicles	14,000	Goodwill	60,000
Stock	400		
Capital – Arbuthnot	44,800		
Barton	44,800		
	112,000		112,000

(b)

Goodwill account

	£		£
Revaluation	60,000	Capital – Arbuthnot	30,000
		Barton	20,000
		Currock	10,000
	60,000		60,000

(c)

Capital accounts

	Arb'not £	B'ton £	Currock £		Arb'not £	B'ton £	Currock £
Goodwill	30,000	20,000	10,000	Balances b/d	65,000	50,000	
				Cash			40,000
Balances c/d	79,800	74,800	30,000	Revaluation	44,800	44,800	
	109,800	94,800	40,000		109,800	94,800	40,000

(d) Arbuthnot, Barton and Currock
Balance sheet as at 1 July 20*4

	£	£
Fixed assets at valuation		
Premises		100,000
Equipment		15,000
Vehicles		20,000
		135,000
Current assets		
Stock	8,500	
Trade debtors	4,600	
Bank	42,500	
	55,600	
Creditors	(6,000)	
		49,600
		184,600
Capital – Arbuthnot		79,800
Barton		74,800
Currock		30,000
		184,600

QUESTION 27
(a)

Revaluation account

	£		£
Equipment	8,000	Premises	40,000
Vehicles	8,000	Goodwill	27,000
Capital – Petteril	25,500		
Eden	20,400		
Calder	5,100		
	67,000		67,000

(b)

Goodwill account

	£		£
Revaluation	27,000	Capital – Eden	18,000
		Calder	9,000
	27,000		27,000

(c)

Capital accounts

	Petteril £	Eden £	Calder £		Petteril £	Eden £	Calder £
Goodwill		18,000	9,000	Balances b/d	50,000	36,000	30,000
Loan a/c	75,500			Revaluation	25,500	20,400	5,100
Balances c/d		38,400	26,100				
	75,500	56,400	35,100		75,500	56,400	35,100
				Balances b/d		38,400	26,100

(d) Eden and Calder
Balance sheet as at 1 October 20*4

	£	£
Fixed assets at valuation		
Premises		100,000
Equipment		6,000
Vehicles		24,000
		130,000
Current assets		
Stock	4,200	
Trade debtors	7,600	
Bank	1,200	
	13,000	
Trade creditors	(3,000)	
		10,000
		140,000
Capital accounts – Eden		38,400
Calder		26,100
		64,500
Loan account – Petteril		75,500
		140,000

QUESTION 29
Stan and Ollie
Balance sheet as at 1 May 20*4

	£	£
Fixed assets at valuation		
Equipment		40,000
Vehicles		8,000
		48,000
Current assets		
Stock	10,000	
Trade debtors	9,000	
Bank	1,500	
	20,500	
Current liabilities		
Trade creditors	(8,500)	
		12,000
		60,000
Capital accounts – Stan		36,500
Ollie		23,500
		60,000

QUESTION 31

(a)

Realisation account

	£		£
Land and buildings	40,000	Discount received	300
Equipment	30,000	Cash (equipment)	17,000
Vehicles	10,000	Sukhdeep (vehicles)	6,000
Stock	3,400	Divya Ltd	60,000
Discount allowed	400	Capital – Pritpal	2,400
Costs	4,300	Sukhdeep	2,400
	88,100		88,100

(b)

Bank account

	£		£
Balance	2,700	Loan – Pritpal	25,000
Debtors	18,000	Creditors	6,100
Realisation	17,000	Realisation – costs	4,300
Divya	30,000	Capital – Pritpal	30,900
		Sukhdeep	1,400
	67,700		67,700

(c)

Capital accounts

	Pritpal £	Sukhdeep £		Pritpal £	Sukhdeep £
Realisation (vehicles)		6,000	Balances b/d	48,300	24,800
Realisation	2,400	2,400			
Divya Ltd (Ord shares)	15,000	15,000			
Cash	30,900	1,400			
	48,300	24,800		48,300	24,800

QUESTION 33

(a)

Realisation account

	£		£
Equipment	42,000	Discount received	140
Stock	17,000	Capital – Jacques (stock)	15,000
Discount allowed	300	Bank (equipment)	25,000
Bank (costs)	8,300	Capital – Jacques	13,730
		Marcel	9,153
		Guillaume	4,577
	67,600		67,600

(b)

Bank account

	£		£
Balance b/d	800	Loan – Guillaume	30,000
Debtors	3,200	Creditors	6,260
Realisation (equipment)	25,000	Costs	8,300
Capital – Jacques	18,082	Capital – Guillaume	2,522
	47,082		47,082

(c)

Capital accounts

	J'ques £	M'cel £	G'me £		J'ques £	M'cel £	G'me £
Realisation (stock)	15,000			Bal b/d	15,000	1,900	10,000
Realisation	13,730	9,153	4,577	Capital – Jacques		4,352	
Capital – M'l			2,901	Guillaume		2,901	
Bank	4,352		2,522	Bank	18,082		
	33,082	9,153	10,000		33,082	9,153	10,000

CHAPTER SIX

QUESTION 1
Purlin plc
Profit and loss appropriation account for the year ended 30 November 20*4

	£000	£000
Profit before taxation		642
Taxation		120
Profit after taxation		522
Transfer to general reserves		100
		422
Dividends – preference shares	35	
ordinary shares	95	
		130
Retained profits for year		292

QUESTION 3
Sleerock plc
Trading and profit and loss account for the year ended 31 July 20*4

	£000	£000
Sales		757
Less Cost of sales		
Stock	83	
Purchases	312	
	395	
Stock	74	
		321
Gross profit		436
Selling and distribution expenses		(89)
Administration expenses		(112)
Operating profit		235
Financial charges		(36)
Profit before taxation		199
Taxation		(39)
Profit after taxation		160
Dividends – preference shares		(40)
ordinary shares		(70)
Retained profit for year		50

QUESTION 5
Typleat plc
Balance sheet as at 28 February 20*5

	£000	£000
Fixed assets		1,836
Current assets	657	
Creditors	349	
		308
		2,144

Share capital and reserves

	£000
Ordinary shares of £1 each	1,500
Share premium account	50
Profit and loss account	594
	2,144

QUESTION 7
Pitcherdy plc
Profit and loss account for the year ended 31 December 20*4

	£000
Gross profit	746
Selling and distribution expenses	(88)
Administration expenses	(124)
Operating profit	534
Interest payable	(36)
Profit before taxation	498
Taxation	(160)
Profit after taxation	338
Transfer to asset replacement reserve	(50)
	288
Dividends – preference – paid	(6)
proposed	(6)
ordinary – paid	(14)
proposed	(20)
	242
Retained profit for year	242

QUESTION 9
Masqik plc
Balance sheet as at 1 December 20*4

	£000
Share capital and reserves	
Ordinary shares of £1 each	1,800
8% preference shares of £1 each	400
Share premium account	112
Profit and loss account	228
	2,540

QUESTION 11
Klobule plc
Summarised balance sheet as at 30 September 20*4

	£000
Net assets	3,373
Share capital and reserves	
Ordinary shares of 25p each	1,640
Share premium account	600
Profit and loss account	1,133
	3,373

QUESTION 13
Ardbeck plc
Balance sheet as at 31 July 20*4

	£000
Net assets	2,500
Share capital and reserves	
Ordinary shares of 10p each	1,800

	£000
Share premium	400
Profit and loss account	300
	2,500

QUESTION 15
McTavish-Jones plc
Balance sheet extract as at 31 March 20*5

	£000
Share capital and reserves	
Ordinary shares of £1 each	2,000
6% preference shares of £1 each	120
Share premium	1,800
Profit and loss account	218
	4,318

QUESTION 17
Omerdoh plc
Balance sheet as at 31 December 20*4

Fixed assets	Valuation £	Cost £	Depreciation £	Net £
Premises	250,000			250,000
Equipment		86,000	56,000	30,000
Vehicles		76,000	57,000	19,000
	250,000	162,000	113,000	299,000
Current assets				
Stock		60,000		
Debtors		47,000		
Bank balance		58,000		
		165,000		
Creditors			(21,000)	144,000
				443,000
Share capital and reserves				
Ordinary shares of £1 each				360,000
Revaluation reserve				76,000
Profit and loss account				7,000
				443,000

CHAPTER SEVEN

QUESTION 1
No. The brand name should not be capitalised. Internally developed intangible assets should be capitalised only where they have an ascertainable market value.

QUESTION 3
No. Internally generated goodwill should not be capitalised.

QUESTION 5
The property may be revalued. Depreciation should then be charged on the revalued amount over the useful lifetime of the property.

QUESTION 7
The finance director is correct. Purchase cost includes transportation and installation costs. All costs to enable the machinery to function.

CHAPTER EIGHT

QUESTION 1

Cash inflows	£000	Cash outflows	£000
Decrease in debtors	14	Purchase of fixed assets	584
Increase in creditors	9	Increase in stock	13
Share issue (100 + prem 300)	400	Taxation	48
Profits	289	Dividends	60
Total cash inflows	712	Total cash outflows	705

Increase in profit and loss account + provision for taxation + proposed dividend

166 +   53   +   70

QUESTION 3

Operating profit for the year ended 31 March 20*5

	£
	463,000
Less Interest	27,000*
Profit before taxation	436,000
Taxation	112,000*
	324,000
Transfer to general reserve	20,000*
	304,000
Dividends	80,000*
Retained profit for year	224,000*

(Put in all the information supplied * then fill in the missing sub-totals until you arrive at the operating profit.)

QUESTION 5

Fixed assets account

	£		£
Balance b/d	2,160	Disposal	850 (1)
Bank	1,180 (6)	Balance c/d	2,490 (4)
	3,340		3,340
Balance b/d	2,490 (4)		

Depreciation of fixed assets account

	£		£
Disposal	610 (2)	Balance b/d	830
Balance c/d	910 (5)	P & L a/c	690 (7)
	1,520		1,520
		Balance b/d	910 (5)

Disposal account

	£		£
Fixed asset	850 (1)	Depreciation	610 (2)
		Bank	170 (3)
		P & L a/c (loss on disposal)	70 (3)
	850		850

Entries not shown:
(3) Dr Bank 170
(6) Dr Bank 1,180
(7) Dr P & L a/c 690
(8) Dr P & L a/c 70

(6) Cr Bank 850

The cash inflows are £170,000 plus the reduction in profit of £690,000 and profit of £70,000 which will not reduce cash but needs to be added to reported profits to obtain cash inflow. £1,180,000 cash outflow for purchase of fixed assets.

QUESTION 7

	Cash inflow	Cash outflow
	£	£
Premises		9,000
Stock		1,900
Debtors	200	
Creditors	150	

QUESTION 9
Shakoor Ltd

Cash inflows	£	Cash outflows	£
Increase in depreciation	38,000	Purchase of fixed assets	132,000
Decrease in debtors	1,980	Increase in stock	3,500
Provision for taxation	38,000	Decrease in creditors	4,610
Proposed dividends	30,000	Taxation paid	40,000
Issue of shares	100,000	Dividends paid	36,000
Retained profit for year	7,330		
Decrease in bank balance during the year	800		
	216,110		216,110

QUESTION 11

Depreciation of £10,000 needs to be added to reported profits to obtain the cash inflow for the year.

QUESTION 13

Plant account

	£		£
Balance b/d	240,000	Disposal	32,000
		Balance c/d	208,000
	240,000		240,000
Balance b/d	208,000		

Provision for depreciation account

	£		£
Disposal	20,000	Balance b/d	100,000
Balance c/d	111,800	P & L a/c	31,800
	131,800		131,800
		Balance b/d	111,800

Disposal account

	£		£
Plant	32,000	Depreciation	20,000
P & L a/c	1,200	Bank	13,200
	33,200		33,200

The cash inflow is £13,200 plus the reduction in reported profits of £31,800 depreciation debited to the profit and loss account. £1,200 profit on disposal should be deducted from operating profit.

QUESTION 15

Only one cash inflow: £200,000 from the issue of 6% preference shares.

QUESTION 17
Reconciliation of operating profit to net cash inflow from operating activities

	£000	
Operating profit	67	(196,000 – £136,000 + £7,000)
Depreciation	140	
Profit on disposal	(7)	
Increase in stocks	(4)	
Decrease in debtors	8	
Decrease in creditors	(5)	
Net cash inflows from operating activities	199	

Fixed assets

£	£
362	70
198	490
490	

Depreciation

60	140
220	140
	220

Disposal

70	60
7	17

QUESTION 19

Reconciliation of operating profit to net cash inflow from operating activities

	£000	
Operating profit	77	
Depreciation	113	(£1,443 − £1,384 + £18)
Loss on disposal	5	
Increase in stocks	(8)	
Decrease in debtors	4	
Increase in creditors	3	
Net cash flow from operating activities	194	

Machinery		Depreciation	
488	102	87	236
145	531	262	113
531			262

Disposal	
102	87
	10
	5

QUESTION 21

Reconciliation of net cash to movement in net debt

	£000	
Increase in cash during period	24	
Increase in debenture stock	(500)	
Increase in long-term loan	(50)	
	(526)	
Net debt as at 1 July 20*3	(1,622)	(1,750 − 128)
Net debt as at 30 June 20*4	(2,148)	(2,300 − 152)

QUESTION 23

Reconciliation of net cash to movement in net debt

	£000	
Decrease in cash during period	(235)	
Cash used to repurchase debentures	700	
Increase in long-term loan	(350)	
Change in net debt	115	
Net debt as at 1 May 20*4	(2,282)	(2,400 − 118)
Net debt as at 30 April 20*5	(2,167)	(2,050 + 130 − 13)

QUESTION 25

McDonnel and Prince plc
Cash flow statement for the year ended 31 January 20*5

	£000	£000
Operating activities		
Net cash inflows from operating activities		2,345
Returns on investments and servicing of finance		
Interest paid	(40)	
Preference dividend paid	(180)	
		(220)
Taxation		
Corporation tax paid		(298)
Capital expenditure and financial investments		
Payments to acquire tangible fixed assets	(1,400)	
Receipts from the sale of fixed assets	47	
		(1,353)
Equity dividends paid		
Equity dividends paid during year		(460)
Net cash inflow before financing		14
Financing		
Receipts from issue of shares		2,000
Increase in cash		2,014

Reconciliation of operating profit to net cash inflow from operating activities

	£000
Operating profit	2,167
Depreciation	214
Profit on disposal of fixed assets	(18)
Increase in stocks	(12)
Decrease in debtors	17
Decrease in creditors	(23)
	2,345

QUESTION 27

Workings

Cash in	£	Cash out	£
Depreciation	20	Equity – dividend – interim	14
Increase in creditors	7	Purchase – intangible assets	405
Debenture issue	10	Purchase – land and buildings	72
Share issue	400	Increase in stocks	10
Operating profit	129	Increase in debtors	12
Interest received	12	Tax paid	38
		Proposed equity div (20*3)	29
		Interest paid	8
Total cash inflow	578	Total cash outflow	588

(a) Sagoo and Simpson
Cash flow statement for the year ended 31 July 20*4

	£000	£000
Operating activities		
Net cash inflow from operating activities		134
Returns on investments and servicing of finance		
Interest paid	(8)	
Interest received	12	
		4
Taxation		
Corporation tax paid		(38)
Capital expenditure and financial investments		
Payments to acquire intangible fixed assets	(405)	
Payments to acquire tangible fixed assets	(72)	
		(477)
Equity dividends paid		
Equity dividends paid during year		(43)
Net cash before financing		(420)
Financing		
Receipts from issue of debentures	10	
Receipts from issue of shares	400	
		410
Decrease in cash		(10)

(b) Reconciliation of operating profit to net cash inflow from operating activities

	£000
Operating profit	129
Depreciation	20
Increase in stocks	(10)
Increase in debtors	(12)
Increase in creditors	7
	134

(c) Reconciliation of net cash to movement in net debt

Gray & Lyons plc
Cash flow statement for the year ended 28 February 20*5

	£000	£000
Operating activities		
Net cash inflow from operating activities		394
Returns on investments and servicing of finance		
Interest paid	(12)	
Preference dividends paid	(28)	
		(40)
Taxation		
Corporation tax paid		(146)
Capital expenditure and financial investments		
Payments to acquire fixed assets	(100)	
Payments to acquire investments	(10)	
Receipts from sale of fixed assets	20	
		(90)
Equity dividends paid		
Equity dividends paid during year		(65)
Net cash inflow before financing		53
Financing		
Repayment of debenture stock		(160)
Decrease in cash		(107)

Reconciliation of operating profit to net cash inflow from operating activities

	£000
Operating profit	325
Depreciation – land and buildings	12
machinery	47
vehicles	144
Loss on disposal of machinery	5
Increase in stock	(104)
Increase in debtors	(74)
Increase in creditors	39
	394

Reconciliation of net cash to movement in net debt

	£000
Decrease in cash during period	(107)
Cash used to repurchase debentures	160
Change in net debt	53
Net debt as at 1 March 20*4	(130)
Net debt as at 28 February 20*5	(77)

CHAPTER NINE

QUESTION 1
(a)

	20*4	20*5
$\dfrac{\text{Gross profit}}{\text{Cost of sales}} \times 100$	52.31%	56.82%
$\dfrac{\text{Gross profit}}{\text{Sales}} \times 100$	34.35%	36.23%
$\dfrac{\text{Net profit}}{\text{Sales}} \times 100$	22.70%	23.23% uses operating profit
$\dfrac{\text{Expenses}}{\text{Sales}} \times 100$	11.65%	13.00%
$\dfrac{\text{Net profit}}{\text{Capital employed}} \times 100$	16.14%	16.03%

(b) There has been an improvement in the first three ratios calculated. The mark-up has

---

	£000
Decrease in cash during period	(10)
Cash received from issue of debentures	(10)
Change in net debt	(20)
Net debt as at 1 August 20*3	(28)
Net debt as at 31 July 20*4	(48)

QUESTION 29
Workings

Cash inflow	£000	Cash outflow	£000
Operating profit	1,123	Interest paid	29
Amortised patents	24	Profit on premises	50
Sale of premises	175	Purchase of machine	225
Depreciation of premises	12	Increase in stock	298
Depreciation of machinery	99	Increase in debtors	149
Increase in creditors	50	Taxation paid	363
Issue of shares	150	Dividend paid	134
Total cash inflow	1,633	Total cash outflow	1,248

Increase in cash over the year £385,000

Dratas plc
Cash flow statement for the year ended 31 August 20*4

	£000
Operating activities	
Net cash inflow from operating activities	811
Returns on investment and servicing of finance	
Interest paid	(29)
Taxation	
Corporation tax paid	(363)
Capital expenditure and financial investment	
Payment to acquire fixed assets	(225)
Receipts from sale of fixed assets	175
	(50)
Equity dividends	
Equity dividends paid during year	(134)
Net cash inflow before financing	235
Financing	
Issue of ordinary shares	150
Increase in cash	385

Reconciliation of operating profit to net cash inflow from operating activities

	£000
Operating profit	1,123
Amortisation of patents	24
Depreciation of premises	12
Depreciation of machinery	99
Increase in stocks	(298)
Increase in debtors	(149)
Increase in creditors	50
Profit on sale of premises	(50)
	811

Reconciliation of net cash to movement in net debt

	£000
Increase in cash during period	385
Net debt as at 1 September 20*3	(223)
Net debt as at 31 August 20*4	162

QUESTION 31

increased from 52.31% to 56.82% (an increase of 8.6% over the year). This is reflected in both margins. Gross margin has improved from 34.35% to 36.23% (an increase of 5.47%), while net margin has improved by 0.53% to 23.23%. The lower rate of increase in net margin is because of the increase in the proportion of expenditure on overheads over the year from 11.65% to 13.00%.

The return on capital employed has remained almost static.

QUESTION 3

(a)

	20*3	20*4
Current ratio = $\dfrac{\text{Current assets}}{\text{Current liabilities}}$	4:1	3.09:1
Liquid ratio = $\dfrac{\text{Current assets − stock}}{\text{Current liabilities}}$	2.93:1	2.09:1
Debtors' collection period = $\dfrac{\text{Debtors} \times 365}{\text{Credit sales}}$	38 days	35 days
Creditors' payment period = $\dfrac{\text{Creditors} \times 365}{\text{Credit purchases}}$	32 days	35 days
Rate of stock turn = $\dfrac{\text{Cost of sales}}{\text{Average stock}}$	11.44 times	10.88 times
OR $\dfrac{\text{Average stock} \times 365}{\text{Cost of sales}}$	33 days	34 days
Working capital cycle	39 days	34 days

(b) There has been an improvement in debtor days; it is getting closer to the 'accepted' 30 days. There has been an improvement in creditor days, although care must be taken not to increase it too much and antagonise suppliers.

In year 20*3, the creditors were being paid rather too quickly – six days on average before debtors settled. There has been an improvement in year 20*4 where the figures match – further improvement should be sought.

QUESTION 5

i) Interest cover = 4.47 times.
ii) Earnings per share = 54.4 pence.
iii) Ordinary dividend cover = 1.7.
iv) Dividend yield = 4.7%.
v) Price/earnings ratio = 12.5%.
vi) Dividend paid per share = 32 pence.
vii) Gearing = 69.48% (very highly geared).

QUESTION 7

(a) Interest cover = $\dfrac{\text{Operating profit}}{\text{Interest paid}}$ = 17.86 times

Earnings per share = $\dfrac{\text{Profit after tax and preference dividends}}{\text{Number of ordinary shares}}$ = 22.55 pence

Dividend paid per share = $\dfrac{\text{Ordinary dividend}}{\text{Number of ordinary shares}}$ = 3.4 pence

Price/earnings ratio = $\dfrac{\text{Market price per share}}{\text{Earnings per share}}$ = 24.39%

Dividend yield = $\dfrac{\text{Dividend per share}}{\text{Market price per share}} \times 100$ = 0.62%

Gearing = $\dfrac{\text{Fixed cost capital}}{\text{Total capital}} \times 100$ = 30%

(b) Interest cover is improving each year. If the debentures have remained the same over the three years, the improvement has been caused by a larger operating profit each year. EPS is improving, again probably because of increased profitability. Dividend per share has improved each year – rather slowly, but shareholders should not be dissatisfied. P/E ratio remains similar to previous years. The dividend yield remains low. Gearing has stayed low but there has been a significant increase in 20*5 – this could affect earnings potential if increased further.

QUESTION 9

(a)

	Baliaba plc	Firty Leaves plc
i) Gearing ratio	20.62%	58.04%
ii) Interest cover		5.24 times
iii) EPS	95.9 pence	20 pence
iv) Dividend paid per share	19.49 pence	5.25 pence
v) Dividend yield	4.6%	3.75%
vi) Price/earnings ratio	4.38	7

(b) Baliaba is a low-geared company (less than 50% of funding is provided by fixed cost capital), whereas Firty Leaves is highly geared (more than 50% of funding is provided by fixed-cost capital). Firty is able to cover its current interest payments more than five times. Baliaba appears to be more successful than Firty Leaves as its earnings per share are more than four times greater. Around a fifth of earnings per share is paid to shareholders, leaving 76 pence of earnings to be 'ploughed back' into the company. Firty Leaves plc has slightly less earnings per share and retained profits, however, it is significant to note that the ordinary shares of Firty Leaves plc are 25p compared with the nominal value of £1 per ordinary share in Baliaba. If adjustment were to be made for this then EPS for Firty Leaves would be 80p and dividend paid per share 21p. This is a more valid comparison. Baliaba's dividend yield is slightly better than that of Firty Leaves. Shareholders in Firty Leaves appear to have more confidence in the company than shareholders in Baliaba – indicated by a higher P/E ratio.

QUESTION 11

Gross profit margin = $\dfrac{\text{GP}}{\text{Sales}} \times 100 = \dfrac{59{,}248}{148{,}120} \times 100$ = 40%

Net profit margin = $\dfrac{\text{NP}}{\text{Sales}} \times 100 = \dfrac{13{,}437}{148{,}120} \times 100$ = 9.1%

ROCE = $\dfrac{\text{Net profit}}{\text{Capital employed}} \times 100 = \dfrac{13{,}437}{14{,}800} \times 100$ = 90.79%

Current ratio = $\dfrac{\text{Current assets}}{\text{Current liabilities}} = \dfrac{10{,}998}{9{,}098}$ = 1.2:1

Liquid ratio = $\dfrac{\text{Current assets − Stock}}{\text{Current liabilities}} = \dfrac{6{,}348}{9{,}098}$ = 0.70:1

There has been a steady improvement in the gross margin over the five years, with a larger than usual increase in 20*2. However, this larger than usual increase was unsustained in subsequent years. There has been an improvement of £4.8 for every £100 of takings over the five years.

The net margin has also shown a steady improvement (£2 per £100 of takings), reflecting that observed in the gross margin.

There has been a greater than usual increase in expenses in the final year. Having been relatively stable at £29.4 and £29.6 for the past three years, they have now risen to £30.9 per £100 of takings in 20*5 – although this is only £1.30 per £100 of takings this should be investigated to determine the cause of this slight deterioration in control of expenses.

The current ratio has deteriorated steadily over the past five years. Whether this is cause for concern will depend largely on the type of business. The liquid ratio too is falling but again identifying the type of business would be important before commenting. The proportion of stock held is falling each year.

QUESTION 13

	20*4	20*5
i) Gross margin	49.36%	49.37%
ii) Net margin	19.23%	17.19%
iii) Operating expenses/sales	30.13%	32.17%
iv) ROCE	19.19%	16.75%
v) Current ratio	0.86:1	0.85:1
vi) Liquid ratio	0.76:1	0.74:1
vii) Interest cover	37.5 times	32.3 times
viii) Dividend cover	2.56 times	2.93 times
ix) Earnings per share	12.6 pence	11.9 pence
x) Price/earnings ratio	7.14	9.24
xi) Gearing ratio	6.4% (low)	6.48% (lower)
xii) Dividend yield	5.44%	4.82%
xiii) Rate of stock turn	–	31 days
xiv) Debtors' ratio	–	106 days

Interest cover has worsened over the two years but it is still very good. Interest could have been paid over 30 times before profits disappeared.

Dividend cover shows how many times the current dividend could be paid out of current profits; the cover has improved over the year.

Earnings per share has deteriorated; profits have gone down; the ratio is an easy to calculate measure of the success of the business.

The price/earnings ratio has improved, perhaps indicating that ordinary shareholders have greater confidence in the future of the company.

Both gearing ratios indicate that a small proportion of the funds invested in the business are provided by long-term creditors.

QUESTION 15

(a)

	Del Tipper	Tanka Continental Traders Ltd	With notional manager's salary
Gross margin	54.56%	57.28%	
Net margin	29.56%	30.1%	16.32%
Expenses/Sales	25%	27.18%	38.24%
ROCE	32.59%	38.04%	18%
Current ratio	11.68:1	1.46:1	
Liquid ratio	10.8:1	0.82:1	
Debtors ratio	15 days	43 days	
Creditors ratio	8 days	199 days	
Rate of stock turn	12 days	125 days	

(b) The gross margin for the two businesses is very similar. This could be expected since they are in the same line of business. TCT Ltd has a slightly better ratio and this may be caused by economies of scale (purchases of £460,000 compared with only £60,000 in Del's business).

After adjusting for the notional manager's salary, Dels's net margin falls from almost 30% to around half of this figure to 16.32% – 16.32% is a fairer representation of his net margin and his ROCE. Using both these ratios, it can be seen that TCT has a better set of figures. Comparison of the amounts devoted to overheads reveals that TCT is managing overheads much more effectively, spending over £11 less per £100 of takings than Del.

It should be remembered that the ROCE calculation depends on the accuracy of the valuation of assets and if these are undervalued (using cost concept, especially in Del's case) then different results could be revealed.

Del's current ratio is much higher than TCT's; in fact, it may be too high. For every £1 owed to trade creditors he has £11.68 of current assets. Perhaps the bank balance could be reduced and the money used in a more productive capacity. The liquid ratio shows that almost £11 current assets cover every £1 of trade creditors – very high. Although TCT's current and liquid ratios are low, they do not pose too much of a problem.

There are great differences between the last three ratios calculated: is Del too strict in getting his debtors to pay? He is certainly paying his creditors too quickly. In fact, he pays his creditors in eight days while receiving money from debtors a week later. TCT, on the other hand, receives money from debtors in 43 days – a little on the long side, especially considering that this is an average collection period – are some debtors taking even longer? The longer debts are outstanding, the greater the chance of them proving to be bad. It is taking TCT almost seven months on average to pay creditors – this is likely to cause problems with suppliers.

Finally, Del's rate of stock turn is very much shorter than that of TCT – who are keeping four months stock in hand. This would seem excessive given that Del keeps stock for only 12 days before sale. Clearly, more would need to be known about each business in order to comment on the efficiency of these figures.

TCT is overtrading – comparatively large stocks; high proportion of debtors; and high proportion of creditors to liquid assets.

(c) Del currently earns £40,200:

■ If he employed a manager and sought employment elsewhere, he would earn £22,200 plus any income from another employment.

■ If he sold the business and sough employment elsewhere he would receive £123,350 which would currently yield £9,868 per annum. If the business assets were worth in excess of £123,350 and a purchaser purchased goodwill too, the annual income from investing the capital sum might be much greater than £9,868 per annum. In addition there would be the salary earned from the other employment.

CHAPTER TWELVE

QUESTION 1

Receipts	Issues	Stock	Workings
(a) FIFO			
1 @ £100		£100	1 @ £100
6 @ £100		£700	6 @ £100
	4	£300	3 @ £100
5 @ £110		£850	3 @ £100, 5 @ £110
	6	£220	2 @ £110
7 @ £120		£1,060	2 @ £110, 7 @ £120
	6	£360	3 @ £120

Stock values: FIFO £360; LIFO £320; AVCO £350.83
Gross profit: FIFO £1,470; LIFO £1,430; AVCO £1,460.83

QUESTION 3
(a) i) FIFO 3 @ £18 = £54
ii) LIFO 2 @ £16 + 1 @ 17 = £49
(b) i)

Trading accounts for August

	FIFO £	FIFO £	LIFO £	LIFO £
Sales		400		400
Less Cost of sales				
Purchases	226		226	
Stock as at 31 August	54		49	
		172		177
Gross profit		228		223

QUESTION 5

	£
Stock as per stock-take of 5 January 20*5	26,870
Less Purchases less returns	(1,868)
Add Sales less returns (3930/1.33)	2,955
Stock as at 31 December 20*4	27,957

QUESTION 7
(a)

FIFO	Receipts	Issues	Balance	£
	5 @ £4		20.00	5 @ £4
		4	4.00	1 @ £4
	17 @ £5		89.00	1 @ £4, 17 @ £5
		15	15.00	3 @ £5
	10 @ £6		75.00	3 @ £5, 10 @ £6
		7	36.00	6 @ £6

(b)

LIFO	Receipts	Issues	Balance	£
	5 @ £4		20.00	5 @ £4
		4	4.00	1 @ £4
	17 @ £5		89.00	1 @ £4, 17 @ £5
		15	14.00	1 @ £4, 2 @ £5
	10 @ £6		74.00	1 @ £4, 2 @ £5, 10 @ £6
		7	32.00	1 @ £4, 2 @ £5, 3 @ £6

(c)

	Receipts	Issues	Balance	£
	5 @ £4		20.00	£20/4 = £4
		4	4.00	1 @ £4
	17 @ £5		89.00	£89/18 = £4.94
		15	14.82	3 @ £4.94
	10 @ £6		74.82	£74.82/13 = £5.76
		7	34.56	6 @ £5.76

QUESTION 9
(a) i) FIFO 1 @ £220
ii) LIFO 1 @ £200

QUESTION 11

(a)

	£	
8 @ £12	96.00	8 @ £12
10 @ £12	216.00	8 @ £12, 10 @ £12
15	36.00	3 @ £12
12 @ £8	132.00	3 @ £12, 12 @ £8
15 @ £7	237.00	3 @ £12, 12 @ £8, 15 @ £7
28	24.00	2 @ £12

(b) Trading account for the month ending 31 August

	£	£
Sales		645
Less Cost of sales		
Stock as at 1 August	96	
Purchases	321	
	417	
Stock as at 31 August	24	
		393
Gross profit		252

QUESTION 13

(a)

Receipts	Issues		Balance	
		£	£	
1 @ £15			15.00	15.00
8 @ £15			135.00	£135/9 = £15
	6		45.00	3 @ £15
12 @ £16			237.00	£237/15 = £15.80
	10		79.00	5 @ £15.80
8 @ £17			215.00	£215/13 = £16.54
	6		115.78	7 @ £16.54

(b) Trading account for the month ended 30 September

	£	£
Sales		880.00
Less Cost of sales		
Stock as at 1 September	15.00	
Purchases	448.00	
	463.00	
Stock 30 September	115.78	
		347.22
Gross profit		532.78

QUESTION 15

	£
Stock as per stock-take of 7 May 20*5	2,940
Add Sales (£1,200/1.25)	960
Less Purchases	(420)
Stock as at 30 April 20*5	3,480

QUESTION 17

(a)

	£
Stock as per stock-take of 4 June 20*4	14,880
Add Sales less returns (2364/1.2)	1,970
Less Purchases less returns	(766)
Stock as at 31 May 20*4	16,084

(b) Stock has increased by £1,204, therefore profit shown on draft accounts will be increased to £186,954.

QUESTION 19

(a)

	£
Stock as per stock-take of 9 August 20*4	2,000
Add Sales less returns (£1,734/1.7)	1,020
Goods on sale or return (£510/1.7)	300
Less Purchases less returns	(1,520)
Stock as at 31 July 20*4	1,800

(b) Stock has reduced by £200, therefore profit shown on draft accounts will be reduced to £42,670.

CHAPTER THIRTEEN

QUESTION 1

(a) Absorption costing statement for Tucon for August 20*4

	£000
Direct materials	938
Direct labour	461
Manufacturing royalties	20
PRIME COST	1,419
Indirect materials	463
Indirect labour	726
Other indirect costs	84
Depreciation of factory machinery	100
Total production costs	2,792
Selling and distribution costs	612
Administration costs	300
Depreciation of office equipment	48
Total cost	3,752

(b) $\frac{£3,752,000}{4,000,000}$ = Production cost for one 'sepyt'

= £0.938

= 93.8 pence.

QUESTION 3

Total cost of producing one 'dible' = $\frac{£127,000}{20,000}$

= £6.35

Selling price = £6.35 + £2.18 = £8.53.

QUESTION 5

Total cost of producing 'treamils' = £159,000
Profit margin = 25% Mark-up = 33⅓%
So selling price = £159,000 x 1.33% = £212,000/45,000 = £4.71 per unit.

QUESTION 7

Overhead	Total cost £	Basis of apportionment	Dept 1 £	Dept 2 £	Dept 3 £
Rent	36,000	Floor area	6,000	12,000	18,000
Depreciation – premises	6,000	Floor area	1,000	2,000	3,000
machinery	210,000	Cost of machinery	30,000	60,000	120,000
Heating and light	9,000	Floor area	1,500	3,000	4,500
Supervisors' wages	160,000	No of workers	32,000	72,000	56,000
	421,000		70,500	149,000	201,500

QUESTION 9

Overhead	Total £	Basis of apportionment	Department Z1 £	Y2 £	X3 £	W4 £	Maintenance £
Total maintenance	974,200		386,100	227,300	180,400	110,500	69,900
		Number of machines	32,620	20,970	11,650	4,660	(69,900)
	974,200		418,720	248,270	192,050	115,160	

QUESTION 11

	Production departments 11/R £	12/S £	13/T £	Service departments UV £	WX £
Total costs	60,000	120,000	45,000	30,000	20,000
Apportionment of Dept UV costs	7,500	15,000	6,000	(30,000)	1,500
	67,500	135,000	51,000		21,500
Apportionment of Dept WX costs	4,300	6,450	8,600	2,150	(21,500)
	71,800	141,450	59,600		

QUESTION 13

Total direct labour hours 3,000 (felto) + 8,400 (hevo) = 11,400.
Labour hour overhead absorption rate = £72,732 = £6.38 per hour.
                                        11,400

(a) Overhead absorption rate for each product:
Felto = 0.2 hours × £6.38 = £1.276
Hevo = 1.4 hours × £6.38 = £8.932

(b) If budgets are met then the total overheads will be absorbed as follows:

	£	
15,000 feltos will absorb	19,140	15,000 × £1.276
6,000 hevos will absorb	53,592	6,000 × £8.932
Total overheads absorbed	72,732	

QUESTION 15

Total direct machine hours 48,000 (klaka) + 84,000 (klova) = 132,000.

Machine hour overhead absorption rate for each product £166,320 = £1.26.
                                                        132,000

(a) Overhead absorption rate for each product:
Klaka = 2.4 × £1.26 = £3.024
Klova = 0.6 × £1.26 = £0.756

(b) If budgets are met the the total overheads will be absorbed as follows:

	£
20,000 klakas will absorb	60,480
140,000 klovas will absorb	105,840
Total overheads absorbed	166,320

QUESTION 17

(a) **Department P:**
OAR using labour hours = £34.875 (£182,466/5232)
OAR using machine hours = £4.50 (£182,466/40,548)
Department N:
OAR using labour hours = £9.25 (£262,145/28,340)
OAR using machine hours = £120.25 (£262,145/2180)

(b) Department P is more capital intensive so choose machine hours.
Department N is more labour intensive so choose labour hours.

(c)

Sporidge takes 9.3 hours in dept P so	41.85
6.5 hours in dept N so	60.125
Total overheads to be absorbed by a sporidge	101.975

QUESTION 19

Overhead	Total cost £	Basis of apportionment	Department B £	C £	D £	E £
Rent	90,000	Floor area	36,000	27,000	18,000	9,000
Rates	15,000	Floor area	6,000	4,500	3,000	1,500
Insurance	21,000	Floor area	8,400	6,300	4,200	2,100
Depreciation	7,000	Floor area	2,800	2,100	1,400	700
Heating	18,000	Floor area	7,200	5,400	3,600	1,800
Machinery insurance	24,000	Replacement cost	9,000	6,000	4,500	4,500
Machinery depreciation	27,000	Cost of machinery	16,200	5,400	3,600	1,800
	202,000		85,600	56,700	38,300	21,400

QUESTION 21

(a)

Overhead	Total £	Basis of apportionment	Departments D £	E £	F £	Canteen £
Rent & rates	19,350	Floor area	7,740	6,772.5	2,902.5	1,935
Insurance of machine	35,100	Cost of machinery	22,950	6,102	5,994	54
Heat and light	11,460	Floor area	4,584	4,011	1,719	1,146
Supervisory wages	29,000	Number of workers	8,990	10,150	8,120	1,740
Power	28,400	Kwh	11,360	7,100	8,520	1,420
Depreciation – machinery	14,950	Cost of machinery	9,775	2,599	2,553	23
	138,260		65,399	36,734.5	29,808.5	6,318

(b)

Canteen (figures rounded)	138,260	Number of workers	2,084	2,352	1,882	(6,318)
			67,483	39,086.5	31,690.5	

CHAPTER FOURTEEN

QUESTION 1

T. Cupp should accept the order. It will make a positive contribution of £2.80 per service (£15.00 − £12.20) – a total contribution of £8,400.

QUESTION 3

George should accept the order. It will make a positive contribution of 10p per candle (£1.00 − 90p) – a total contribution of £100.

QUESTION 5

Renting the room to the bridge club will make a positive contribution of £14, therefore the bowling club should accept the bridge club's offer.

QUESTION 7

Pierre should not accept the offer from Italy. At present his marginal costs are £240 (£40 + £170 + £30) so contribution is £770. Purchasing from Engelo the marginal costs will be:

	£
Fireplace	200
Delivery	180
Distribution	30
Total marginal costs	410

Contribution will fall to £600. Pierre will be worse off if he accepts Angelo's offer.

QUESTION 9

'Comfy' slippers should be manufactured. They would yield a positive contribution of £15 compared with a contribution of £14 from the 'Warmy' slippers.

QUESTION 11

(a) Tables, then chairs, then headboards.
(b) All 300 tables.
    500 chairs.

QUESTION 13

(a) Gents', then Ladies', then Children's.
(b) Gents' 10,000 pairs; Ladies' 8,000 pairs; Children's 250 pairs.

QUESTION 15

(a) Break even = $\dfrac{\text{Total fixed costs}}{\text{Contribution per unit}} = \dfrac{40,000}{9} = 4,445$ units

(b) £88,900.
(c) 5,555 units

QUESTION 17

(a) c/v ratio = $\dfrac{\text{Sales} - \text{variable costs}}{\text{Sales}} = \dfrac{244,000}{356,000} = 0.685$

(b) Break-even = £218,978.

QUESTION 19

(b) 32,000 kilos.
(c) 68,000 kilos.
(d) £3,000 loss.
(e) £2,000 profit.

QUESTION 23

Overhead

	Total	Basis of apportionment	XY	ZA	BC	Canteen	Maintenance
Rent and rates	21,120	Floor area	7,920	2,640	5,280	1,320	3,960
Heat and light	17,040	Floor area	6,390	2,130	4,260	1,065	3,195
Supervisory wages	220,000	Number of workers	83,600	26,400	66,000	17,600	26,400
Power	29,610	Kwh	14,805	6,909	5,922	658	1,316
Depreciation – machinery	24,000	Cost of machinery	3,600	7,500	4,500	2,400	6,000
premises	16,800	Floor area	6,300	2,100	4,200	1,050	3,150
Insurance							
– machinery	21,720	Cost of machinery	3,258	6,787.5	4,072.5	2,172	5,430
premises	14,112	Floor area	5,292	1,764	3,528	882	2,646
	364,402		131,165	56,230.5	97,762.5	27,147	52,097
Maintenance		Number of machines	28,052	12,022	8,015	4,008	(52,097)
			159,217	68,252.5	105,777.5	31,155	
Canteen		Number of workers	14,799	4,673	11,683	(31,155)	*
	364,402		174,016	72,925.5	117,460.5		

*Ignores maintenance workers.

QUESTION 25

(a)

Overhead	Total £	Basis of apportionment	AZ £	BY £	Machinery £	Canteen £
Rent and rates	47,840	Area	15,600	26,000	5,200	1,040
Supervisory wages	172,500	No of workers	46,000	92,000	23,000	11,500
Depreciation of machinery	55,000	Book value of machinery	32,500	12,500	6,000	4,000
	275,340		94,100	130,500	34,200	16,540
Maintenance			22,800	8,550	(34,200)	2,850
			116,900	139,050		19,390
Canteen	275,340		6,463	12,927		(19,390)
			123,363	151,977		

(b) OAR AZ = machine hours = $\dfrac{123,363}{8,310}$ = £14.85

OAR BY = labour hours = $\dfrac{151,977}{4,800}$ = £31.66

(c) Job PR/72

	£
Direct materials	47.50
Direct labour	34.00
2 hours in Dept AZ	29.70
3 hours in Dept BY	94.98
Total cost	206.18
Mark-up 70%	144.33
Selling price	350.51

375

QUESTION 3

Sq × Sp
2,900 × 200 = £580,000
Aq × Sp
3,100 × 200 = £620,000
Aq × Ap
3,100 × 220 = £682,000

£40,000 adverse material usage sub-variance
£62,000 adverse materials price sub-variance
£102,000 adverse total direct material variance

QUESTION 5

Sq × Sp
9,000 × £1.60 = £14,400
Aq × Sp
9,100 × £1.60 = £14,560
Aq × Ap
9,100 × £1.40 = £12,740

£160 adverse direct material usage sub-variance
£1,820 favourable direct material price sub-variance
£1,660 favourable total direct material variance

QUESTION 7

Sq × Sp
1,400 × £9.50 = £13,300
Aq × Sp
1,350 × £9.50 = £12,825
Aq × Ap
1,350 × £9.60 = £12,960

£475 favourable direct labour efficiency sub-variance
£135 adverse direct labour rate sub-variance
£340 favourable direct labour variance

QUESTION 9

Direct materials
Sq × Sp
1,720 × £1.80 = £3,096.00
Aq × Sp
1,735 × £1.80 = £3,123.00
Aq × Ap
1,735 × £1.75 = £3,036.25

£27 adverse material usage sub-variance
£86.75 favourable material price sub-variance
£59.75 favourable total direct materials variance

Direct labour
Sq × Sp
810 × £8.40 = £6,804
Aq × Sp
834 × £8.40 = £7,005.60
Aq × Ap
834 × £8.50 = £7,089

£201.60 adverse direct labour efficiency sub-variance
£83.40 adverse direct labour rate sub-variance
£285 adverse total direct labour variance

	£	
Total direct material variance	59.75	favourable
Total direct labour variance	285.00	adverse
Total direct expenses variance	225.25	adverse

QUESTION 21

Muriel should accept. The meeting will provide a positive contribution of £0.71 per meal or £213 in total.

QUESTION 23

(a) First CQ/4; second AP/7; third DS/8; then BR/9.
(b) 1,000 CQ/4s; 5,000 AP/7s; 500 DS/8s.
(c)

QUESTION 25

(a) VC £21.50; Contribution £18.50
Break-even = Total fixed costs / Contribution per unit = 119,000 / 18.50 = 6,433 units
(b) Margin of safety = 7,567 units.

QUESTION 27

(b) 750 units.
(c) £18,750.
(d) 1,250 units.
(e) Loss £2,800.
(f) Loss £1,200.
(g) Profit £400.

QUESTION 29

(a) Marginal cost statement for April 20*5

	£
Sales	80,000
Direct materials	20,000
Direct labour	30,000
Royalties	2,000
	52,000
Contribution	28,000
Fixed costs	7,000
Profit	21,000

(b) c/v ratio = 28,000 / 80,000 = 0.35.

Break-even = Total fixed costs / c/v ratio

= 7,000 / 0.35 = £20,000.

CHAPTER FIFTEEN

QUESTION 1

Sq × Sp
7,000 × £2.50 = £17,500
Aq × Sp
6,900 × £2.50 = £17,250
Aq × Ap
6,900 × £2.40 = £16,560

£250 favourable materials usage sub-variance
£690 favourable price sub-variance
£940 favourable total material variance

QUESTION 11

The flexed budget figures are:

Direct materials: 10,500 units at £4.00 per unit
Direct labour: 700 hours at £13.50 per hour

Direct materials:

Sq × Sp
10,500 × £4.00 = £42,000
Aq × Sp
10,600 × £4.00 = £42,400   £400 adverse direct material usage sub-variances
Aq × Ap
10,600 × £3.85 = £40,810   £1,590 favourable direct material price sub-variance
                            £1,190 favourable total direct material variance

Direct labour: 700 × £13.50 = £9,450

705 × £13.50 = £9,517.50   £67.50 adverse direct labour efficiency sub-variance

705 × £13.40 = £9,447   £70.50 favourable direct labour rate sub-variance

£3.00 Favourable direct labour variance

QUESTION 13

Sq × Sp
29,300 × £7.96 = £233,228
Aq × Sp
29,250 × £7.96 = £232,830   £398 adverse sales volume sub-variance
Aq × Ap
29,250 × £8.03 = £234,877.50   £2,047.50 favourable sales price sub-variance
                                £1,649.50 Favourable total sales variance

QUESTION 15

Cheaper workers being used who are less skilled and so take longer to complete work.

QUESTION 17

One possible inter-relationship: more materials have been used because of wastage – more highly skilled workers used to attempt to cut down on the wastage. Also poor machinery used.

QUESTION 19

Sq × Sp
4,200 × £3.40 = £14,280
Aq × Sp
4,150 × £3.40 = £14,110   £170 favourable direct material usage sub-variance
Aq × Ap
4,150 × £3.50 = £14,525   £415 adverse direct material price sub-variance
                           £245 adverse total direct materials variance

QUESTION 21

Sq × Sp
1,200 × £8.50 = £10,200
Aq × Sp
1,400 × £8.50 = £11,900   £1,700 adverse direct labour efficiency sub-variance
Aq × Ap
1,400 × £8.60 = £12,040   £140 adverse direct labour rate sub-variance
                           £1,840 adverse total direct labour variance

QUESTION 23

Direct materials:

17,300 × £1.82 = £31,486
17,250 × £1.82 = £31,395   £91 favourable direct material usage sub-variance
17,250 × £1.80 = £31,050   £345 favourable direct material price sub-variance
                            £436 favourable total direct materials variance

Direct labour:

410 × £9.40 = £3,854
440 × £9.40 = £4,136   £282 adverse direct labour efficiency sub-variance
440 × £9.50 = £4,180   £44 adverse direct labour rate sub-variance
                        £326 adverse direct labour variance.

g) Total direct expenses variance is £110 favourable.
h) £91 saved – perhaps using better-quality materials, although price has decreased. Less wastage – perhaps using better machinery. Higher wage bill might indicate higher level of skilled workers being used.
i) Pay rise – higher skilled workforce hired; some overtime being worked at premium rates.

QUESTION 25

400,000 × £0.87 = £348,000
450,000 × £0.87 = £391,500   £43,500 favourable sales volume sub-variance
450,000 × £0.85 = £382,500   £9,000 adverse sales price sub-variance
                              £34,500 favourable sales variance

QUESTION 27

Flexed budget:
Direct materials:

14,400 × £6.10 = £87,840
14,500 × £6.10 = £88,450   £610 adverse direct materials usage sub-variance
14,500 × £6.00 = £87,000   £1,450 favourable direct material price sub-variance
                            £840 Favourable total direct material variance

Flexed budget
Direct labour:

37,800 × £6.80 = £257,040
37,500 × £6.80 = £255,000   £2,040 favourable direct labour efficiency sub-variance
37,500 × £6.75 = £253,125   £1,875 favourable direct labour rate sub-variance
                             £3,915 favourable total direct labour variance

Material wastage; cheaper materials purchased; labour worked more efficiently; labour prepared to take lower wages perhaps to secure jobs.

	Proposal 1 Cash inflows/(outflows)	Proposal 2 Cash inflows/(outflows)
	£	£
Year 0	(100,000)	(110,000)
Year 1	40,000	38,000
Year 2	43,000	44,000
Year 3	45,000	47,000
Year 4	47,000	50,000
Year 5	50,000	44,000

(a) Payback period for Proposal 2 = 2.38 years.
Payback period for Proposal 2 = 2.6 years.
(b) Adopt Proposal 1.

QUESTION 7
(a) Accounting rate of return = $\dfrac{\text{Average profit}}{\text{Average investment}}$ = $\dfrac{£11,400}{£50,000}$ = 22.8%.
(b) The directors should not proceed with production of the new product as the return is less than that required.

QUESTION 9
(a)
Project 321: Average investment = $\dfrac{300,000 + \text{no scrap value}}{2}$ = £150,000

Project 322: Average investment = $\dfrac{300,000 + 0}{2}$ = £150,000

Accounting rate of return – Project 321 = $\dfrac{30,000}{150,000} \times 100$ = 20%.

Accounting rate of return – Project 322 = $\dfrac{35,000}{150,000} \times 100$ = 23.3%.

(b) The directors should undertake Project 322 since it yields the higher accounting rate of return.

QUESTION 11
(a)

	Cash flows	Discount factor	NPV
	£		£
Year 0	(80,000)	1	(80,000)
Year 1	25,000	0.926	23,150
Year 2	30,000	0.857	25,710
Year 3	27,000	0.794	21,438
Year 4	26,000	0.735	19,110
			9,408

QUESTION 29
Flexed budget:
Direct materials:
725 × £16.40 = £11,890.00
732 × £16.40 = £12,004.80   £114.80 adverse direct material usage sub-variance
732 × £18.30 = £13,395.60   £1,390.80 adverse direct material price sub-variance
         £1,505.60 adverse direct material variance

Flexed budget:
Direct labour:
1,087.5 × £8.35 = £9,080.63   £20.87 adverse direct labour efficiency sub-variance

1,090 × £8.35 = £9,101.50   £163.50 favourable direct labour rate sub-variance
1,090 × £8.20 = £8,938   £142.63 favourable total direct labour variance

More wastage; increase price; more hours worked perhaps because of less good materials; lower wage rate paid perhaps because of less skilled workers being employed.

CHAPTER SIXTEEN

QUESTION 1
a Project 24/JJ – payback is 2.2 years.
Project 25/SM – payback is 2 years.
b Project 25/SM should be chosen.

QUESTION 3

	Project Minor Cash inflows/(outflows)	Project Nixto Cash inflows/(outflows)
	£000	£000
Year 0	(8,800)	(7,400)
Year 1	3,600	1,700
Year 2	4,600	2,200
Year 3	5,600	2,700
Year 4	5,600	3,200
Year 5	5,600	2,700

a Payback period for Project Minor – 2.11 years.
Payback period for Project Nixto – 3.25 years.
b Project Minor should be chosen as it has the shorter payback period.

(b) The machine should be purchased because it yields a positive NPV of £9,408.

QUESTION 13

(a)

	Plant PAQ/73			Plant BAX/482		
	Cash flows	Discount factor	NPV	Cash flows	Discount factor	NPV
	£m		£m	£m		£m
Year 0	(6.0)	1	(6.0)	(11.5)	1	(11.5)
Year 1	0.9	0.917	0.8253	3.0	0.917	2.751
Year 2	2.9	0.842	2.4418	4.0	0.842	3.368
Year 3	3.4	0.772	2.6248	3.7	0.772	2.8564
Year 4	3.5	0.708	2.478	3.6	0.708	2.5488
Year 5	4.4	0.650	2.860	4.0	0.650	2.60
		Net present value	5.2299			2.6242

(b) Plant PAQ/73 should be purchased as it yields the larger NPV of £5,031,900.

QUESTION 15

Year	Cash flow	Discount factor	NPV
	£000		£000
0	(400)	1	(400)
1	250	0.935	233.75
2	260	0.873	226.98
3	270	0.816	220.32
4	280	0.763	213.64

Payback will occur part-way through Year 2.
400 − 233.75 = 166.25
166.25/226.98 = .732
226.98
Payback = 1.732 years.

QUESTION 17

(a) 3.73 years.
(b) (£35,000) + (£7,616 + £8,163 + £8,640 + £9,053 + £9,408) = £7,880.
(c) 4.16 years or 4 years 58 days; or 4 years 8.32 weeks; or 4 years 1.9 months.

QUESTION 19

(a) i) Payback period of facility R is 4.49 years.
Payback period of facility S is 3.06 years.
Payback period of facility T is 3.64 years.
ii) NPV up to Year 5:

	R	S	T
	£	£	£
	182.7	(52.2)	252.3
	381.78	287.28	695.52
	348.74	296.1	717.22
	286.00	280.28	629.20
	258.44	248.50	596.40
	(542.34)	259.96	(109.36) NPV

iii) Only Facility S will pay back within the five years – 3.06 years –.
(b) Facility S has the fastest payback period and is the only facility to yield a positive NPV after the five years. However, it appears to be the smallest facility – the cash inflows are significantly less than the other two facilities – does this mean that it produces less electricity? If it appears so – if this is the case – this could have an effect on the living standards of the Kapokian people and the nation's business world.
The Government should build Facility T. It has a slightly longer payback period using both methods and will yield a positive NPV by the end of Year 6. It will provide significantly more electricity which may be important for the economic development and living standards in the future.

QUESTION 21

(a) i)   YP/32 = 4.65 years
          WQ/43 = 2.72 years
          XR/17 = 3.74 years
ii) Profits = cash flows – depreciation

$$\text{Average investment} = \frac{\text{Initial investment} + \text{scrap value}}{2}$$

$$VP/32 = \frac{3,000}{38,000} = 7.89\%$$

$$WQ/43 = \frac{5,000}{38,000} = 13.16\%$$

$$XR/17 = \frac{3,250}{38,000} = 8.55\%$$

iii)

	VP/32	WQ/43	XR/17
	£	£	£
Year 0	(68,000)	(68,000)	(68,000)
Year 1	11,112	23,150	16,668
Year 2	8,570	21,425	15,426
Year 3	11,910	26,202	14,292
Year 4	13,230		19,845
Year 5	19,068		
NPV	(4,110)	2,777	(1,769)

iv) Only Project WQ/43 will pay back and this will only occur on the final day of Year 3 when the investment yields a scrap value.

(b) Only WQ/43 yields a positive NPV so it should be chosen. It has the highest ARR and is the only machine to cover its outlay when using discounted payback as a method of appraisal.

INDEX